Measuring National Well-being 2013

In replacement of 'Social Trends'

The data displayed in this document was correct at the time of downloading 09/12/13

Contents:

CD containing reference tables relating to:

15 February 2013

Household Satellite Accounts, Valuing Informal Childcare in the UK

Author Name(s): **Valerie Fender, Rosemary Foster, Atif Khan, Sue Punt and Gerard Carolan; Office for National Statistics**

Abstract

This article reports on the measurement and valuation of the output of the household production of childcare. This includes all care given by parents, family members, friends and focuses on the numbers of children looked after, rather than those giving the care. It is the first in a series of articles to update the full household satellite accounts (HHSA) for the UK. The methodology remains under development and any estimates reported here, or in forthcoming publications, should be considered experimental and interpreted with caution.

Key Points

- This article reports on the measurement of informal childcare by households which is outside the scope of National Accounts and therefore Gross Domestic Product (GDP).
- Formal childcare per child for children under 5 years old increased by 36.4% between 1995 and 2010.
- Between 1995 and 2010 there was a movement away from informal childcare in the household towards formal childcare for children aged under 5 years old.
- The value of informal childcare in 2010 was £343 billion (valued using gross wages), this is equivalent to 23% of GDP.

Introduction to the Household Satellite Accounts

In 2002 the Office for National Statistics (ONS) published the first Household Satellite Account (HHSA) for the UK, which measured and valued the unpaid goods and services produced by households (ONS, 2002; Holloway, Short & Tamplin, 2002).

Following the publication of the Report by the Commission for the Measurement of Economic Performance and Social Progress (2009) there has been fresh interest in valuing household production. As such, as part of the Measuring National Well-being programme ONS is currently updating the HHSA which measure household production in the UK. The value of informal childcare is the first of the eight HHSA modules to be updated.

Household production is all unpaid goods and services produced by households in the UK. Conventional National Accounts measurements, such as GDP, do not fully take into account of these goods and services. However, if these goods and services are paid for they are included as part of the National Accounts. For example, if I were to iron my own clothes this service would not be included, however, if I were to pay someone to do it for me it would.

The HHSA provide a means by which the influence of changing patterns of unpaid work on the economy can be measured. The information will also be of use to policy makers who need to take significant amounts of unpaid work into account.

This work falls outside the scope of the UK National Accounts. This is because the inclusion of all activity which is productive in the economic sense but which does not have a monetary value, would swamp the monetary flows, obscure what is happening in the markets, and reduce the usefulness of National Accounts data for analysis. HHSA is therefore separate from, but conceptually consistent with the UK National Accounts.

The HHSA extends the National Accounts boundary to include all activity that could be delegated to another person. This activity is divided into several principal functions providing housing, transport, nutrition, clothing, laundry services, adult care, child care and voluntary work. The approach being taken by the ONS is to focus on the outputs of these principal functions.

The methodology remains under development and any estimates reported here, or in forthcoming publications, should be considered experimental and interpreted with caution. ONS welcomes comments and feedback on all aspects of the methodology used and the assumptions made, and seek suggestions for further/alternative data sources. A more detailed description of the methodology and assumptions made can be found in the appendices of this article.

What is Formal and Informal Childcare?

As most of the childcare carried out by household members or their networks (family members or neighbours) could be delegated to another person, it is deemed to be part of the productive role of households.

The definitions of formal and informal childcare vary between different surveys and projects. Definitions of formal childcare can vary from including only childcare that is registered and paid for (for example registered childminder places for the under 8's), to also including care which is formalised by payment but unregistered (for example unregistered childminders and nannies).

Reflecting this, the definition of informal childcare can also vary. Informal childcare is often defined as unpaid care. This usually refers to care given by family members such as grandparents and siblings, as well as friends; but does not usually include care given by parents. Alternatively, informal childcare can be defined as care which is unregistered even if paid for, so paid babysitters and unregistered childminders could fall into this category. This is still referred to as informal care because the arrangements are not formalised with contracts or employment rights.

The HHSA definition of informal childcare is all care which does not involve a monetary transaction and therefore includes the childcare of parents and other family members. It is the total amount of childcare required (total number of children in the population multiplied by twenty four hours a day) less any formal childcare, defined as all paid childcare, whether it is registered or unregistered.

Within this definition of informal childcare we have not tried to distinguish between physical acts of supervision or help and the building of parent-child relationships, which obviously cannot be delegated. By using a residual approach to estimate informal childcare we are accounting for all the time a child needs supervision. This supervision can be 'active' or 'passive'. Passive care includes the time when an adult may not be directly interacting with the child, but is still responsible for them. The important point is that if no unpaid carer were available, a third person would have to be paid to take their place. Therefore passive care is part of the productive role of households and is included in our estimates. One simple way of distinguishing between passive and active childcare is to look at waking and sleeping time. If we assume a child under 5 sleeps for twelve hours, we can say that 50% of their childcare is passive, and so on.

As children get older, some of them are left unsupervised for varying amounts of time. An allowance has been made for this, so that the amount of informal care is reduced for older children.

Formal Childcare Hours

Formal childcare is all childcare which involves a monetary transaction and total hours of formal childcare can be affected by several factors – the duration of time that children spend in childcare, the total number of children who attend formal childcare and the total number of children in the population. However, as the time spent in each type of formal care is assumed to remain constant over the period, the changes actually reflect changes in the uptake of childcare places and the population size.

Chart 1 - UK Child Population

United Kingdom

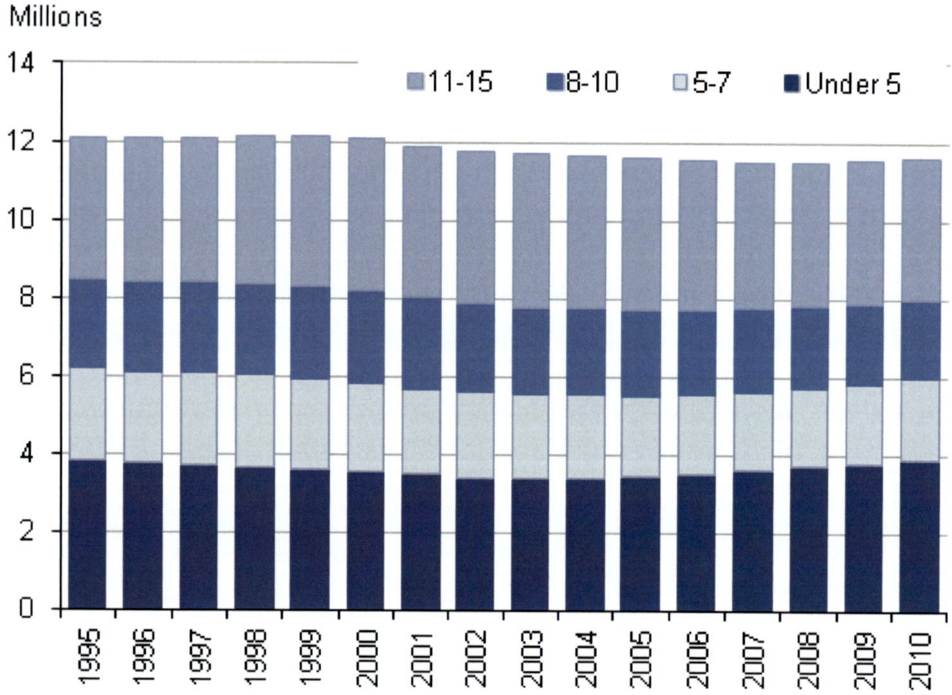

Source: Office for National Statistics

Download chart

XLS XLS format
(20 Kb)

The number of children in the population will affect some formal childcare places more immediately than others. If the population increases, the number of school places will increase. Provision for the under 5's will be more sensitive to changing preferences, changes in the labour market and/or changes in government policy.

Overall, the number of children in the UK has fallen 4.1% between 1995 and 2010. This is reflected in estimates of formal childcare hours for the UK. Formal childcare per child for children aged 5 to 15 has remained relatively stable, increasing 4.5% over the 15 year period. However, formal childcare per child for children under 5 years old increased substantially, and was 36.4% higher in 2010 than in 1995. Relative to this, population growth has been slower (in 2010, there were just 0.6% more children under 5 years old than in 1995).

Despite a substantial increase in formal childcare of those under 5 years old between 1995 and 2005, on average, children under 5 years old spend much less time in formal care than those 5 to 15 years old.

Table 1: Estimated UK Formal Childcare Hours per Child

United Kingdom

Hours

	1995	2000	2005	2010	% change 1995-2010
Under 5	490	621	642	668	36.4
5 - 7	1243	1267	1299	1344	8.0
8 - 10	1214	1237	1256	1268	4.5
11 - 15	1321	1301	1320	1350	2.1
Total	**1023**	**1081**	**1103**	**1108**	**8.3**

Table source: Office for National Statistics

Download table

XLS XLS format
(28.5 Kb)

This is in line with government policies in the early 2000's encouraging under 5's into formal childcare. Over the same period, the percentage of mothers in employment also increased (ONS, Mothers in the Labour Market, 2011).

Informal Childcare Hours

Table 2: Estimated UK Informal Childcare Hours per Child

United Kingdom

Hours

	1995	2000	2005	2010	% change 1995-2010
Under 5	8270	8139	8118	8092	-2.2
5 - 7	7517	7493	7461	7416	-1.3
8 - 10	7546	7523	7504	7492	-0.7
11 - 15	6045	6090	6036	6011	-0.6
Total	**7316**	**7242**	**7187**	**7216**	**-1.4**

Table source: Office for National Statistics

Download table

XLS XLS format
(28.5 Kb)

Reflecting movements in the population and formal childcare, informal childcare hours per child remained relatively stable in the late 1990's before falling. Overall, between 1995 and 2010 there was a fall of 1.4%. This was driven by falls in informal childcare of those under 5 years old, particularly between 1995 and 2005.

Chart 2 looks at the ratio of informal to formal childcare. This shows that in the 10 years between 1995 and 2005, there was a considerable change in the ratio of informal to formal childcare for the under 5's. In 1995, total annual hours of informal childcare was 16.9 times greater than formal childcare. By 2005, this had fallen to 12.7 times greater. Since 2005 the ratio of informal to formal childcare of those aged under 5 has remained more stable and was 12.1 in 2010. By contrast, the ratio for all other age groups has remained relatively stable over the whole period. This highlights the movement away from informal childcare in the home towards formal childcare for children of pre-school age.

Chart 2 - Ratio of Formal to Informal Childcare

United Kingdom

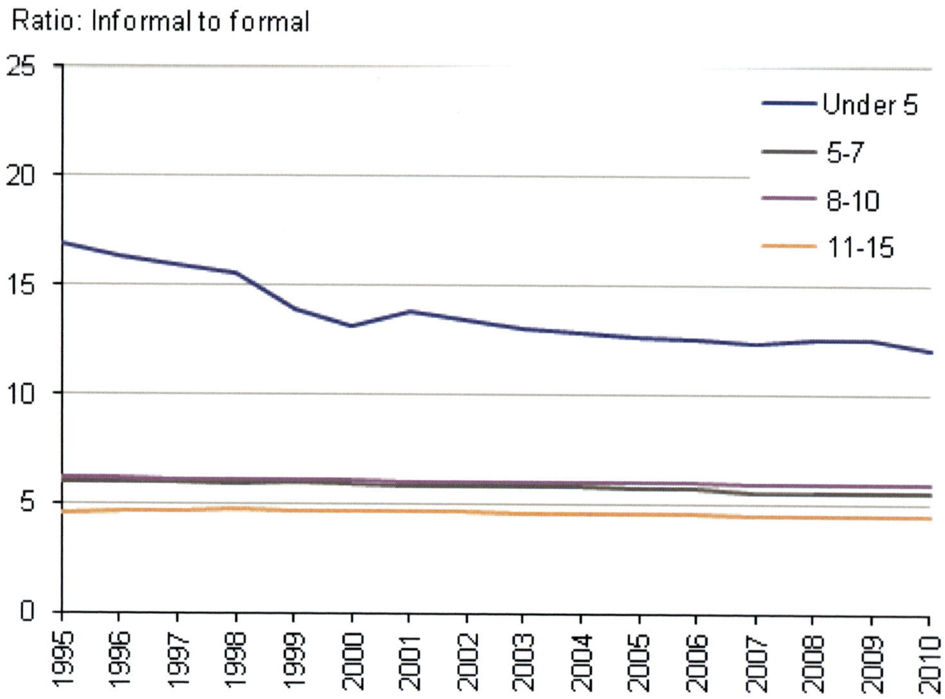

Source: Office for National Statistics

Download chart

XLS [XLS format](#)
(19.5 Kb)

Value of Informal Childcare

The services provided by a live in nanny have been deemed the closest market equivalent to the services provided by parents and other informal carers, so their rate per child hour has been used to value informal childcare. The wages of live-in nannies have been taken from the Professional Nanny/Nannytax Annual Survey, which gives average wages by geographical area and for the UK.

Chart 3 - Estimated Rate per Child Hour (net and gross)

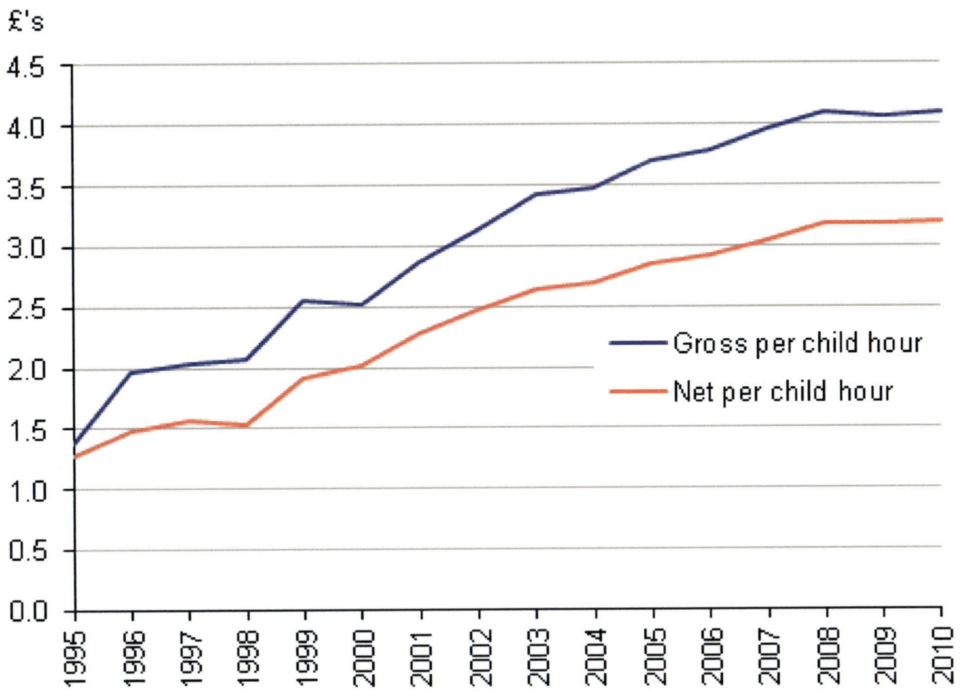

Source: Office for National Statistics

Download chart

XLS [XLS format](#)
(28 Kb)

Chart 3 shows there were sharp increases in average wages between 1995 and 1996, and between 1998 and 1999. While there are likely to be many factors which have contributed to this growth, one of the key influences could have been the introduction of the National Minimum Wage. A shortage of nannies may also have contributed to higher wages. More recently, the wages of nannies have also been affected by the recession, with little growth evident since 2008.

The averages conceal a huge degree of variation, particularly regionally; as such we have used the average wage for 'other cities' (i.e. excluding London) to value informal childcare. Additionally, the wage used to value informal childcare has been adjusted for payments in kind – a nanny is often paid in accommodation, food and sometime additional perks such as the use of a car. Finally, nannies do not charge for their services by the hour or by the child, therefore we have assumed that on average a nanny works a 48 hour week and looks after an average of 2 children. Obviously, the estimation of the value of informal childcare is sensitive to these adjustments and assumptions.

We consider both gross and net wages. The value using a rate based on gross wages is equivalent to the cost to households were they to employ a nanny to provide the childcare they give. The value based on net wages is the equivalent of what informal carers would receive were they to be paid the same rate as nannies.

Table 3 shows the value of informal childcare using both gross and net wages. It shows that for both methods of valuing informal childcare, the result is a substantial increase between 1995 and 2010. However, these values of informal childcare do not take account of inflation and this rise is against a backdrop of a fall in informal childcare hours. As such we can conclude that the increase in the value of informal childcare is driven by an increase in the price of childcare.

Table 3: Estimated Value of Informal Childcare

United Kingdom

	Billion hours	£bn	
	Informal Hours	**Value - Gross**	**Value - net**
1995	88.6	122	113
1996	88.4	174	131
1997	88.5	180	136
1998	88.4	183	139
1999	88.0	225	168
2000	87.5	220	177
2001	85.8	246	196
2002	85.0	266	209
2003	84.3	289	223
2004	83.7	291	225
2005	83.3	308	237
2006	82.9	314	242
2007	82.7	328	251
2008	82.9	340	264
2009	83.3	339	266

2010	83.8	343	268

Table source: Office for National Statistics

Download table

XLS [XLS format](#)
(21 Kb)

This can be broken down by age groups, which shows that all age groups experienced an increase in the value of informal childcare and in all cases this was driven by an increase in the price of childcare. In both the 5 to 7 age group and the 8 to 10 age group, this was partially offset by a slight reduction in the number of informal childcare hours.

The valuation of informal childcare is equivalent to either 18% or 23% of GDP (in current prices) in 2010 depending on the rate used. Using gross wages (representing the cost to households were they to employ a nanny to provide the childcare they give) informal childcare is valued at the equivalent of 23% of GDP in 2010, an increase from 16% in 1995. Using net wages (representing what informal carers would receive were they to be paid the same rate as nannies) informal childcare is valued at the equivalent of 18% of GDP in 2010, an increase from 15% in 1995.

Chart 4 shows that between 1995 and 2002 the value of informal childcare as a percentage of GDP increased, reflecting the increases in the value of informal childcare through this period. However, since then informal childcare as a proportion of GDP has fallen slightly again.

Chart 4 - Informal Childcare as a Proportion of GDP

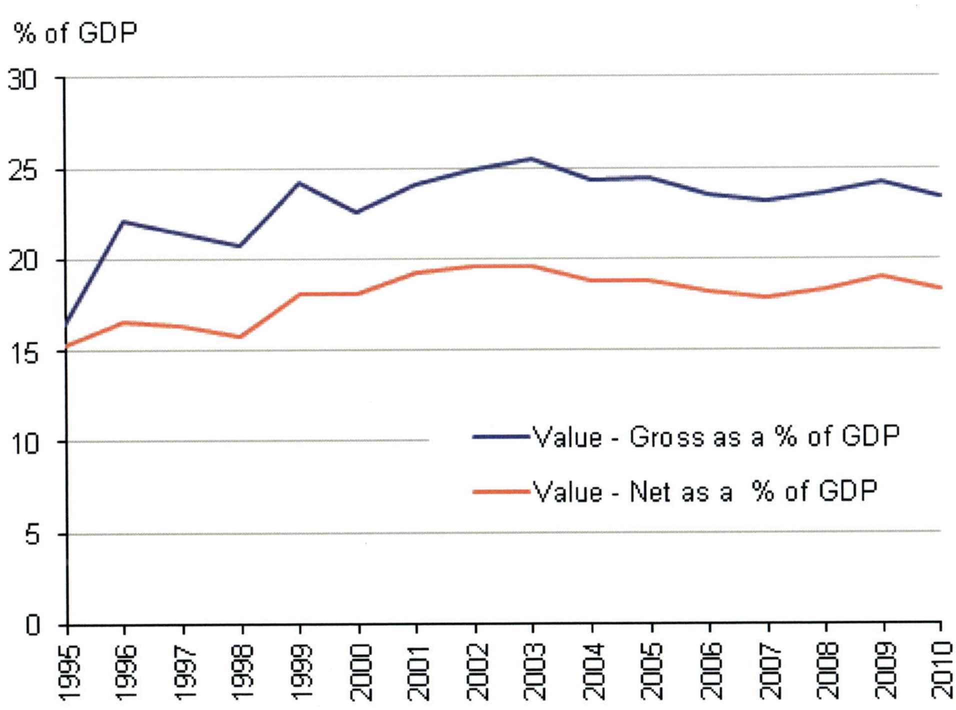

Source: Office for National Statistics

Download chart

XLS XLS format
(34.5 Kb)

Background notes

1. Details of the policy governing the release of new data are available by visiting www.statisticsauthority.gov.uk/assessment/code-of-practice/index.html or from the Media Relations Office email: media.relations@ons.gsi.gov.uk

Copyright

This document is also available on our website at www.ons.gov.uk.

Supporting Information

Further information

Mothers in the Labour Market
Analysis of the employment trends and characteristics of working mothers, compared to women without children and working fathers.

About the Household Satellite Account
Further information about the ONS Household Satellite Account (HHSA) (experimental)

References

1. Stiglitz, J. Sen, A. Fitoussi, J.P. (2009). Commission on the Measurement of Economic Performance and Social Progress.

2. Holloway, Short and Tamplin (2002). Household Satellite Account (Experimental) Methodology. Office for National Statistics.

3. Office for National Statistics (2002). Complete Household Satellite Accounts.

Appendix A: Methodology

Input and Output Methodologies

There are two possibilities for measuring household production, to measure inputs or outputs. Measuring inputs focuses on the time spent on productive activities and relies principally on time-use data. This usually takes the form of a diary, which the survey respondent is asked to complete, giving information about their principal activities throughout a 24-hour period.

The alternative is to attempt to measure outputs, this is the approach being taken by ONS. The output method values what the household produces, for example the number of children cared for or the number of meals prepared. This is important because it is often easier to value outputs than inputs, particularly when there is a market equivalent to the service being produced. Output measurement is also more consistent with the way the rest of the National Accounts are constructed and reflects household productivity. It may be possible to construct a historical series using this approach, even in the absence of time-use data. Outputs can be estimated through surveys that specifically request this type of information.

An estimate of gross unpaid production is obtainable by multiplying the volume of output by an appropriate market value or price. This in itself is problematic due to the difficulties in applying a market price or wage rate to outputs without any information on the variation in quality between households. The methodology is essentially the same for all of the principal functions except voluntary work.

The development of the UK Household Satellite Account was the first attempt to estimate the volume of outputs for each of the principle functions and to produce a value for total household production based on this approach.

Methodology for Childcare

The remainder of this annex will look at the estimation of household production of childcare (one element of the household satellite accounts) using the output approach.

As most of the childcare carried out by the household members or their networks (family members or neighbours) could be delegated to another person, it is deemed to be part of the productive role of households. ONS have not tried to distinguish between physical acts of supervision or help and the building of parent-child relationships, which obviously cannot be delegated.

The HHSA definition of informal childcare is all care which does not involve a monetary transaction. It is the total amount of childcare required (total number of children in the population multiplied by twenty four hours a day) less any formal childcare, defined as all paid childcare, whether it is registered or unregistered. However the estimates do not include some paid care which takes place, but for which ONS has been unable to find any data. This includes care by babysitters and au-pairs, as well as out-of-school clubs and holiday play schemes for children over 8 years old.

As children get older, some of them are left unsupervised for varying amounts of time. An allowance has been made for this, so that the amount of informal care is reduced for older children. There is limited hard data on the actual amount of unsupervised time. If, in fact, the assumptions ONS have made lead to informal childcare being underestimated (i.e. including too much unsupervised time), this will be offset to some extent by the unmeasured formal care which has not been included.

By using a residual approach to estimate informal childcare ONS is accounting for all the time a child needs supervision. This supervision can be active or passive. Passive care includes the time when an adult may not be directly interacting with the child, but is still responsible for them. The important point is that if no unpaid carer were available, a third person would have to be paid to take their place. Therefore passive care is part of the productive role of households and is included in the estimates.

Estimating Formal Childcare Hours

Information on different types of formal care has been collected for each UK country. This mainly takes the form of the numbers of childcare places available, and in all cases ONS have assumed 100% take-up of places. The requirement for and use of formal childcare varies for children of different ages, so the places have been allocated to the following categories:

- Age Group 1: under 5 years old
- Age Group 2: 5 to 7 years old
- Age Group 2: 8 to 10 years old
- Age Group 4: 11 to 15 years old

As formal childcare availability varies by the time of the year, the year has been split into four types of day:

- Weekend – 104 days
- Week Day School Day = 180 days (36 weeks x 5 days)
- Week Day Working Holiday = 28 days (4 weeks x 5 days plus 8 bank holidays)
- Week Day School Holiday = 53 days (12 weeks holiday minus bank holidays)

The estimates for each age group, by time and type of day, have been aggregated to obtain a figure for the total number of hours spent by all children in the UK in formal care in any one year.

As for the original estimates produced in 2002, for each separate type of day and age group, assumptions were made about the length of time the various types of childcare provision were available. ONS continue to review the assumptions and would welcome any information on further sources to inform this process. Although the length of time the various types of childcare provision is available may change over time, the HHSA assumes this to be constant. Full details of the assumptions made about each type of formal care can be found in appendix B.

ONS assume those children in foster places and children's homes are cared for 24 hours a day all year round, with the exception of attending school for 6.5 hours a day. Similarly, full time boarders are assumed to be in formal care 24 hours a day on school days and at weekends. Weekly boarders are assumed to be in formal care 24 hours a day on weekdays in term time. This means that for some individual children ONS may be double counting the total number of hours spent in formal care; for example, a foster child, a child living in a children's home or a boarder may attend other formal care activities (such as holiday play schemes or out of school clubs). Due to this double counting, the total number of formal hours may be slightly over estimated; this will result in an underestimate of informal hours.

Assumptions have also been made in order to divide the geographic data between the three different age groups. If the data is already broken down into different age groups from the ones outlined above, then the data is prorated using the UK country and year specific population age structure. If only the total number of children in a care category is available, then the proportion in each age group from the England data has been applied to the total numbers. Finally, if data is split down into the age groups for only some years, then the average split between the age groups has been applied to the years when only the total is available. Missing data points have been estimated by predicting the trend between existing data points.

To ensure a consistent approach across all four countries of the UK the population estimates were taken before any adjustments for the 2011 Census had taken place. Therefore at this stage the population estimates are not consistent with the 2011 Census.

Estimating Informal Childcare Hours

ONS estimate the volume of informal care by subtracting the hours spent in formal care, plus an allowance for the hours a child aged 12 to 15 may be left unsupervised, from the child population multiplied by the total number of hours in a year. As with formal care, the total hours of informal care can be broken down by age group and time, and type of day.

The assumption about the time children aged between 11 and 15 spend unsupervised is critical in calculating informal hours, and is perhaps the most difficult to support with hard evidence. To estimate the number of hours spent in informal care, the number of hours a child is left unsupervised, plus the hours spent in formal childcare activities, needs to be subtracted from the total population hours. This time unsupervised by adults could be when a child is spending time with their friends, being looked after by an older sibling, or when they are on their own.

The data available for when children are left unsupervised by their parents is very sensitive to reporting errors. This is due to social norms and beliefs about the amount of time children should spend alone. A survey carried out by Kids Club Network in 1997, sponsored by Nestlé, estimated that 6% of children return home to an empty house. A similar survey (the Make Space Youth Review) conducted by 4Children in 2007 suggests that an estimated 34% of all teenagers return home to an empty house. The sensitivity of the issues suggests that there is under-reporting by parents. Because of the lack of data about the length of time left unsupervised, ONS have started from the working assumption outlined below.

In the HHSA ONS have assumed that no child aged 11 or under is left unsupervised and that 10% of 12 year olds, 20% of 13 year olds, 30% of 14 year olds and 50% of 15 year olds spend time without adult supervision. In every case, ONS have not included any allowance for time spent unsupervised during four weeks holiday plus Bank Holidays. These assumptions can be interpreted as a mix of two extremes. ONS could say that 10% of children aged 12 are left unsupervised all the time. ONS could also say that out of 337 days (365 days minus four weeks paid holiday of parent/carer minus eight days bank holiday) an individual 12-year-old would spend a total of 10% of their time unsupervised.

As the unspervised time figure shows, for a 12 year old, this unsupervised time could typically include an hour in the morning before school, plus an hour and a half after school (e.g. walking themselves to and from school), plus being left unsupervised by an adult between 8.00 a.m. and 4.00 p.m. in the school holidays while a parent is at work. This scenario assumes no time unsupervised in the evenings or at the weekends. For a 15-year old, the assumption includes the same times of day as a 12 year old, plus additional hours after school on school days, in the evenings in the school holidays and at the weekend. Informal care in the HHSA is therefore care of children by adults, as care of children by other children is included in the assumption of time unsupervised.

Unsupervised time

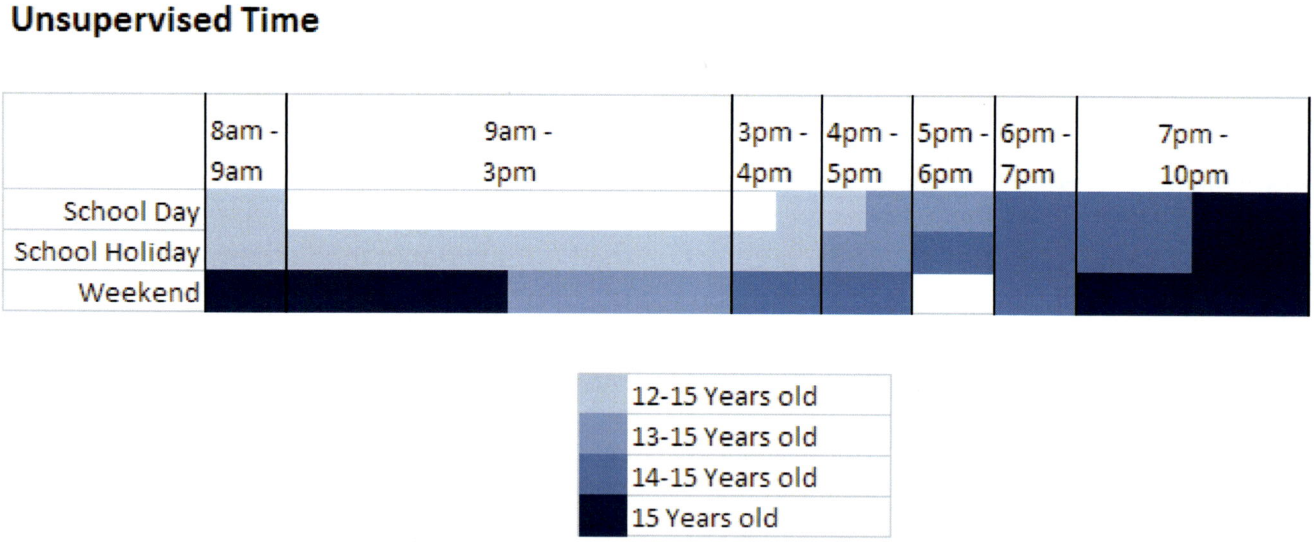

Valuation of Informal Childcare

As mentioned earlier the requirement for and use of informal childcare varies for children of different ages, as well as by different times of the day and different days of the year. It is possible to value all informal hours at a single market price or to take into consideration the time of the year, time of the day and the age of the child. Because ONS is valuing the output of childcare, i.e. the number of children cared for multiplied by the total time in a year when they receive this care; the market price must also be a rate per child.

The services provided by an employed live-in nanny are deemed to be the nearest market equivalent to the services provided by parents and other informal carers, so their rate per child hour has been used to value informal care. The wages of live-in nannies have been taken from the Professional Nanny/Nannytax Annual Survey, which gives average wages by geographical area for the UK.

However, the averages conceal considerable variation. For example, the Nannytax survey shows that for live out nannies in 2010, the net weekly wages was £490 in London, but just £360 outside of London and the Home Counties. ONS have used the average wage for other cities. i.e. excluding London.

A live-in nanny is paid not just in wages but also in accommodation and food, with some nannies receiving additional perks such as the use of a car. Because of this the live-in nanny wage rate is lower than the daily nanny rate. The Nannytax survey gives data for both live in nannies and live out nannies, with a difference of £110 per week in net wages in central London in 2010.

ONS have made an adjustment for payment in kind, comparing the live-in and daily rate for nannies working the same number of hours per week. This results in an upward adjustment to the net wage rate of 8.5% and the gross wage rate of 10%.

Nannies do not charge for their services by the hour or per child. ONS have assumed that the average live-in nanny works 48 hours a week looking after an average of two children. This information is used to adjust the gross and net weekly wages.

Further Areas for Development

There are several ongoing methodological challenges which ONS will continue to develop while updating the accounts. Of primary concern is the use of the 'time-unsupervised' assumption; this assumption could be tested by examining whole household data in the 2000 Time Use Survey and estimating time spent unsupervised by age. Additionally, the alternatives for pricing passive care will be investigated.

ONS acknowledge the advantages of using time-use data to complement the output approach. The main advantage of using time-use data is that socio-demographic information can be applied to the data to answer question's such as 'who is providing informal childcare?'. The data sources used in the UK accounts, at present, do not allow linkages to be made between the outputs of household production and types of individual. This question can be addressed by looking at time-use data, such as the UK Time Use Survey from 2000, allowing the comparison of relative contributions of different socio-demographic groups.

It is also possible to make assumptions about the amount of time children of different age groups are asleep, and therefore the childcare is passive rather than active. By splitting informal care into passive and active care, different prices can be applied reflecting the different valuation of passive and active care.

Appendix B: Data Sources

Household Satellite Accounts - Valuing Informal Childcare in the UK uses a vast array of data sources. Full details of the data sources used and assumptions made can be found in the reference table (55.5 Kb Excel sheet) accompanying this appendix.

About the ONS Measuring National Well-being Programme

NWB logo 2

This article is published as part of the ONS Measuring National Well-being Programme.

The programme aims to produce accepted and trusted measures of the well-being of the nation - how the UK as a whole is doing.

Measuring National Well-being is about looking at 'GDP and beyond'. It includes headline indicators in areas such as health, relationships, job satisfaction, economic security, education, environmental conditions and measures of 'subjective well-being' (individuals' assessment of their own well-being).

Find out more on the Measuring National Well-being webiste pages.

Measuring National Well-being - Older People's Neighbourhoods, 2013

Author Name(s): **Helen Lofts Office for National Statistics**

Abstract

This is the first in a series of short articles examining the well-being of older people aged 50 and over using measures related to the Measuring National Well-being Programme. The Office for National Statistics measures of well-being are organised into ten domains with each domain having between three and five separate indicators. More information about all the measures can be found in the 'National Well-being wheel of measures' (ONS 2012a).

Introduction

One of the indicators in the 'Where we live' domain is the percentage of people who agree that they belong to their neighbourhood. The information for this measure is taken from Understanding Society, the UK Household Longitudinal Study (UKHLS) which collects information each year about the social and economic circumstances and attitudes of people. Respondents to this survey were asked if they felt they belonged to their neighbourhood and were also asked whether the friendships and associations they had with other people in their neighbourhood meant a lot to them. Having a strong sense of belonging to one's neighbourhood and a circle of local friends and associates has been shown to be related to greater community cohesion and a higher sense of security. Belonging strongly to a neighbourhood has also been shown to have a positive effect on health and well-being (Windsor et al, 2012).

Key points

In the UK in 2009–10 for older people aged 50 and over:

- In each older age group a higher percentage reported that they felt that they belonged to their neighbourhood and that local friendships and associations meant a lot to them, compared with the average for all aged 16 and over.
- The percentage of older people who agreed that they belonged to their neighbourhood increased with age, from 69% of those aged 50 to 54 to 84% of those aged 70 and over.
- About 82% of those who agreed that they belonged to their neighbourhood also reported that they were satisfied with their life overall compared with 53% of those who disagreed.
- Those who agreed that local friendships and associations meant a lot to them increased with age from 64% of those aged 50 to 54 to over 80% of those aged 70 and over.

- About 81% of those who agreed that local friendships and associations meant a lot to them were satisfied with their lives overall compared with 64% of those who disagreed.

Feelings of belonging to the neighbourhood

In 2009–10, 69% of people aged 50 to 54 in the UK agreed or strongly agreed that they belonged to their neighbourhood. This rose to 84% for those aged 70 and over. In each older age group the percentage agreeing that they belonged to their neighbourhood was higher than the average for all respondents aged 16 and over (66%).

Figure 1: Belonging to the neighbourhood: by selected age groups and sex (1), 2009–10

United Kingdom

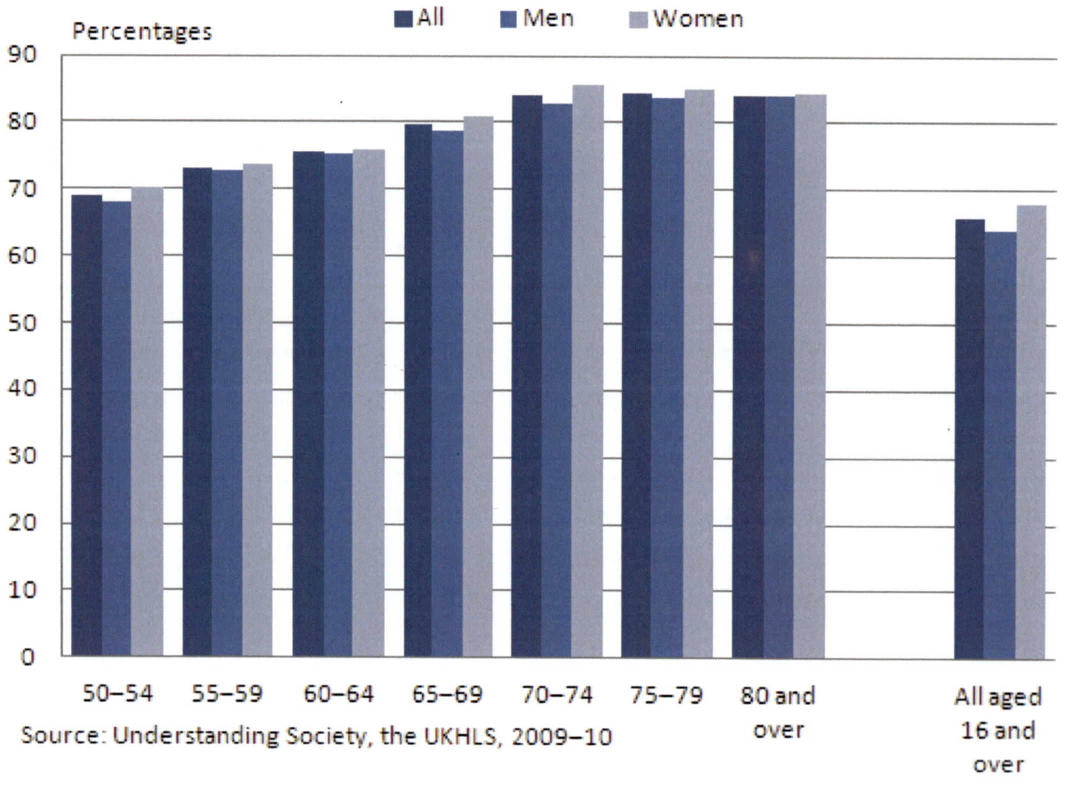

Notes:

1. Respondents were asked to indicate whether they 'strongly agree, agree, neither agree or disagree, disagree or strongly disagree' with the statement 'I feel like I belong to this neighbourhood'.

Download chart

XLS XLS format
(28 Kb)

Feelings of belonging to one's neighbourhood also varied slightly by sex for all respondents aged 16 and over: a higher proportion of women (68%) agreed or strongly agreed that they belonged to their neighbourhood than men (64%). For those aged 50 and over there were only small differences between the sexes in each age group **(Figure 1).**

Figure 2: Satisfaction with life (1): by belonging to their neighbourhood (2), 2009–10

United Kingdom

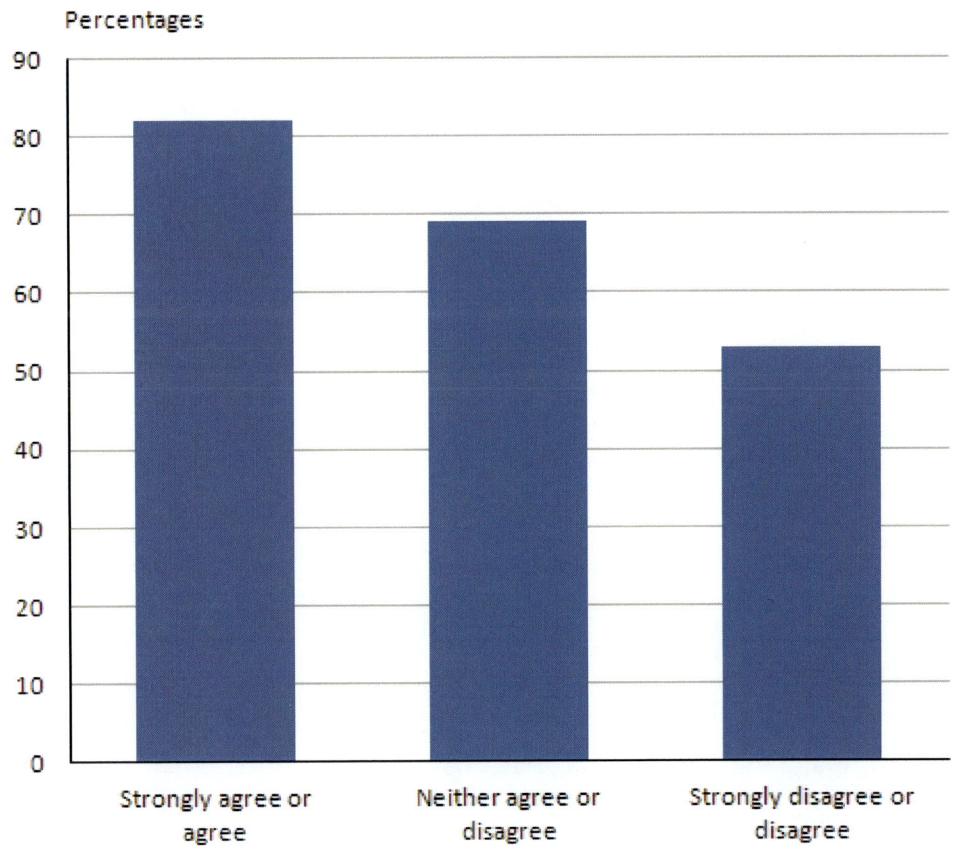

Source: Understanding Society, the UKHLS, 2009–10

Notes:

1. Includes those who were completely, mostly or somewhat satisfied with their life overall.

2. Respondents were asked to indicate whether they 'strongly agree, agree, neither agree or disagree, disagree or strongly disagree' with the statement 'I feel like I belong to this neighbourhood'.

Download chart

XLS XLS format
(27.5 Kb)

There was a relationship between overall life satisfaction and feelings about belonging to the neighbourhood. About 82% of those aged 50 and over who agreed that they belonged to their neighbourhood were satisfied with their lives overall compared with about 53% of those who disagreed (**Figure 2**).

Importance of friends in the neighbourhood

Having friends that live locally can be one of the things that make a person feel that they belong to their neighbourhood. Friends are part of a person's support system and, unlike family, are chosen by the individual. They may often give advice on decisions and are companions in life who share interests and can be confided in (ONS 2012b).

Figure 3: Friendships in the neighbourhood: by selected age groups and sex (1), 2009–10

United Kingdom

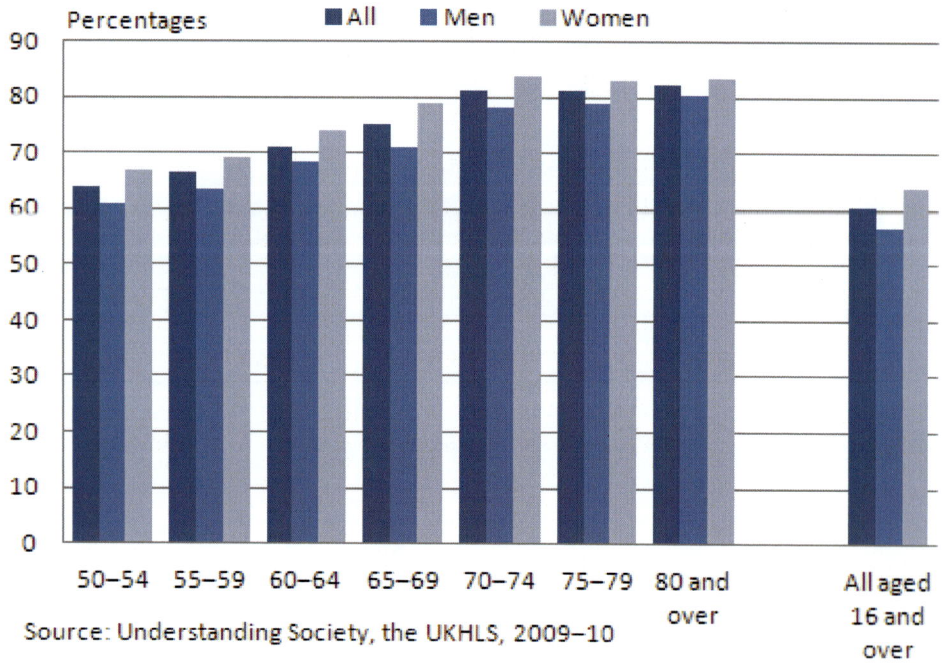

Notes:

1. Respondents were asked to indicate whether they 'strongly agree, agree, neither agree or disagree, disagree or strongly disagree' with the statement 'The friendships and associations I have with other people in my neighbourhood mean a lot to me'.

Download chart

XLS [XLS format]
(28 Kb)

The 2009–10 UKHLS asked respondents if friendships and associations they have with other people in their neighbourhood meant a lot to them. Overall, 60% of respondents aged 16 and over reported that local friends meant a lot to them, with women (64%) more likely to report this than men (57%). Of those aged 50 to 54 years old, 64% agreed or strongly agreed that local friends meant a lot to them. This rose to over 80% of those aged 70 and over. In each older age group a larger percentage of respondents said that local friends meant a lot to them than the average for all aged 16 and over (**Figure 3**).

Just as with feelings of belonging to one's neighbourhood there was a relationship between levels of overall life satisfaction and having local friends and associations. About 81% of those who agreed or strongly agreed that local friends and associations meant a lot to them were satisfied with their lives overall compared to those who disagreed (about 64%).

About the ONS Measuring National Well-being Programme

NWB logo 2

This article is published as part of the ONS Measuring National Well-being Programme.

The programme aims to produce accepted and trusted measures of the well-being of the nation - how the UK as a whole is doing. It is about looking at 'GDP and beyond' and includes:

- Greater analysis of the national economic accounts, especially to understand household income, expenditure and wealth.
- Further accounts linked to the national accounts, including the UK Environmental Accounts and valuing household production and 'human capital'.
- Quality of life measures, looking at different areas of national well-being such as health, relationships, job satisfaction, economic security, education environmental conditions.
- Working with others to include the measurement of the well-being of children and young people as part of national well-being.

- Measures of 'subjective well-being' - individuals' assessment of their own well-being.
- Headline indicators to summarise national well-being and the progress we are making as a society.

The programme is underpinned by a communication and engagement workstream, providing links with Cabinet Office and policy departments, international developments, the public and other stakeholders. The programme is working closely with Defra on the measurement of 'sustainable development' to provide a complete picture of national well-being, progress and sustainable development.

Find out more on the Measuring National Well-being website pages.

Background notes

1. **Understanding Society, the UK Household Longitudinal Study**
   Understanding Society is a unique and valuable academic study that captures important information every year about the social and economic circumstances and attitudes of people living in 40,000 UK households. It also collects additional health information from around 20,000 of the people who take part.

   Information from the longitudinal survey is primarily used by academics, researchers and policy makers in their work, but the findings are of interest to a much wider group of people including those working in the third sector, health practitioners, business, the media and the general public.

   Key facts

   - 40,000 households – 2,640 postcode sectors in England, Scotland and Wales – 2,400 addresses from Northern Ireland.
   - £48.9 million funding (until 2015).
   - Approximately 3 billion data points of information.
   - Innovation Panel of 1,500 respondents.
   - Participants aged 10 and older.
   - Building on 18 years of British Household Panel Survey.
   - 35 to 60 minutes: the average time to complete each face to face interview.

   How does it work?

   Interviews began in 2009 with all eligible members of the selected households.

   - Adults are interviewed every 12 months either face to face or over the phone using Computer Assisted Interviewing.
   - 10 to 15 year olds fill in a paper self-completion questionnaire.

   From 2010 some 20,000 participants aged over 16 also received nurse visits and provided a blood sample and some basic physical measurements (height, weight, blood pressure, grip strength).

Data used in this analysis

The data in this analysis is from the adult self completion questionnaire of Wave 1 of the Survey and has been weighted using the interview with self completion individual cross-sectional weight (a_indscus_xw).

Throughout this article 'agree' refers to those who strongly agree or agree and 'satisfied' refers to those who report being completely, mostly or somewhat satisfied.

For more information about the UKHLS see Understanding Society

2. Details of the policy governing the release of new data are available by visiting www.statisticsauthority.gov.uk/assessment/code-of-practice/index.html or from the Media Relations Office email: media.relations@ons.gsi.gov.uk

Copyright

This document is also available on our website at www.ons.gov.uk.

References

1. ONS 2012a National Well-being interactive wheel of measures. Accessed at National Well-being interactive wheel of measures [Adobe Flash]

2. ONS2012b Randall C (2012): Measuring National Well-being – Our Relationships, 2012, ONS. Accessed at Our relationships

3. Windsor et al, 2012: National Seniors Productive Ageing Centre (2012) Windsor T, Pearson E, Crisp A, Butterworth P, and Anstey K (2012): Neighbourhood Characteristics: Shaping the well-being of older Australians. Accessed at: http://www.productiveageing.com.au/userfiles/file/NeighbourhoodCharacteristics.pdf

04 April 2013

Measuring National Well-being - Children's well-being, 2013

Author Name(s): **Jen Beaumont Office for National Statistics**

Abstract

The article 'Measuring National Well-being - Children's Well-being, 2012' (ONSa) reported children's views on some aspects of their lives. This was based on data from the 2009–10 Understanding Society, the UK Household Longitudinal Study (UKHLS).This summary further explores children's reports of their well-being based on the 2010–11 study.

Introduction

During the national debate 'What matters to you' (ONSb), children were asked what was important to their overall well-being. They reported that their family, friends, school and appearance were very important.

To quote a respondent to the national debate on measuring well-being;

'My children matter to me. Most of all, their well-being and future prospects are the single most important thing in my life. If they are happy and well cared for, I am happy'.

Throughout this analysis 'relatively happy' refers to all those who were completely, mostly or somewhat happy.

Key points

- In 2010–11, 89 per cent of children said that they were relatively happy with their lives overall and 4 per cent reported being relatively unhappy.
- A much higher percentage reported being completely happy with their friends and family than with their school, their school work or, particularly, their appearance.

- Boys were more likely than girls to report being happy with their life overall, their friends and their appearance, while girls were more likely than boys to report being happy with their school work.
- Children's responses to all the UKHLS 2010–11 questions about their feelings to aspects about their lives were very similar to those in 2009–10.

Children's levels of happiness

In 2010–11 children aged 10 to 15 who took part in the UKHLS were most positive about their friends (96 per cent relatively happy) and family (95 per cent relatively happy) and least positive about their appearance (75 per cent relatively happy). Just over a third of children were completely happy with their lives overall (34 per cent). However, well over half of respondents were completely happy with their friends (56 per cent) and family (62 per cent). By contrast, less than one in five respondents were completely happy with their school work or appearance (both 19 per cent) (**Figure 1**).

Figure 1: Reported level of children's happiness with life overall and aspects of their lives, (1), 2010–11

United Kingdom

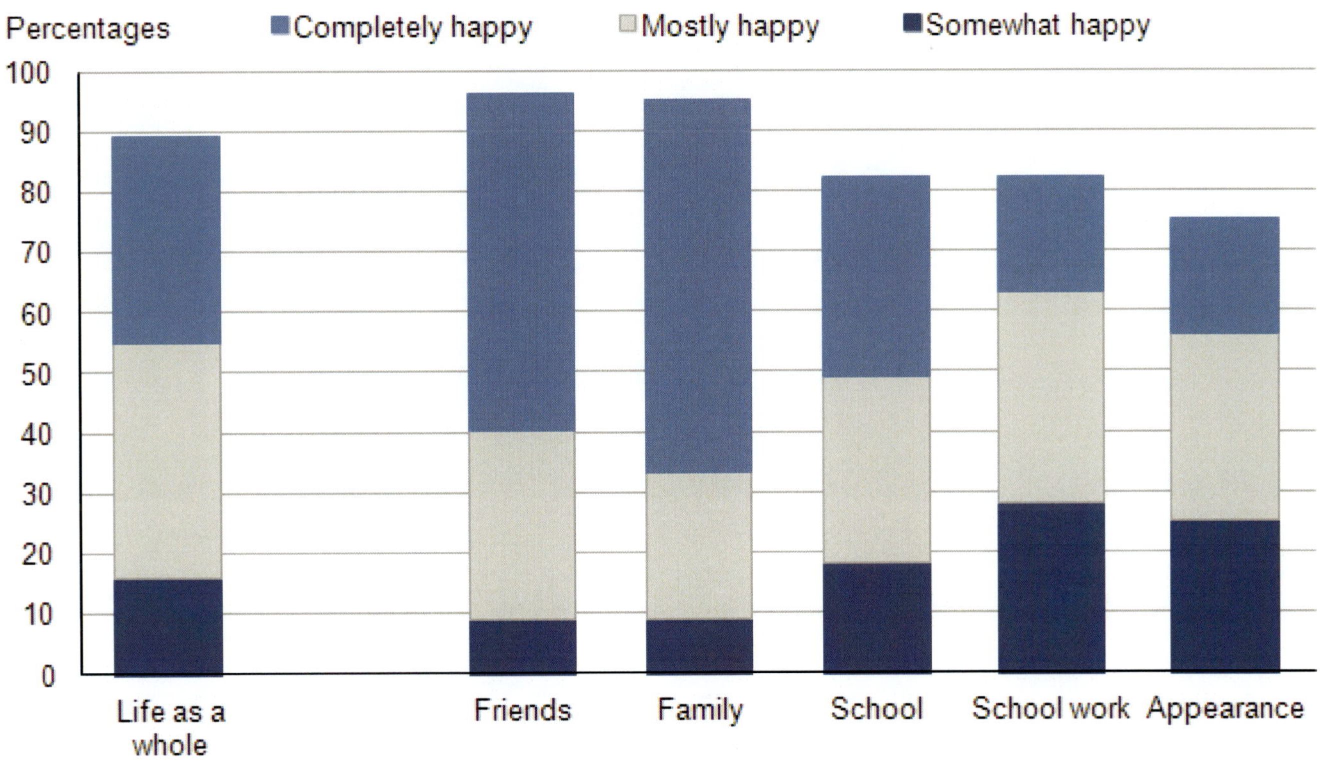

Source: Youth Module of the UK Household Longitudinal Study, 2010-11

Notes:

1. Children aged 10 to 15 were asked 'How do you feel about your .... life as a whole, friends, family, school. school work, appearance?' Responses were on a seven point scale from 'completely happy' to 'not at all happy'

Download chart

XLS XLS format
(28.5 Kb)

Differences by sex

Overall, a higher percentage of girls than boys said they were relatively happy with their school work while a higher percentage of boys than girls reported being relatively happy with life as a whole and their appearance (**Figure 2**).

Figure 2: Percentage of children who were relatively happy with life overall and aspects of their lives by sex, (1), 2010–11

United Kingdom

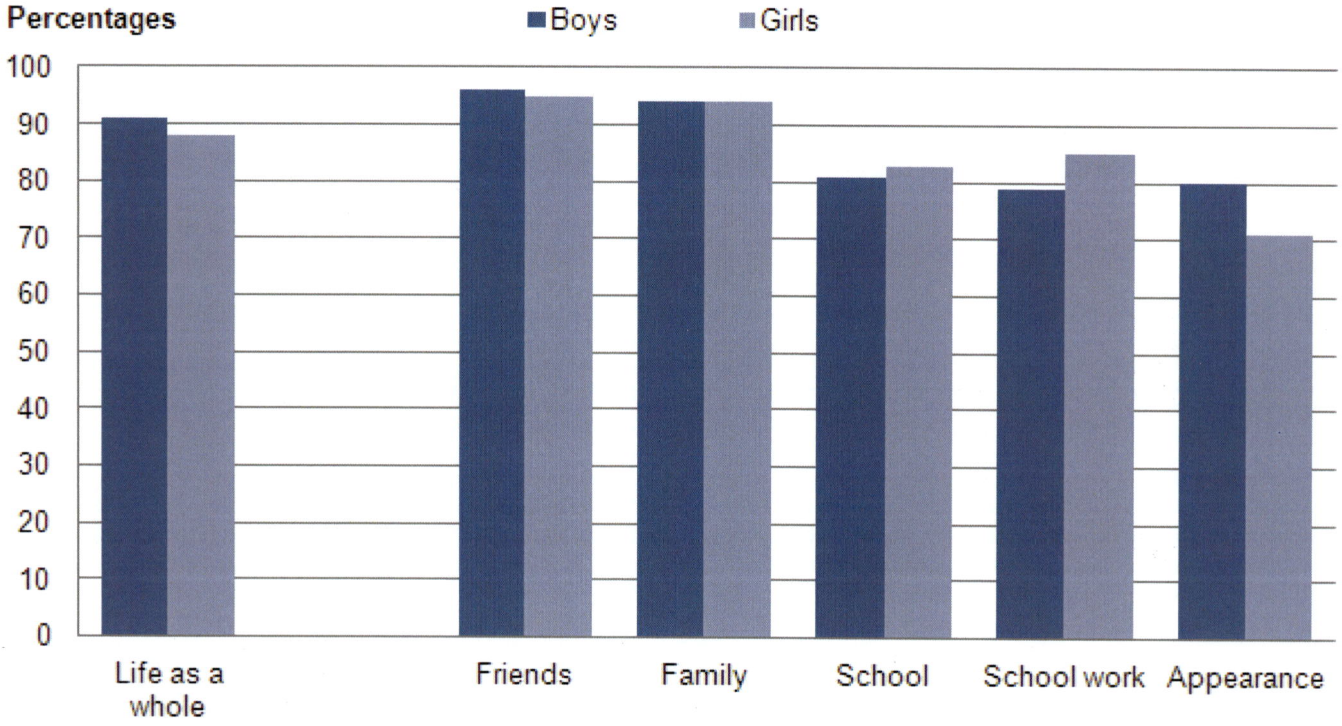

Source: Youth Module of the UK Household Longitudinal Study, 2010-11

Notes:

1. Children aged 10 to 15 were asked 'How do you feel about your .... life as a whole, friends, family, school. school work, appearance?' Responses were on a seven point scale from 'completely happy' to 'not at all happy'

Download chart

XLS XLS format
(29 Kb)

Children's well-being and the Good Childhood Index

The overall findings are similar to those of research in England by the Children's Society. This found a significant association between a child's self reported well-being and the 10 aspects of children's lives included in the Good Childhood Index (The Good Childhood Report, 2012). Other key findings in this report include:

- Choice and family have the biggest impact on children's happiness.
- The quality of children's relationships with their families is far more important than the structure of the family that they live in.
- Children in families who have experienced a reduction in income are more likely to have low well-being.
- Children who do not have clothes to 'fit in' with their peers are more than three times as likely to be unhappy with their appearance.

Further information

Some other aspects of children's well-being were discussed in the article 'Measuring National Well-being - Children's Well-being, 2012' Measuring National Well-being - Measuring children's Well-being

The paper 'Review of available sources and measures for children and young people's well-being' (January 2013) gives information about data which already exists and discusses some of the limitations of these data. Find this on the Measuring National Well-being website pages.

The Good Childhood Report, 2012 (Children's Society) http://www.childrenssociety.org.uk/what-we-do/research/well-being/good-childhood-report-2012

About the ONS Measuring National Well-being Programme

NWB logo 2

This article is published as part of the ONS Measuring National Well-being Programme.

The programme aims to produce accepted and trusted measures of the well-being of the nation - how the UK as a whole is doing.

Measuring National Well-being is about looking at 'GDP and beyond'. It includes headline indicators in areas such as health, relationships, job satisfaction, economic security, education, environmental conditions and measures of 'subjective well-being' (individuals' assessment of their own well-being).

Find out more on the Measuring National Well-being website pages.

Background notes

1. **UK Longitudinal Study**

The Youth Module of the UK Longitudinal Study is a self-completed questionnaire answered by those aged 11 to 15. The questions used in this analysis are:

'How do you feel about your...

life as a whole

schoolwork

appearance

family

friends

school?'

Responses were on a 7-point scale 'completely happy, 2, 3. 4, 5, 6 not at all happy'. In this analysis, responses completely happy, 2 (mostly happy) and 3 (somewhat happy) are described as relatively happy, a response of 4 is considered neutral and 5 (somewhat unhappy), 6 (mostly unhappy) and not at all happy are considered as relatively unhappy.

Source: University of Essex. Institute for Social and Economic Research and National Centre for Social Research, Understanding Society: Wave 1-2, 2009-2011 [computer file]. 4th Edition. Colchester, Essex: UK Data Archive [distributor], December 2012. SN: 6614, http://dx.doi.org/10.5255/UKDA-SN-6614-4.

The Good Childhood Index

The Good Childhood Index is published by the Children' Society. It is produced using surveys in England

http://www.childrenssociety.org.uk/what-we-do/research/well-being/background-programme/good-childhood-index

The main measure of overall subjective well-being included in the index consists of five statements to which children are asked to respond on a five-point scale from 'strongly disagree' to 'strongly agree':

- My life is going well

- My life is just right
- I wish I had a different kind of life
- I have a good life
- I have what I want in life

This measure is derived from a longer seven-item measure originally developed by Huebner (1994) in the United States. Children's responses to each question are coded on a scale from zero ('strongly disagree') to four ('strongly agree'), with the score for the middle statement being reversed. Then these scores are added together to create an overall scale from 0 to 20.

2. Details of the policy governing the release of new data are available by visiting www.statisticsauthority.gov.uk/assessment/code-of-practice/index.html or from the Media Relations Office email: media.relations@ons.gsi.gov.uk

Copyright

This document is also available on our website at www.ons.gov.uk.

References

1. ONSa Joloza, T (2012): Measuring National Well-being – Children's Well-being, 2012, ONS. Accessed at Measuring National Well-being - Measuring children's Well-being

2. ONSb "Measuring what Matters: National Statistician's Reflections on the National Debate on Measuring National Well-being' - published 25 July 2011. Find this on the Measuring National Well-being website pages.

3. University of Essex. Institute for Social and Economic Research and National Centre for Social Research, Understanding Society: Wave 1-2, 2009-2011 [computer file]. 4th Edition. Colchester, Essex: UK Data Archive [distributor], December 2012. SN: 6614, http://dx.doi.org/10.5255/UKDA-SN-6614-4.

11 April 2013

Measuring National Well-being: Older people's leisure time and volunteering, 2013

Author Name(s): **Theodore Joloza, Office for National Statistics**

Abstract

This article analyses for those aged 50 and over two measures which are currently used for Measuring National Well-being. These are 'the percentage of people who say they are satisfied with the amount of their leisure time' and 'the percentage of people who have volunteered more than once in the last 12 months'. The data are from Understanding Society, The UK Household Longitudinal Study, 2010-11 (UKHLS).

Introduction

This is part of a series of analyses examining the well-being of older people aged 50 and over. The Office for National Statistics' measures of well-being are organised into ten domains with each domain having between three and five separate indicators. More information about all the measures can be found in the 'National Well-being wheel of measures' (ONS, 2012a). Throughout this analysis 'satisfied' includes those who responded that they were completely, mostly or somewhat satisfied.

Key points

- A higher percentage of people aged 50 and over (70%) were satisfied with the amount of their leisure time compared with all those aged 16 and over (61%).
- The percentage of respondents who were satisfied with the amount of their leisure time increased steadily between the ages of 50 to 54 (51%) and 65 to 69 (84%) and then stayed at a similar level for those aged 69 and over (just over 80%).
- A higher percentage of those who were satisfied with the amount of their leisure time were also satisfied with their life overall.
- About 1 in 5 people aged 50 and over had volunteered more than once in the last 12 months but this varied by age group.
- Volunteering was associated with greater overall life satisfaction.

Satisfaction with the amount of leisure time

"The amount and quality of leisure time is important for people's well-being for the direct satisfaction it brings. Additionally leisure, taken in certain ways, is important for physical and mental health. Leisure also contributes to the well-being of people other than the person directly enjoying leisure. When a person engages in leisure, the benefits gained are shared with others in a multitude of ways, including improvements in personal relationships, family functioning, and in terms of creation of social capital networks." (OECD, 2009)

The measure 'the proportion of people who are satisfied with the amount of leisure time' has been used as one of the headline indicators of measuring national well-being in the area of 'What we do'. This section focuses on how satisfied older people were with the amount of their leisure time.

Data from the second wave of UKHLS show that a higher proportion of older people aged 50 and over (70%) reported being satisfied with the amount of leisure time they had compared to all respondents aged 16 and over (61%). Among the older respondents there was little difference by sex, with about 70% of both men and women being satisfied with the amount of their leisure time.

There was a relationship between age and satisfaction with leisure time. There was a gradual increase in the percentage of those who were satisfied with the amount of their leisure time from 51% of those aged 50 to 54 to 84% of those aged 65 to 69. This is presumably because the time used caring for school age children and being in paid work reduces at this stage of individuals' lives. After the age of 69 there was little change in the percentage of those satisfied with the amount of their leisure time. There is a slight reduction for those aged 80 and over (80%).

Figure 1: Satisfaction with the amount of leisure time by selected age group and sex (2010–2011)

United Kingdom

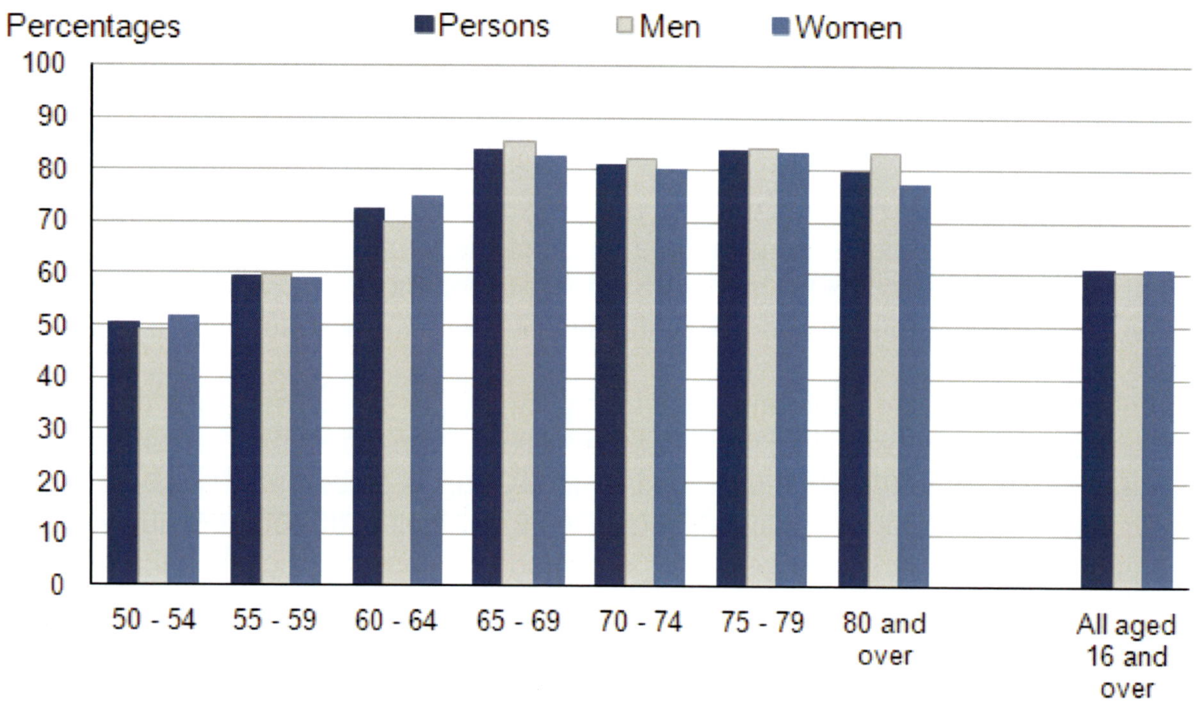

Notes:

1. Respondents were asked 'How dissatisfied or satisfied they were with the amount of their leisure time?' Responses were on a 7 point scale from 'completely dissatisfied to 'completely satisfied'.
2. Non-respondents not included
3. Source: Understanding Society, Wave 2, 2010–11

Download chart

XLS XLS format
(28.5 Kb)

There is a relationship between satisfaction with the amount of leisure time and satisfaction with life overall. **Figure 2** shows that 91% of older people who were satisfied with the amount of their leisure time were also satisfied with life overall. Only 40% of those who said they were dissatisfied with their amount of leisure said they were satisfied with their life overall.

Figure 2: Satisfaction with life overall by satisfaction with amount of leisure time

United Kingdom

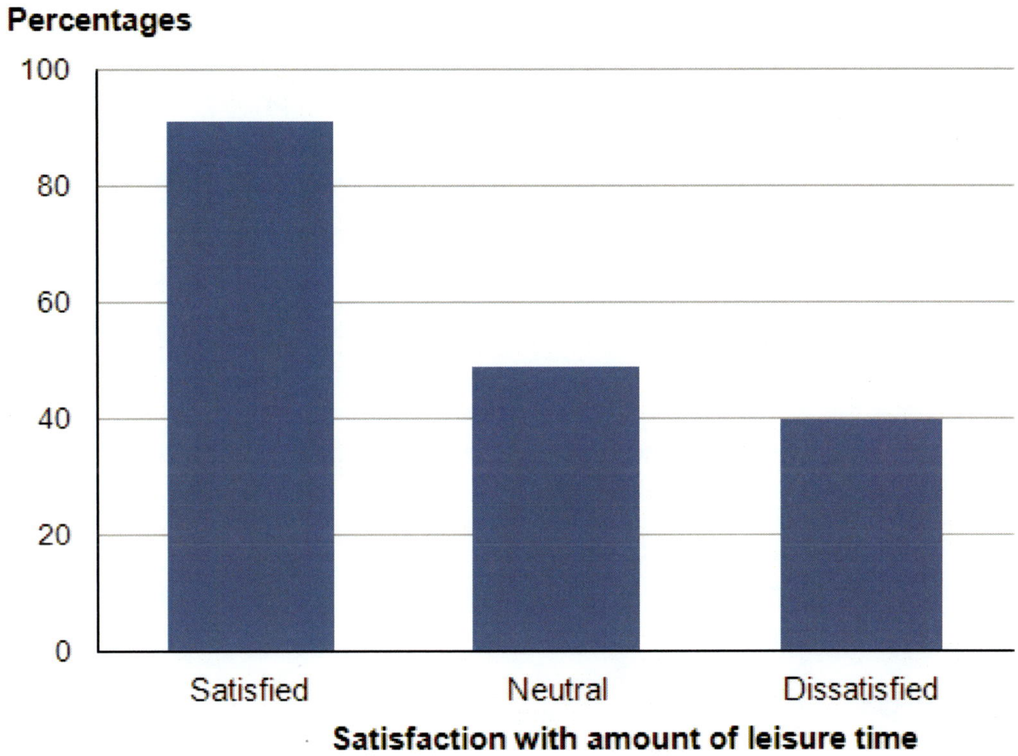

Notes:

1. 'Satisfaction with life overall' includes those who responded that they strongly agree, agree or slightly agree that they were satisfied with their life
2. Non-respondents not included
3. Source: Understanding Society, Wave 2, 2010–11

Download chart

XLS XLS format
(28 Kb)

Volunteering

Research on the influence of volunteering on well-being has considered older people. According to Plagnol and Huppert (2010), the research has often been guided by the observation that older people appear to benefit more from volunteering than younger people. These authors offer a possible explanation that volunteering gives older people a new sense of purpose, which may be more significant for this group because of evidence suggesting that older people tend to be more prone to feeling lonely (McCloughan et all, 2011).

Analysis of the English Longitudinal Study of Ageing data from 2006 and 2008 showed that there are benefits to volunteering in later life.The higher the frequency of volunteering the better the well-being measured by the life satisfaction, quality of life, social isolation and depression of the individuals involved. People who volunteered in both years had improvements in their well-being scores compared to those who did not. The study also found that there was a relationship between the frequency of volunteering and improvements in individual well-being. Those who volunteered frequently had higher levels of individual well-being compared to those who had not volunteered. The difference in individual well-being between those who had volunteered once and those who had not volunteered at all was minimal and not significant (Nazroo and Matthews, 2012).

The UKHLS asked whether respondents had volunteered in the 12 months before their interview and if so how often. Nearly 20% of older people had volunteered in the last 12 months compared to about 17% of all those aged 16 and over.

Figure 3: Volunteering more than once by age

United Kingdom

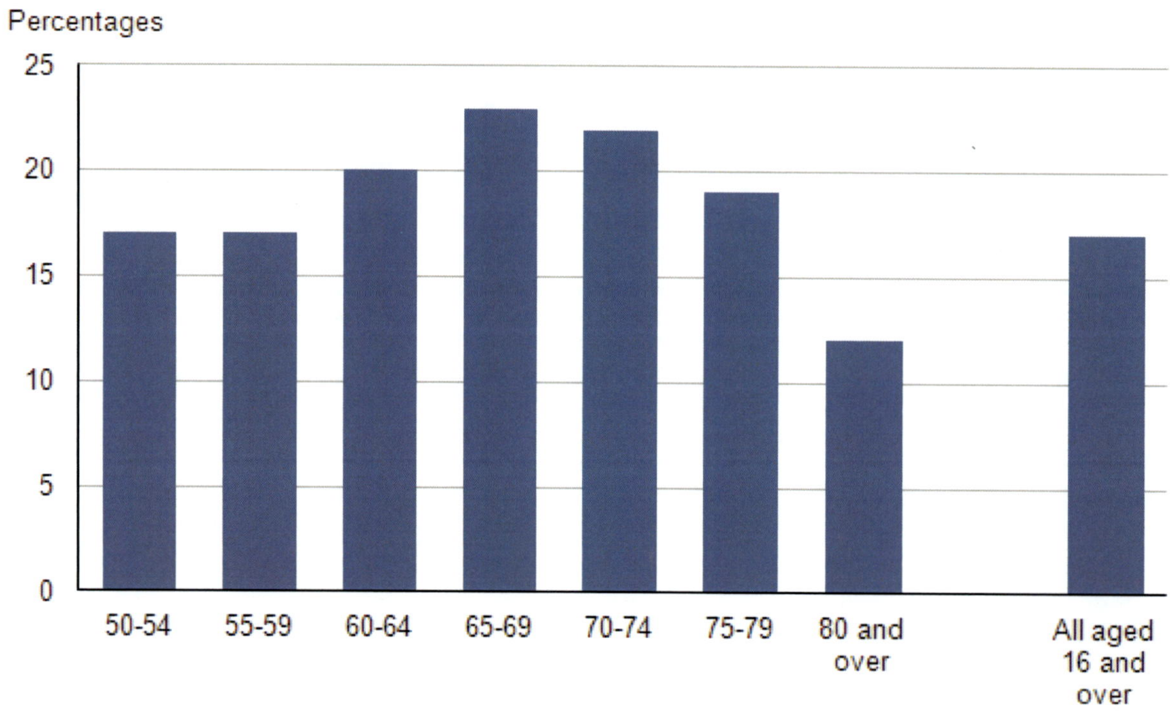

Notes:

1. Respondents were asked whether they have volunteered at all in the last 12 months and if so how often.
2. Non-respondents are not included
3. Source: Understanding Society, Wave 2, 2010–11

Download chart

XLS XLS format
(27.5 Kb)

The data also showed that there was a relationship between age and how often people volunteer. The proportion of people who volunteered more than once increased with age. For those aged between 50 and 59 it was about 17%. The highest proportion of older people who volunteered more than once was in those aged 65 and 69 at 23% (Figure 3). This is the same group that also had the highest proportion of people saying they were satisfied with their amount of leisure time.

There was a relationship between volunteering at least once in the last 12 months and life satisfaction. For older people the proportion of those who volunteered and said they were satisfied with their lives overall was higher at 84%. For those who did not volunteer 75% said they were satisfied with their life overall.

Background notes

1. Details of the policy governing the release of new data are available by visiting www.statisticsauthority.gov.uk/assessment/code-of-practice/index.html or from the Media Relations Office email: media.relations@ons.gsi.gov.uk

Copyright

This document is also available on our website at www.ons.gov.uk.

References

1. McCloughan, P, Batt, WH, Costine M and Scully, D (2011), Participation in volunteering and unpaid work, http://www.eurofound.europa.eu/pubdocs/2011/02/en/1/EF1102EN.pdf

2. Nazroo, J. and Matthews, K. (2012) 'The Impact of Volunteering on Wellbeing in Later Life', http://www.wrvs.org.uk/Uploads/Documents/Reports%20and%20Reviews/the_impact_of_volunteering_on_wellbeing_in_later_life.pdf, accessed on 19/03/13

3. OECD (2009), Special Focus: Measuring Leisure in OECD Countries http://www.oecd.org/berlin/42675407.pdf accessed on 26 March 2013

4. ONS, 2012a, National Well-being wheel of measures, http://www.ons.gov.uk/ons/interactive/well-being-wheel-of-measures/index.html

5. Plagnol, A. C., and Huppert, F. A. (2010). Happy to help? Exploring the factors associated with variations in rates of volunteering across Europe. Social Indicators Research, 97, 157-176.

6. University of Essex, Institute for Social and Economic Research and National Centre for Social Research, *Understanding Society: Wave 1-2, 2009-2011* [computer file]. 4th *Edition*. Colchester, Essex: UK Data Archive [distributor], December 2012. SN: 6614, http://dx.doi.org/10.5255/UKDA-SN-6614-4.

About the ONS Measuring National Well-being Programme

NWB logo 2

This article is published as part of the ONS Measuring National Well-being Programme.

The programme aims to produce accepted and trusted measures of the well-being of the nation - how the UK as a whole is doing. It is about looking at 'GDP and beyond' and includes:

- Greater analysis of the national economic accounts, especially to understand household income, expenditure and wealth.
- Further accounts linked to the national accounts, including the UK Environmental Accounts and valuing household production and 'human capital'.
- Quality of life measures, looking at different areas of national well-being such as health, relationships, job satisfaction, economic security, education environmental conditions.
- Working with others to include the measurement of the well-being of children and young people as part of national well-being.

- Measures of 'subjective well-being' - individuals' assessment of their own well-being.
- Headline indicators to summarise national well-being and the progress we are making as a society.

The programme is underpinned by a communication and engagement workstream, providing links with Cabinet Office and policy departments, international developments, the public and other stakeholders. The programme is working closely with Defra on the measurement of 'sustainable development' to provide a complete picture of national well-being, progress and sustainable development.

Find out more on the Measuring National Well-being website pages.

About Understanding Society

Understanding Society, the UK Household Longitudinal Study
Understanding Society is a unique and valuable academic study that captures important information every year about the social and economic circumstances and attitudes of people living in 40,000 UK households. It also collects additional health information from around 20,000 of the people who take part.

Information from the longitudinal survey is primarily used by academics, researchers and policy makers in their work, but the findings are of interest to a much wider group of people including those working in the third sector, health practitioners, business, the media and the general public.

Key facts

- 40,000 households – 2,640 postcode sectors in England, Scotland and Wales – 2,400 addresses from Northern Ireland.
- £48.9 million funding (until 2015).
- Approximately 3 billion data points of information.
- Innovation Panel of 1,500 respondents.
- Participants aged 10 and older.
- Building on 18 years of British Household Panel Survey.
- 35 to 60 minutes: the average time to complete each face to face interview.

How does it work?

Interviews began in 2009 with all eligible members of the selected households.

- Adults are interviewed every 12 months either face to face or over the phone using Computer Assisted Interviewing.
- 10 to 15 year olds fill in a paper self-completion questionnaire.

From 2010 some 20,000 participants aged over 16 also received nurse visits and provided a blood sample and some basic physical measurements (height, weight, blood pressure, grip strength).

Data used in this analysis

The data in this analysis is from the adult self completion questionnaire of Wave 1 of the Survey and has been weighted using the interview with self completion individual cross-sectional weight (a_indscus_xw).

Throughout this article 'agree' refers to those who strongly agree or agree and 'satisfied' refers to those who report being completely, mostly or somewhat satisfied.

For more information about the UKHLS see Understanding Society

Measuring National Well-being - Older people and loneliness, 2013

Author Name(s): **Jen Beaumont Office for National Statistics**

Abstract

This is the part of a series of short articles examining the well-being of older people. It provides an analysis of reported feelings of loneliness by people aged 52 and over using 2009–10 data from the English Longitudinal Study of Ageing (ELSA).

Introduction

Loneliness is a complex and usually unpleasant emotion which typically includes anxious feelings about a lack of connectedness or communality with others. As such, loneliness can be felt even when surrounded by other people. Research has shown that loneliness is widely prevalent throughout society among people in marriages or relationships, and among those who have families and successful careers (Peplau et al, 1982). Loneliness has also been described as social pain — a psychological mechanism meant to alert an individual to feelings of isolation and motivate him/her to seek social connections (Caciopone et al, 2008). One way of thinking about loneliness is as a discrepancy between one's desired and achieved levels of social interaction, while solitude is simply the lack of contact with people. People can be lonely while in the middle of a crowd. Conversely, one can be alone and not feel lonely. Loneliness is therefore a subjective experience; if a person thinks they are lonely, then they are lonely.

Key points

Information from English Longitudinal Study of Ageing in 2009-10 for those aged 52 and over:

- Two thirds (66 per cent) of respondents reported being lonely hardly ever or never, 25 per cent said they felt lonely sometimes and only 9 per cent said they felt lonely often.
- A higher percentage of those aged 80 and over reported feeling lonely some of the time or often when compared to other age groups (46 per cent of those aged 80 and over compared to the average of 34 per cent for all aged 52 and over).
- Those who report feeling lonely sometimes or often are much more likely to report a lower level of satisfaction with their lives overall.
- Two in every five individuals who lived alone reported that they hardly ever or never felt lonely.
- People who had been widowed, separated or divorced or those who were in poor health were more likely to report feeling lonely.

- There is a strong association between reported feelings of loneliness and reported limitations in performing daily activities.
- Limitations in daily activities together with other changes in circumstances such as loss of partner or losing touch with friends as age increases are likely to contribute to the increase in reported feelings of loneliness in the oldest age groups.
- In all age groups a higher percentage of women than men reported feeling lonely some of the time or often, the differences were larger in the older age groups
- Some of the difference between women and men in reported loneliness could be explained by the characteristics of the sample who responded to this survey: in the older age groups there were considerably more women than men and women were more likely than men to be widowed.

Frequency of feeling lonely by age and sex

In 2009-10 one question asked on the English Longitudinal Study of Ageing (ELSA) was how often individuals felt lonely. About 46 per cent of those aged 80 and over reported being lonely often or some of the time compared to about third (34 per cent) of all aged 52 and over. Those aged 80 and over were also considerably more likely to report being lonely often than other age groups: 17 per cent of this oldest age group reported being lonely often compared to an average of 9 per cent of all respondents (**Figure 1**).

Figure 1: Frequency of feeling lonely by age group (1), 2009–10

England

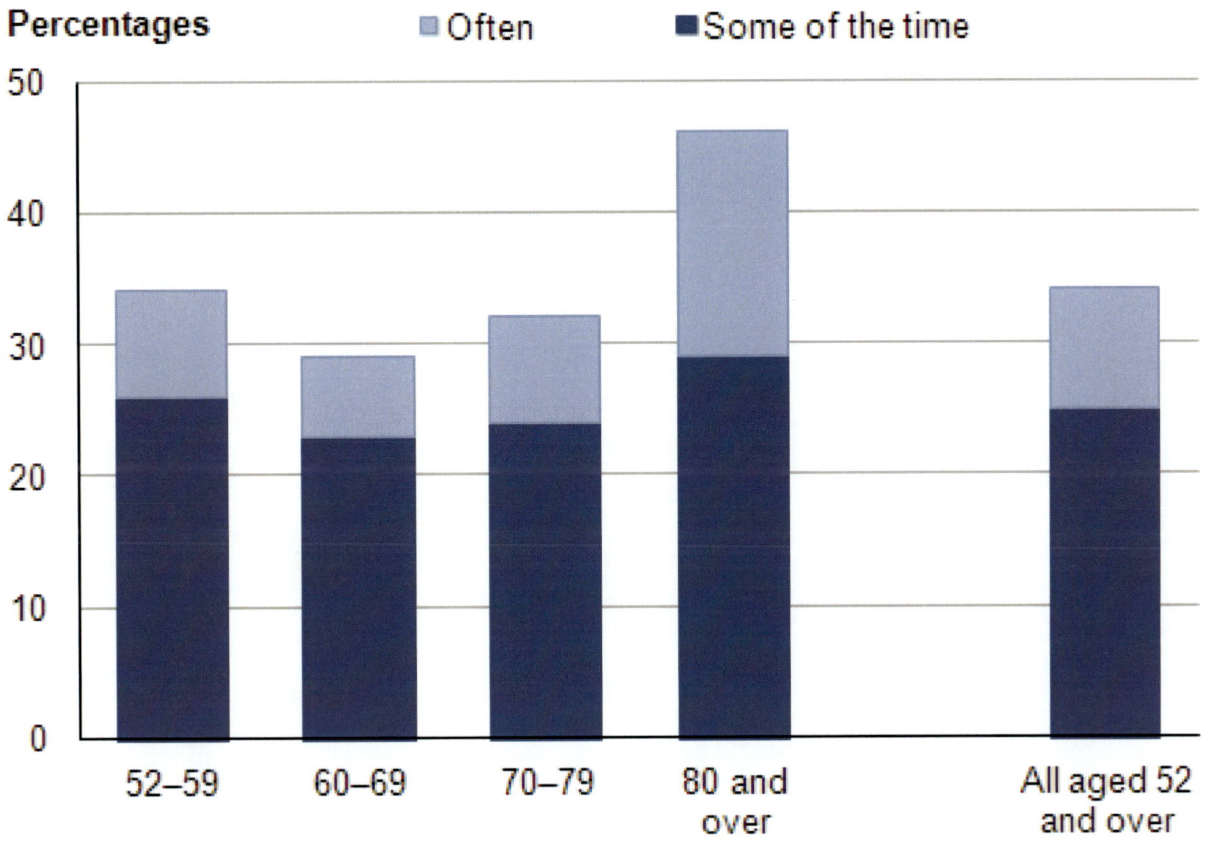

Notes:

1. Respondents were asked 'How often do you feel lonely' and responded 'Hardly ever or never', 'Some of the time' or 'Often'
2. Source: English Longitudinal Study of Ageing, Wave 5, 2009–10

Download chart

XLS XLS format
(28.5 Kb)

A higher percentage of women than men reported feeling lonely some of the time or often in each age group: 39 per cent of all women aged 52 and over reported this frequency of feeling lonely compared to 27 per cent of men. **(Figure 2)** In this survey the characteristics of the respondents also vary by age and sex which may explain some of this difference. See 'Loneliness and other characteristics' for further discussion.

Figure 2: Feeling lonely: by age group and sex (1), 2009–10

England

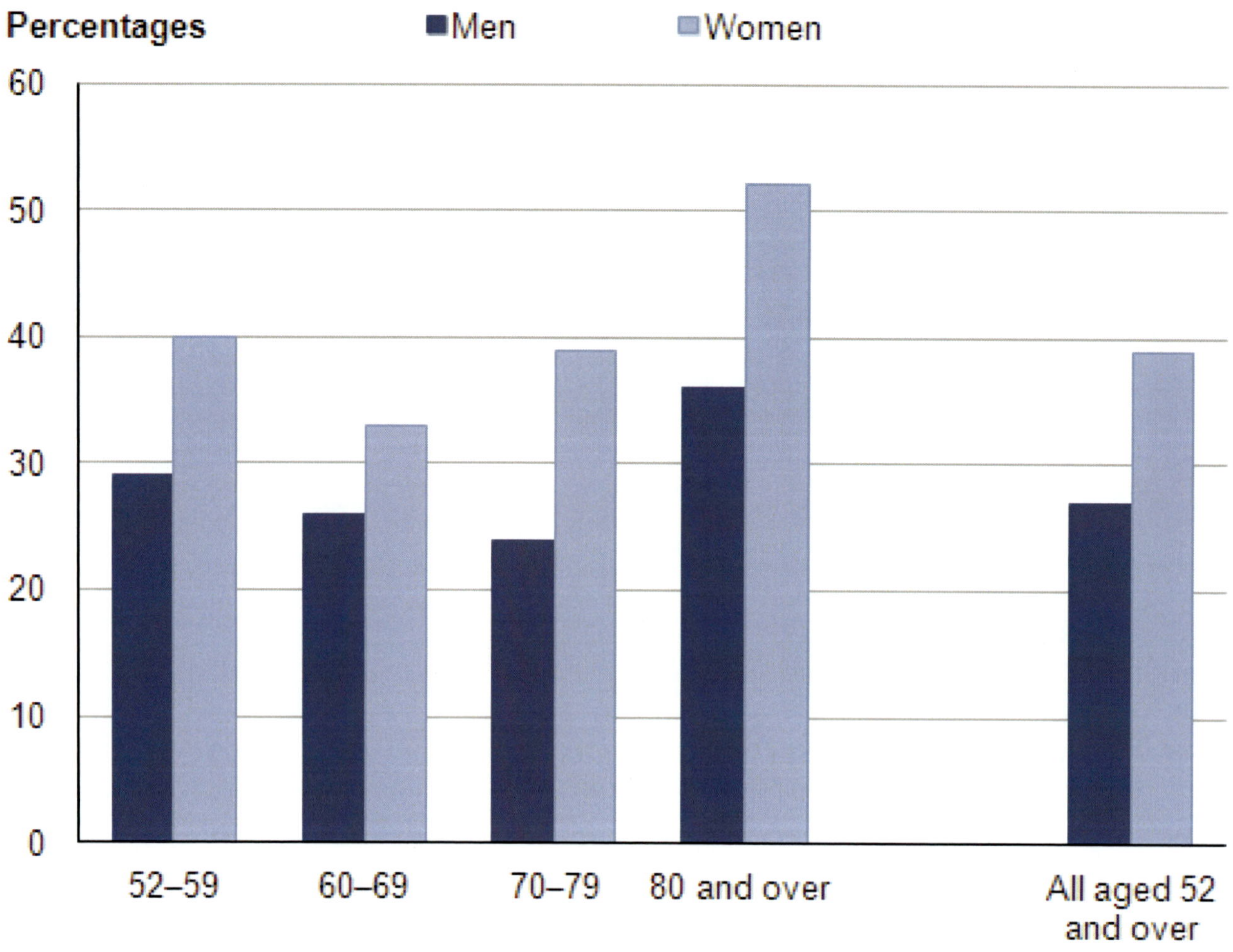

Notes:

1. Respondents were asked 'How often do you feel lonely' and responded 'Hardly ever or never', 'Some of the time' or 'Often'
2. Source: English Longitudinal Study of Ageing, Wave 5, 2009–10

Download chart

XLS XLS format
(28.5 Kb)

Frequency of feeling lonely and life satisfaction

Another question asked in ELSA was about how satisfied individuals were with their lives overall. The reported frequency of feeling lonely is strongly related to respondents' views of their own lives: the percentage of respondents who reported very positive views of satisfaction with their lives overall is highest for those who hardly ever feel lonely (89 per cent) and lowest for those who report feeling lonely often (38 per cent) (**Figure 3**).

Figure 3: Satisfaction with life overall: by frequency of loneliness (1), 2009–10

England

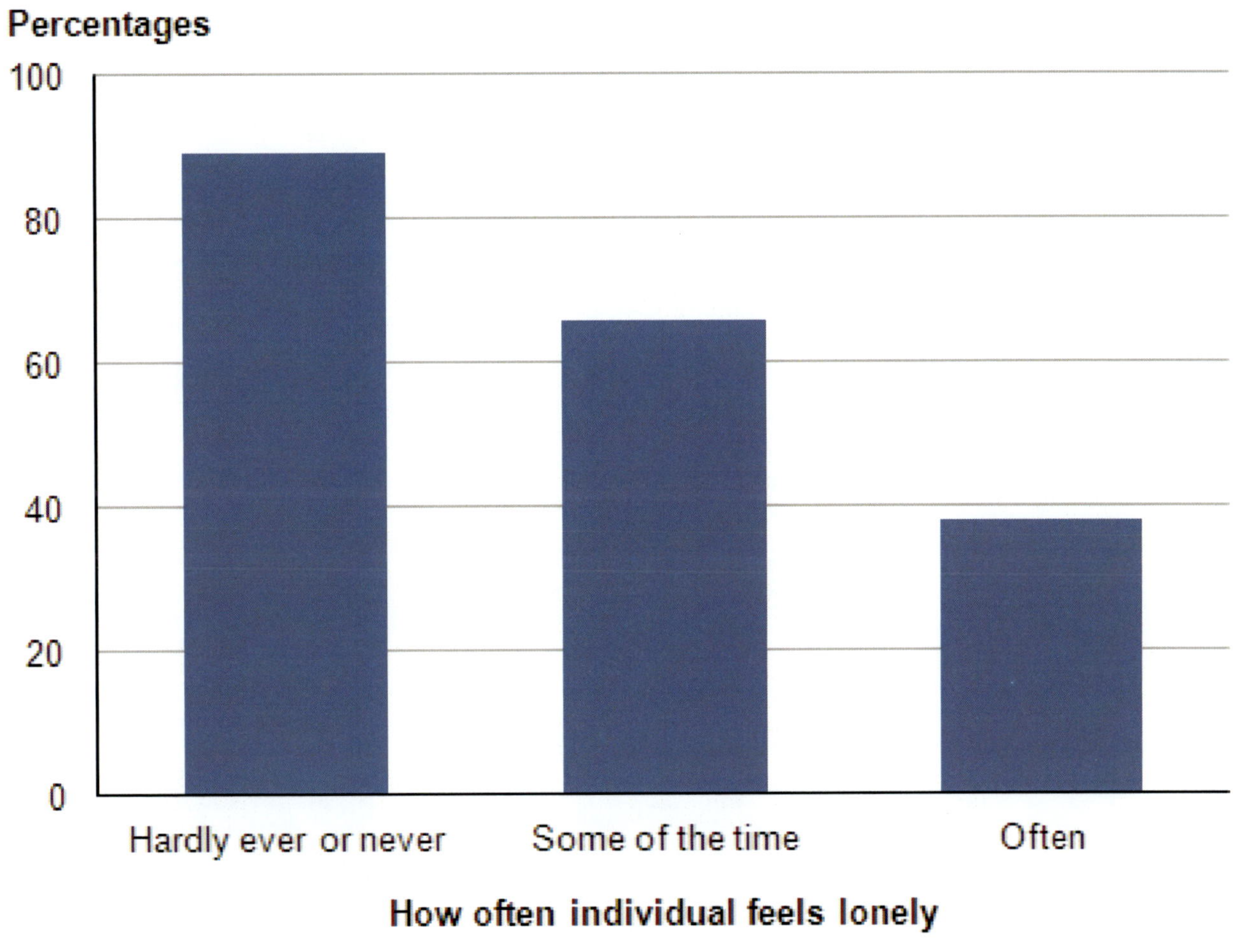

Notes:

1. 'Satisfaction with life overall' includes those who responded that they were strongly agree, agree or slightly agree that they were satisfied with their life
2. Source: English Longitudinal Study of Ageing, Wave 5, 2009–10

Download chart

XLS XLS format
(28 Kb)

Impaired activities of daily living and feeling lonely

An analysis of well-being and health related issues based on data from respondents to Wave 4 of the English Longitudinal Study of Ageing (ELSA) showed that limitations in activities of daily living (ADL) were a major correlate of well-being as measured by elevated depressive symptoms in middle-aged and older people (Demakakos, McMunn and Steptoe, 2010). The differences in loneliness associated with impaired ADL were among the greatest observed in this analysis irrespective of age.

The data analysed here show that there is a considerable difference in the percentage of those who report feeling lonely some of the time or often according to whether any reported long standing illness is also said to limit daily activities. About 27 per cent of those who did not report that they had any long standing illness said that they had been lonely some of the time or often compared to about 29 per cent of those with a long standing illness which did not limit their activities. However, nearly 45 per cent of those with a long standing illness that did limit their activities reported feeling lonely some of the time or often **(Figure 4)**.

Figure 4: Frequency of loneliness (1): by status of long standing illness (2), 2009–10

England

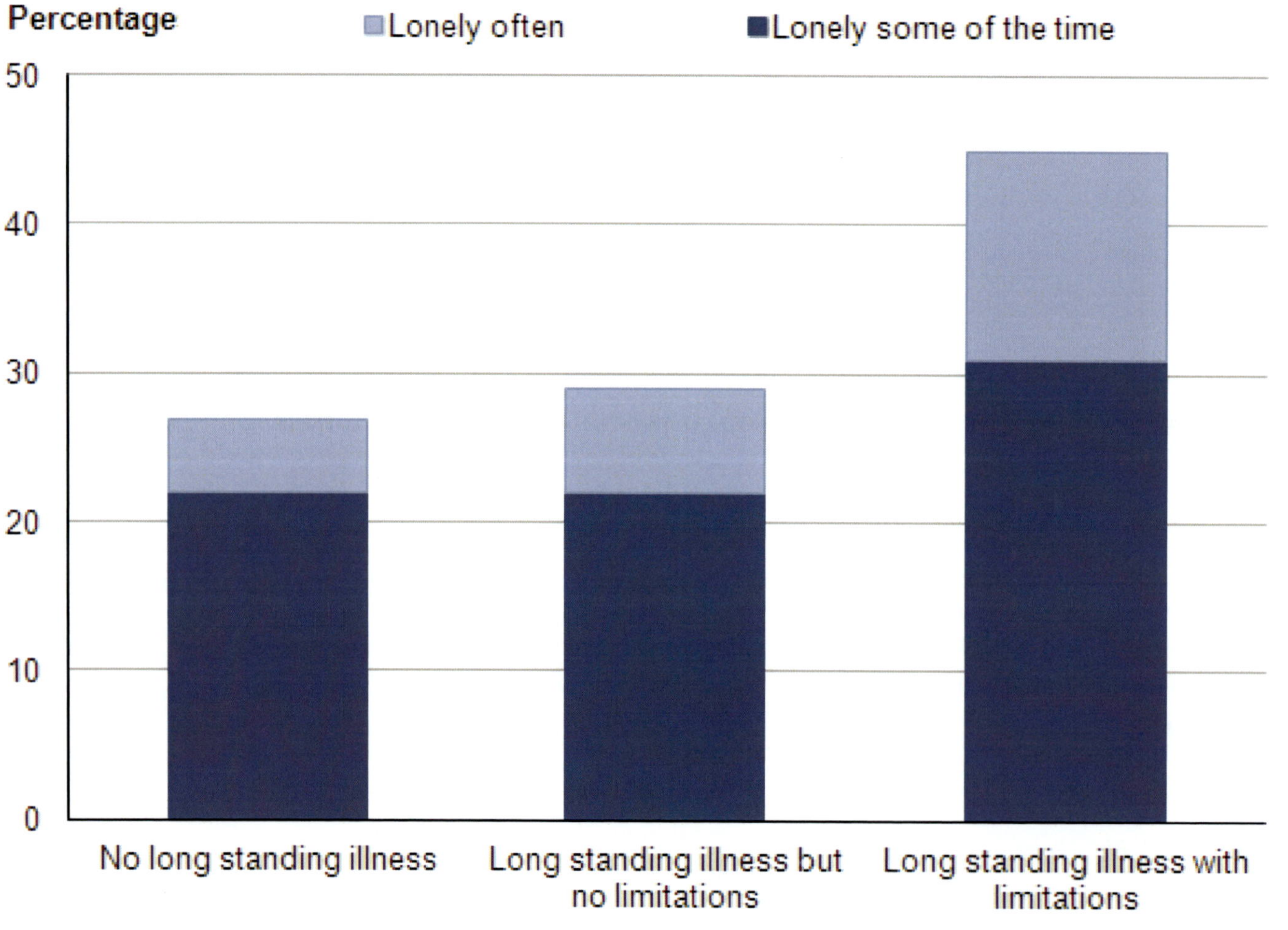

Notes:

1. Respondents were asked 'How often do you feel lonely' and responded 'Hardly ever or never', 'Some of the time' or 'Often'
2. Respondents were asked whether they had a long standing illness and whether it limited their daily activities such as pushing a vacuum cleaner
3. Source: English Longitudinal Study of Ageing, Wave 5, 2009–10

Download chart

XLS XLS format
(28.5 Kb)

Loneliness and other characteristics

As was reported at the beginning of this paper feeling lonely is not the same as being alone. Indeed some individuals welcome and prefer solitude to being with others all of the time. However, both living arrangements and marital status are related to feeling lonely. One in five (20 per cent) of those aged 52 and over who lived on their own reported being lonely often and an additional two in five (39 per cent) reported being lonely some of the time. Of course those who live on their own are more likely to be single, widowed, separated or divorced and a relatively high percentage of these groups report that they were lonely often or some of the time, with a particularly high percentage of those who were widowed (63 per cent). The percentage of those who reported poor health and being lonely some of the time or often (59 per cent) was nearly three times the percentage of as those who reported excellent health and loneliness some of the time or often (21 per cent) **(Table 1).**

Table 1: Frequency of loneliness (1): by marital status, number of people in household and reported health status, 2009–10

England (Percentages (2))

		Hardly ever or never	Some of the time	Often
Marital status				
	Married, remarried or in a legal partnership	77	19	4
	Single, that is never married	57	30	13
	Separated or divorced	49	37	14
	Widowed	38	41	22
Household size				
	1	41	39	20
	2	76	19	4
	3	69	26	5
	4 or more	67	25	8
Health status				
	Excellent	80	18	3
	Very good	76	20	4

	Good	67	25	7
	Fair	52	33	14
	Poor	41	36	23
Limiting long standing illness or disability				
	No long standing illness	73	22	5
	Long standing illness but no limitations	71	22	7
	Long standing illness with limitations	55	31	14
All aged 52 and over		66	25	9

Source: English Longitudinal Study of Ageing, Wave 5, 2009–10

Table notes:

1. Respondents were asked 'How often do you feel lonely' and responded 'Hardly ever or never', 'Some of the time' or 'Often'.
2. Percentages may not sum to 100 because of rounding.

Download table

XLS XLS format
(30 Kb)

The age and sex differences in feelings of loneliness which were discussed in the section 'Frequency of feeling lonely by age and sex' might be explained by the distribution of other characteristics of the respondents to ELSA. The Survey is longitudinal (the same households are interviewed during each wave) so that this sample for Wave 5 reflects the changes over time that result from men tending to die at a younger age. There are a much higher number of women than men in the older age groups and a much higher percentage of women than men have been widowed.

The distribution of characteristics within the sample might explain some of the variation in reported frequency of feeling lonely. The percentages of both men and women in all age groups are very similar for each reported health status. However, women in this sample were more likely than men to be widowed in each age group, but particularly in the 70-79 and 80 and over age groups. As approximately four in five of those who are widowed also lived on their own at the time of the Survey, women were also more likely to live on their own. Losing one's partner and living alone can result in a reduction in an individual's social interaction and, therefore, an increase in feelings of loneliness **(Table 2).**

Table 2: Marital status and household size: by selected age groups and sex, 2009–10

England (Percentages (1))

		Men 70–79	Women 70–79	Men 80 and over	Women 80 and over
Marital status					
	Married, remarried or in a legal partnership	75	53	65	22
	Single, that is never married	6	4	1	6
	Separated or divorced	8	11	3	5
	Widowed	11	32	31	67
Household size					
	1	21	39	31	68
	2	70	55	63	27
	3	8	4	3	4
	4 or more	2	2	2	1

Source: English Longitudinal Study of Ageing, Wave 5, 2009–10

Table notes:

1. Percentages may not sum to 100 because of rounding.

Download table

XLS XLS format
(19 Kb)

Background notes

1. **The English Longitudinal Study of Ageing (ELSA)**

   This is an interdisciplinary data resource on health, economic position and quality of life as people age. The primary objective of the ELSA is to collect longitudinal multidisciplinary data from a representative sample of the English population aged 50 and older. It collects both objective and subjective data relating to health and disability, biological markers of disease, economic circumstance, social participation, networks and well-being.

   For more information see ***[http://www.ifs.org.uk/ELSA/data]***

Data used in this analysis

The data in this analysis is from the adult self completion questionnaire of ELSA Wave 5 of the Survey and has been weighted using the self completion individual cross-sectional weight

Throughout this article 'agree' refers to those who strongly agree or agree and 'satisfied' refers to those who report being completely, mostly or somewhat satisfied.

2. Details of the policy governing the release of new data are available by visiting www.statisticsauthority.gov.uk/assessment/code-of-practice/index.html or from the Media Relations Office email: media.relations@ons.gsi.gov.uk

Copyright

References

1. Peplau, L.A. & Perlman, D. (1982). Perspectives on loneliness. In L. A. Peplau & D. Perlman (Eds.), Loneliness: A sourcebook of current theory, research and therapy. (pp. 1-18). New York: John Wiley and Sons

2. Cacioppo, John; Patrick, William, *Loneliness: Human Nature and the Need for Social Connection*, New York : W.W. Norton & Co., 2008. ISBN 978-0-393-06170-3. Science of Loneliness.com

About the ONS Measuring National Well-being Programme

NWB logo 2

This article is published as part of the ONS Measuring National Well-being Programme.

The programme aims to produce accepted and trusted measures of the well-being of the nation - how the UK as a whole is doing.

Measuring National Well-being is about looking at 'GDP and beyond'. It includes headline indicators in areas such as health, relationships, job satisfaction, economic security, education, environmental conditions and measures of 'subjective well-being' (individuals' assessment of their own well-being).

Find out more on the Measuring National Well-being website pages.

30 April 2013

Differences in well-being by ethnicity

Author Name(s): **Stephen Hicks Office for National Statisitcs**

Abstract

This short story looks at people's assessment of their own well-being by different ethnic groups using the April 2011 to March 2012 Annual Population Survey. As well as providing estimates for ethnic groups and ethnic group by sex, it provides further information that may explain some of the differences observed.

Introduction

Asking people to provide their own assessment of their own well-being is part of ONS's approach to measuring the well-being of the nation. Showing differences for different population groups is important as it allows for debate about why these differences may exist and provides useful information for policy making. This short story considers the differences in well-being between different ethnic groups and offers some potential reasons for these observed differences. It is published as part of the ONS's Measuring National Well-being programme which aims to monitor and understand the well-being of the UK.

Key Points

- People from the Black ethnic group[1] were on average least satisfied with their lives out of all the broad ethnic groups in the UK (6.7 out of 10). Bangladeshi (7.0 out of 10) and Mixed/multiple groups (7.1 out of 10) also gave lower ratings on average than the White ethnic group (7.4 out of 10).
- All other ethnic groups, gave on average, lower ratings than the White ethnic group when asked to assess the extent they feel the things they do in life are worthwhile. Bangladeshi gave the lowest average ratings (7.3 out of 10) compared with the White group (7.7 out of 10).
- Day-to-day emotions including happiness and anxiety also differ by ethnic group. Indian respondents reported higher levels of anxiety yesterday (3.4 out of 10) compared with the White ethnic group (3.1 out of 10), which is in contrast to happiness yesterday, life satisfaction, and worthwhile things in life where their responses were similar.
- On average all ethnic groups reported higher levels of anxiety than the White ethnic group.
- Within each ethnic group, there was little difference between men's and women's assessment of their own well-being.
- The differences observed between ethnic groups in subjective well-being may in part be caused by the way that different people with different ethnic backgrounds respond to these questions, but also the varied responses reflect the different circumstances that people find themselves in.

For example, the unemployment rate for Pakistani, Bangladeshi and Black ethnic groups are amongst the highest for the different ethnic groups in the UK.

Notes

1. The Black ethnic group is made up of Black, African, Caribbean and Black British people.

Differences by Ethnic Group

As well as a range of demographic and labour market questions the Annual Population Survey asks a cross section of 165,000 adults aged 16 and over to make their own assessment of how they feel about their lives.

Life Satisfaction

Figure 1 shows that when asked how satisfied people are with their lives, respondents from the White ethnic group gave an average rating of 7.4 out of 10 in 2011-12.

This was in contrast with people from the Black ethnic group who gave the lowest ratings with an average of 6.7 out of 10. This was also lower than the Bangladeshi (7.0 out of 10) and Mixed/ multiple ethnic groups (7.1 out of 10) who also gave significantly lower ratings on average than the White ethnic group. The Black ethnic group is made up of Black, African, Caribbean and Black British people.

In contrast, people who identified themselves as Indian (7.5 out of 10), Chinese (7.4 out of 10) and Other Asian backgrounds (7.4 out of 10) gave similar ratings on average to the White population.

Figure 1. Average (mean) life satisfaction, ratings (1): by ethnic group, 2011 - 2012

United Kingdom

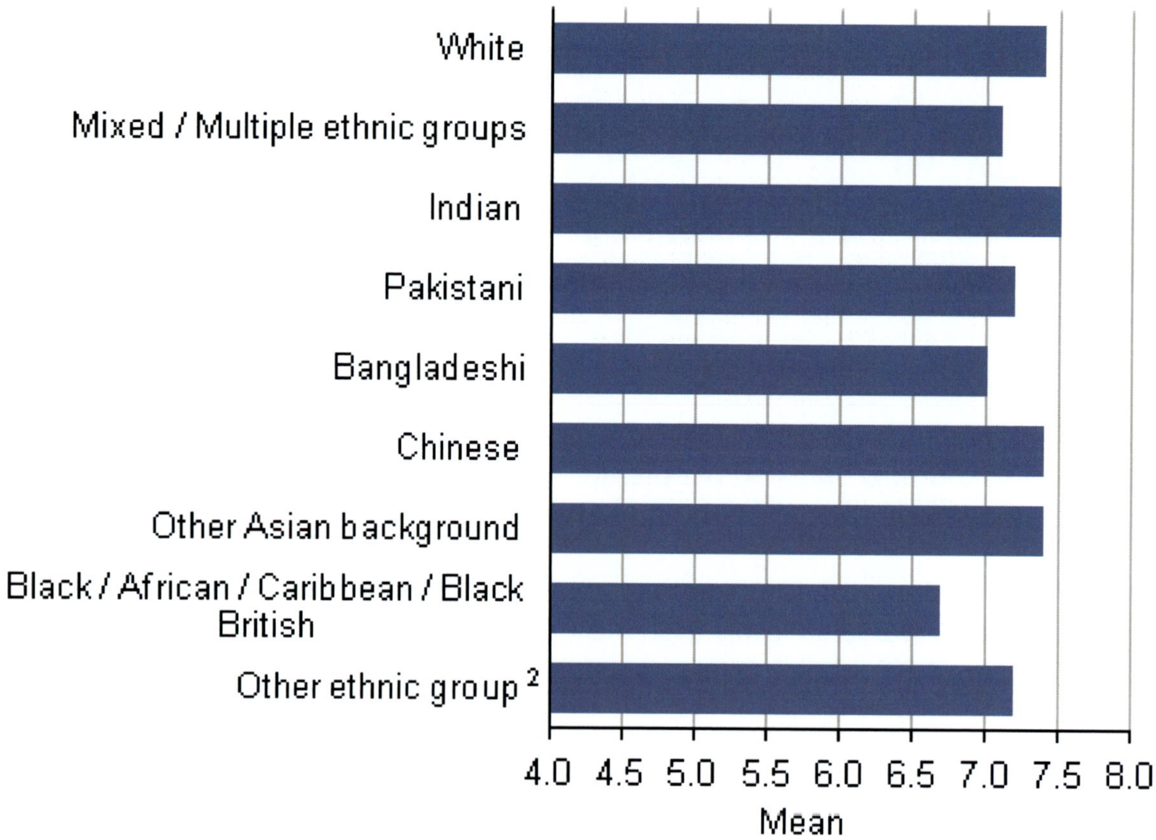

Source: Annual Population Survey (APS) - Office for National Statistics

Notes:

1. Adults aged 16 and over were asked 'Overall, how satisfied are you with your life nowadays? Where nought is 'not at all' and 10 is 'completely'.
2. Including Arab.

Download chart

XLS XLS format
(29.5 Kb)

Worthwhile things in life

As well as asking about how satisfied people are with their lives, the Annual Population Survey also asks to what extent people feel the things that they do in their lives are worthwhile.

The White ethnic group, with an average rating of 7.7 out of 10, was higher than all the other ethnic groups. The lowest average rating for this question was given by Bangladeshi respondents who reported an average of 7.3 out of 10.

Pakistani, Chinese, Black, and the Other ethnic group all reported a rating of 7.4 out of 10.

Day-to-day emotions

As well as asking people to make an assessment of how their lives are going overall, it is also important to understand how people's day-to-day emotions differ when making an assessment of people's well-being. For example, the Annual Population Survey asks about how happy and anxious people felt in the previous day.

The ethnic group that provided the lowest average rating for the 'happy yesterday' question was the Black ethnic group (6.9 out of 10), significantly lower than the average for the White group (7.3 out of 10). The Indian and Other Asian background groups both reported the highest ratings of 7.4 out of 10.

Figure 2 shows that for 'anxiety yesterday', all other ethnic groups reported on average higher levels of anxiety than the White ethnic group.

Indian respondents reported significantly higher levels of anxiety (3.4 out of 10) compared with the White ethnic group, which is in contrast to happiness yesterday, life satisfaction and worthwhile things in life, where their responses were similar. Bangladeshi (3.6 out of 10) and Pakistani (3.5 out of 10) groups also reported significantly higher ratings compared with the White group (3.1 out of 10) meaning that on average people who identified with these ethnic groups reported being more anxious in the day before interview.

Figure 2. Average (mean) anxious yesterday ratings (1): by ethnic group, 2011 - 2012

United Kingdom

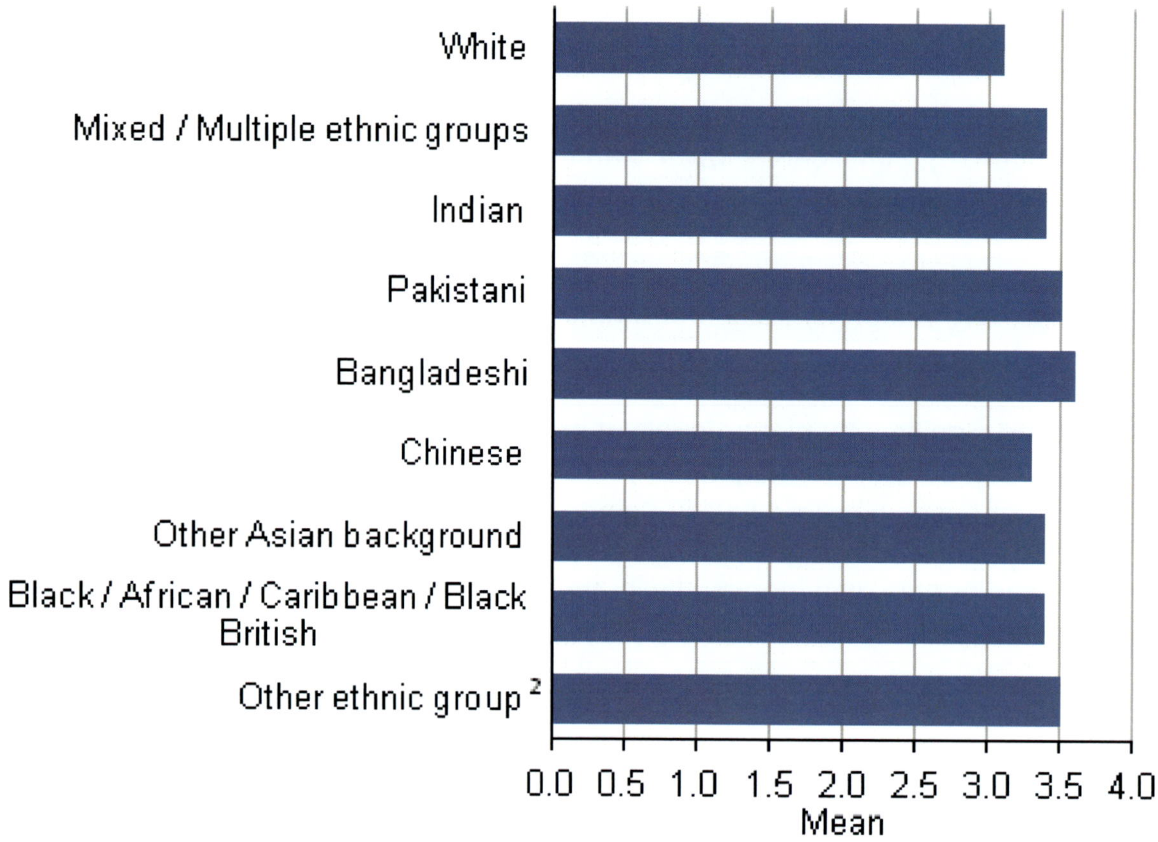

Source: Annual Population Survey (APS) - Office for National Statistics

Notes:

1. Adults aged 16 and over were asked 'Overall, how anxious did you feel yesterday? Where nought is 'not at all' and 10 is 'completely'.
2. Including Arab.

Download chart

XLS XLS format
(29.5 Kb)

Differences for men and women in each ethnic group

Overall, regardless of ethnic group, according to the 2011-12 Annual Population Survey women in the UK reported on average slightly higher levels of life satisfaction, worthwhile things in life, the same levels of happiness yesterday, but higher levels of anxiety yesterday than men (ONS, 2012).

Figure 3 shows that when looking at the differences between men and women broken down by ethnic group the differences were also small for each group. Given for some ethnic groups the sample sizes are small, caution should be adopted when interpreting the differences between men and women as they will often not be statistically significant.

Some of the largest differences between men and women for different ethnic groups were for the average ratings for the question that asked about the extent to which people feel the things they do in their life are worthwhile. The averages for White men and women for this question were 7.6 and 7.8 out of 10 respectively.

The largest difference between men and women were for the:

- Pakistani ethnic group (7.2 for men vs. 7.6 for women), the
- Bangladeshi ethnic group (7.1 for men vs. 7.5 for women), and the
- Other ethnic group (7.3 for men vs. 7.7 for women).

However, sample sizes are small, particularly for the Bangladeshi group which is not a statistically significant difference. The Chinese group is the only ethnic group where men reported on average higher levels of feeling things are worthwhile than women, however again the sample is small and this is not a statistically significant difference.

Figure 3. Average (mean) worthwhile ratings: by ethnic group and sex (1), 2011 - 2012

United Kingdom

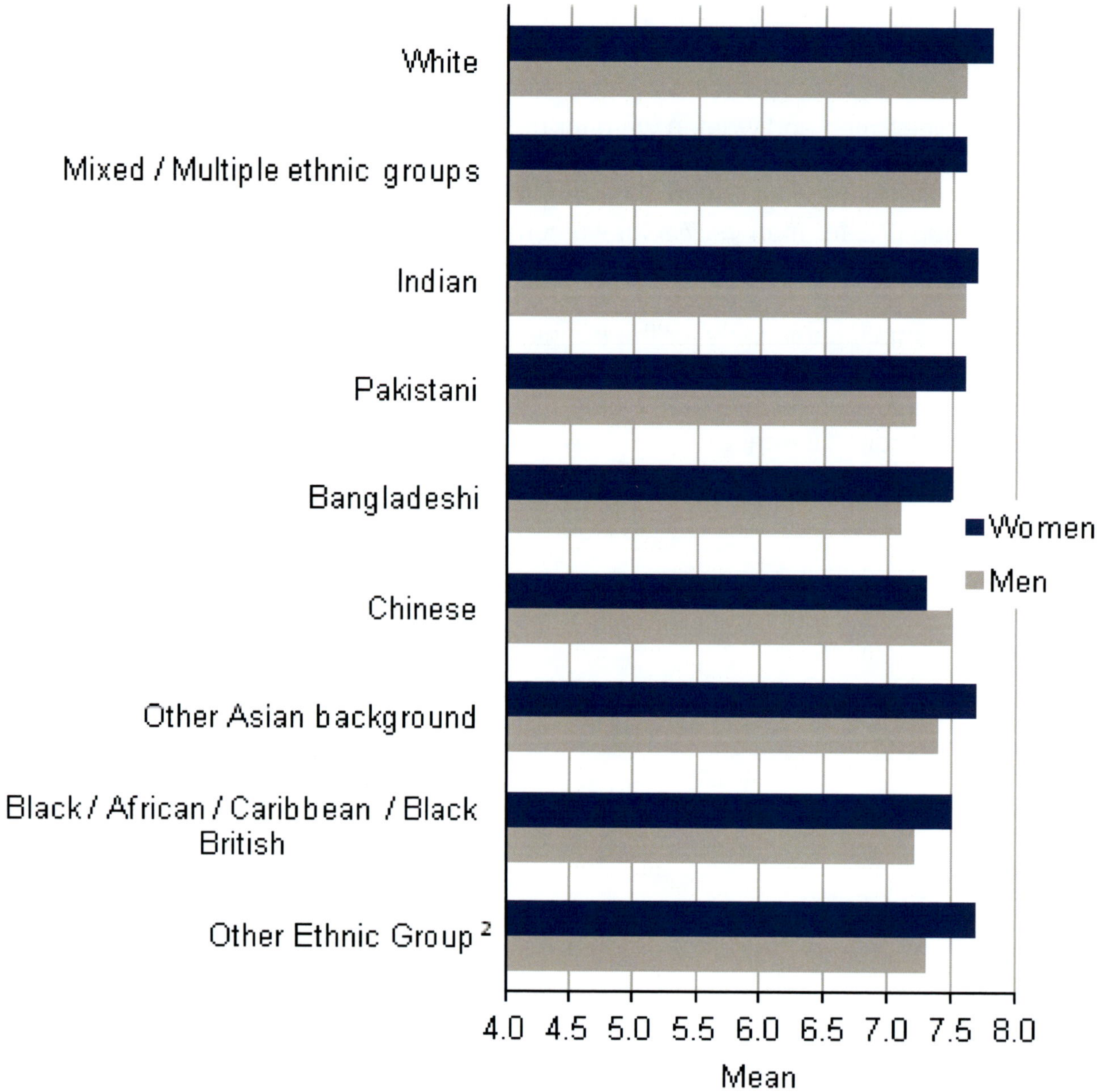

Source: Annual Population Survey (APS) - Office for National Statistics

Notes:

1. Adults aged 16 and over were asked 'Overall, to what extent do you feel the things you do in your life are worthwhile? Where nought is 'not at all' and 10 is 'completely'.
2. Including Arab.

Download chart

XLS XLS format
(29.5 Kb)

Explaining differences by ethnicity

There are distinct differences in the average ratings between ethnic groups, and these are unlikely to be explained by different ratings given by men and women, as these differences are also small.

So what could be the main reasons for the different average ratings given by people in different ethnic groups?

The differences may in part be due to what can be described as 'cultural bias'. This may be because people from different cultures may interpret the question scales differently or be more likely to give more extreme or moderate ratings when asked to make an assessment of their life in this way. However, although the research literature suggests there are some cultural differences in the patterns of observed responses, it is difficult to say to what extent this represents error in the data rather than genuine differences in how people feel, or how they assess their lives (OECD, 2013). This presents a challenging research agenda for the future.

An alternative to the cultural bias theory is that these differences exist because they reflect people's responses to the circumstances that they find themselves in.

- As **Figure 4** shows, unemployment rates for Pakistani, Bangladeshi and the Black ethnic groups are amongst the highest. In October to December 2012 they stood at 18.4%, 20.0% and 15.7% respectively. Given the large association between unemployment and subjective well-being this may go some way to explaining some of the reason for the lower average life satisfaction, worthwhile things, happiness yesterday and higher average anxiety levels for these ethnic groups (ONS, 2013).
- Pakistani and Bangladeshi groups also on average report the highest rates of poor health and limiting and long-standing illness or disability (ONS, 2008), other factors highly associated with subjective well-being.
- Within the broader ethnic groupings, pupils of any Black background have historically been least likely on average to achieve 5 or more GCSEs at grade A* to C or equivalent including English and mathematics GCSEs or iGCSEs (DfE, 2013).

Figure 4. Unemployment rates (aged 16+): by ethnic group, October to December 2012

United Kingdom

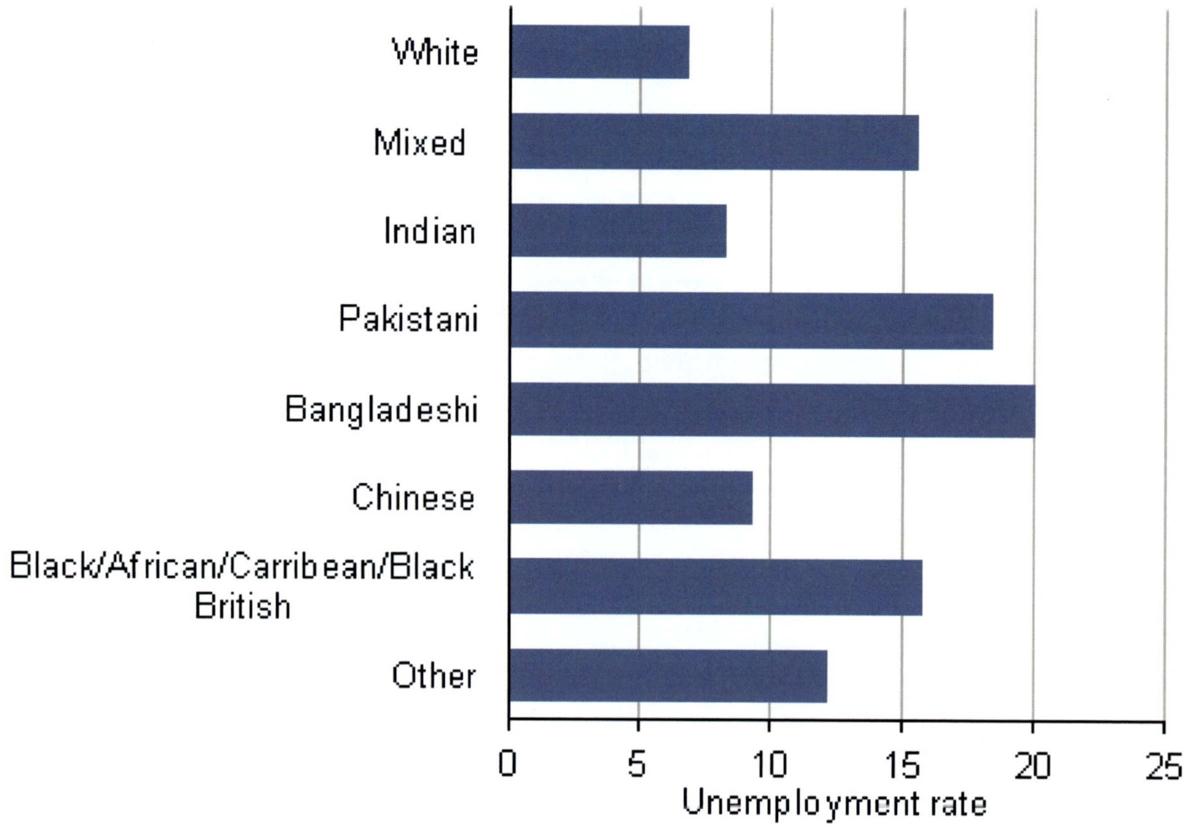

Source: Annual Population Survey (APS) - Office for National Statistics

Download chart

XLS XLS format
(27 Kb)

Further, more complex analysis is required to look in more detail to better determine how much these differences in circumstances can explain the observed differences in average ratings of subjective well-being between ethnic groups. The Annual Population Survey with its large sample and wide variety of different variables of interest is a useful source for further research in this area.

Many of the specific measures that are related to an individual's well-being are also related to each other such as age, employment status, marital status and health. ONS is currently analysing[1] the relationship between each measure and subjective well-being. A methodological report providing more detailed results will be published in May 2013.

Notes

1. Regression analysis - a statistical procedure that determines a relationship between one set of variables or measurements and another.

Measuring Subjective Well-being

Choice of questions

The questions developed and included in the Annual Population Survey were developed with expert academic advice as well as benefiting from discussions between members of the National Statistician's Measuring National Well-being Advisory Forum and Technical Advisory Group.

The questions that ONS has asked on the Annual Population Survey include:

- Overall, how satisfied are you with your life nowadays? (Evaluative approach),
- Overall, to what extent do you feel the things you do in your life are worthwhile? (Eudemonic approach),
- Overall, how happy did you feel yesterday? (Experience approach),
- Overall, how anxious did you feel yesterday? (Experience approach).

All answered using a 0 to 10 scale where nought is 'not at all' and 10 is 'completely'

Further information on the ONS approach to measuring subjective well-being can be found in the paper 'Measuring Subjective Well-being' (240.8 Kb Pdf) published by ONS in July 2011.

Interpreting subjective well-being estimates

When comparing differences between mean ratings for groups or areas it is important to realise that these comparisons are made using aggregate statistics based on samples with those characteristics. Just because the average of the sample has a certain rating of subjective well-being does not necessarily mean that all people with that certain characteristic have that particular outcome.

For example, even though women on average have higher life satisfaction than men, it is important not to infer that all women are more satisfied with their lives than men.

It is also important to note that although subjective well-being estimates in this report have been analysed by people with different characteristics we are not inferring causation, even though some groups are more likely to give higher life satisfaction ratings on average, it may not be the particular characteristic that is causing them to have higher subjective well-being.

There are other factors that could also be influencing people's ratings which would need to be controlled for in a regression model, and even then causation is often difficult to infer.

The size of differences between mean ratings of subjective well-being for groups of people with certain characteristics or in different circumstances can appear fairly small. These differences must be interpreted in light of the fact that subjective well-being is affected by many different life circumstances with a variety of factors having a bearing on a person's subjective well-being.

For example, if someone is in poor health, that is only one aspect of their lives so when making a cognitive judgment about how satisfied they are with their lives overall, although their poor health may have a bearing, other factors may mitigate against that and mean they do not give such a low score as we may perhaps first expect.

The Annual Population Survey

The Annual Population Survey, first conducted in 2004, combines results from waves one and five of the Labour Force Survey and the English, Welsh and Scottish LFS boosts. The survey asks 155,000 households and 360,000 people per dataset about their own circumstances and experiences regarding a range of subjects including housing, employment and education.

The survey provides enhanced data on key social and socio-economic variables. For the subjective well-being questions responses by proxy are not collected. That is only people who respond directly to the survey are included rather than including responses made on behalf of other people. For this reason the sample size for the subjective well-being data is around 165,000.

One of the benefits of collecting subjective well-being data on a large scale survey such as Annual Population Survey is that large sample sizes, all else being equal, produce smaller standard errors. The standard error is an indication of the accuracy of an estimate and gives users an indication of how close the sample estimator (in this case the mean subjective well-being rating) is to the population value: the larger the standard error, the less precise the estimator. Large sample sizes also allow for comparisons across population groups and areas. The Annual Population Survey is a mixed mode survey and uses both face-to-face and telephone interviews. Different collection modes can affect responses and subjective well-being estimates are no exception.

About the Measuring National Well-being programme

NWB logo 2

This article is published as part of the ONS Measuring National Well-being Programme.

The programme aims to produce accepted and trusted measures of the well-being of the nation - how the UK as a whole is doing.

Measuring National Well-being is about looking at 'GDP and beyond'. It includes headline indicators in areas such as health, relationships, job satisfaction, economic security, education, environmental conditions and measures of 'subjective well-being' (individuals' assessment of their own well-being).

Find out more on the Measuring National Well-being website pages.

Background notes

1. These statistics are experimental in nature and published at an early stage to gain feedback from users. Should users have comments on the ONS approach to the measurement of subjective well-being and or the presentation of the subjective well-being questions they can email ONS at national.well-being@ons.gov.uk. It is the role of the UK Statistics Authority to designate these statistics as National Statistics and this is one of the aspirations of the National Well-being programme to see these statistics gain National Statistics status.

2. The data analysed in this report are derived from a customised weighted 12 month APS microdataset. This dataset is not part of the regularly produced APS datasets and was produced specifically for the analysis of subjective well-being data. ONS is making the experimental APS microdata available to approved researchers to allow them to undertake further analysis of these experimental questions at an early stage and to provide further feedback to ONS.

3. All data (unless otherwise stated) is from the Annual Population Survey April 2011 to March 2012. All data is weighted and non-respondents are not included.

4. Details of the policy governing the release of new data are available by visiting the UK Statistics Authority or from the Media Relations Office

5.

6. Details of the policy governing the release of new data are available by visiting www.statisticsauthority.gov.uk/assessment/code-of-practice/index.html or from the Media Relations Office email: media.relations@ons.gsi.gov.uk

Copyright

References

1. DfE (2013), GCSE and equivalent attainment by pupil characteristics in England Statistical Bulletin, Department of Education.

2. OECD (2013), OECD Guidelines on Measuring Subjective Well-being, OECD Publishing.

3. ONS (2008), Diversity and different experiences in the UK, National Statistician's Annual Article on Society (286.5 Kb Pdf), Office for National Statistics.

4. ONS (2011), Measuring Subjective Well-being (240.8 Kb Pdf), Office for National Statistics.

5. ONS (2012), First Annual ONS Experimental Subjective Well-being Results, Office for National Statistics.

6. ONS (2013), Labour Market Statisitcs, February 2013, Office for National Statisics. Table A09: Labour market status by ethnic group.

The Economy - International Comparisons

Coverage: **International**
Date: **14 May 2013**
Geographical Area: **Country**
Theme: **Economy**
Theme: **People and Places**

Key Points

- The economy is a key consideration when attempting to measure National Well-being and comparing the relative performance of different countries is an important aspect
- In international comparisons of household income the UK has dropped from 5th place in 2005 to 12th place in 2011. This is partly as a result of the devaluation of sterling seen in this period.
- Since 2009 inflation has remained high compared to the US, France and Germany but has been relatively less volatile
- Despite falling 12 places between 2005 and 2011 when looking at rankings based on unemployment, the UK labour market has been more resilient in than previous recessions
- In terms of household spending and wealth, the UK has remained relatively strong compared with other OECD countries
- Despite falling two places in the rankings since 2005, the UK still fares relatively better under Net National Income than Gross Domestic Product

Introduction

This article is published as part of the ONS Measuring National Well-being Programme. The programme aims to produce accepted and trusted measures of the well-being of the nation. This article focuses on one aspect of well-being, the economy, and is part of a series of articles which aim to explore in more detail the different areas that have been considered as important for the measurement of national well-being. These areas have been termed 'domains' The article describes how the UK has fared relative to other countries in the domain of the economy.

The scope of this domain includes measures of economic output and stock. These measures reflect the 'household perspective' as recommended in the Report from the Commission on the Measurement of Economic Performance and Social Progress published in 2009.

The article looks at each of these indicators within 'the economy' - in addition to a number of other relevant indicators - and compares the UK with other countries. We are comparing the UK with 33 other countries that are members of the Organisation for Economic Co-operation and Development (OECD). The first section of the article focuses on measures of household income, spending and wealth. The article then moves on to look at wider indicators of the economy as a whole.

Further information regarding the technical definitions of each of the indicators can be found in the supporting information at the end of the article.

Household Income

The well-being of individuals in a country is best reflected by looking at the experiences of households. Most households will not consider their share of national measures, but rather the income they actually have in their pockets after deductions such as income tax or pension contributions – this measure is household disposable income.

To allow for true international comparisons, in this section household disposable income is adjusted for services provided by government such as healthcare and education. Whilst these are largely free to households in some countries (such as the UK) they are not in all, meaning households in some countries would have to pay for these services out of their income. As a result, when making international comparisons on standards of living or well-being, it is important to adjust for this difference. This services adjusted indicator is referred to in this paper as household actual disposable income. We also adjust for the size of a country by looking at 'per head' measures.

Up until 2010 the UK had seen a prolonged period of growth in this adjusted measure of household income. Including 2008 and 2009, where household incomes grew despite the onset of the recession. This is because household incomes were supported by low mortgage interest rates and a stronger labour market than experienced in any previous recessions. Over the course of the recession, as unemployment rose, people paid less taxes and claimed more benefits – causing less of a strain on household income. However, as the economy emerged from the first period of contraction (measured by GDP), households began to feel the squeeze on their incomes as these effects wore off.

It is interesting to look at developments in the income of UK households relative to other countries, as this should provide a good comparison of international standards of living. In 2011, the UK was ranked 12th against other OECD countries when looking at household actual disposable income per head (see Figure 1).

Figure 1: Household Actual Disposable Income Per Head in 2011

OECD Countries, UK=100

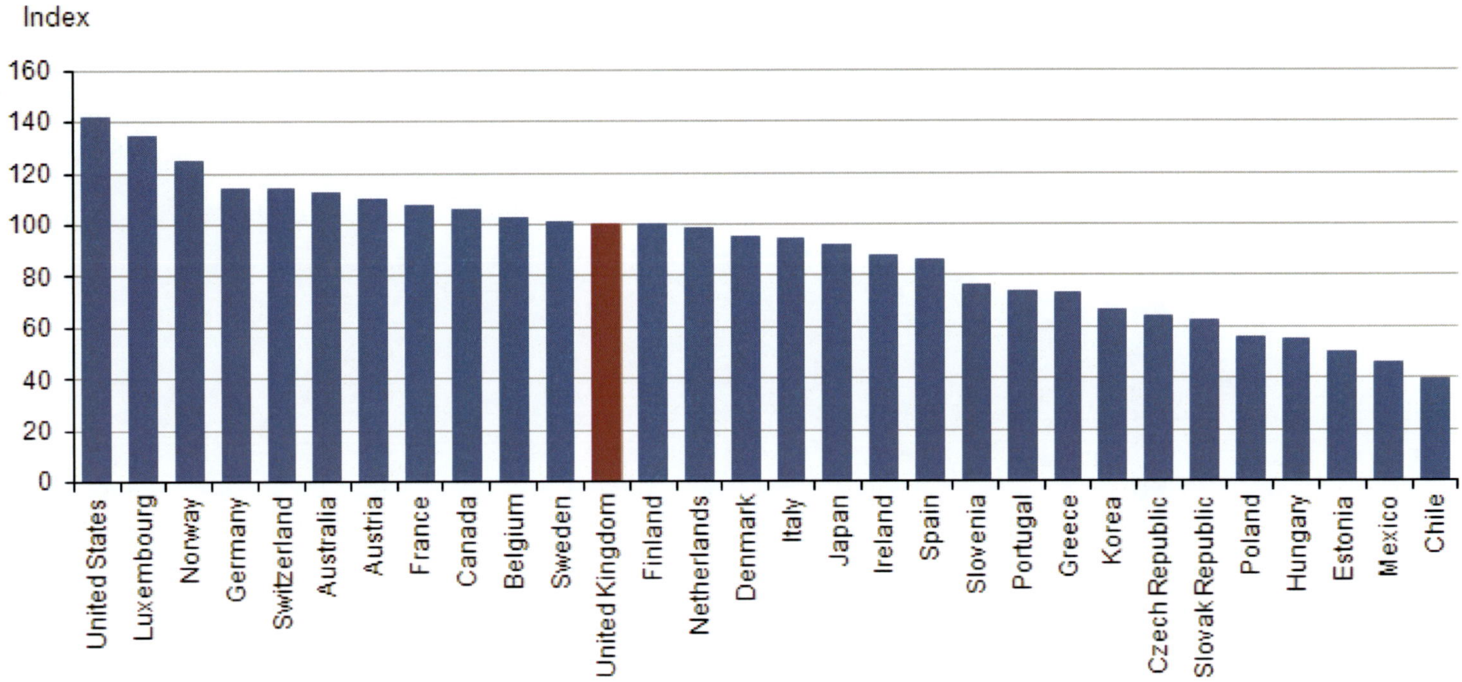

Notes:

1. Source: OECD
2. Current prices and current PPPs
3. Data for Iceland, Israel, New Zealand and Turkey are not available

Download chart

XLS XLS format
(39 Kb)

In previous years, the UK has fared better when comparing household income internationally. When looking at 2005 data, the UK ranks 5th – this highlights the relative experience of UK households since the recession which started in 2008. Figure 2, shows the UK's ranking in 2011 is seven places lower when compared to 2005.

Figure 2: Household Actual Disposable Income Per Head rankings over time (2005 and 2011)

OECD Countries

Rank	2005	2011
1	United States	United States
2	Luxembourg	Luxembourg
3	Norway	Norway
4	Germany	Germany
5	United Kingdom	Switzerland
6	Australia	Australia
7	Austria	Austria
8	Switzerland	France
9	France	Canada
10	Canada	Belgium
11	Belgium	Sweden
12	Netherlands	United Kingdom
13	Ireland	Finland
14	Italy	Netherlands
15	Japan	Denmark

Notes:

1. Source: OECD

Download chart

XLS XLS format
(30 Kb)

To allow for international comparisons, household actual disposable income per head has been adjusted to equivalise the spending power across countries. This means it reflects not just the level of income but also how much can be bought with it (the purchasing power). Between 2005 and 2011 the prices of goods and services in the UK has increased relative to other countries. As a result, although household income in the UK has grown, when compared to other countries that income doesn't stretch as far. This goes some way in explaining why the UK ranks relatively lower than it did in 2005.

Household Spending

Trends in household income and inflation will impact on household spending decisions. Households have a choice as to what they do with their disposable income - they can either spend it on current consumption or save it for future consumption. This means an increase in income may not be spent straight away, and therefore in addition to income it is important to look at household spending to fully gauge any change to well-being. While income signifies potential material living standards, spending better signifies actual material living standards.

Like household income, this section adjusts household final consumption expenditure for services provided by the government, such as healthcare and education. This adjusted measure is known as

Household Actual Consumption. It is the value of the goods and services consumed by households - whether these goods and services are purchased and paid for by households, by government or by non-profit organisations. We also adjust this section for the size of a country by looking at the 'per head' measure.

The increase in household incomes seen in the early period of the 2008 recession was not matched by equivalent growth in household spending in the UK. The pattern of household spending followed the prolonged period of growth (seen in income) up to 2007. In 2008, the two measures diverge: household spending starts to fall despite the growth in household income. This fall in spending was therefore accompanied by an increase in saving, possibly reflecting the uncertainty facing households and the need to pay down debt.

This is reflected in the international comparisons of household spending per head, as measured by household actual consumption per head in Figure 3. The UK dropped to 7th place in 2011 - although this is an improvement from the ranking seen with household income per head (where the UK ranked 12th for the same year), it is not as strong as in previous years. This can be seen when comparing 2011 with 2005 data, in which the UK ranks 5th place.

Figure 3: Household Actual Consumption Per Head in 2011

OECD Countries, UK=100

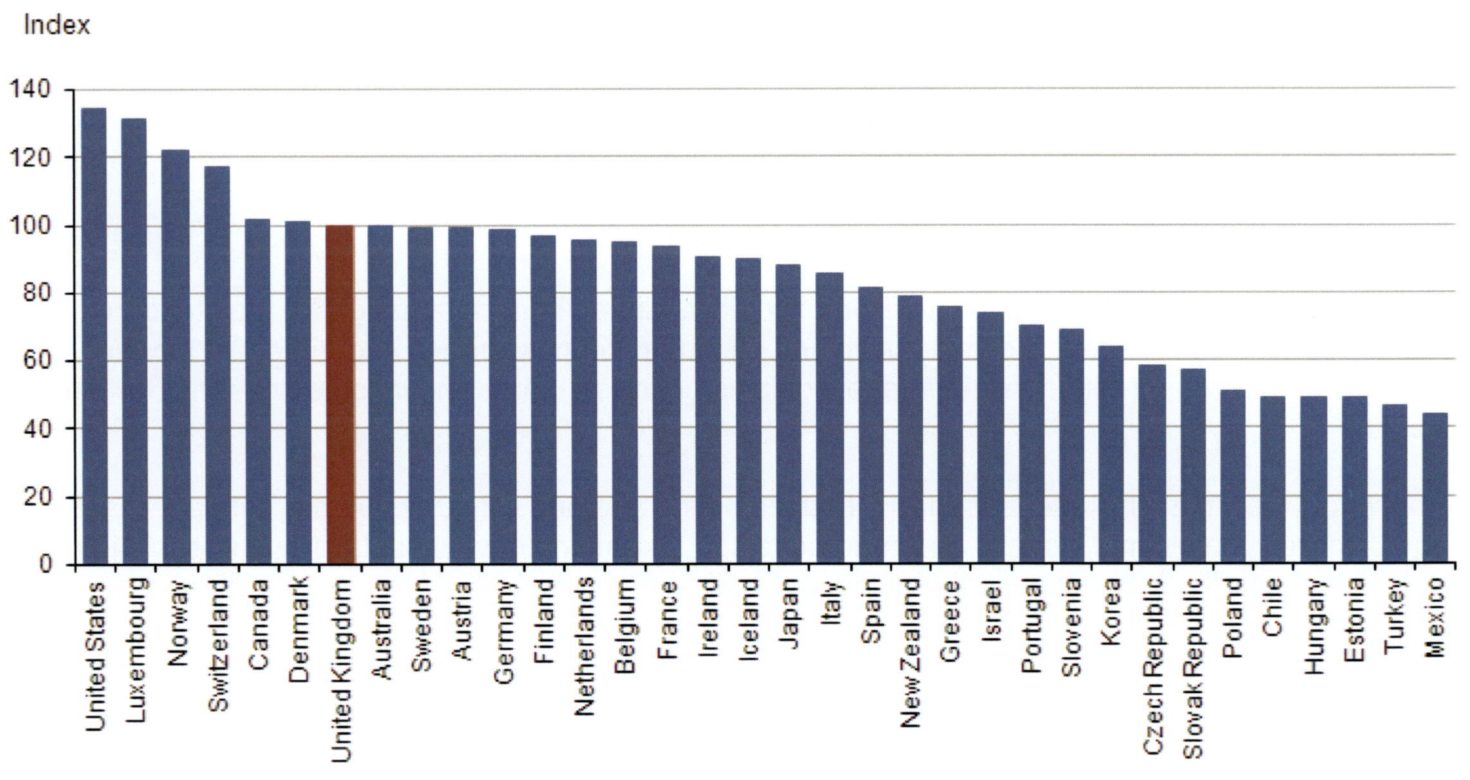

Notes:

1. Source: OECD
2. Current prices and current PPPs

Download chart

XLS XLS format
(39.5 Kb)

It is worth highlighting that the gap between 5th place (Canada) and 11th place (Germany) is quite small and, in terms of household spending, the UK remains close to the countries around it in the rankings. As a result this change in the rankings may not really be significant in terms of relative experiences through the recession.

As we have seen, the UK's ranking for household spending per head is higher and much more stable than for household income per head. This would suggest that the relative material living standards of households in the UK are better than household income per head may indicate. It is worth noting that both Germany and France rank much lower under household spending per head, reflecting the different spending and saving decisions made by households in the UK compared to France and Germany. This shows that although household spending is a good indicator of living standards, cultural differences in saving priorities may affect any international comparison.

Between 2005 and 2011, the household saving rate was, on average, 11.8% for France, 10.9% for Germany and -1.1% for the UK. This figure is so low for the UK due to saving culture before the recession. From 2009, the savings ratio has been positive in the UK. This highlights that from 2005 to 2008, UK households were actually living beyond their means, spending not just from their income but also their savings (or borrowing to fund spending). This highlights the importance of considering household wealth when looking at well-being – giving an indication of the sustainability of current income and spending flows.

Household Wealth

Measures of household income and consumption flows are an important gauge for the standard of living today, but in the end it is consumption and consumption possibilities over time that matter. A low-income household with above-average wealth is better off than a low-income household without wealth.

Household wealth is also one reason why household income and consumption are not necessarily equal; for a given income, consumption can be raised by running down assets or by increasing debt, and consumption can be reduced by saving and adding to assets.

In the UK, household net financial wealth saw growth from 2003 to 2006, but shrunk in 2007 and 2008. This reduction in financial wealth reflects falls in the value of household assets (for example shares and other equities) and may be attributed turmoil on the stock market as the financial crisis deepened. Household net financial wealth started to recover after 2008 but is unsteady, this is likely to be because of the UK's volatile mortgage market.

Figure 4 shows household financial net wealth per head relative to other countries in 2011. As with the other indicators, we adjust for the size of a country by looking at 'per head' measures. This shows that the UK was in 7th place amongst OECD countries. The UK's financial net wealth of households is double that of Ireland and four times as much as Chile.

Figure 4: Financial Net Wealth of Households and NPISH Per Head in 2011

OECD Countries, UK=100

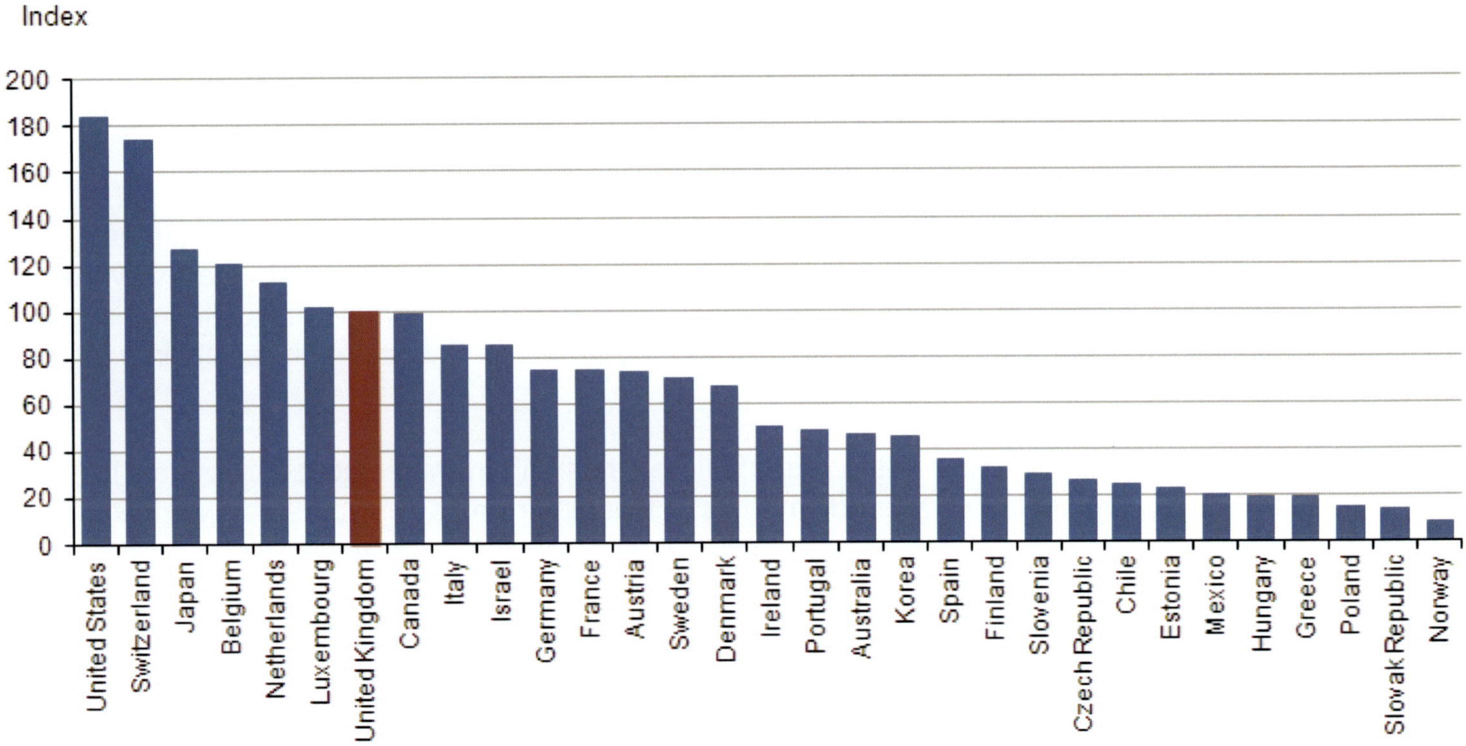

Notes:

1. Source: OECD
2. Current prices and current PPPs
3. Data for Iceland, New Zealand and Turkey are not available

Download chart

XLS XLS format
(30 Kb)

The financial net wealth of households in the UK remained relatively stable over this period, only ranking 7th or 8th place from 2005 to 2011.

It is interesting to note that several countries which ranked higher than the UK in some of the previous indicators now rank closer to or well below the UK, for example - Luxembourg and Germany. Furthermore, Italy, Israel and Japan have moved considerably up the rankings, meaning that their households' are, on the whole, getting wealthier over the period.

Differences in the net wealth of countries can arise for a number of reasons. They may be due to the importance placed on other assets over financial assets. This in turn may be reflected in the extent to which households participate in the financial markets. Finally, differences in social security systems across the countries may encourage some households to take out private pensions and life insurance.

Inflation

Inflation is another key factor that can influence well-being. The main channel through which inflation impacts households, and therefore well-being, is through the erosion of household incomes. As prices rise faster than people's incomes, over time people find their income purchases a lower quantity of goods and services - therefore they feel worse off.

In addition to the impact on household income, a high rate of inflation reduces the real value of wealth held in cash terms - the higher the rate of inflation the greater the reduction in the real value of wealth held in cash. In addition, if inflation is above the interest rate the value of wealth in the form of savings also falls in real terms. The opposite is true for debtors, as this scenario results in a fall of the real value of debt.

Therefore the rate of inflation relative to the rate of interest has important distributional effects for well-being; a relatively high inflation rate redistributes net wealth from savers to debtors and vice versa.

Figure 5 shows inflation as measured by the HICP (CPI) for the UK, the US, France and Germany. The recession saw a fall in house prices, consumer confidence and thus consumer demand, and an increase in savings. This is clearly reflected by the fall in inflation for the UK to 2.2% in 2009. However, in the same year, prices grew by only 0.1% in France and 0.2% in Germany and actually fell by 0.8% in the USA.

Following this, the UK experienced relatively high inflation between 2010 and 2011, again much above that of France, Germany or the US. While other countries appear to have experienced a similar trend to the UK when looking at inflation, the UK has been higher but less volatile than the France Germany and the US since 2009.

Figure 5: Annual Change in Harmonised Index of Consumer Prices (HICP)

Selected OECD Countries

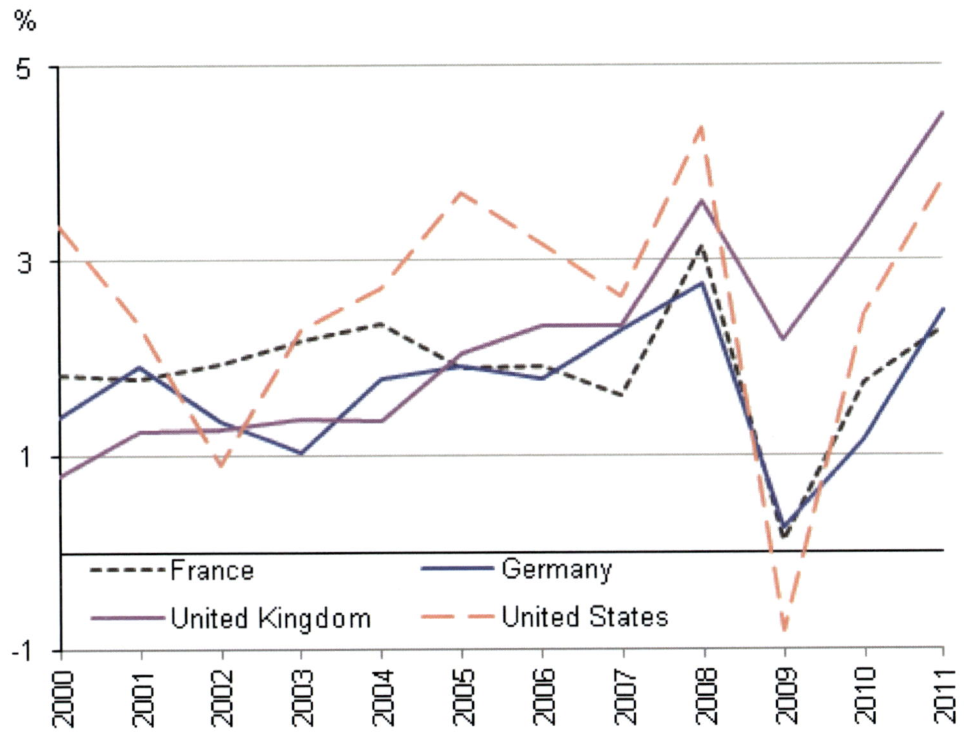

Notes:

1. Source: OECD

Download chart

XLS XLS format
(28 Kb)

Unemployment

A substantial proportion of household income comes from earnings from employment; unemployment can therefore reduce income and subsequently well-being. Any deterioration in employment is expected to have a negative impact on income growth.

In addition to reducing household income per head, unemployment also has a direct, and strongly negative, impact on individual well-being. ONS Experimental Subjective Well-being results showed that forty-five per cent of unemployed people rated their life satisfaction as 'low' or 'very low'; over twice the proportion reported by employed people.

Although the impact of the recession on employment was more muted in 2008 than previous recessions (employment did not fall as far and unemployment did not rise as much), it is also important to see how the UK unemployment compares internationally as well as historically. Looking at the falls in employment relative to those experienced in other countries give an international picture of the UK's relative well-being over the recession.

Figure 6: Harmonised Unemployment Rates in 2011

OECD Countries

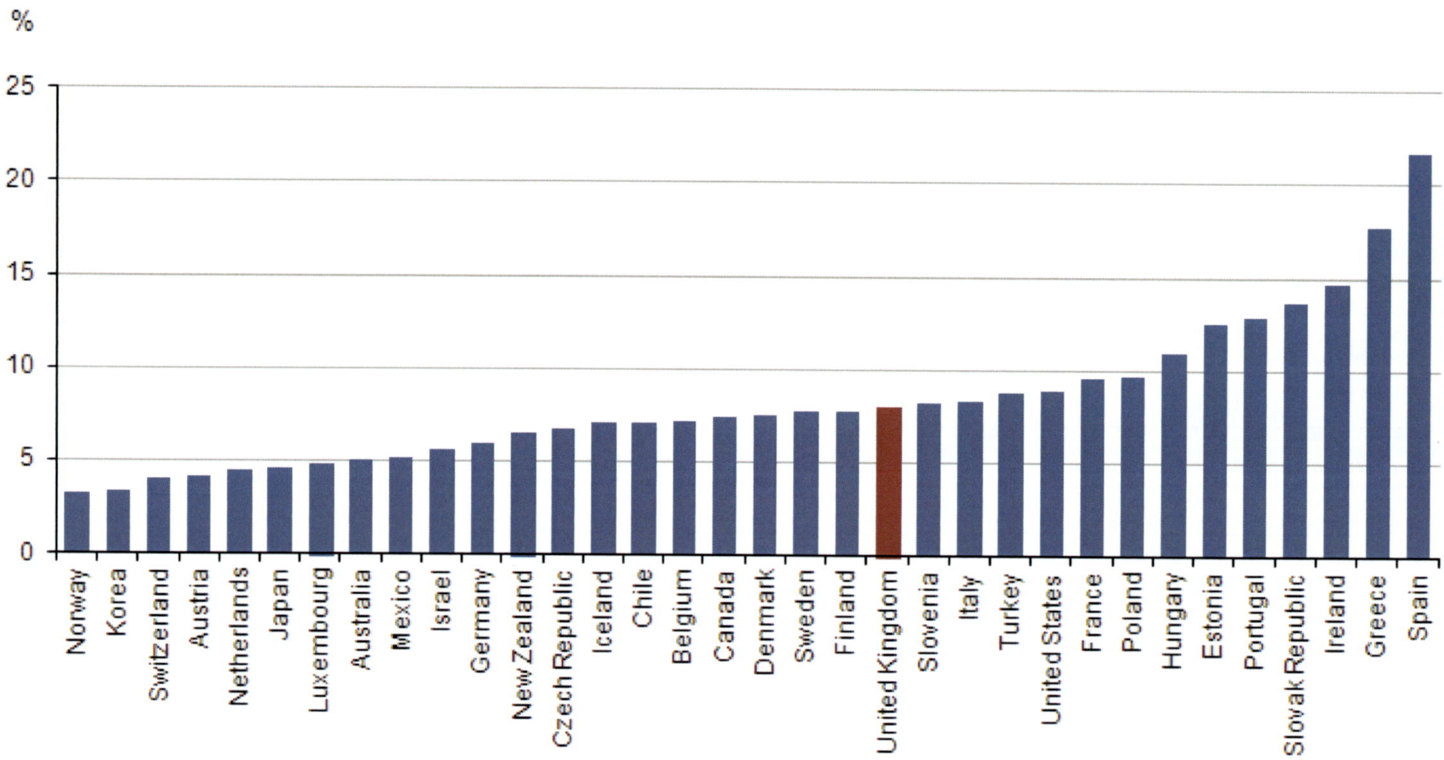

Notes:

1. Source: OECD

Download chart

XLS XLS format
(30 Kb)

Figure 6 shows OECD countries ranked from lowest unemployment rate (Norway) to the highest (Spain). From the point of view of well-being, a lower employment rate would have a positive impact (both directly and indirectly) on society. In 2011 the UK ranked somewhere near the middle of the order when looking at unemployment. This is 12 places below the ranking of 9th seen in 2005. However, with a rate of 8.0% in 2011, UK unemployment still remains well below unemployment rates seen in Greece (17.7%) or Spain (21.6%) and closer to Norway. Unemployment in Norway has remained the lowest since 2008, and in 2011 the unemployment rate was 3.3%. Luxembourg, Australia and Austria maintained a relatively stable rate of unemployment over the 6 years. This might help to explain why they are also amongst the top ranking countries for household income per head.

Figure 7 shows some of the 'big movers' in terms of the unemployment rate since 2005 - showing that while unemployment in the UK has increased, it is not the only economy to have experienced a weakening labour market over the recession. Unemployment in the US echoes that of the UK, with the US falling 13 places down the OECD rankings between 2005 and 2011. Against the background of recession, Germany has seen the biggest improvement (of those countries compared in Figure 7) in the unemployment rate, decreasing from 11.3% in 2005 to 6.0% in 2011.

The fall in the international rankings of the UK and US should be taken in context. As Figure 4 indicates, though the UK and the US have seen growth in their unemployment rates, the extent of this growth has not been as severe as other countries (such as Spain, Greece, Portugal and Ireland). Many of the countries that have overtaken the UK and US in the rankings are smaller economies, less exposed to the 2008 downturn, which centred on the US and Europe. The fall of 12 places in the international rankings for the UK has therefore come despite historically the most stable labour market seen in a UK recession.

Figure 7: Harmonised Unemployment Rates

Selected OECD Countries

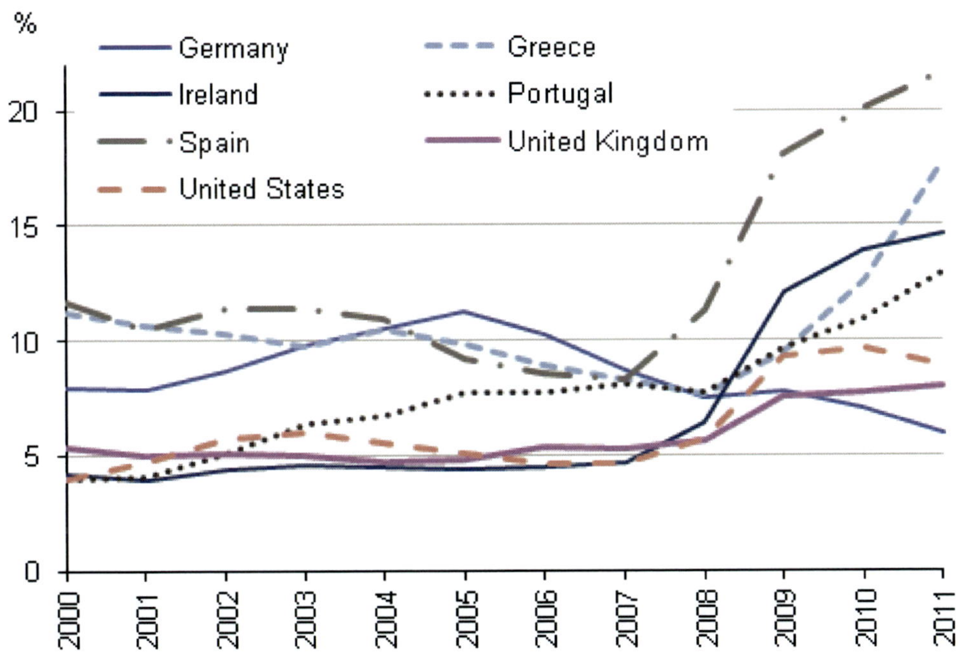

Notes:

1. Source: OECD

Download chart

XLS XLS format

(29 Kb)

The National Economy

Although it is important to look at the household perspective, it is also important to understand the performance of an economy overall. This section of the article looks at the economy as a whole, using Gross Domestic Product (GDP) per head as a starting point and then considering, Net National Income (NNI) per head and Gross Public Debt as a percentage of GDP. The role of GDP in this release is to provide a starting point from which other measures can be discussed and used to provide greater insight on how the UK fares internationally.

GDP is the most well-known macroeconomic indicator, and can be considered as either the total of income, expenditure or production within an economy. It can be defined as the value of all the goods and services produced within the economic territory of a country, in other words its entire output, during a given period (it can also be defined in a similar way as the total income or expenditure of an economy).

GDP is often used for judging how well an economy is doing. A country with a higher figure for GDP is said to have a 'bigger economy'. When GDP is increasing, the economy is said to be growing. The term 'recession' is often defined as two consecutive quarters of declining GDP.

Figure 8 shows how OECD countries compare against each other when looking at real GDP per head. Again, this is on a per head basis and adjusted to reflect relative purchasing power.

Figure 8: Real GDP Per Head for 2011

OECD Countries, UK=100

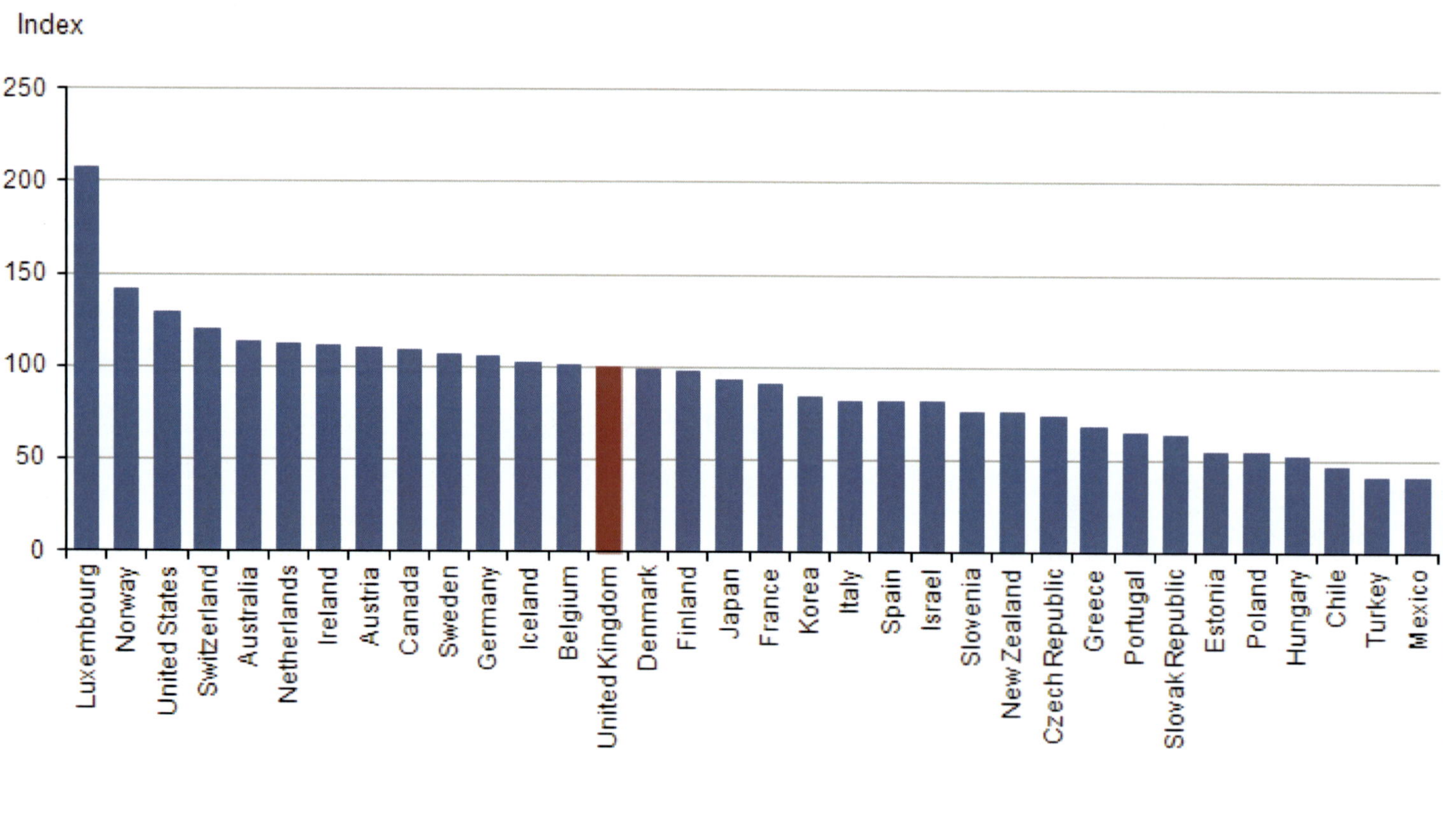

Notes:

1. Source: OECD
2. Constant prices and constant PPPs

Download chart

XLS XLS format
(30.5 Kb)

In 2010, the UK ranked 14th place with a GDP per head less than half that of Luxembourg in first place but almost three times that of Mexico at the other end of the scale.

Although GDP has traditionally been considered a measure of living standards, it was not designed for this purpose. GDP measures production and not material well-being. Living standards are more closely aligned with NNI which better measures the total income available to residents of that country.

NNI is a measure of the total income of a country and is different from GDP in two ways. Firstly, it includes only the income from UK production (in other words, the share of GDP) that can be claimed by individuals and organisations resident in the UK. It then adds to this the income that these residents can claim from the GDP of other countries. This production is still part of the UK's income even though it does not take place within its national boundaries. For example the following would all be included in GDP but excluded from NNI as they are not income available to the residents:

- A non-UK resident receiving wages for seasonal work undertaken in this country
- The profits of a UK based subsidiary that are repatriated to its parent company in another country
- A pensioner resident abroad receiving dividends on shares held in a British business

Additionally NNI is adjusted for capital depreciation - that is to say the day-to-day wear and tear on vehicles, machinery, buildings and other fixed capital used in the productive process. This takes account of income that is used to simply replace or repair existing vehicles, machinery, buildings and other fixed capital as this does not increase the well-being of a nation.

Figure 9 graphically represents how GDP is adjusted to take account of depreciation and net income from abroad to derive NNI.

Figure 9: Deriving NNI from GDP

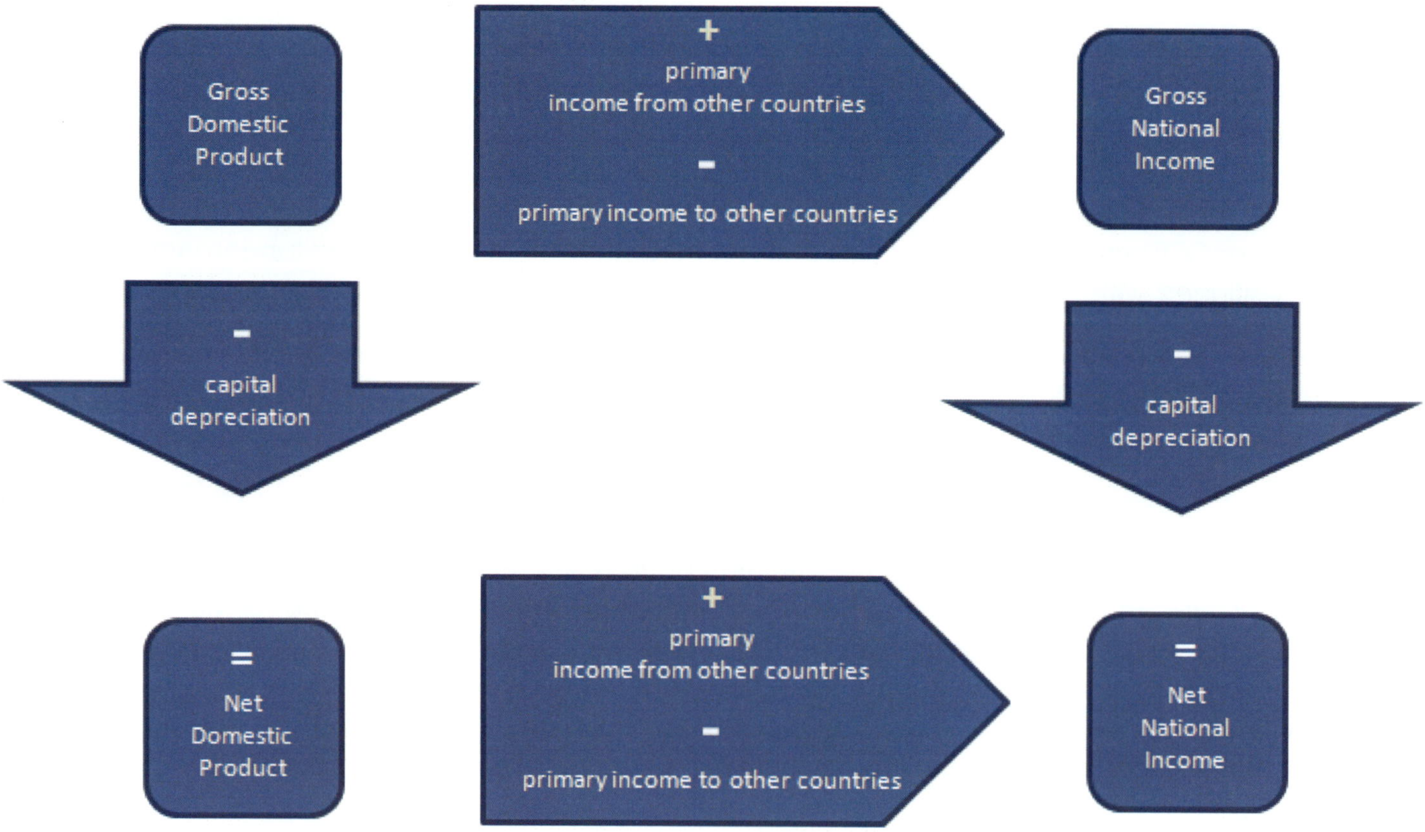

A full comparison of GDP per head and NNI per head in the UK can be found in The Economy article. It shows that for the second quarter of 2012 the UK NNI per head in real terms was 13.2% below its level in the first quarter of 2008; a sharper fall in living standards than the GDP data alone indicate.

Figure 10 shows how the UK compares to other OECD countries when using real NNI per head. In 2011 the UK ranked 9th place – higher than the ranking under GDP per head. Using NNI per head has resulted in the UK overtaking Austria and Germany. However, the UK remains behind Netherlands, Sweden and Canada. The UK fell by two places when comparing its position in 2005 with its position in 2011. However, the gap (as a ratio of UK NNI per head) between Luxembourg and the UK narrowed by 14 percentage points during the same period.

Figure 10: Real NNI Per Head for 2011

OECD Countries, UK=100

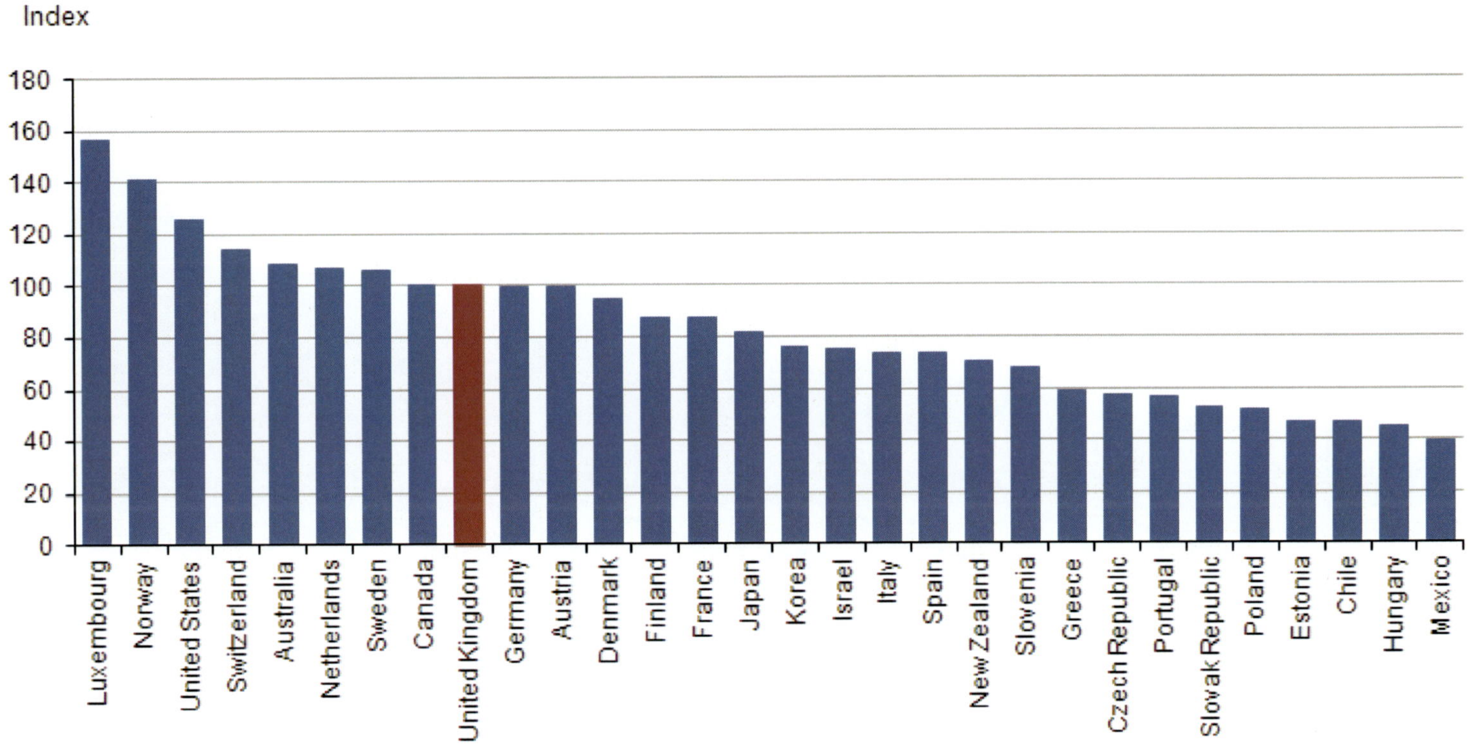

Notes:

1. Source: OECD
2. Constant prices and constant PPPs
3. Data for Ireland, Iceland, Belgium and Turkey are not available.

Download chart

XLS XLS format
(30 Kb)

Interestingly, Luxembourg's NNI per head is 31.9% smaller than its GDP per head. As a result, the NNI per head of the UK is now greater than half that of Luxembourg's. Luxembourg has a significant number of workers commuting from neighbouring countries. Consequently, there is a large outflow of income earned by foreign nationals in Luxembourg which explains why Luxembourg's NNI per head is much less than it's GDP per head. Nevertheless, Luxembourg still retains in 1st place in the rankings.

Given the extent of the fall in NNI over the recession that started in 2008 (see the Economy Article) it is also interesting to look at the impact this has had on the international rankings. Figure 11 shows real NNI per head from 2000 to 2011 for the UK, US, France and Germany. Between 2000 and 2007 there is a notable increase in NNI per head overall, which corresponds with a general increase in material living standards during this period. The general decline in the rate of growth between 2007 and 2009 is indicative of the global recession.

Figure 11: Real NNI Per Head

Selected OECD Countries

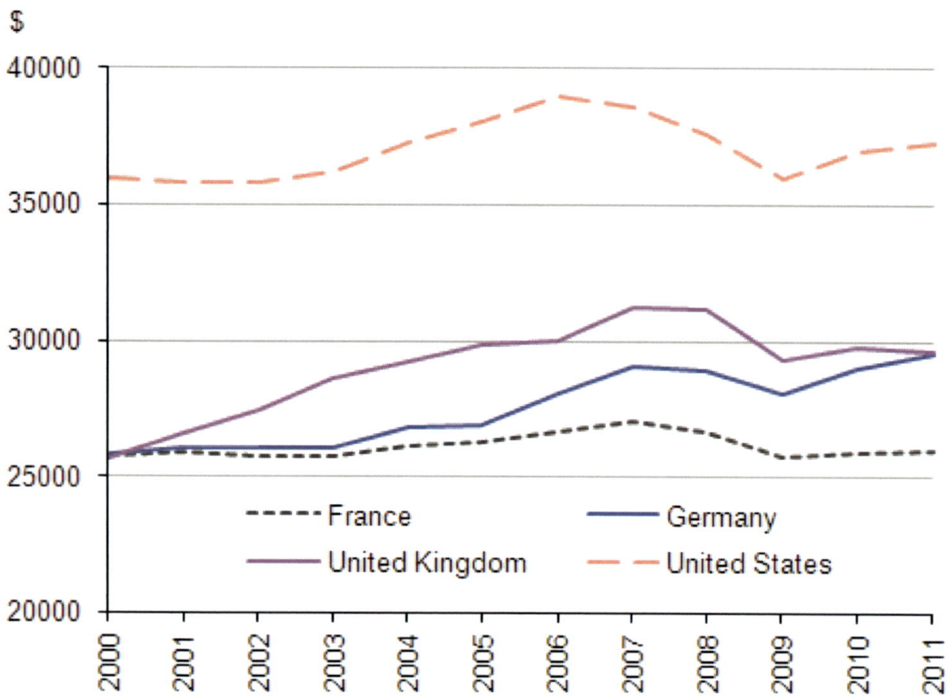

Notes:

1. Source: OECD
2. Constant prices and constant PPPs

Download chart

XLS XLS format
(27.5 Kb)

The UK saw, relatively, the largest growth in the early 2000s with an average growth rate of 2.8% between 2000 and 2007. However, like France, it did not recover well after the recession. Germany experienced more stable growth and a stronger recovery.

In 2008 and 2009 the effect of the recession is clear in all four economies. France was taken to its lowest NNI per head since 2000 and the UK was pushed back to close to its 2004 level. Germany fared comparably well, falling less severely. By 2010, Germany had recovered to its pre-recession level of NNI per head. However the UK recovery lags behind, in 2011 NNI was still 5% below its 2008 level.

Germany, France and the UK had a similar level of NNI per head in 2000 and although the UK grew more strongly than Germany between 2000 and 2007, the weaker recovery in the UK has resulted in Germany and the UK having similar levels of NNI again in 2011. Comparatively France saw weaker growth to 2007 and a relatively weak recovery, leaving NNI per head in France 12.3 per cent lower than the UK.

Conversely, in 2000 the US NNI per head was 39.9% bigger than that of the UK. Over the period, despite relatively strong growth in the US between 2004 and 2006, the gap between the US and the other countries (including the UK) reduced. By 2011, the gap had shrank 14 percent points to 25.9% of UK NNI per head. This reflects stronger growth in the UK between 2000 and 2008, and comes despite a weaker recovery.

Public Sector Debt

As with households, while national income flows are important for current income, it is also important to consider Public Sector Debt – giving an indication of the sustainability of current public spending. While NNI per head tells us about what is happening in the economy here and now, levels of debt give us an indication of how the current situation may affect the future. Debt effectively transfers the burden of paying for current consumption from the present to the future. Personal debt remains the liability of the individual (at least until their death). However, Public Sector Debt is government debt and can be transferred from one generation of tax payers to the next. However, it is worth highlighting that future economic progress can increase when debt is spent on investment in assets and capital, which generate income over their lifetime.

This article looks at Gross Public Sector Debt to indicate sustainability of public spending, this is internationally comparable. This is notably a different measure to that used to influence UK fiscal policy, Public Sector Net Debt, which we are not able to compare across countries. Figure 12 compares the UK and Euro Area countries in terms of Gross Public Sector Debt as a percentage of GDP, a comparison that is often used as it gives an indication of the sustainability of debt. There is no precise ratio as to what level of debt is sustainable; this depends on a variety of country specific risks and ultimately debt sustainability is decided by the financial markets. Growth in GDP, however, is seen as a critical element in reducing the risks.

Figure 12: Gross Public Debt as a percentage of GDP

United Kingdom and Euro Area

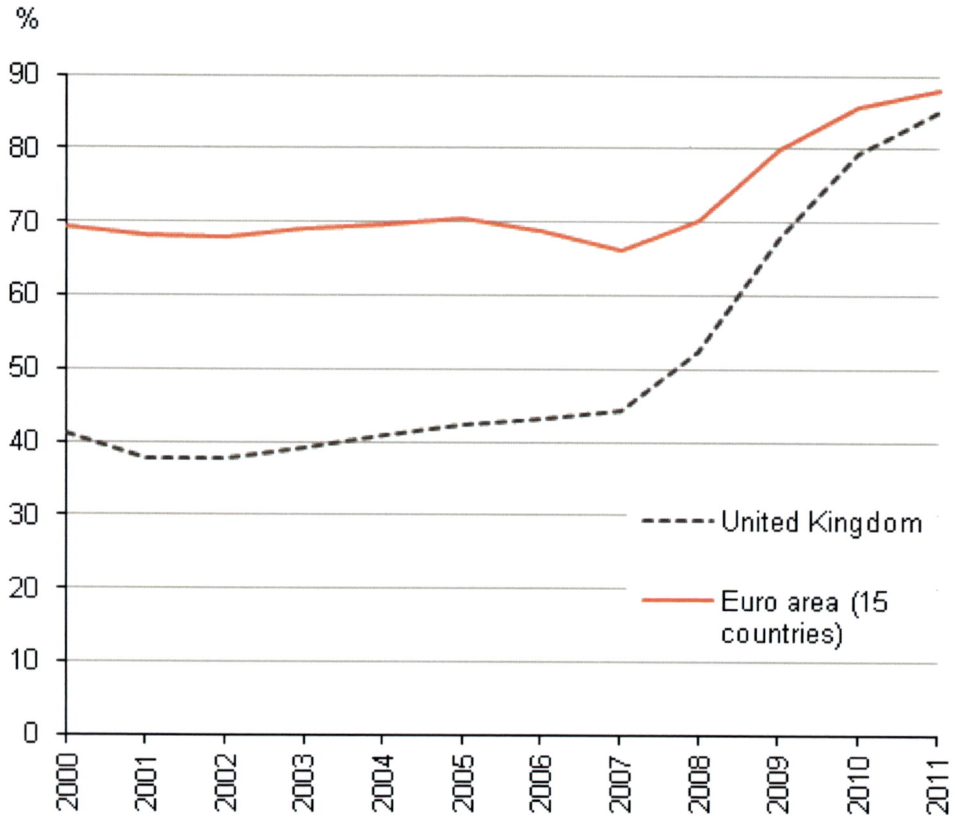

Notes:

1. Source: OECD

Download chart

XLS [XLS format](#)
(27.5 Kb)

In 2000, the level of UK debt was 41.1% of GDP, which is notably lower than the 69.2% for the Euro area. Between 2007 and 2011, with the effects of the financial crisis, the two levels of debt converge, increasing to 85% for the UK and 88.1% for the Euro area countries. By 2012, Gross Public Sector Debt as a percentage of GDP for the UK was over twice as much as it was in 2000.

Unsurprisingly given Figure 12, the UK has moved up the rankings when considering Gross Public Sector Debt (see Figure 13) from the 15th most indebted OECD country in 2000 to the 7th most indebted OECD country in 2011. Other countries who also saw a big rise in their relative debt levels by 2011 were Greece, France, Hungary and Norway who all moved up by two places, when compared to 2000. Notable countries at the top of the ranking include Greece, Italy, Portugal and Ireland all of whom have experienced problems with sustainability of debt in recent years.

Figure 13: Gross Public Debt as a Percentage of GDP in 2011

OECD Countries

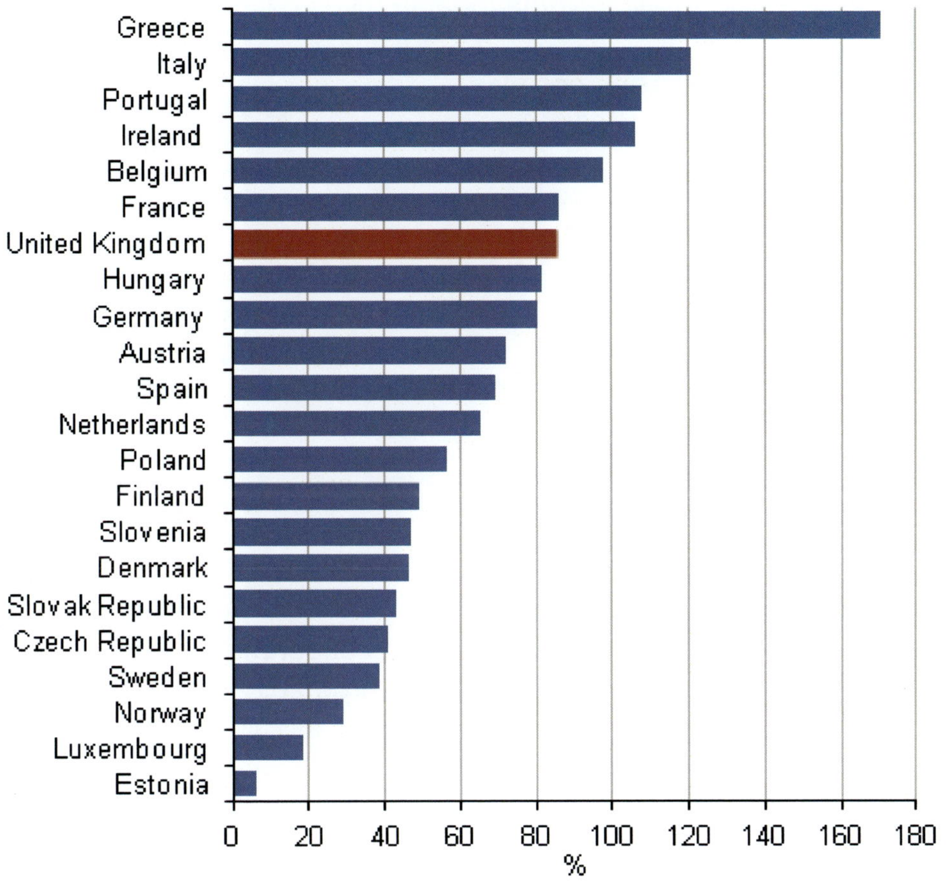

Notes:

1. Source: OECD

Download chart

XLS [XLS format](#)
(29.5 Kb)

Background notes

1. Details of the policy governing the release of new data are available by visiting www.statisticsauthority.gov.uk/assessment/code-of-practice/index.html or from the Media Relations Office email: media.relations@ons.gsi.gov.uk

Copyright

Supporting Information

Further information

Measuring National Well-being, The Economy
The article describes how economic well-being has evolved over the last decade and focuses on the period beginning with the 2008 recession.

Measuring National Well-being, Summary of Proposed Domains and Measures, July 2012
Summary of proposed domains and measures of national well-being

First Annual ONS Experimental Subjective Well-being Results
This article presents estimates of subjective well-being from the first annual experimental Annual Population Survey (APS) Subjective Well-being dataset for April 2011 to March 2012

Related Internet Links

Stiglitz J E, Sen A & Fitoussi J-P (2009) 'Report by the Commission on the Measurement of Economic Performance and Social Progress'.
Stiglitz J E, Sen A & Fitoussi J-P (2009) 'Report by the Commission on the Measurement of Economic Performance and Social Progress'.

OECD: Main Economic Indicators (MEI)

Glossary

Gross Public Sector Debt

The measure of Public Sector Debt used in this article is Gross public sector debt. Gross public sector debt measures the nominal value of consolidated general government financial liabilities including currency, bills, bonds and loans. It is different to the Measuring National Well-being Economy Domain indicator of public sector net debt excluding the temporary effects of financial interventions which is calculated as financial liabilities less liquid assets with both scored at face value. Liquid assets mainly comprise foreign exchange reserves and bank deposits. We have used the former definition in this article to allow international comparability.

Household Income (Household Actual Income)

The measure of household income used in this article is Household Actual Disposable Income (or household gross adjusted disposable income) in current prices and per head. This is a measure composed of total household income (employment earnings, property income, interest, dividends, pensions and social security benefits) plus the value of social transfers in kind receivable by households less payments of taxes, social security contributions, other current transfers, insurance premiums and the value of social transfers in kind payable by households.

Household Spending (Household Actual Consumption)

The measure of household spending used in this article is Household Actual Consumption (or household actual individual consumption). This is a measure of the value of consumption goods and services acquired by households, either through purchase or transfer from government or non-public institutions serving households (NPISH).

Household wealth

The measure of household wealth used in this article is household and NPISH net financial worth per head. Household financial worth is the sum of financial assets less financial liabilities. Financial assets include currency and deposits, securities other than shares, loans, and shares and other equity, net equity of households in life insurance reserves and pension funds, prepayments of premiums and other accounts receivable. Financial liabilities include loans, house purchase loans, and other accounts payable and where applicable securities other than shares (except financial derivatives), net equity of households in pension funds, and prepayments of premiums.

Inflation

The measure of inflation used in this article is the Harmonised Index of Consumer Prices (HICP). This is equivalent to the UK headline measure of inflation (Consumer Price Index – CPI).

Unemployment

The measure of unemployment used in this article is the Harmonised Rate of Unemployment. The Harmonised unemployment rates are based on the International Labour Organisation definition and are all sourced from the European Union Labour Force Survey. Unemployed persons are defined as persons aged 15 to 74 who are without work, are available to start work within the next two weeks and who have actively sought employment at some time during the previous four weeks. The unemployment rate is the number of people unemployed as a percentage of the labour force (the total number of people employed and unemployed).

30 May 2013

Measuring National Well-being - Review of domains and measures, 2013

Author Name(s): **Abigail Self and Chris Randall, Office for National Statistics**

Abstract

This article is published as part of the ONS Measuring National Well-being Programme. The programme aims to produce accepted and trusted measures of the well-being of the nation - how the UK as a whole is doing. It outlines the latest review of domains and measures of national well-being and is part of the ongoing refinement of measures.

Introduction

The aim of the MNW programme is to, 'develop and publish an accepted and trusted set of National Statistics which help people to monitor national well-being'. Critical to achieving this aim is the development of an agreed set of domains and measures. The initial list of domains and measures was developed based on responses to the National Debate, which took place between November 2010 and April 2011; existing research and international initiatives.

The measures were the subject of a public consultation which ran between October 2011 and January 2012. A summary and discussion of responses received was published in July 2012 in the paper, 'Measuring National Well-being: Report on consultation responses on proposed domains and measures'[1]. No significant changes were made to the set of measures at that time.

This review of domains and measures honours a commitment made in November 2012 in 'Measuring National Well-being: Life in the UK, 2012'[2] that ONS would 'review and further refine domains and measures of well-being and the criteria used to select them'. Feedback is invited on the changes made and a further refined set will be published in the Autumn. Please send feedback to: nationalwell-being@ons.gsi.gov.uk (for more information see 'Next steps')

The review has largely focused on revisiting the public consultation which ran between October 2011 and January 2012 as well as any feedback received since, for example, emails received by the Programme. ONS also took into account the large proportion of respondents who answered 'no' to the question asked in each domain, 'should any of the measures in this domain be removed' (around 80% to 90%). Informal discussions have also been held with relevant Government departments to ensure any proposed changes are in keeping with policy priorities.

The outcome of the review of measures is described domain by domain on the following pages. An interactive 'wheel of measures' and an expanded set of interactive graphs are available showing the latest data for each domain[2]. Data including time series for each measure (where available) are also provided in the data section of this publication.

Notes

1. Report on consultation responses on proposed domains and measures (524.4 Kb Pdf)

2. National Well-being

Key points

- Five measures have been added to reflect: arts and culture, participation in sport, access to services, satisfaction with accommodation and household recycling.
- Three measures have been removed namely satisfaction with leisure time, trust in parliament and air pollutants PM_{10}.
- The 'Individual well-being' domain has been renamed 'Personal well-being'
- The need for measures to be 'available for the UK' is classified as 'aspirational', to prevent important components of well-being being excluded on the basis of data availability.

Review of criteria

A proposal was made in the July 2012 report [1] to review and where appropriate, refresh the criteria used to select measures of national well-being.

The existing criteria are available in the National Statistician's report[2] on the findings from the national debate. Most of the criteria have been retained. As part of the review, criteria have been classified as 'aspirational' or 'essential'.

Essential

Measures of national well-being must be:

- Statistically robust.
- Have a time series and likely to be available in the future.
- Based on broad support (New) and be policy relevant.
- Nationally representative (New).
- Timely (New).

Aspirational

Where possible, measures of national well-being should be:

- Available for the UK.

- Capable of disaggregation for geographical areas and specific sub groups, for example, age, sex, socio-economic status, ethnicity, household type or other population group.
- Internationally comparable.

The most notable change compared with the original criteria is classifying 'available for the UK' as aspirational. The original need to ensure that measures reflect the UK meant that important contributors to well-being, for example, measures relating to arts and culture were excluded as there is no single UK measure. Classing the UK criterion as aspirational provides a more balanced approach. Every effort will still be made to include UK measures. Where this is not possible, flexibility exists to ensure that measures widely considered important for inclusion in the set of measures of national well-being can still be adopted.

Where data are not available for the UK within a single source, a 'nationally representative' data set should be chosen for the headline measure. This has been added to the 'essential criteria' to ensure that measures selected have sufficient coverage of the population to be used as a proxy for the UK. In most if not all cases, this is likely to be an England data set and equivalent data from the devolved administrations will be sign posted where available.

Disaggregation of data to sub-groups has also been defined as 'aspirational'. This again reflects a general lack of data to meet this need, rather than a shift in importance. The MNW programme remains committed to exploring well-being data for both sub-groups and sub-UK geographies and will continue work in this area. International comparability has been classed as aspirational to reflect the need to balance domestic priorities with international comparability when considering new measures.

In the essential criteria list, the 'policy relevant' criteria has been expanded to reflect the programme's ongoing engagement with a broad range of stakeholders in order to determine 'what matters'. In order to meet the Programme aim for the measures to be 'accepted', there needs to be wide support for the measures chosen so they report on a broadly shared understanding of well-being - including those which are policy relevant.

A final addition to the 'essential' criteria is that data should be 'timely'. This means that data should be collected and reported regularly to ensure measures are providing up-to-date information. The frequency for data updates should be appropriate to the measure concerned.

Original criteria relating to measures being a 'small set' and 'covering scope of domain without overlapping' have been removed. The need to have a manageable and non-overlapping set of measures remains important, but these are ambitions for the overall set rather than criteria which should be applied to individual measures.

Notes

1. Report on consultation responses on proposed domains and measures (524.4 Kb Pdf)

2. Measuring what matters: National Statistician's reflections on the national debate on measuring National Well-being (1.16 Mb Pdf)

Review of domains

The consultation showed that there was general support for all the domain names. Some concern was raised over the ease with which 'Governance' could be understood. Consideration was given to renaming this domain, 'democratic engagement' to more clearly describe the measures within it. However, following international interest in developing 'Governance' as a fourth pillar of well-being, alongside society, the economy and the environment, the name 'Governance' will be retained and revisited at a later date when the international picture is clearer.

Concern has also been raised at the use of 'individual well-being' as a domain name. Feedback was received during the consultation and in more recent focus groups which looked at what 'subjective well-being' meant to people and how the data should be presented. Candidates in the focus groups were presented with alternative names for subjective well-being, including 'individual well-being' and 'personal well-being'. 'Personal well-being' was chosen as being the most easily understood. For this reason, the individual well-being domain has been renamed 'personal well-being'.

Review of measures

The review of measures has largely focused on revisiting the public consultation which ran between October 2011 and January 2012 as well as any feedback received since, for example, emails received by the Programme. Informal discussions have also been held with relevant Government departments to ensure any proposed changes are in keeping with policy priorities.

Personal well-being

Summary

- No changes have been made to measures in this domain.
- ONS have committed to the inclusion of a measure of mental well-being from the Warwick-Edinburgh Mental Well-being Scale (WEMWbS). Work is underway to include this measure in the Autumn 2013 release.

Overview

At the time of consultation, the individual well-being domain comprised only one measure – life satisfaction. Life satisfaction was used as a placeholder for the four measures shown in Table 1 which were added following the release of the first annual dataset of subjective well-being data in July 2012. The inclusion of these additional measures also reflected consultation responses which suggested more measures be included within the domain.

A measure of mental well-being was also proposed during the consultation, either instead of or as well as the ‘percentage with some evidence of probable psychological disturbance or mental ill health’ measure which is taken from the 12 item General Health Questionnaire (GHQ-12). Following further discussion with the programme's Technical Advisory Group, it was agreed that a measure of mental well-being based on the Warwick Edinburgh Mental Well-being Scale (WEMWbS) should be added to the personal well-being domain in order to provide a more holistic view of subjective well-being. This would be in addition to the GHQ–12 measure in the health domain. Discussions on this and other aspects of the WEMWbS measure are ongoing, with the aim to include a suitable measure in the next update of domains and measures scheduled for Autumn 2013.

Table 1: Personal well-being measures

Measures	Geography	Source	Revision summary
Percentage with medium/high rating of satisfaction with their lives overall	UK	Annual Population Survey, ONS	No change
Percentage with medium/high rating of how worthwhile the things they do are	UK	Annual Population Survey, ONS	No change
Percentage who rated their happiness yesterday as medium/ high	UK	Annual Population Survey, ONS	No change
Percentage who rated how anxious they were yesterday as medium/ low	UK	Annual Population Survey, ONS	No change

Download table

XLS XLS format
(26.5 Kb)

Our relationships

Summary

- The ‘percentage who said they had someone they could really count on in a crisis’ has been replaced with an alternative measure of social support from the Understanding Society, UK Household Longitudinal survey.
- The source for ‘percentage who were somewhat, mostly or completely satisfied with their social life' has been changed to the European Quality of Life Survey (EQLS).

Overview

The main change in this domain is the replacement of the measure ‘percentage who said they had someone they could really count on in a crisis’, which provides an indication of social support network. This original question has not been carried forward from the original source, the British Household Panel Survey (BHPS), to the Understanding Society UK Household Longitudinal survey (UKHLS)[1]. Therefore the measure has been replaced by, ‘the percentage of people that have a spouse, family member or friend to rely on if they have a serious problem’- see Table 2. The measure combines three questions asked on Understanding Society, the UKHLS. In the same way, the question relating to the ‘percentage who were somewhat, mostly or completely satisfied with their social life’ was not carried forward from the BHPS to the Understanding Society UKHLS. The EQLS is proposed as a suitable alternative source.

Responses to the consultation included proposals for measures on religion/belief and on working relationships. Measures on religion and belief are not included here for reasons reported previously 2. A measure of satisfaction with work colleagues or workplace relationships was considered but it was decided that as not everyone in the UK has a job, it should not be included as a headline measure.

Table 2: Our relationships measures

Measures	Geography	Source	Revision summary
Average rating of satisfaction with family life	UK	European Quality of Life Survey, Eurofound	No change
Average rating of satisfaction with social life	UK	European Quality of Life Survey, Eurofound	Replacement - source changed
Percentage of people that have a spouse, family member or friend to rely on if they have a serious problem	UK	Understanding Society, the UK Household Longitudinal Study	Replacement

Download table

XLS XLS format
(27 Kb)

Notes

1. For more information about the UKHLS see Understanding Society

2. Report on consultation responses on proposed domains and measures (524.4 Kb Pdf)

Health

Summary

- No changes have been made to measures within this domain.

Overview

The consultation proposed measures on lifestyles (e.g. physical fitness, outdoor activities and sport). The proposals echoed comments made in relation to the 'What we do' domain, where a sports participation measure has now been added.

Table 3: Health measures

Measures	Geography	Source	Revision summary
Healthy life expectancy at birth by sex	UK	ONS	No change
Percentage who reported a long term illness and a disability	UK	Labour Force Survey, ONS	No change
Percentage who were somewhat, mostly or completely satisfied with their health	UK	Understanding Society, the UK Household Longitudinal Study	No change
Percentage with some evidence indicating probable psychological disturbance or mental ill health	UK	Understanding Society, the UK Household Longitudinal Study	No change

Download table

XLS XLS format
(26.5 Kb)

What we do

Summary

- The measure, 'Percentage who were somewhat, mostly or completely satisfied with their use of leisure time' has been removed.
- Two new measures have been added to reflect arts and culture; and sport.

Overview

Four of the existing measures in this domain have been retained (see Table 4). The measure, 'Percentage who were somewhat, mostly or completely satisfied with their use of leisure time' has been removed as this question is not asked on the Understanding Society, the UK Household Longitudinal Study (UKHLS), which replaces the previous source, the British Household Panel Survey (BHPS). It is also considered to overlap with the 'satisfaction with amount of leisure time' measure.

The most commonly requested additions during the consultation were measures to reflect arts, culture and sport. ONS had previously excluded these measures due to lack of UK data for these topics. However, ONS have been convinced by the weight of evidence in favour of including measures to reflect these areas. In addition, as part of this review, the criteria for selecting measures has been amended to ensure that whilst measures for the UK are preferable, measures which are 'nationally representative' will be accepted, with UK coverage being aspirational.

Consideration was given as to whether the measure should separate arts and culture or combine them and whether a combined measure would prove too broad a measure to be meaningful. Another consideration was whether the measure should cover engagement or participation. The final proposal of the 'percentage of people who have engaged with, or participated in, arts or cultural activity at least three times in the last year' taken from the Taking Part Survey was based on advice from the Department for Culture, Media & Sport (DCMS). The measure excludes 'reading for pleasure' as this was thought to have covered most people. Measures of arts and culture used by Scotland, Wales and Northern Ireland are signposted in the data section of this publication.

It was also acknowledged that the measures of well-being were incomplete without some measure of sports participation. The proposed measure is the percentage of respondents who had done 30 minutes or more of moderate intensity sport at least once a week in the last four weeks of being interviewed (note that recreational walking and cycling is excluded). The measure selected was based upon the advice of the DCMS and Sport England. The Taking Part Survey (DCMS) was considered as a source but it was decided to use the Active People Survey (Sport England) as this has a larger sample size. Measures of sport used by Scotland, Wales and Northern Ireland are signposted in the data spreadsheet.

Table 4: What we do measures

Measures	Geography	Source	Revision summary
Unemployment rate	UK	Labour Force Survey, ONS	No change
Percentage who were somewhat, mostly or completely satisfied with their job	UK	Understanding Society, the UK Household Longitudinal Study	No change
Percentage who were somewhat, mostly or completely satisfied with their amount of leisure time	UK	Understanding Society, the UK Household Longitudinal Study	No change
Percentage who volunteered more than once a year	UK	Understanding Society, the UK Household Longitudinal Study	No change
Percentage of people who have engaged with, or participated in, arts or cultural activity at least 3 times in the last year	England [1]	Taking Part Survey, Department for Culture, Media and Sport	New
Adult participation in 30 minutes of moderate intensity sport [2]	England [1]	Active People Survey, Sport England	New
Percentage who were somewhat, mostly or completely satisfied with their use of leisure time	UK	British Household Panel Survey	Removed

Table notes:

1. Similar devolved administration data available for this measure - see data section of this publication.
2. At least four sessions in the previous 28 days.

Download table

XLS XLS format
(27.5 Kb)

Where we live

Summary

- The measure, 'percentage that feel very or fairly safe walking alone after dark' (England and Wales) has been amended to highlight data for men and women, as opposed to an overall total.
- 'Percentage of those who were very or fairly satisfied with their accommodation' has been added to reflect the need for a housing measure in the 'Where we live' domain.
- A measure of access to key services has been added to reflect consultation responses.

Overview

Feedback was received during the consultation on the 'percentage who felt very or fairly safe walking alone after dark'. Comments related to the inclusion only of the measure relating to 'after dark'; the potential influence the media, as opposed to levels of crime itself, in determining people's answers; and of the difference between data for men and women which was masked by providing an overall total. Alternative measures of perception of crime were explored, including what people felt about levels of crime nationally and in their local area. However, it was felt that a measure which related to personal behaviour and crime was important to include. The existing measure has therefore been retained with the differences between men and women more clearly highlighted (see Table 5).

The measure 'Percentage of those who were very or fairly satisfied with their accommodation' has been added to reflect the need for a housing measure in the 'Where we live' domain. The measure was selected following a review of responses to the consultation, available data and discussions with the Department for Communities and Local Government (DCLG). Data for groups such as private renters and owner occupiers are provided in the underlying data spreadsheet, providing scope for further analysis. Further analysis might include: understanding the differences between groups and changes over time by looking at the root causes for differing levels of satisfaction, spanning issues of affordability, homelessness, overcrowding, and decent homes.

An accessibility measure has also been added. Increasing car use has provided greater opportunity for people to travel and access the services they require. However 1 in 4 households do not have access to a car. These people rely on other forms of transport such as public transport, walking, lifts from friends etc. The reliance on such 'networks', which may be limited, can lead to social exclusion and may affect a person's sense of well-being.

Table 5: Where we live measures

Measures	Geography	Source	Revision summary
Crimes against the person (per 1,000 adults)	England and Wales[1]	Crime Survey for England and Wales, ONS	No change
Percentage of men and women that feel very or fairly safe walking alone after dark	England and Wales	Crime Survey for England and Wales, ONS	Changed from all persons to men and women
Percentage who accessed the natural environment at least once a week in the last 12 months	England[1]	Natural England	No change
Percentage who agreed or agreed strongly that they felt they belonged to their neighbourhood	UK	Understanding Society, the UK Household Longitudinal Study	No change
Households with good transport access to key services or work[2]	England[3]	Accessibility Statistics, Department for Transport	New
Percentage of those who were very or fairly satisfied with their accommodation	England[3]	English Housing Survey, full household sample, Department for Communities and Local Government	New

Table notes:

1. Similar devolved administration data available for this measure - see data section of this publication.
2. This indicator relates the car ownership rate to the average public transport time to seven key services. The indicator is indexed (as a score of 100) to the England average for 2010.
3. No similar data for other devolved administrations were found.

Download table

XLS XLS format
(28 Kb)

Personal finance

Summary

- No changes have been made to measures within this domain

Table 6: Personal finance measures

Measures	Geography	Source	Revision summary
Percentage of individuals living in households with less than 60 per cent of median income after housing costs	UK	The Family Resources Survey, Department for Work and Pensions	No change
Median wealth per household, including pension wealth	Great Britain	Wealth and Assets Survey, ONS	No change
Percentage who were somewhat, mostly or completely satisfied with the income of their household	UK	Understanding Society, the UK Household Longitudinal Study	No change
Percentage who report finding it quite or very difficult to get by financially	UK	Understanding Society, the UK Household Longitudinal Study	No change

Download table

XLS XLS format
(27 Kb)

Education and skills

Summary

- No changes have been made to measures within this domain.

Overview

The importance of continued and life-long learning was highlighted in the consultation for its role in enhancing personal development and employability which in turn may affect a person's well-being. Further research to find a single viable measure that would encapsulate all aspects of life-long learning was carried out. ONS will continue to investigate potential measures for inclusion in future domain analyses.

Table 7: Education and skills measures

Measures	Geography	Source	Revision summary
Human capital - the value of individuals' skills, knowledge and competences in the labour market	UK	ONS	No change
Percentage with five or more GCSE grades A* – C (including English and Mathematics)	UK	Department for Education; Welsh Government; Scottish Government; Northern Ireland Department of Education	No change
Percentage of UK residents aged 16–64 with no qualifications	UK	Labour Force Survey, ONS	No change

Download table

XLS XLS format
(27 Kb)

The economy

Summary

- No changes have been made to measures within this domain.

Table 8: The economy measures

Measures	Geography	Source	Revision summary
Real household actual income per head	UK	National Accounts, ONS	No change
Real net national income per head	UK	National Accounts, ONS	No change
UK public sector net debt as a percentage of Gross Domestic Product	UK	National Accounts, ONS	No change
Inflation rate (as measured by the CPI)	UK	ONS	No change

Download table

XLS XLS format
(26.5 Kb)

Governance

Summary

- The measure 'percentage of those who have trust in national Parliament' has been removed as it was considered similar to the measure 'Percentage of those who have trust in national Government'.

Table 9: Governance measures

Measures	Geography	Source	Revision summary
Percentage of registered voters who voted	UK	International Institute for Democracy and Electoral Assistance	No change
Percentage of those who have trust in national Government	UK	Eurobarometer	No change
Percentage of those who have trust in national Parliament	UK	Eurobarometer	Removed

Download table

XLS XLS format
(26.5 Kb)

The natural environment

Summary

- The measure, 'Air pollutants - PM_{10}' has been removed.
- A measure of household recycling has been added.

Overview

Recycling was the most commonly cited proposed addition to the Natural Environment domain during the consultation. After discussions with Defra, ONS decided that the measure - 'percentage of household waste that is recycled' would be added to this domain. It is a readily available well known indicator giving an indication of the priority households are now giving to protecting the natural environment. It also shows how we are making best use of the natural resources and minimising the use of land fill sites. Recycled waste also includes waste that is composted or reused. As the measure is England only, similar data for Wales, Scotland and Northern Ireland are provided in the data section of this publication.

The measure of air pollutant PM_{10} has been removed as it is not widely understood and air emissions are already covered in the measure to be retained on green house gas (GHG) emissions. This measure shows the contribution the UK is making in reducing world GHG emissions. Global green house gas emissions are a major concern to the population with its links to climate change.

This is linked to the measure of energy consumed from renewable sources which has also been retained.

Concerns were raised over the usefulness of 'extent of protected areas' measure and whether a measure which better reflects how environmental quality is changing would be better. A more suitable approach may be to consider a measure of land use and discussions will continue as to whether there is an appropriate measure.

Finally, ONS were encouraged to consider the weather and natural disasters and the effect they had on people's well-being. Currently there are no suitable measures for this area or means of assessing progress but this will be kept under review.

Table 10: The natural environment measures

Measures	Geography	Source	Revision summary
Total green house gas emissions	UK	Department of Energy and Climate Change	No change
The extent of protected areas in the UK	UK	Department for Environment, Food and Rural Affairs	No change
Energy consumed within the UK from renewable sources	UK	ONS	No change
Percentage of household waste that is recycled (including composted and reused)	England[1]	The Department for Communities and Local Government	New
Air pollutants - PM_{10}	UK	ONS	Removed

Table notes:

1. Similar devolved administration data available for this measure - see data section of this publication.

Download table

XLS XLS format
(27 Kb)

Next steps

ONS seek and welcome feedback about the changes outlined in this article, in particular:

- Changes made to the criteria used to select the measures.
- The change in domain name from 'individual well-being' to 'personal well-being'.
- The measures which have been added.
- The measures which have been removed.
- Any suggestions for further variants on the measures which could be more appropriate.

ONS will consider feedback received and the measures will be further refined and republished in Autumn 2013.

Please send feedback to the following email or postal address:

Email: nationalwell-being@ons.gsi.gov.uk

Measuring National Well-being, Room 2.164,

Office for National Statistics,

Government Buildings,

Cardiff Road,

Newport,

South Wales, NP10 8XG

For further information about this article, please contact Abigail Self:

Telephone: +44 (0)1633 455855

Email: Abigail.self@ons.gsi.gov.uk

About the ONS Measuring National Well-being Programme

NWB logo 2

This article is published as part of the ONS Measuring National Well-being Programme.

The programme aims to produce accepted and trusted measures of the well-being of the nation - how the UK as a whole is doing.

Measuring National Well-being is about looking at 'GDP and beyond'. It includes headline indicators in areas such as health, relationships, job satisfaction, economic security, education, environmental conditions and measures of 'subjective well-being' (individuals' assessment of their own well-being).

Find out more on the Measuring National Well-being website pages.

Background notes

1. Details of the policy governing the release of new data are available by visiting www.statisticsauthority.gov.uk/assessment/code-of-practice/index.html or from the Media Relations Office email: media.relations@ons.gsi.gov.uk

Copyright

30 May 2013

Measuring National Well-being - What matters most to Personal Well-being?

Author Name(s): **Sebnem Oguz, Salah Merad, Dawn Snape, Office for National Statistics**

Abstract

This article uses data from the Annual Population Survey collected between April 2011 and March 2012 which includes measures of personal well-being. It describes the results of regression analysis – a statistical technique which analyses variation in well-being outcomes by specific characteristics and circumstances of individuals while holding all other characteristics equal. This allows for a better understanding of what matters most to personal well-being than when different factors are considered separately.

Introduction

This article is published as part of the Office for National Statistics Measuring National Well-being Programme. The programme aims to produce accepted and trusted measures of the well-being of the nation - how the UK as a whole is doing. The Office for National Statistics measures of well-being are organised into ten domains with each domain having between three and five separate indicators. More information about the measures can be found in the 'National Well-being wheel of measures' (ONS 2012). The aim of the Programme is to achieve an accepted and trusted set of National Statistics to help people understand and monitor national well-being.

As part of the Programme four measures of the personal well-being of individuals were developed (Tinkler & Hicks 2011). Since April 2011 these have been collected from respondents to the Annual Population Survey and asked of adults aged 16 and over. A number of analyses of these data have been released by ONS already which examine the measures and their distribution by specific characteristics.

These analyses considered how different factors are associated with personal well-being separately, for example, how self-reported health is related to the different measures of personal well-being. The regression analysis (see section 5.1) in this report takes factors from within the large scale Annual Population Survey together and considers how these are related to personal well-being. So when looking at how self-reported health is associated with personal well-being, it also controls for a range of other factors for example people's age and sex and ethnicity to name a few. This allows for a better understanding of what matters most to personal well-being as the relationship between the variable in question and personal well-being is considered knowing that other factors included in the analysis are held equal.

Although the regression analysis can show the nature, size and strength of the relationship between a specific personal characteristic or circumstance and personal well-being, we cannot say with certainty that the characteristic or circumstance has caused greater or lesser well-being. As this data is like a snapshot of one point in time, we cannot establish whether a person's circumstances have contributed to their level of well-being or indeed whether their level of well-being has contributed to their current circumstances.

Key points

According to regression analysis of the 2011/12 Annual Population Survey in Great Britain, holding other variables equal:

- Self-reported health had the strongest association with all the measures of personal well-being, the second strongest association was employment status and the third was relationship status.
- People's sense of choice and contentment with their situation appear to be associated with personal well-being. For example, people who are employed but want a different or additional job have lower levels of personal well-being (including higher 'anxious yesterday' levels) than employed people who are not looking for another job.
- Some circumstances or characteristics appear to have a more global effect on all aspects of personal well-being, while others have a more discrete effect on only one or two areas. For example, self-reported health makes a large contribution to the explained variance between individuals across all four measures of personal well-being while age explains a moderate amount of the variance in relation to life satisfaction, but less on the other three measures of well-being.

Below are other interesting findings from across the well-being domains which are statistically significant but have smaller effects on ratings of personal well-being than the factors noted above:

- Living alone is negatively related to our personal well-being, regardless of relationship status. All household types where two or more people live together give higher ratings for 'worthwhile' and 'life satisfaction' than those living alone.
- People in the Black/African/Caribbean/Black British ethnic group rate their 'life satisfaction' and 'happiness yesterday' lower on average than the White group.
- People who say that they have a religious affiliation, rate their levels of 'happiness yesterday', 'life satisfaction' and 'worthwhile' higher than people who said they have no religious affiliation.
- People with the highest educational attainment have higher ratings of 'anxiety yesterday' on average than people with lower educational attainment.
- People in higher managerial and professional occupations give higher scores for 'anxious yesterday' levels on average than those in lower supervisory and technical occupations.
- Among a sub-sample of employees only, those who earn higher wages from their job give higher ratings for 'life satisfaction' on average than those earning less, but ratings for 'worthwhile', 'happy yesterday' and 'anxiety yesterday' were not related to earnings.
- People living in London gave similar ratings of their 'life satisfaction' than people living in other urban areas in Great Britain, but people living in the rural areas of almost all regions gave higher 'life satisfaction' ratings than people living in London.
- People living in the least deprived local areas reported slightly higher levels of 'anxiety yesterday' than people living in more deprived local areas.

Table 1 provides an overview of the size of the unique contribution that each variable in the analysis makes to personal well-being. The link beneath the table will take readers to the data on which the summary table is based.

Table 1: The size of the unique contribution that each variable makes to the explained variance in personal well-being

Factor	'Life satisfaction' (R^2)	'Worthwhile' (R^2)	'Happiness yesterday' (R^2)	'Anxious yesterday' (R^2)
Self-reported health	Large	Large	Large	Large
Economic activity	Large	Large	Moderate	Moderate
Marital status	Large	Moderate	Moderate	Very Small
Age	Moderate	Very Small	Small	Small
Mode of interview	Small	Small	Very Small	Very Small
Ethnicity	Small	Very Small	Very Small	Very Small
Region	Small	Small	Very Small	Small
Tenure	Small	Small	Very Small	Very Small
Religion	Very Small	Small	Small	Very Small
Socio-economic status	Very Small	Very Small	Very Small	Very Small
Index of multiple deprivation decile	Very Small	Very Small	Very Small	Very Small
Education	Very Small	Very Small	Very Small	Small
Gender	Very Small	Small	Very Small	Small
Disability	Very Small	Very Small	Very Small	Very Small
Migration	Very Small	Very Small	Very Small	Very Small
Children	Very Small	Small	Very Small	Very Small

Table source: Office for National Statistics

Table notes:

1. Large = contribution of 1.0 percentage point or more to R-square; Moderate= contribution of .05 < 1.0 percentage point to R-square; Small= contribution of 0.1 < 0.5 percentage point to R-square; Very small= contribution of less than 0.10 percentage point to R-square.

Download table

XLS XLS format
(37.5 Kb)

Summary

Introduction

The analysis in this report is based on data from the Annual Population Survey (APS) collected from April 2011 to March 2012. The survey included the following four questions on personal well-being which ONS first added to the survey in April 2011:

- Overall, how satisfied are you with your life nowadays?
- Overall, to what extent do you feel the things you do in your life are worthwhile?
- Overall, how happy did you feel yesterday?
- Overall, how anxious did you feel yesterday?

Those taking part in the survey are asked to give their answers on a scale of 0 to 10 where 0 is 'not at all' and 10 is 'completely'.

The APS also collects a range of other information. These can be used to see how responses to each of the four personal well-being questions differ by a range of characteristics and circumstances. This article presents the results of regression analysis, a statistical technique which analyses the variation in responses to the personal well-being questions by specific characteristics and circumstances of individuals while holding all other characteristics equal. The key benefit of regression analysis is that it provides a better method of identifying those factors which matter most to personal well-being than an analysis looking at the relationship between only two variables at a time.

What matters most to personal well-being?

People's self-reported health was the most important factor associated with personal well-being, followed by their work situation and then their relationship status.

Even after holding other personal characteristics and circumstances equal:

- People who reported very bad health gave much lower ratings of personal well-being than those in good health. On the eleven point scale above (from 0 to 10), people in very bad health rated their 'life satisfaction' 2.4 points lower, their 'happiness yesterday' 2.6 points lower, the sense that what they are doing is 'worthwhile' 2.0 points lower than people in good health. Also, people in very bad health rated their 'anxiety yesterday' levels 2.1 points higher than people in good health.
- The second largest association with the four personal well-being questions was found to be employment status. Holding all else equal those who are unemployed rated their levels of 'life satisfaction', 'happiness yesterday' and the sense that what they are doing is 'worthwhile' significantly lower on average than people who are employed.
- Among the areas examined here, the nature of our relationships is the final area that should be highlighted as having an important influence on personal well-being. Holding all else equal and comparing people according to their relationship status shows that married people and those in civil partnerships rate their 'life satisfaction', the sense that their activities are 'worthwhile' and 'happiness yesterday' significantly higher than cohabiting couples, single, divorced and widowed people. Single people rated their 'happiness yesterday' on average 0.4 of a point lower than

those who are married or in civil partnerships. Widowed people rate their 'happiness yesterday' score 0.6 of a point lower on average than married people or people in civil partnerships. The 'anxiety yesterday' ratings of single, divorced and widowed people were also significantly higher than those of married people (between 0.1 and 0.2 of a point higher).

Other factors such as people's age, sex, ethnic group, migration status, religious affiliation, level of qualification, presence of children, reasons for inactivity, occupation, home ownership, and area where they live were also associated in different ways to personal well-being, but none to the same extent as health, unemployment and relationship status.

How does people's sense of choice and contentment with their situation affect their personal well-being?

People's sense of choice and contentment with their current situation also appears to be associated with their levels of personal well-being. It appears that it is more about where they are in life compared to where they want to be. For example:

- It is not just about having a job that matters to personal well-being, but also being content with that job. Permanent employees who wanted a different or additional job had lower levels of life satisfaction, a sense that what they do in life was worthwhile, feelings of happiness and increased levels of anxiety than those who did not want a different or additional job. Permanent employees who wanted a different job rated their 'life satisfaction' 0.7 points on average below that of permanent employees who didn't want a different or additional job. Similarly, their average ratings for both 'worthwhile' and 'happy yesterday' were 0.5 points below those of permanent employees who didn't want another job. In addition the anxiety ratings for those who wanted another job were 0.6 higher than those who didn't.
- Also those who are economically inactive and in caring roles but would rather be in paid work have lower personal well-being than those who are working and content with their jobs. In contrast, there is no difference in life satisfaction between people who are working and content with their job and those who are economically inactive and in a caring role with which they are content.

Some factors are more important to specific aspects of personal well-being than others

Finally, some circumstances are associated differently with the various aspects of personal well-being. For example, even after holding other personal characteristics and circumstances equal:

- People living with dependent children have a higher sense that what they do in life is worthwhile compared to those with no dependent children in the household. On the eleven point scale above (0 to 10), people with dependent children in the household gave ratings for 'worthwhile' almost 0.2 points higher on average than those with no dependent children in the household.
- Increased earnings of employees are associated with higher levels of life satisfaction but not with the sense that their activities are worthwhile nor with their day-to-day emotions. Employees with higher earnings therefore do not appear to have a sense that their activities are more worthwhile any more than those employees with lower earnings nor do they report significantly higher levels of happiness or lower levels of anxiety.

Further research

This analysis illustrates how the APS can be used to examine how different factors are associated with personal well-being. The strength of the APS is the large sample and range of variables about people's characteristics and circumstances, particularly labour market related variables. It is however, a cross-sectional sample survey and as such is not well suited to exploring how individual well-being may change over time. Given the large sample of the APS, it lends itself to further examination of small sub-groups of the population and of small geographic areas. These types of analyses would potentially offer new insights to help policy-makers identify areas of need and target policies.

1. Taking a closer look at what matters most to personal well-being

Personal well-being, often referred to as subjective well-being, is people's own assessment of their own well-being. Many factors have been shown to be related to personal well-being such as health, disability, age, ethnic group, employment situation, relationships, religious beliefs and participation, etc. However, studies comparing the importance of any specific circumstance or characteristic to personal well-being cannot provide a clear picture of which of the many possible personal characteristics and circumstances that may affect us actually make the strongest contribution to how we experience our lives and our sense of well-being. Special statistical techniques such as regression analysis (see section 5.1) are required to do this which look at the relationship of each characteristic or circumstance to personal well-being while holding other possible influences on well-being equal. This article presents the results of regression analysis undertaken by ONS to understand more about at what matters most to personal well-being.

Before moving on to the findings from this study, it is important to note that previous research in this area shows that our genes and personality explain much of the differences between people's levels of personal well-being. Indeed, it has been estimated that these differences may explain up to half of the variation observed between people in their level of personal well-being (Diener 1996).

This study uses data from the Annual Population Survey which does not include any measurement of personality or genetic differences. Excluding these important areas, we would hope to be able to explain up to 50% of the differences in personal well-being between people. In our analysis, we have explained between 10% and 19% of the differences in levels of well-being between people.

2. Research methods

2.1 How people were asked to rate their well-being

The research is based on data from the Annual Population Survey (APS) from April 2011 to March 2012. The survey provides a representative sample of people living in residential households in the UK and includes about 165,000 respondents.

In April 2011, ONS included four questions on the APS which focus on 3 aspects of personal well-being: how we assess our life satisfaction; whether we feel our lives have meaning and purpose;

and our recent experiences of positive and negative emotions. These ideas are measured by asking people aged 16 and over four questions:

- Overall, how satisfied are you with your life nowadays?
- Overall, to what extent do you feel the things you do in your life are worthwhile?
- Overall, how happy did you feel yesterday?
- Overall, how anxious did you feel yesterday?

Those taking part in the survey are asked to give their answers on a scale of 0 to 10 where 10 is 'completely' and 0 is 'not at all'. For the first three questions which are about positive aspects of personal well-being, a higher score indicates higher personal well-being. However, the fourth question asks about anxiety which is a negative emotion so a higher score here indicates lower personal well-being. In this report the abbreviations 'life satisfaction', 'worthwhile' 'happy yesterday' or 'happiness yesterday' and 'anxious yesterday' or 'anxiety yesterday' are used to refer to the four overall monitoring questions.

Interviewing for the survey goes on throughout the year and on every day of the week except Sundays. As researchers have found that people remember their emotions accurately only for the very recent past, the questions on daily emotions ask about happiness and anxiety yesterday. The fact that yesterday may not have been very typical of someone's normal emotional state will average out across the 165,000 people in the study to provide a good estimate of levels of happiness and anxiety in the UK overall.

2.2 Why ask people about their well-being?

The reason for asking people to assess these aspects of their lives is ultimately to help understand more about how people in the UK think their lives are going and what is most important in shaping their views. This is one part of the much larger ONS Measuring National Well-being Programme.

Overall, the Programme uses both objective information as well as information based on people's own views to monitor the well-being of the UK. This includes a wide range of measures developed after extensive public consultation undertaken in 2010-11 during the National Debate (Office for National Statistics 2011) to ask people what matters most to them. The Programme aims to provide information about how the UK is doing which moves beyond GDP as the main measure of societal progress. The goal is to provide policy makers with information which will enable them to take into account the likely impacts of their ideas on the well-being of the people and environment of the UK and therefore to make better decisions.

2.3 Approach to the regression analysis

There were three stages involved in the analysis. These were:

- Construction of the main model which was used in separate regressions with each of the four personal well-being questions;
- Construction of an another model used among employees only, a sub-set of the sample, in order to explore how earnings are related to personal well-being; and
- Analysis of each of the models using two different regression techniques, ordered probit regression and then replicating the analysis using ordinary least squares regression.

Constructing the main model

From the outset, the aim was to develop two models: one for the whole population and one specifically for employees to address the fact that the APS does not include household income data but does have earnings data for employees. The variables used in the models were chosen to capture specific aspects of the different ONS well-being domains including: our health, our relationships, what we do, where we live, our finances, and basic personal characteristics.

This also presented an opportunity to further knowledge about personal well-being by attempting to replicate the findings of others or to use alternative measures. This work represented an extension to the basic regression project. Findings from the alternative models are discussed in section 5 and the results of each model are presented in full in Reference Table 4 (770 Kb Excel sheet).

For some domains, such as 'Where we live', there is minimal data available directly from the APS. For this reason, a variable was added to the APS to try to capture more of the differences between places. This is based on the Indices of Multiple Deprivation (IMD) of England, Wales and Scotland. As some of the place related variables, such as IMD deciles and rural/urban identification, could not be created from the data available. The analysis reported here therefore does not include respondents from Northern Ireland and focuses on Great Britain rather than the United Kingdom. Excluding Northern Ireland, the total sample size is approximately 163,000.

As noted, once the model was developed, the same basic set of variables was used in regressions with each of the four personal well-being questions. This included the following:

- Age (both age and age^2)
- Sex
- Ethnicity
- Migration status
- Relationship status
- Economic activity status
- Housing tenure
- Self-reported health
- Self-reported disability
- Highest qualification held
- Socio-economic status,
- Presence of dependent and non-dependent children in the household,
- Religious affiliation,
- Geographical region,
- The relative deprivation of the area in which the individual lives,
- Whether the area is urban or rural,
- Mode of interview (telephone or personal interview)

Creating a model for exploring earnings and personal well-being

The next stage of work involved the specification of a model for use with employees for whom earnings information is available, a sub-sample of those included in the main analysis. Although household income has been shown by other research (Kahneman 2010; Pishke, 2011) to play a role in our personal well-being, the Annual Population Survey does not include this information. Other variables which might provide a rough indication of the individual's financial situation were included in earlier versions of the regression models to see how well they worked, such as the Income Deprivation domain of the Indices of Multiple Deprivation and the individual's benefit status. Analysis was also undertaken using average household income in the areas where each respondent lives (using MSOA level data), but the results showed that it was not a significant factor in explaining personal well-being. This is probably because average household income in an area is not a very good substitute for individual household income.

The same approach was taken to this analysis as described above for the main sample and using the same variables noted above, but with additional variables on individual net earnings in the previous week, either as the log of last week's net wage or as a decile, (i.e. relative distribution of the net wage). Another variation used the same variables as in the main model, but also included information about household net earnings in the previous week using the same approach as for individual earnings. These were included in the models with employees in order to understand more about how income from work, either individually or at a household level, may influence personal well-being. The variables for household net earnings were created specially for this analysis using data available in the APS.

Approach to the analysis

The final stage of the work involved analysis of each model, first using ordered probit regression and then replicating it using OLS. This was done because the ordered probit technique is best suited to ordered nature of the responses to the personal well-being questions (ie, with responses on a scale from 0 to 10). However, the results of ordered probit analysis are difficult to explain to a wide audience in an accessible way. For this reason, it is generally considered acceptable to undertake the analysis first in ordered probit and then to replicate in OLS. If the findings are very similar, then they can be reported using the OLS regression results. In this case, the statistical significance, the signs and the relative sizes of the regression coefficients were very similar between the two methods and the choice of the regression method made little difference to the overall findings. This is also consistent with other similar research (Ferrer-i Carbonell and Frijters 2004; Stevenson and Wolfers 2008; Fleche et al., 2011).

The findings in this report are therefore based on the results of the OLS regressions for the sake of simplicity and ease of interpretation, but the results from both types of regression are included in the reference tables to enable comparisons.

Interpreting what the numbers mean

The numbers included throughout the text and in the tables at the beginning of each section are the unstandardised coefficients for each variable included in the main regression models. This shows the size of the effect that the variable has on the specific aspect of personal well-being considered. Numbers to indicate the size of the effects are presented only if they are from the main regression models and they are statistically significant. Where findings from the alternative models shed light on specific aspects of well-being, these are referred to in the text but no references are made to the coefficients to avoid direct comparisons with the main models. As noted, reference tables with the coefficients from the alternative models are available via links in each section.

In interpreting the findings, it is important to remember that these numbers represent the difference between two groups when all other variables in the model have been held equal. The comparisons are therefore between two people who are otherwise the same in every respect apart from the particular characteristic or circumstance being considered. This helps to isolate the effect of any specific characteristic or circumstance on personal well-being.

Throughout, in order to give a sense of the size of the relationship found between each individual characteristic and personal well-being, we have used the following schema. This summarises the size of the difference between how an individual from the reference group would rate their well-being for each question compared to how an individual from another group would rate the same question, holding other variables equal.

Under the tables, when results are referred to as 'significant at the 5% level', this means there is a probability of less than .05 (or less than one in twenty) that the result could have occurred by chance.

Schema for comparing the size of the relationship between each variable and personal well-being:

Large- a difference of 1.0 points or more between the average rating of the reference group and the group being studied after controlling for other factors

Moderate- 0.5 points < 1.0 points difference between the groups

Small- 0.1 points < 0.5 points difference between the groups

Very small- a difference of less than 0.10 points but which is still statistically significant

3. Our findings

The results of the regression analyses are summarised in the sections which follow. A table which provides a summary of the results for all the variables in the main model is available in Reference Table 1 (141.5 Kb Excel sheet). In order to illustrate the findings relevant to each section, an extract from Reference Table 1 is included in each section showing the results for the variables in that section.

3.1 Does who we are affect our personal well-being?

As noted earlier, aspects of who we are, such as our genes and our personality, have been shown to have an important influence on our sense of personal well-being. But beyond that, do our 'objective' personal characteristics like whether we are a man or a woman, our age or our ethnicity have a role to play?

3.1.1 Summary of findings on age, sex, ethnicity, migration and religion

Holding other factors equal:

- Personal well-being is highest among younger and older adults and dips in middle age
- Differences in personal well-being between men and women are small, but women report higher 'life satisfaction', 'worthwhile' and 'happy yesterday' levels. Women also reported slightly higher levels of 'anxious yesterday' than men
- People of Black/African/Caribbean/Black British ethnicities rated their 'life satisfaction' lower on average than White people. The size of this relationship was moderate.
- Indian and Pakistani people also rated their 'anxiety yesterday' higher than White people. The size of the differences found between these ethnic groups and the white reference group were small.
- People who have migrated to the UK rate their 'life satisfaction' and 'happiness yesterday' more highly on average than those who were born in the UK. Immigrants who settled in the UK more recently give slightly higher ratings for 'happy yesterday' than those who have been living in the UK for 12 years or more. Overall, the size of the relationship between migration status and personal well-being is small.
- People who say that they have a religious affiliation rate their levels of 'happiness yesterday', 'life satisfaction' and 'worthwhile' higher than people who said they have no religious affiliation. The size of relationship between religious affiliation and personal well-being is small.

3.1.2 Age

Looking first at age, the analysis shows that the relationship between age and the four subjective well-being measures is statistically significant but generally small. The findings are shown in **Table 2**.

After controlling for all the other factors, personal well-being is highest among younger people and older people. This is in line with previous ONS findings and other research that shows that the relationship between age and personal well-being is U-shaped. That is, our sense of personal well-being is highest among younger people and older people and is lowest among people in their middle years.

There may be two possible explanations for this. Firstly, this may be a 'cohort effect' in which people born in different eras have different experiences and expectations which shape their sense of well-being. If the age curve represents a cohort effect, we might expect that people born around the same time would maintain a similar level of well-being throughout their lives regardless of their age.

Another possible explanation is that our level of personal well-being may change as we move through our lives, have new experiences, and possibly change the way we look at things. A growing body of research (The Economist 2010; Dolan et al., 2008) notes that the U-shaped curve observed between age and well-being has been found consistently over 40 years of data collection. These differences consistently appear at particular points in the life cycle and after controlling for many other characteristics and circumstances which may influence personal well-being. This has led some researchers to suggest that the different levels of well-being observed at different points in life may be the result of internal changes within the individual rather than external circumstances.

For example, some recent studies have suggested the dip in well-being in middle age and the subsequent rise later in life may represent what has been called, the "death of ambition and birth of acceptance". That is, people may come to accept their strengths and weaknesses and, "give up hoping to become chief executive or have a picture shown in the Royal Academy, and learn to be satisfied as assistant branch manager, with their watercolour on display at the church fete." (The Economist 2010).

Overall, further research exploring the dynamics of well-being and how it changes over time and throughout the life cycle would be helpful. Analysis of longitudinal data which follows the same people over time would be particularly useful in shedding light on what happens to personal well-being as we age and why.

Table 2: Effects of age and sex on well-being ratings after controlling for individual characteristics

Great Britain

Coefficients

	Life satisfaction	Worthwhile	Happy yesterday	Anxious yesterday
Age	-0.066*	-0.016*	-0.039*	0.05*
Age squared	0.001*	0*	0*	-0.001*
Sex				
Reference group: male[1]				
Female	0.1*	0.23*	0.046*	0.254*

Table source: Office for National Statistics

Table notes:

1. The reference group for sex is 'male'.
2. * shows that the relationship is statistically significant at the 5% level.

Download table

XLS XLS format
(30.5 Kb)

3.1.3 Sex

Turning to the relationship between a person's sex and well-being, the results show that holding other factors equal, women rate their levels of 'life satisfaction', 'happiness yesterday' and 'worthwhile' higher on average than men, but the size of the differences between the sexes is small. For example, women rated their life satisfaction 0.1 points higher on average than men and worthwhile 0.2 points higher.

However, women also rated their level of 'anxiety yesterday' 0.3 points higher on average than men. So all things being equal, women view their lives a bit more positively and report more 'happiness yesterday', but they also experience more anxiety.

Some studies that have also found differences in the well-being of men and women suggest that this could be due to women being more socially connected and involved than men. The implication is that women may care more what others think and this may make them more prone to anxiety. However, there are other studies that have found no differences between the sexes after controlling for other factors (Dolan et al., 2008).

The results here (see Table 2) suggest that in comparison to the other characteristics and circumstances included in the analysis, one's sex is not as important to well-being as many other factors.

3.1.4 How do ethnicity and immigration relate to personal well-being?

Ethnicity

The findings here suggest that there is a relationship between ethnicity and personal well-being once other factors are taken into account. However, the size of the relationship is small. **Table 3** summarises the effects of ethnicity on personal well-being ratings.

Findings of note are that, after controlling for individual characteristics, people from the Black/African/Caribbean/Black British ethnic group rated their life satisfaction 0.5 points lower on average than the White group. They also rate their 'happiness yesterday' 0.2 points lower on average than the White group.

People in the Bangladeshi ethnic group also rated both their life satisfaction and a sense that their activities are worthwhile lower than the White group (0.3 points lower and 0.2 lower respectively).

Those in both the Indian and Pakistani ethnic groups rated their levels of anxiety yesterday higher on average than those in the White group (0.2 points higher). Furthermore, Pakistani people also rated the 'worthwhile' question 0.2 points lower on average than White people.

The differences may in part be due to what can be described as 'cultural bias'. This may be because people from different cultures may interpret the question scales differently or be more likely to give more extreme or moderate ratings when asked to make an assessment of their life in this way. However, although the research literature suggests there are some cultural differences in the patterns of observed responses, it is difficult to say to what extent this represents error in the data rather than genuine differences in how people feel, or how they assess their lives (OECD, 2013). This presents a challenging research agenda for the future.

An alternative to the cultural bias theory is that these differences exist because they reflect people's responses to the circumstances that they find themselves in.

How does the personal well-being of migrants to the UK compare to the well-being of people born in Britain?

Some studies suggest that levels of personal well-being may differ between those who migrate to a country and those of people who were born there (Findlay et al., 2010; Gibson et al., 2012). There is also research which suggests that the personal well-being of new migrants to a country may be different to that of immigrants who have lived there for a longer time. For example, the initial experience of disorientation and unhappiness which may be associated with recent migration may gradually disappear as people adapt to life in a new country in terms of language, customs, working and family lives.

In order to explore how the personal well-being of people who have come to the UK as migrants differs to that of people who were born in the UK, the regression analysis included variables indicating whether the respondent was born in the UK or not. If they were born in another country, information about how long ago they came to the UK is also included. The results are shown in Table 3.

After controlling for other factors, people who have migrated to the UK are somewhat happier and more satisfied with their lives than people who were born in the UK, but the size of the differences between them were small (around no more than 0.2 points difference in how they rated 'happy yesterday' and 'life satisfaction'). There were no statistically significant differences between people who were born in the UK and those who migrated from elsewhere in terms of their ratings for 'anxiety yesterday' or a sense that the things they do are 'worthwhile'.

This analysis went a bit further by comparing the well-being of those who were born in the UK to those who migrated to the UK more recently or those who have lived here for a longer time. The results indicate that people who settled in the UK more than 12 years ago rate their 'life satisfaction' 0.1 points higher on average than people who were born in the UK. Those who settled in the UK more recently (since 2009) rate their 'happiness yesterday' 0.2 points higher than those who were born in the UK. Although this may suggest interesting areas for further study, the differences between the well-being ratings for each of these groups are small.

Similarly to ethnicity, there may be cultural differences or linguistic differences in how people from different countries respond to the personal well-being questions, therefore these results should be treated with caution.

Finally, in constructing the models, analysis was also undertaken on an individual's nationality. This was not included in the final model because of the high correlation between the ethnicity and migration status, but the results of the analysis can be found in Reference Table 4 (770 Kb Excel sheet).

Table 3: Effects of ethnicity and migration on personal well-being after controlling for individual characteristics

Great Britain

Coefficients

	Life satisfaction	Worthwhile	Happy yesterday	Anxious yesterday
Reference group: White[1]				
Mixed/multiple ethnic groups	-0.145	0.019	0.039	0.158
Indian	-0.037	-0.057	0.02	0.205*
Pakistani	-0.112	-0.242*	-0.12	0.217*
Bangladeshi	-0.305*	-0.216*	0.001	0.311
Chinese	-0.095	-0.189	0.013	0.094
Any other Asian background	0.036	-0.072	0.066	0.017
Black/African/ Caribbean/Black British	-0.473*	-0.102*	-0.195*	0
Arab	-0.236	-0.118	-0.179	0.34
Other ethnic groups (including gypsy travellers)	-0.131*	-0.157*	-0.074	0.151
Not stated or missing	-0.379	-0.058	-0.194	-0.15
Reference group: not a migrant[1]				
New migrant (since 2009)	0.04	-0.032	0.197*	0.076
Medium term migrant (came between 2000-2009)	0.004	-0.081*	0.167*	0.073
Long term migrant (came before 2000)	0.124*	0.038	0.058	-0.058

Table source: Office for National Statistics

Table notes:

1. The reference group for ethnicity is 'White' and the reference group for migration status is 'not a migrant'.
2. * shows that the relationship is statistically significant at the 5% level.

Download table

XLS XLS format
(32.5 Kb)

3.1.5 How does religious affiliation relate to personal well-being?

The Annual Population Survey does not ask about people's political, philosophical, religious or other beliefs, but it does ask about their religious affiliation[1]. This is just a simple indication of whether someone identifies themselves with a religion or not and can only be considered a first look at the well-being of those who say that they have a religion compared to those who do not. Other studies that have looked at the relationship between religion and well-being have explored degree of religious conviction, attendance at religious services, and social connections made through participation in religious activities. This would be an interesting area for further research, but the Annual Population Survey does not have any information on these topics.

The findings which are summarised in **Table 4** show that, other things being equal, respondents who said that they have a religious affiliation rate their levels of 'happiness yesterday', 'life satisfaction' and 'worthwhile' higher on average than people who said they do not have a religious affiliation. Specifically, those with a religious affiliation, rate their life satisfaction 0.1 points higher, 'worthwhile' 0.2 points higher and 'happiness yesterday' 0.2 points higher on average than those who do not have a religious affiliation. All of these differences would be considered small.

There is also a very small, but statistically significant difference between the two groups in ratings for 'anxiety yesterday'. Those with a religious affiliation give higher ratings for their anxiety levels.

Several studies have demonstrated that religious faith and spirituality can contribute to a person's mental and physical well-being. Some of these have found a positive relationship between higher levels of well-being and religious beliefs or activities and concluded that this could be due to several factors including religion helping people to cope with troubling life circumstances such as sickness or death of a loved one. However, other studies have found that religious faith can impact negatively on a person's well-being. For example, personal relationships may suffer if those we care about do not share the same religious convictions (James & Wells 2003).

Table 4: Effects of religious affiliation on personal well-being after controlling for individual characteristics

Great Britain

Coefficients

	Life satisfaction	Worthwhile	Happy yesterday	Anxious yesterday
Reference group: No religious affiliation[1]				
Any religion reported	0.132*	0.206*	0.169*	0.067*
Not stated or missing	-0.091	0.031	0.052	0.109

Table source: Office for National Statistics

Table notes:

1. The reference group for religious affiliation is 'no religious affiliation'.
2. * shows that the relationship is statistically significant at the 5% level.

Download table

XLS XLS format
(20.5 Kb)

3.2 How important are health and disability to well-being?

The National Debate (Office for National Statistics 2011) highlighted the importance of health among the things that really matter to personal well-being and this has been confirmed by numerous studies. Previous ONS publications have also highlighted a very clear positive relationship between self-reported health and 'life satisfaction', a sense that our activities are 'worthwhile' and 'happy yesterday', and a negative relationship between health and 'anxious yesterday'. These findings are from bi-variate analysis looking only at the relationship between self-reported health and personal well-being. The regression analysis enables us to go further and to look at the size and strength of the relationship between self-reported health and personal well-being when other factors are held equal.

3.2.1 Key points

Holding other factors equal:

- The size of the relationship between self-reported health and personal well-being is larger than any other variable included in the regression model.
- 'Life satisfaction' scores for people who say they have very bad health are much lower on average than for people who say they have good or very good health.

- There is also a large and positive relationship between people's assessments of their health and their ratings of 'happiness yesterday' and 'worthwhile'. People who say their health is bad report higher levels of 'anxiety yesterday' on average than people who say their health is good.
- People who reported a disability gave lower ratings on average for life satisfaction and 'happiness yesterday' and higher ratings for 'anxiety yesterday' than people who did not report a disability.
- The size of the relationship between self-reported disability and personal well-being is small.

3.2.2 The challenge of measuring the relationship between health and personal well-being

An important question in the regression analysis was which variable representing health should be included in the model in order to best capture the relationship between health and personal well-being. The following were two of the key considerations taken into account in developing the model:

- Health and disability are both likely to be related to personal well-being, but they are closely related to each other and this makes it is difficult to be sure that the effects of each are captured while holding the other equal.
- The data from the Annual Population Survey include information about health and disability based on people's own assessments. This means that we are using people's **views** about their health and whether they have a disability rather than relying on more objective information from a source such as medical records. It may be that our views about our health and disability are related to our sense of well-being in different ways than objective measures of health and disability would be.

In order to explore these issues, several different ways of approaching the analysis were tried before opting for the version reported here in the main model. The results from each of these models can be found in Reference Table 4 (770 Kb Excel sheet) and more detailed discussion of the factors taken into account in deciding which variables to use to measure health and disability are discussed further in section 5.3.3.

Table 5: Effects of self-reported health and self-reported disability on personal well-being after controlling for individual characteristics

Great Britain

Coefficients

	Life satisfaction	Worthwhile	Happy yesterday	Anxious yesterday
Reference group: not disabled[1]				
Disabled - both DDA and work-limiting	-0.112*	-0.007	-0.06*	0.183*
Not stated or missing	0.016	0.058	-0.005	-0.008
Reference group: good health[1]				
very good	0.422*	0.364*	0.458*	-0.481*
fair	-0.531*	-0.419*	-0.544*	0.631*
bad	-1.463*	-1.162*	-1.466*	1.333*
very bad	-2.428*	-1.958*	-2.561*	2.107*
Not stated or missing	-0.667*	-0.492*	-0.577*	0.668*

Table source: Office for National Statistics

Table notes:

1. The reference group for self-reported disability is 'not disabled' and the reference group for self-reported health is 'good health'.
2. * shows that the relationship is statistically significant at the 5% level.

Download table

XLS XLS format
(22 Kb)

3.2.3 The bigger picture on the relationship between self-reported health, self-reported disability and personal well-being

The key finding from this analysis is that self-reported health has a large and significant relationship with personal well-being. Self-reported disability has a significant but much smaller relationship with well-being when other variables are held equal including self-reported health.

The main model includes both self-reported disability and self-reported health, and the correlation between the two is high but not perfect. For example, people who report that they have a disability are also more likely to report that they are in fair, bad or very bad health than people who do not report a disability. However, a third of those who said they have a disability also said their health is good or very good. This suggests that there is quite a lot of overlap between the variables, but they are not measuring exactly the same thing.

How much difference does self-reported health make to ratings of personal well-being?

Other things being equal, 'life satisfaction' scores for people who said they were in very bad health were 2.4 points lower on average than for people who said they were in good health and almost 3 points lower than for people who said they were in very good health.

There is also a strong association between health, 'happy yesterday' and feeling that one's activities are 'worthwhile'. For example, on average, people who reported very bad health rated their 'happiness yesterday' 2.6 points lower on average than people who reported good health and 3 points lower on average than people who reported very good health.

As might be expected, bad health is related to increased anxiety. Holding all else equal, the 'anxious yesterday' ratings for people who said they have very bad health were on average around 2 points higher than people who said they have good health and 2.5 points higher than people who reported very good health. **Figure 1** illustrates the relationship between how people rate their health and how they rate each aspect of their personal well-being, after holding other variables equal.

Figure 1: How self-assessed health relates to personal well-being after controlling for personal characterisitics

Great Britain

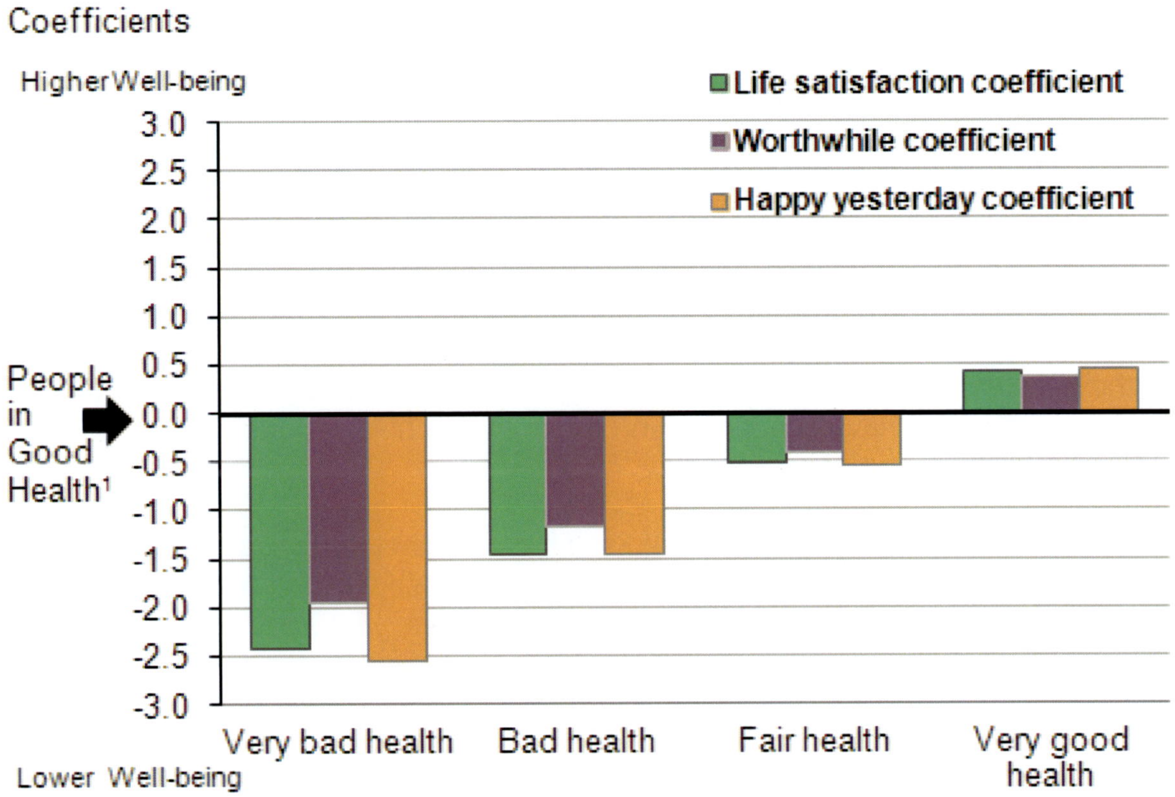

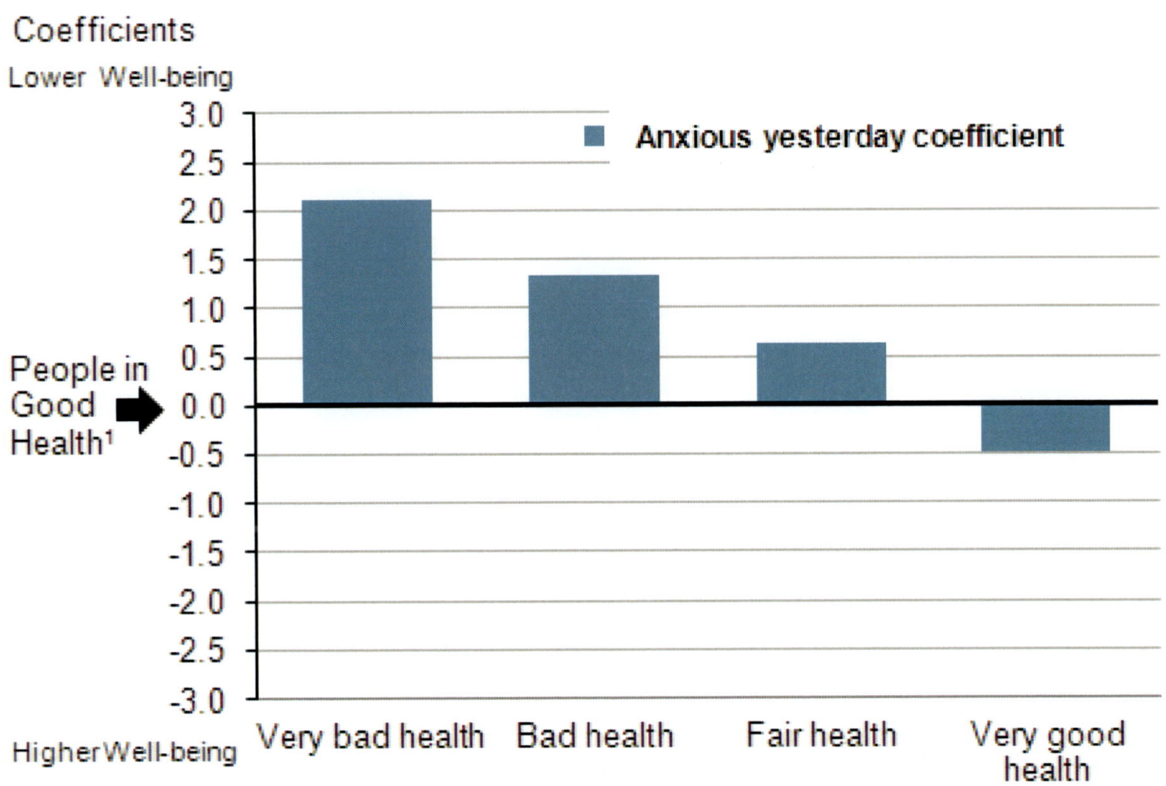

Source: Annual Population Survey (APS) - Office for National Statistics

Notes:

1. Reference group at 0 is a baseline of people who rated their health as good.

Download chart

XLS XLS format
(30.5 Kb)

How much difference does self-reported disability make to ratings of personal well-being?

People who said that they have a disability according to the definition of the Disability Discrimination Act (DDA) or those who said that they have a work-limiting disability are both included in this analysis of self-reported disability.

Holding other factors equal, those who said they have a disability rated their life satisfaction 0.1 points lower and their happiness yesterday 0.1 points lower than those who did not report a disability. People who reported a disability also rated their level of anxiety yesterday 0.2 points higher than those without a disability.

Based on these findings, the size of the relationship between self-reported disability and personal well-being is small.

3.2.4 Final thoughts on the relationship between self-reported health and personal well-being

Research consistently shows that both physical health and psychological health are strongly associated with well-being and that psychological health is highly correlated with personal well-being.

As Dolan et.al (2008) notes, some of the association may be caused by the impact that well-being has on health. That is, people who are in good physical and mental health may be happier, but happy people may be less likely to fall ill than unhappy people.

A significant relationship between personal well-being and health may also be due to personality differences and without controlling for these the size of the relationship between health and personal well-being may be not captured accurately.

Finally, in the absence of an ‘objective’ health variable, using a person’s own assessment of health to control the relationship between health and personal well-being in the regression may exaggerate the apparent relationship between health and well-being. For this reason, we have been careful to refer to the relationship between self-reported health and personal well-being as we have not used an objective measure of health.

However, other research has also shown that subjective evaluations of health status matter more than objective measures in terms of the relationship with personal well-being (Brown et. al., 2010; Diener et al., 1999).

3.3 How does educational attainment relate to personal well-being?

3.3.1 Key Points

Holding other factors equal:

- Those with qualifications below A level give lower ratings on average for 'worthwhile' than people with A level qualifications and above.
- People with the highest educational attainment have higher ratings of 'anxiety yesterday' on average than people with lower educational attainment. They also have lower life satisfaction ratings than those with lower educational attainment.
- There were no statistically significant differences between the average life satisfaction ratings of people with no qualifications and those with A levels.
- Overall, the findings here show that size of the relationship between educational attainment and personal well-being is either small or very small.

The analysis here suggests that the level of education we reach is related to personal well-being, but the size of the relationship is small or very small. The findings are shown in **Table 6**.

Statistically significant findings did emerge when comparing those with A level qualifications to those with lower level or no qualifications. For example, those with no qualifications rate 'worthwhile' 0.1 points lower on average than those with A level or equivalent qualifications. There were no statistically significant differences in 'worthwhile' between those with A level qualifications and those with higher level qualifications.

Additionally, those with the highest qualifications rated 'anxious yesterday' 0.1 points higher on average than those with A levels and higher than all those with lower educational attainment.

There were no statistically significant differences found between the life satisfaction ratings of those with no qualifications and those with A level qualifications.

Finally, as a word of caution, it should be noted that approximately 18% of the respondents in the Annual Population Survey have a missing value regarding their highest qualification. Most of those were among those aged 60 years and over and this is probably due to the fact that the question on highest qualification is only asked of those of working age (up to the age of 69). Beyond this age, it is only asked of those who are still in work and who have qualifications. This suggests that there may be other datasets that could provide a more comprehensive picture of the relationship between educational attainment and personal well-being.

Other studies have found a positive correlation between educational attainment and personal well-being which disappears after controlling for other factors such as income and health (Dolan et al., 2008; Brown et al., (2010). This suggests that education may not be related to personal well-being directly, but only indirectly via its relationships with other factors like income and health.

Table 6: Effects of educational attainment on ratings of personal well-being after controlling for individual characteristics

Great Britain

Coefficients

	Life satisfaction	Worthwhile	Happy yesterday	Anxious yesterday
Reference group: GCE A-level or equivalent[1]				
Degree or equivalent and higher	-0.04*	0.013	-0.025	0.116*
Higher education	-0.073*	-0.018	-0.023	0.023
GCSE grades A*-C or equivalent	-0.058*	-0.056*	-0.005	-0.059
Other qualifications	-0.024	-0.074*	0.011	-0.035
No qualification	-0.006	-0.124*	-0.02	0.055
Not stated or missing	-0.28*	-0.19*	-0.184*	0.21*

Table source: Office for National Statistics

Table notes:

1. The reference group for educational attainment is 'GCE A-level or equivalent'.
2. * shows that the relationship is statistically significant at the 5% level.

Download table

XLS XLS format
(21 Kb)

3.4 How are relationship status and children in the household related to personal well-being?

This section focuses on how our closest relationships, those with spouses, partners and children, relate to personal well-being. There are many other relationships that it would also be helpful to explore, such as those with friends, colleagues and neighbours, but this analysis uses the data available in the APS to take a basic look at how relationship status and children in the household relate to personal well-being.

3.4.1 Key Points

Holding other factors equal:

- People who are married or in a civil partnership gave higher ratings for 'life satisfaction', feelings that the things they do in their lives are 'worthwhile', and 'happiness yesterday' than those in the other relationship categories.
- People who are widowed, divorced, or separated gave lower ratings for 'life satisfaction', feelings that the things they do in their lives are 'worthwhile', and 'happiness yesterday' than other groups.
- People who are married or in civil partnerships rate their level of 'anxiety yesterday' lower than other groups.
- People who live with dependent children on average give higher ratings when asked if they feel that the things they do in life are 'worthwhile', compared to people who do not live with children.
- Those living in households with two or more people (including children) rate their 'life satisfaction' more highly than those living alone.
- Overall, the size of the association between relationship status and personal well-being could be described as moderate while the relationship between children in the household and personal well-being is small or very small.

3.4.2 Delving deeply into our relationships

The analysis looked at current relationship status and considered whether being married, cohabiting, divorced, separated, single or widowed is related to personal well-being when other factors are held equal.

The results of the analysis are shown in **Table 7**. Holding other factors equal, those who are single, widowed, divorced or separated all have lower average ratings for 'life satisfaction', 'worthwhile' and 'happy yesterday' than people who are married or in a civil partnership.

Looking at the scale of the differences in personal well-being associated with these different relationship situations, other things being equal, single people rate their 'life satisfaction' 0.5 points lower on average than married people or those in a civil partnership. The 'life satisfaction' scores of people who are widowed and living alone is on average 0.7 points lower than that of married people or those in a civil partnership. People who are divorced or separated and living alone similarly rate their 'life satisfaction' 0.6 points lower on average than married people or those in civil partnerships. The size of the association between relationship status and personal well-being would be considered moderate. These findings are shown graphically in **Figure 2**.

Although people who are cohabiting also give lower ratings on average than married people/civil partners for 'life satisfaction', 'worthwhile' and 'happy yesterday', the scale of the difference between their ratings and those of people in a marriage/civil partnership is much smaller than the difference between married people/civil partners and those in all the other relationship status categories.

In terms of anxiety, all the relationship groups considered here report higher 'anxiety yesterday' than married people and those in civil partnerships, but size effects were small (on average, around 0.1 to 0.2 points). These findings are illustrated in Figure 2.

These results are consistent with findings from other studies and confirm that relationships are a key ingredient of personal well-being (Dolan et al., 2008). However, it is important to note that factors that are not measured here may also contribute to a person's relationship status. For example, if people who tend to be happier are also more likely to get married or to enter into a civil partnership, then the differences in personal well-being observed between those who are married or in civil partnership and those who are not may actually be a reflection of underlying personality differences rather than relationship status per se.

Although this cannot be explored fully using the data available in the Annual Population Survey, the significance and the size effects as well as evidence from other studies all suggest that our relationships are very important to personal well-being.

Figure 2: How relationship status affects personal well-being after controlling for individual characterisitcs

Great Britain

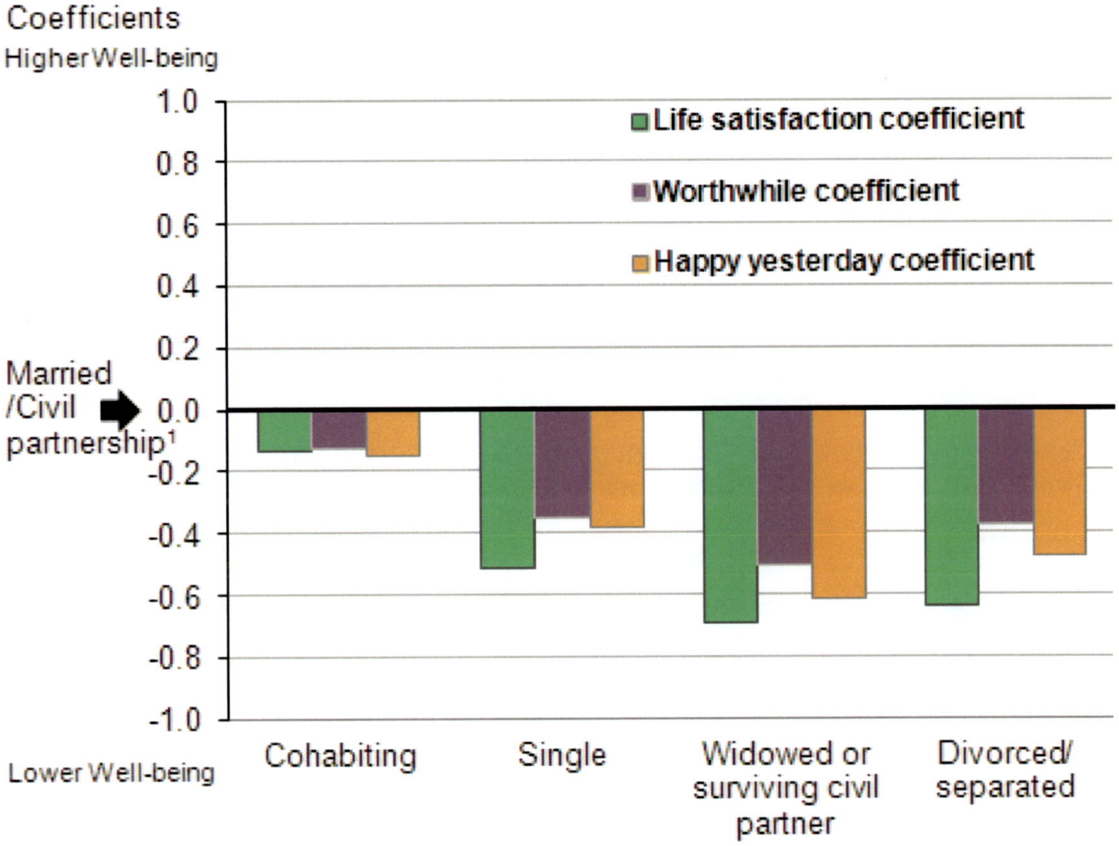

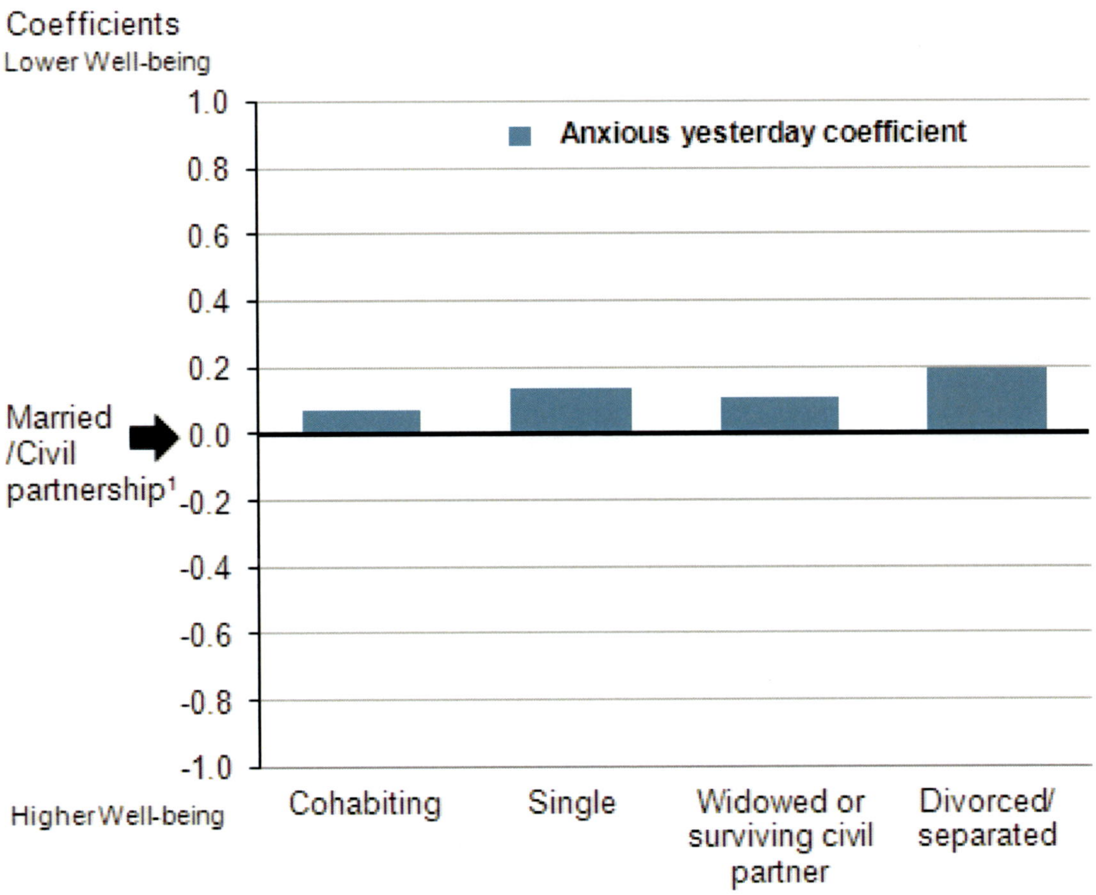

Source: Annual Population Survey (APS) - Office for National Statistics

Notes:

1. Reference group at 0 is a baseline of people who are married or within a civil partnership.

Download chart

XLS XLS format
(30.5 Kb)

3.4.3 How's life with children?

The results are shown in Table 7 and they indicate that living with children has a small association with personal well-being which is focused primarily on the sense that our activities are worthwhile.

The analysis here makes a distinction between dependent children (defined as aged 0 to 15 or aged 16 to 18 and in full-time education) and non-dependent children (aged 16 to 18 and not in full-time education or over the age of 18).

Holding other factors equal, people who live with dependent children rate 'worthwhile' 0.2 points higher on average than those who do not live with children. This suggests that living with and looking after children is linked to an enhanced perception that what we are doing in life is 'worthwhile'. Indeed, there is evidence from other studies that the presence of young children in the household may increase parents' well-being levels, but this may reflect a temporary boost to well-being when a new child arrives which subsides with time (Dolan et al., 2008).

Holding all else equal, there was no statistically significant difference between people living in households with or without children in terms of their ratings of 'happy yesterday' or 'anxious yesterday' and there was only a very small association with 'life satisfaction'.

Table 7: Effects of relationship status and presence of children in the household on ratings of personal well-being after controlling for individual characteristics

Great Britain

Coefficients

	Life satisfaction	Worthwhile	Happy yesterday	Anxious yesterday
Reference group: married or with civil partner[1]				
Cohabiting(include all people cohabiting, different or same sex couples, whether they are separated, widowed or "single")	-0.136*	-0.13*	-0.147*	0.072*
Single, never married (and not cohabiting)	-0.518*	-0.349*	-0.386*	0.137*
Widowed or surviving civil partner(living alone, not cohabiting)	-0.691*	-0.506*	-0.613*	0.104*
Divorced/ separated, former civil partner legally dissolved, separated civil partner (living	-0.637*	-0.377*	-0.472*	0.192*

alone, not cohabiting)				
Reference group: no children in the household[1]				
Dependent children only	0.016	0.179*	0.025	-0.001
Non-dependent children only	-0.053*	-0.007	-0.034	-0.02
Both dependent and non-dependent children	0.052	0.132*	0.073	-0.088

Table source: Office for National Statistics

Table notes:

1. The reference group for relationship status is 'married or with civil partner' and the reference group for presence of children in the household is 'no children in the household'.
2. * shows that the relationship is statistically significant at the 5% level.

Download table

XLS XLS format
(23.5 Kb)

3.4.4 How does who we live with affect personal well-being?

Another way to explore whether our household circumstances affect our personal well-being is to compare the well-being of people living in different situations. In addition to looking at relationship status and presence of children in the household separately, as reported above, further analysis was done using information about people living in different types of households. This is a variation on the main regression model, the details of which can be found in Reference Table 4. (770 Kb Excel sheet)

On the whole, this analysis shows that living alone is negatively related to our personal well-being, regardless of relationship status. For example, all the household types where two or more people live together give higher ratings than those living alone when asked if they feel the things they do in life are 'worthwhile'.

Similarly, people living in households with two or more people also rate their 'life satisfaction' more highly than those living alone.

Looking only at households where two or more people live together, married people (particularly those not living with children) and same sex couples give the highest ratings for well-being (except in the case of 'anxious yesterday').

Taken together, these results suggest that living as part of a married couple or in a civil partnership is associated with higher levels of well-being and living alone is associated with lower well-being. Living with children in the household appears to affect personal well-being only marginally.

3.5 How does employment status relate to personal well-being?

This section looks at how employment status relates to our personal well-being. The analysis also considers how satisfied people are with their employment situation as this may contribute to personal well-being.

3.5.1 Key Points

Holding other factors equal:

- People who are unemployed have significantly lower levels of 'life satisfaction', 'happy yesterday', and feelings that their activities are 'worthwhile' than those who are employed and most groups of economically inactive people. Unemployed people also have higher 'anxious yesterday' levels compared with people in other work situations.
- People who are employed but want a different or additional job have lower levels of personal well-being (including higher 'anxious yesterday' levels) on average than employed people who are not looking for another job.
- Retired people who said that they do not want to work and those who said they do not need to work have on average higher levels of well-being than people who are working and satisfied with their jobs.
- People who are economically inactive due to ill health or disability have particularly low ratings for personal well-being.
- People in higher managerial or professional occupations rate their life satisfaction higher on average than those in other occupational groups. They also give slightly higher ratings when asked if they think the things they do are 'worthwhile'. However, on average the difference in their ratings on these aspects of their well-being compared to those in other occupational groups was small or very small.
- People in higher managerial and professional occupations give higher scores for 'anxious yesterday' levels on average than those in lower supervisory and technical occupations.
- Among a sub-sample of employees only, those who earn higher wages from their job give higher ratings for 'life satisfaction' on average than those earning less, but ratings for 'worthwhile' and 'happy yesterday' and 'anxiety yesterday' were not related to earnings.

3.5.2 How do employment, unemployment and economic inactivity relate to personal well-being?

Work is an important aspect of our lives which can provide the obvious tangible benefits of income and a pension, as well as more psychological benefits such as a sense of purpose, social status, social interaction and giving structure to one's day. Employment status is generally split into employment, unemployment and economic inactivity and this section compares the well-being of people in these categories. After controlling for all the other factors included in the analysis, people who are unemployed have significantly lower levels of 'life satisfaction', 'happy yesterday', and feelings that their activities are 'worthwhile' than those who are employed or economically inactive.

The findings here are clear and consistent with those reported elsewhere (Dolan et al., 2008; Clark 2003; Blanchflower & Oswald 1999); unemployment has a strong and negative association with well-being.

There is also an interesting finding about differences in personal well-being related to duration of unemployment. As the duration of unemployment increases, the average ratings for personal well-being decline. The lowest ratings for personal well-being are among those who have been unemployed for between two and four years. Their life satisfaction scores are 1.2 points lower on average than those of people in a permanent job with which they are content. Those who have been unemployed for four years or more have life satisfaction scores that are 1.0 point lower on average than those of people in a permanent job with which they're content. These findings are illustrated in **Figure 3**.

These findings could suggest that people adapt somewhat to their situation as time goes on, but even among those who have been unemployed for four years or more, well-being ratings are still significantly below those of employed people. Longitudinal analysis following the same people over time would be required to examine the possibility of adaption more fully.

Figure 3: How length of unemployment relates to personal well-being after controlling for personal characteristics

Great Britain

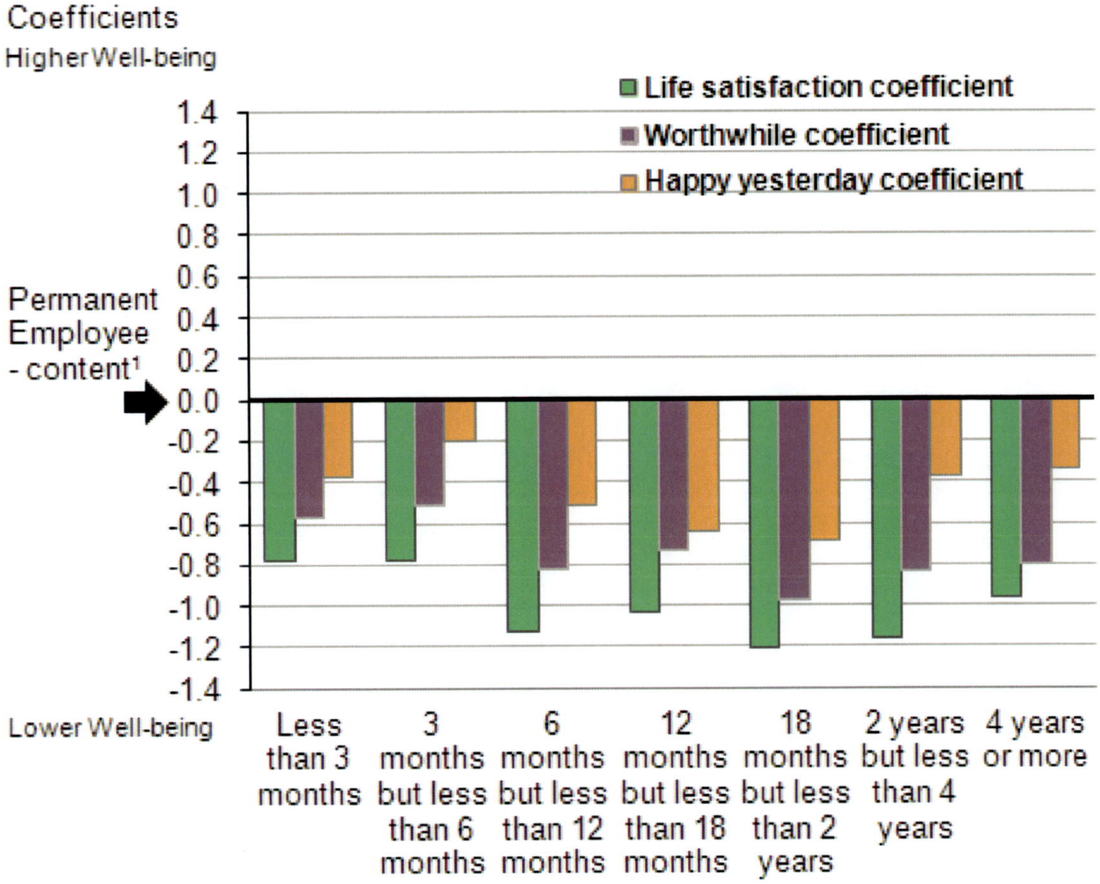

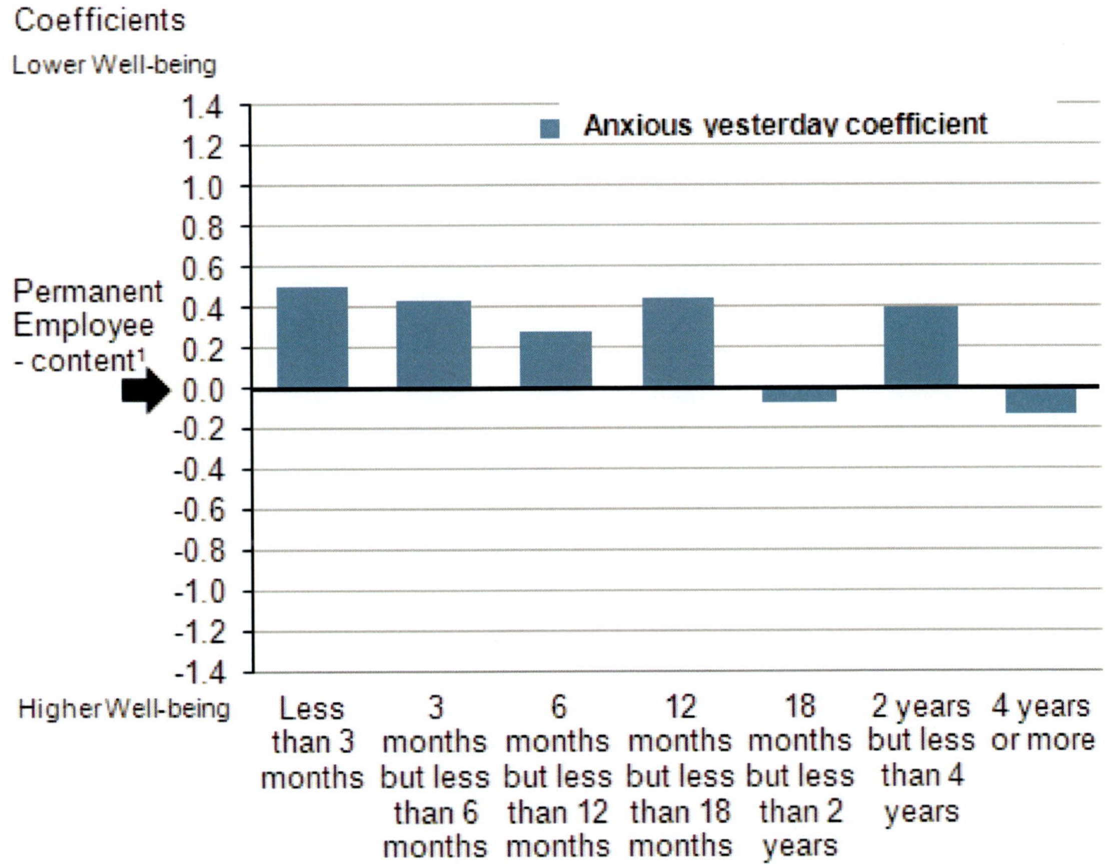

Source: Annual Population Survey (APS) - Office for National Statistics

Notes:

1. Reference group at 0 is a baseline of people who are in permanent employment and don't want different or additional job - content in the job they have.

Download chart

XLS XLS format
(31 Kb)

3.5.3 Is it just about work or about contentment with what we are doing?

While the evidence is clear that employment is better for personal well-being than unemployment, on closer inspection it seems that people who want a different or additional job have lower levels of well-being (including more anxiety) than those who don't. This is regardless of the nature of their current work situation (e.g., full-time or part-time, permanent or non-permanent, employed or self-employed). These findings are illustrated in **Figure 4**.

When people say that they would like a different or additional job they are saying that their current situation is some way off their ideal. This 'satisfaction gap' is likely to affect personal well-being in ways which cannot be captured simply by comparing the specific circumstances of their work.

Furthermore, it is reasonable to suggest that people who express dissatisfaction with some aspect of their working lives are more likely to have experienced negative effects arising from that situation than are others in the same situation who have not said that they are dissatisfied. These negative experiences may also impact on people's sense of personal well-being.

Figure 4: How contentment with employment relates to personal well-being after controlling for individual characteristics

Great Britain

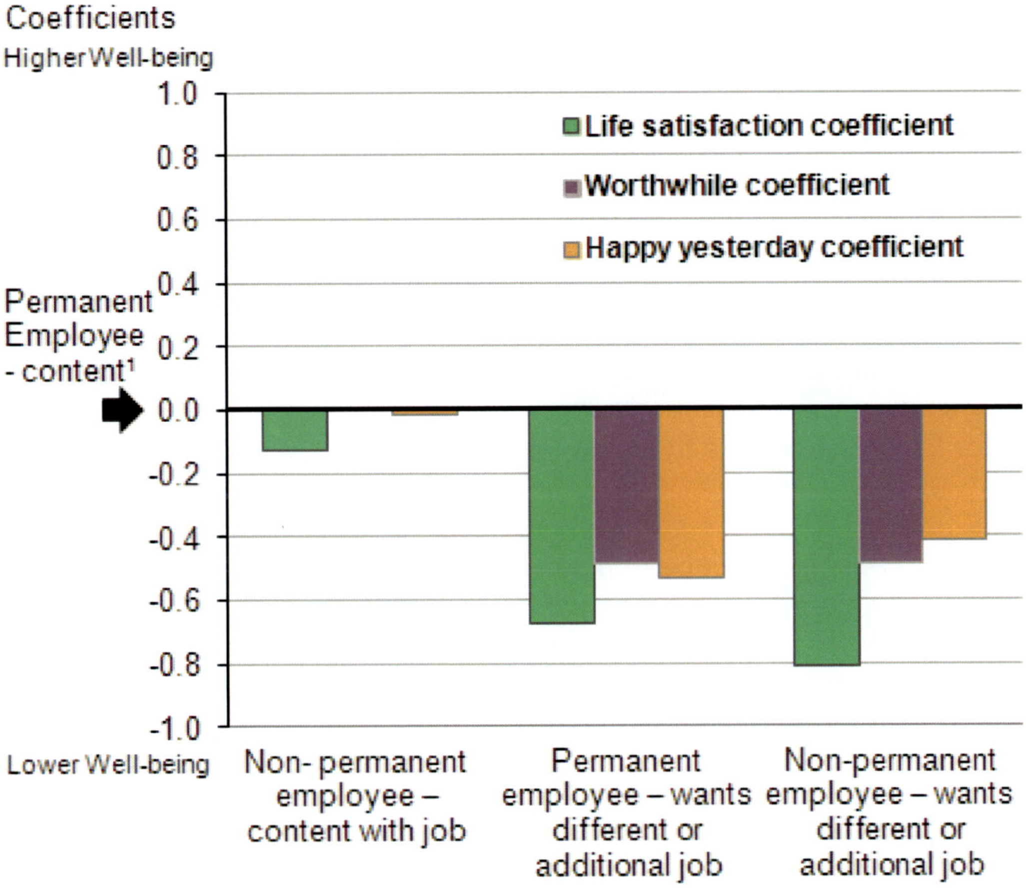

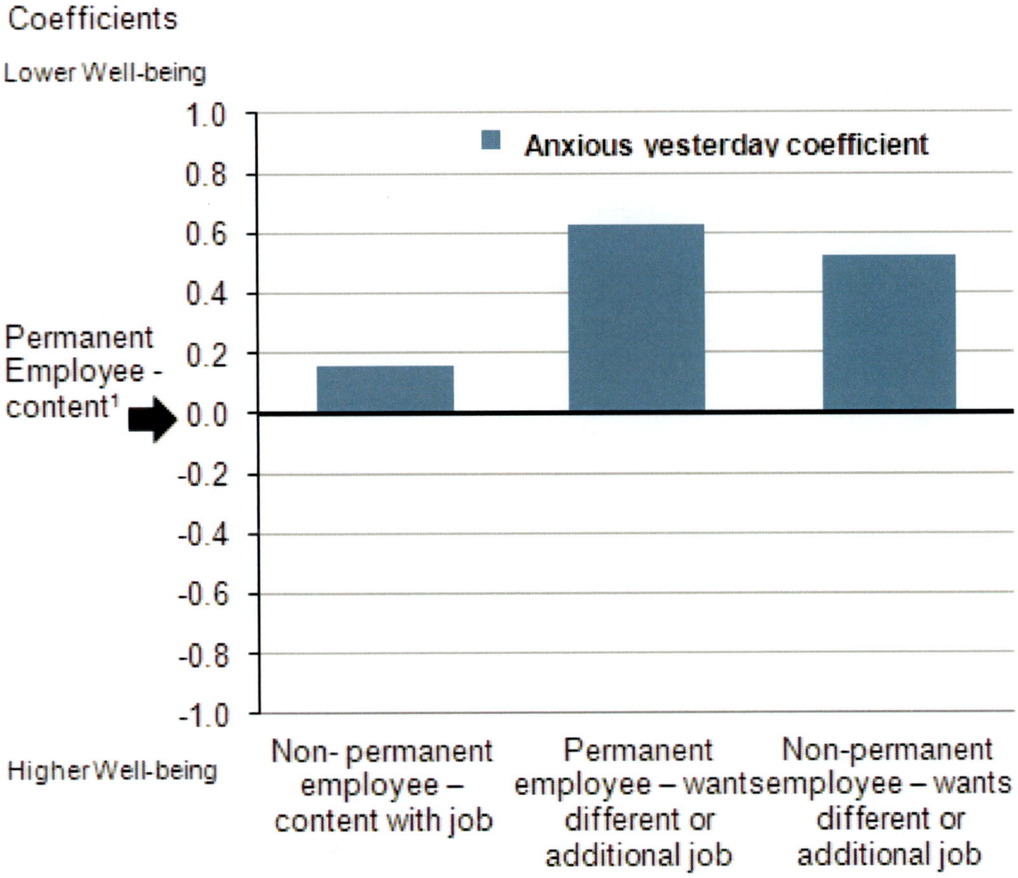

Source: Annual Population Survey (APS) - Office for National Statistics

Notes:

1. Reference group at 0 is a baseline of people who are in permanent employment and don't want different or additional job - content in the job they have.

Download chart

XLS XLS format
(30.5 Kb)

These findings are consistent with several studies which have found that there is a strong positive association between job satisfaction and 'life satisfaction' and a negative association between under-employment or over-employment and well-being (Tam 2010; Blanchflower & Oswald 1999).

3.5.4 How does well-being differ between people in employment and those who are economically inactive?

There are a number of reasons why people may not be in paid work apart from unemployment. These include retirement, being in full-time education, being ill or disabled and unable to work, looking after a home or family, being a carer of another adult, or simply not needing to work. People in all of these situations are referred to as 'economically inactive' which means that they are not participating in the labour market, but their reasons for not doing so are quite diverse as are their circumstances.

Retired people and those who are economically inactive because they do not need to work stand out as quite different to other groups of economically inactive people. Their well-being is higher than all the other economic activity groups including those who are working and content with their jobs.

Holding other factors equal, those who are working and content with their situation generally have higher well-being than people who are working but are not content with their job. They also have higher well-being than all groups of economically inactive people apart from those who are retired and not wanting to work and those who said they don't need to work.

The importance that a sense of choice over and satisfaction with our activities has to personal well-being extends beyond contentment with a job. People looking after family or home who would like to work but were prevented by their circumstances from seeking work reported lower average levels of life satisfaction and 'happy yesterday' than similar people who were content with their situation.

3.5.5 How is personal well-being affected by inactivity in the labour market due to ill health or disability?

There were particularly low average ratings for all four well-being measures in the group who were sick or disabled. There was also a larger impact on well-being ratings among those who say they are temporarily unable to work due to ill health or disability than among those who say they have been unable to work in the longer term for these reasons. This may suggest that people adapt somewhat to ill health or disability as time goes on. As they adjust to new circumstances, their well-being may return to their more usual level. In order to establish clearly that people do adjust over time in this way, research that follows the same people over time would be required rather than the type of data available here which provides a snapshot of a people's lives.

The findings here suggest that it is when disability or ill health is felt to limit one's activities that it affects well-being most. As work is a place where many of us have social relationships as well, an inability to work may also increase a sense of social isolation and this too could affect personal well-being.

3.5.6 How important is occupational status to personal well-being?

Occupational status may affect personal well-being for many reasons such as the link between occupation and financial circumstances, health problems that may affect people in some occupational groups more than others, and people's perceptions about their relative standing in society as reflected by their occupation. This analysis is able to hold some of those factors equal while just comparing differences in well-being associated with occupational status.

The findings are shown in **Table 8**. Other things being equal, people in higher managerial or professional occupations rate their 'life satisfaction' and 'worthwhile' higher on average than those in other occupational groups. However, on average the difference in their ratings on these aspects of their well-being compared to those in other occupational groups was small - other groups gave ratings around 0.1 to 0.2 points lower for 'life satisfaction' and just under 0.1 lower for their ratings of whether their activities are 'worthwhile'.

In relation to 'anxious yesterday', those in higher managerial and professional occupations gave slightly higher scores on average than those in lower supervisory and technical occupations and those in semi-routine occupations. It is not possible to say from the data available here whether this is because the work done by those at more senior levels involves more responsibility and stress or whether those who are more anxious (and push themselves harder) are more likely to reach this occupational level. In terms of ratings for 'happiness yesterday', after controlling for other factors, there were no statistically significant differences found between the different occupational groups.

Table 8: Differences in well-being ratings by occupational group after controlling for individual characteristics

Great Britain

Coefficients

	Life satisfaction	Worthwhile	Happy yesterday	Anxious yesterday
Reference group: higher managerial and professional[1]				
Lower managerial or professional	-0.056*	0.026	0.002	-0.031
Intermediate occupations	-0.139*	-0.086*	-0.043	-0.071
Small employers and own account workers	-0.11*	-0.082*	-0.001	-0.08
Lower supervisory and technical	-0.087*	-0.021	0.031	-0.206*
Semi-routine occupations	-0.155*	-0.082*	-0.036	-0.091*
Routine occupations	-0.149*	-0.102*	-0.039	-0.042
Never worked, unemployed, and not elsewhere classified	0.013	0.028	-0.001	0.059

Table source: Office for National Statistics

Table notes:

1. The reference group for occupational group is 'higher managerial and professional'.
2. * shows that the relationship is statistically significant at the 5% level.

Download table

XLS XLS format
(22 Kb)

3.5.7 How important are earnings to the personal well-being of employees?

The Annual Population Survey does not include information on household income which would enable comparisons of the personal well-being of those in more or less favourable financial positions. However, it does contain information on earnings for people who are employees. This will not give a clear picture of how well people are doing financially overall, but it does help to show how the financial element of our working lives relates to personal well-being.

The information on earnings is only available for those who are employees in paid jobs, so this analysis does not include those who are self-employed. Please see Reference Table 3 (593 Kb Excel sheet) for the full results of this analysis.

The findings show that, other things being equal, higher wages are associated with higher levels of 'life satisfaction', but not with higher levels of 'happiness yesterday' or feeling that what we do is 'worthwhile'. The level of personal earnings also does not affect 'anxious yesterday' levels.

It may seem surprising that how much we earn does not affect our level of 'anxious yesterday', but this may be because financial worries come into play only in the context of the overall financial situation of the household. If we have low wages but access to financial resources from elsewhere, then personal wage levels may not be directly related to our sense of financial security and to our level of anxiety.

In order to explore this, further analysis was carried out on the relationship between total household earnings and personal well-being. For this analysis, a new variable was created to represent 'household earnings'[2]. The findings showed a similar picture to that for individual earnings: household earnings have a positive relationship with 'life satisfaction' but not with other measures of personal well-being. Other studies have found a well established positive correlation between life satisfaction measures and income in individual cross-sectional data (Kahneman 2010; Pishke 2011). These studies suggest that changeable, day-to-day moods (such as happiness and anxiety yesterday) are different from the deeper satisfaction you feel about the way your life is going. Higher earnings are not related to our mood, but they are associated with assessments of whether life is going well overall.

3.6 How do the circumstances of where we live affect our personal well-being?

This analysis looks at four broad aspects of where we live to see how they may be related to personal well-being. These are: housing tenure, the level of deprivation in the local area compared to other areas, the region where we live and whether it is urban or rural. As noted earlier, the APS does not include data on local area deprivation so this was added to the dataset specifically for this analysis. There are many other possible ways to look at the relationship between where we live and personal well-being, such as the sense of belonging in the community, access to green spaces, local noise and air pollution, etc. ONS intends to look in more detail at the relationship between the local area and personal well-being in future analysis.

3.6.1 Key Points

Holding other factors equal:

- People who rent and those with mortgages give lower ratings for their personal well-being on average than those who own their homes outright, but this analysis does not distinguish between private and social renters.

The region of Great Britain that people live in was found to have a small effect on people's personal well-being;

- People living in London gave similar ratings of their 'life satisfaction' as people living in other urban areas in Great Britain. The exceptions to this were among those living in urban areas in North East England and Scotland where people rated their 'life satisfaction' more highly on average than those living in London. Those living in urban areas of the West Midlands also had lower life satisfaction ratings than those in London.
- People living in the rural areas of almost all regions gave higher 'life satisfaction' ratings on average than people living in London, but the size effects were small.
- There were no statistically significant differences in ratings for 'happy yesterday' between those living in London and elsewhere, except among those in rural areas of the North West, Yorkshire and Humberside, South East, South West, Scotland and Wales. In each of these areas, people rated their 'happiness yesterday' marginally higher than people in London.
- When asked if they feel what they do in life is 'worthwhile', people living in London rated this lower on average than those living in most of the other regions. The exception to this is in the West Midlands where people rated this similarly to those in London.
- People in London also rated their 'anxiety yesterday' levels as higher than people living in the rest of the Great Britain.
- People living in the least deprived local areas reported slightly higher levels of 'anxiety yesterday' than people living in more deprived local areas.

3.6.2 Is our well-being affected by whether we rent, have a mortgage or own our home?

The findings for the analysis are shown in **Table 9**. The results show a small but statistically significant relationship between personal well-being and 'housing tenure' which is a term used to classify whether we rent, have a mortgage or own our home outright. The findings show that holding all else equal, people who rent and those with mortgages give lower ratings for personal well-being on average than those who own their homes outright. For example, people who rent and those with mortgages rated their 'life satisfaction' on average 0.2 points lower than people who own their homes outright. They also rated their 'anxiety yesterday' levels 0.1 points higher on average than those who own their homes outright.

The impact of housing tenure on personal well-being could be due to lower disposable income available to people who rent their home or are paying a mortgage and possibly a lower sense of financial security associated with this. It may also be related to perceived differences in social status in the UK among those rent or own their homes. These are issues which can be explored in more detail in future using data for example from the Wealth and Assets Survey or the Survey of English Housing. In future, it would be perhaps also be helpful to explore this further by distinguishing between those who rent from private or social landlords as their experiences may be quite different.

Table 9: Effects of housing tenure on ratings of personal well-being after controlling for individual characteristics

Great Britain

Coefficients

	Life satisfaction	Worthwhile	Happy yesterday	Anxious yesterday
Reference group: owned outright[1]				
Being bought with mortgage or loan	-0.17*	-0.162*	-0.136*	0.101*
Part rent, part mortgage	-0.113	-0.087	0.009	-0.066
Rented	-0.203*	-0.147*	-0.188*	0.129*
Rent free or squatting	-0.037	-0.023	0.017	0.075
Not stated or missing	-0.294	-0.211	-0.463	-0.337

Table source: Office for National Statistics

Table notes:

1. The reference group for housing tenure is 'owned outright'.
2. * shows that the relationship is statistically significant at the 5% level.

Download table

XLS XLS format
(21.5 Kb)

3.6.3 Does the place where we live affect our personal well-being?

As noted, there are many aspects of the place where we live which may potentially affect personal well-being such as whether we live near parks and other green spaces, how close we are to beaches, the types of social and cultural activities that are available, the noise and pollution levels locally and what the neighbourhood is like. Ideally, all these different characteristics of the local area would be explored in the analysis in order to hold all these things equal while looking at how each one relates to personal well-being. However in this analysis we focus only three broad aspects of the local area and how these relate to our personal well-being. These are:

- whether we live in an urban or rural area;
- the level of deprivation in the area where a person lives compared to other areas; and
- the region where we live within Great Britain.

Does living in the city or the country or the region where we live make a difference to personal well-being?

As there was an almost perfect correlation between the variable which was to be used to measure whether an area is urban or rural and the London category of the variable indicating the region where the respondent lives, it was not possible to include both as separate variables in the analysis (see section 5.3.1 for further details). The next best approach was to compare the well-being of those living in urban or rural areas within different regions of Great Britain at the same time. These findings show that generally across regions, people living in rural areas give higher ratings for their well-being than those living in urban areas when other factors have been taken into account. However, the size of the relationship between living in an urban or rural area and personal well-being is small. These findings are shown in **Table 10**.

Table 10: Effects of region on ratings of personal well-being after controlling for individual characteristics

Great Britain

Coefficients

	Life satisfaction	Worthwhile	Happy yesterday	Anxious yesterday
Reference group: London[1]				
North East - Urban	0.152*	0.123*	0.024	-0.159*
North East - Rural	0.143*	0.102	-0.006	-0.182
North West (including Merseyside) - Urban	0.038	0.108*	0.007	-0.167*
North West (including Merseyside) - Rural	0.2*	0.225*	0.243*	-0.295*
Yorkshire and Humberside - Urban	0.064*	0.154*	0.025	-0.212*
Yorkshire and Humberside - Rural	0.081	0.098*	0.108*	-0.394*
East Midlands - Urban	0.058	0.104*	0.077	-0.204*
East Midlands - Rural	0.167*	0.183*	0.112	-0.234*
West Midlands - Urban	-0.083*	-0.05	-0.027	-0.319*
West Midlands - Rural	-0.024	0.029	-0.052	-0.232*
East of England - Urban	0.023	0.06	0.065	-0.259*
East of England - Rural	0.062	0.113*	0.089	-0.156*
South East - Urban	0.038	0.094*	0.023	-0.203*
South East - Rural	0.138*	0.142*	0.098*	-0.282*

South West - Urban	0.044	0.087*	0.042	-0.286*
South West - Rural	0.152*	0.18*	0.104*	-0.24*
Wales - Urban	0.034	0.116*	0.049	-0.183*
Wales - Rural	0.126*	0.189*	0.136*	-0.356*
Scotland - Urban	0.133*	0.091*	0.043	-0.216*
Scotland - Rural	0.217*	0.155*	0.159*	-0.406*

Table source: Office for National Statistics

Table notes:

1. The reference group for region is 'London'.
2. * shows that the relationship is statistically significant at the 5% level.

Download table

XLS XLS format
(24.5 Kb)

Some of the more detailed results show that, other things being equal:

- Generally, people living in London gave similar ratings for their 'life satisfaction' to those living in other urban areas in Great Britain.
- People living in the rural areas of almost all regions reported higher 'life satisfaction' ratings than people living in London. This is probably more about the differences in 'life satisfaction' associated with living in rural or urban areas generally rather than a reflection of life in London per se. For example, other things being equal, the 'life satisfaction' score of a person living in a rural area of Scotland is, on average, 0.2 points higher than the 'life satisfaction' score of the person living in London.
- There were no statistically significant differences in ratings for 'happy yesterday' between those living in London and elsewhere, except among those in rural areas of the North West, Yorkshire and Humberside, South East, South West, Scotland and Wales. In each of these areas, people rated their 'happiness yesterday' marginally higher than people in London.
- When asked if they feel what they do in life is 'worthwhile', people living in London on average rated this lower than those living in most of the other regions. The exception to this is in the West Midlands (both rural and urban) where people rated this similarly to those in London.
- People in London also rated their 'anxiety yesterday' levels as higher than people living in the rest of the Great Britain.

The analysis here suggests that the region where we live and whether we live in an urban or rural area are related to personal well-being, but the relationships are small. However, it should also be noted that these results only reflect the average personal well-being ratings between the regions and countries of Great Britain. This may mask important differences between local areas within each region. Indeed, preliminary analysis of smaller local areas suggests that there may be considerable variation within the larger regions. This is an area which should be explored in future research.

How does the relative level of deprivation in the area where we live affect our personal well-being?

This question has been analysed by comparing local areas on a standard ranking system based on how deprived they are relative to other areas. The ranking system, called the Index of Multiple Deprivation, takes into account a number of different aspects of the local area including economic, social and housing issues and combines them into a single deprivation score for each area.

Table 11: Effects of relative deprivation on ratings of personal well-being after controlling for individual characteristics

Great Britain

Coefficients

	Life satisfaction	Worthwhile	Happy yesterday	Anxious yesterday
Reference group: bottom decile (most deprived)[1]				
2nd decile	0.081*	0.069*	0.112*	-0.029
3rd decile	0.056	0.062*	0.084*	0.031
4th decile	0.062*	0.092*	0.082*	0.029
5th decile	0.058	0.062*	0.097*	-0.010
6th decile	0.056	0.11*	0.145*	0.007
7th decile	0.075*	0.083*	0.104*	0.036
8th decile	0.084*	0.094*	0.092*	0.067
9th decile	0.074*	0.075*	0.072*	0.029
top decile (least deprived)	0.054	0.049	0.082*	0.161*

Table source: Office for National Statistics

Table notes:

1. The reference group for deprivation is the 'bottom decile'.
2. * shows that the relationship is statistically significant at the 5% level.

Download table

XLS XLS format
(21.5 Kb)

The findings from the regression analysis show that other things being equal, those living in relatively less deprived local areas have higher levels of personal well-being on average than those living in the most deprived areas. However, the size effects are very small (less than 0.1 points). These results are shown in **Table 11**.

Contrary to expectations, other things being equal, people living in the areas in the top decile (i.e. the least deprived areas) gave higher ratings on average for 'anxious yesterday' (around 0.2 points higher) compared to people living in the areas in the bottom decile (i.e., the most deprived areas).

In summary, after controlling for individual characteristics, the relationship between region, whether we live in an urban or rural area and the relative deprivation in the area are all related to personal well-being, but the size of the relationships is small.

We suggest that the differences observed in personal well-being among those living in urban or rural areas could be re-visited in further local area analysis. Other recent evidence also suggests that parks, gardens and green spaces in urban areas enhance the well-being of people living near them (Alcock 2013). These findings, as well as our own preliminary analysis at local level suggest that a more finely grained analysis could shed more light on the relationship between where we live and personal well-being.

Notes

1. 'What is your religion?'

2. Within each household, the net earnings of all working adults who are employees are summed, but if a household contains at least one working adult who is an employee but for whom earnings information is missing, then the household is excluded from the analysis.

4. Future work

The results have confirmed much of the existing literature on the subject. As many other studies were carried out using data from much smaller samples, it is useful to have this confirmation from a much larger sample survey.

We are confident that we have been able to identify and confirm some key associations with well-being amongst factors such as health, employment status, and marital status together with some more nuanced results such as the importance of choice and control over one's activities. Throughout, we have given an indication of the relative size of the different relationships between the individual variables in the analysis and personal well-being, holding other factors equal. However, we suggest that exact size effects of these associations should be treated with caution.

Looking ahead, we have made a number of suggestions throughout the analysis as to possible future directions. Overall, it will be helpful for researchers to focus more deeply on individual topics, either by using other more detailed datasets or by adding further data to the APS. We also suggest that further analysis using longitudinal data as this will allow researchers to follow the same individuals over time as their circumstances change.

Suggested areas for further exploration include:

- Sub-regional analysis of personal well-being;
- The relationship between household income and personal well-being;
- The relationship between objective and subjective measures of health and disability and personal well-being; and
- The age curve for personal well-being and whether this relates to cohort effects, age effects or both.

5. Technical annex

5.1 Why undertake a regression analysis?

In analysis which looks at the relationship between two variables, it can be tempting to infer that one variable is directly related to the other. For example, people in one ethnic group may have higher life satisfaction than those in another ethnic group, but can we assume that the differences observed in relation to life satisfaction ratings are primarily about ethnic differences? This conclusion would only be justified if we could show there were no other important differences between the ethnic groups which might affect the findings such as differences in health or employment status.

Regression analysis allows us to do this by holding all the variables in the model equal while measuring the size and strength of the relationship between two specific variables. If the regression results show a significant relationship between ethnicity and life satisfaction, then this means that two people who are identical in every way apart from their ethnicity would indeed rate their life satisfaction differently. This implies a direct relationship between ethnicity and life satisfaction even when the other variables included in the analysis are taken into account. Therefore, the key benefit of regression analysis is that it provides a better method than analysis looking at the relationship between only two variables at a time of indentifying those factors which matter most to personal well-being.

However, every analytical method has its limitations and regression analysis is no exception. The following sections summarise some key considerations which should be borne in mind in terms of the statistical assumptions underlying the techniques used here and the types of inference which can be drawn from the findings.

5.1.1 Using OLS for ordered responses and the robustness of the OLS estimates

A key implicit assumption in OLS regression is that the dependent variable (the outcome we are trying to explain, such as the personal well-being ratings) is continuous. Continuous data is data that can take any value (usually within a range). For example, a person's height could be any value within the range of human heights or time in a race which could even be measured to fractions of a second. The personal well-being survey responses, however, are discrete, i.e., they can only take on a relatively small number of integer values, such as 6 or 10 with no other values such as halves in between.

OLS regression also assumes that the values of the dependent variable (e.g., personal well-being ratings) are cardinal, i.e. the interval between any pair of categories such as between 2 and 3 is of the same magnitude as the interval between any other similar pair such as between 6 and 7. As the personal well-being responses are only rankings we cannot know whether for example the distance between 2 and 3 is the same as the distance between 6 and 7. For example, it may be the case that it doesn't take much for people to move from 2 to 3 in life satisfaction ranking, but it may take a lot more for them to jump from 6 to 7.

Therefore, the OLS regression approach may not be well suited for modelling this kind of dependent variable - however see below.

There are a number of alternatives to OLS for modelling discrete response variables, such as logit or probit regression. In these models the categories of the responses are treated separately (i.e. there is no order to the categories, for example, 4 is not higher than 3). The disadvantage of these methods is that the information contained in the ordering of the personal well-being ratings is lost. However, a way of overcoming this issue is to create two categories, for example rankings below 7 and above 7, but the categories will be artificial.

An alternative method is to treat the response variable as ordinal and use regression techniques, such as ordered logit or ordered probit that are developed to deal with ordinal data. Ordinal data values can be ranked or ordered on a scale such as from 0 to 10 with each higher category representing a higher degree of personal well-being (or lower personal well-being in the case of anxiety) and unlike the OLS method, ordered probit or ordered logit regression does not assume that the differences between the ordinal categories in the personal well-being rankings are equal. They capture the qualitative differences between different scores. It is important to note that ordinal probit/logistic performs several probit/logistic regressions simultaneously, assuming that the models are identical for all scores. The latter assumption can be relaxed but the interpretation of the results becomes more difficult.

In common with much of the existing literature that models subjective well-being we have applied an **ordered probit** model to explore the factors contributing to a person's personal well-being. As Greene (2000) points out, the reasons for favouring one method over the other (such as ordered probit or ordered logit) is practical and in most applications it seems not to make much difference to the results.

The major advantage of such models is that it takes the ordinal nature of the response variable (i.e. personal well-being rankings) into account without assuming equality of distance between the scores. Similarly to OLS, it identifies statistically significant relationships between the explanatory variables (e.g. age, health, etc) and the dependent variable (personal well-being ranking); however, the estimated coefficients have no direct interpretation[1].

The existing literature also suggests that OLS may still be reasonably implemented when there are more than five levels of the ordered categorical responses, particularly when there is a clear ordering of the categories e.g. levels of happiness with 0 representing the lowest category and 10 representing the highest category (for example see Larrabee, 2009). Indeed, several studies applied both methods to personal well-being data and found that there is little difference between the OLS and the theoretically preferable methodologies such as ordered probit. For example, see Ferrer-i-Carbonell and Fritjers (2004) for a detailed discussion of this issue.

The main advantage of OLS is that the interpretation of the regression results is more simple and straightforward than in alternative methods.

So for the sake of completeness, the analysis was conducted in both OLS and probit regression methods. This also acts as a sensitivity check for the robustness of the OLS results as the key assumptions for the OLS regression may not hold for the ordered personal well-being data.

It should be noted that this does not imply that the OLS regression estimates were completely 'robust'. Post regression diagnostics identified some violations of the OLS regression assumptions such as model specification and the normality of residuals. However, as some studies (for example see Osborne and Waters, 2002), suggest that several assumptions of OLS regression are 'robust' to violation such as normal distribution of residuals and others are fulfilled in the proper design of the study such as the independence of observations. In this analysis, using the survey design controlled for the potential dependence of the individual observations with each other (see section 5.2) and applying the survey weights provided some protection against model misspecification.

As there is no formal statistical test that can be used to identify multi-collinearity when the covariates in the model are dummy variables, an informal method of cross-tabulating each pair of dummy variables can be used. When cross-tabulations showed very high correlation between the variables they were not used in the regression. An example where this was the case is between the variables "reported being a Muslim" and "reported being Pakistani"; to get around this problem in this example, the dummy variables for the individual religions from the model were replaced with a single dummy variable "reported a religion".

Stata automatically computes standards errors that are robust to heteroskedasticity when the regressions are estimated incorporating survey design.

Additionally, estimating the models using different specifications as well as two methods (OLS and ordered probit) confirmed that the magnitude and the statistical significance of the parameter estimates did not significantly change and the general inferences from the analysis remained the same.

5.1.2 The explanatory power of the models

It is important to note that the explanatory power of the main regression model used here is relatively low. Indeed, the amount of variance that has been explained by the model is similar to that of other reported regression analyses undertaken on personal well-being. For the 'happy yesterday', 'anxious yesterday' and 'worthwhile' questions, around 10% of the variation between individuals is explained by the variables included in the model. By contrast, a much higher proportion (19%) of the individual variation in ratings for life satisfaction was explained by the model.

The lower explanatory power of the model could be due to leaving out important factors which contribute to personal well-being. For example, genetic and personality factors are thought to account for about half of the variation in personal well-being. It has not been possible to include variables relating to personality or genes in the models as the APS does not include data of this type.

The subjective nature of the outcome variable also means that it is probably measured with some imperfect reliability. The lower the reliability of the outcome variable, the more unclear its correlations with other variables will tend to be.

5.1.3 Omitted variable bias

In an ideal world, a regression model should include all the relevant variables that are associated with the outcome (i.e. variable being analysed such as personal well-being). In reality, however, we either cannot observe all the potential factors affecting well-being (such as personality) or are limited by whatever information is collected in the survey data used in the regression analysis.

If a relevant factor is not included in the model, this may result in the effects of the variables that have been included being mis-estimated. When the omitted variables are correlated with the included variables in the model, the coefficient estimates of those variables will be biased and inconsistent. However, the estimated coefficients are less affected by omitted variables when these are not correlated with the included variables (i.e. the estimates will be unbiased and consistent). In the latter case, the only problem will be an increase in the estimated standard deviations of the coefficients which are likely to give misleading conclusions about the statistical significance of the estimated parameters.

5.1.4 Causality

Regression analysis based on cross-sectional observational data cannot establish with certainty whether relationships found between the independent and dependent variables are causal. This is particularly the case in psychological contexts where there may be a reciprocal relationship between the independent and the dependent variables. For example, the usual assumption is that individual characteristics or circumstances like health or employment status are independent variables which may affect personal well-being (viewed here as a dependent variable). However, some of the association between health and well-being may be caused by the impact of personal well-being on health.

Furthermore, as the data used in the regression analysis here are collected at one point in time (i.e. cross-sectional), they are not able to capture the effect of changes over time and which event preceded another. For example, it is not possible to tell from this data whether the perception of being in bad health precedes a drop in well-being or whether a drop in well-being precedes the perception that one is in bad health. We can only definitely say that the perception of being in bad health is significantly related to lower levels of well-being compared to people who say they are in good health. Therefore, while the regression analysis here can demonstrate that a relationship between two variables exists even after holding other variables in the model constant, these findings should not be taken to infer causality.

5.1.5 Multi-collinearity- dependence (or correlations) among the variables

If two or more independent variables in the regression model are highly correlated with each other, the reliability of the model as a whole is not reduced but the individual regression coefficients cannot be estimated precisely. This means that the analysis may not give valid results either about individual independent variables, or about which independent variables are redundant with respect to others. This problem becomes increasingly important as the size of correlations between the independent variables (i.e. multi-collinearity) increases.

5.2 Taking the design of the APS sample into account in the analysis

The primary sampling unit in the Annual Population Survey is the household. That is, individuals are grouped into households and the households become units in sample selection.

Regression analysis normally assumes that each observation is independent of all the other observations in the dataset. However, members of the same household are likely to be more similar to each other on some or all of the measures of personal well-being than they are to members of different households. If the analysis ignores this within-household correlation, then the standard errors of the coefficient estimates will be biased, which in turn will make significance tests invalid.

Therefore, to correctly analyse the data and to make valid statistical inferences, the regressions are estimated in Stata with the specification of the survey design features. The survey weights were also used in the estimation of the model as these allow for more consistent estimation of the model coefficients and provide some protection against model misspecification.

5.3 Development of the regression models

Overall, eighteen regression models were constructed during this project. Each of these was analysed first using ordered probit and then using OLS. All of these results are available in the Reference Tables. To summarise:

- Reference Table 1 (141.5 Kb Excel sheet) contains a summary of the OLS regression coefficients and their significance for the main model.
- Reference Table 2 (208.5 Kb Excel sheet) contains the full results for the main regression model with the findings provided separately for each of the four personal well-being questions.
- Reference Table 3 (593 Kb Excel sheet) contains the results for the analysis with the employees sub-group and includes separate findings for each variation on the measurement of earnings for each of the four personal well-being questions.
- Reference Table 4 (770 Kb Excel sheet) contains the results for the other alternative specifications to the main model including models with the top level economic activity categories only; with household type replacing separate variables on marital status and children; with self-reported disability only (and dropping self-reported health); with self-reported health only (and dropping self-reported disability); with disability benefit receipt only (and dropping self-reported disability and self-reported health); and with country of birth only (replacing migration status and ethnic group).
- Reference Table 5 (58.5 Kb Excel sheet) contains a summary of sample sizes for each variable in the main model for each of the four personal well-being questions.

5.3.1 Development of the regional model

Further details of the regional analysis

The main regression model originally included Government Office Region (GOR) dummies to indicate where an individual lives and two other place related variables. The latter included a variable indicating whether the area is rural or urban and the relative deprivation of the Local Super Output Area (in terms of Index of Multiple Deprivation deciles) where the respondent lives.

However, as there was an almost perfect correlation between the variable used to indicate whether an area is urban or rural and the variable indicating London in the regional analysis, the final analysis included a dummy variable indicating whether the respondent lives in a rural or urban area within the relevant region (e.g. rural North East, or urban South West).

The analysis found a small but significant association between where people live and their levels of personal well-being. This was the case even before individual controls were introduced into the models. When all the four personal well-being variables were regressed only on GOR dummies or the place characteristics (i.e. urban/rural or relative deprivation) (without the controls for personal characteristics, both objective and subjective) there was a significant but rather small relationship between the region or place characteristics and an individual's personal well-being. After introducing all the individual controls in the models, the conclusion remains the same.

Further information about the Index of Multiple Deprivation and how it was used in this analysis

The Indices of Deprivation measure relative deprivation for small areas (LSOAs). Deprivation is a wider concept than poverty, and so the indices are constructed from a number of different types, or domains, of deprivation. These domains are combined into a single index, the Index of Multiple Deprivation (IMD), which ranks the areas in order of deprivation. A rank of 1 identifies the most deprived area.

The IMD deciles in this analysis are created by treating the most-deprived 10% of these areas as a single (non-adjacent) area, named Decile 1. The next most-deprived 10% are then grouped into a single area, named Decile 2, and so on.

Each of the four Nations of the UK produces its own Index. These Indices are not directly comparable because they use different domains and indicators, reflecting the priorities in the individual countries, and are published on different timescales covering different time periods.

However, the two domains – income and employment- are common to all four national IMDs and they contribute around half the weight of each IMD. They also use similar indicators such as simple percentage of individuals receiving one or more income or employment benefits. This implies they are relatively comparable across countries. For this analysis, the IMD deciles are created separately for each UK nation and then it is matched with the individual data. Although the values of the IMD deciles variable are not comparable across different nations, the variable can be considered a fairly good proxy for the relative deprivation of the area where an individual lives.

The deciles are based on the latest publications of the IMD Indices. These were: the English IMD Index -2010, Scottish IMD Index - 2012 and the Welsh IMD Index - 2011.

5.3.2 Decisions about the use of the Income Domain of the Index of Multiple Deprivation as a proxy for household income

In order to address the lack of household income information in the Annual Population Survey data, a possible alternative that was considered was the Indices of Multiple Deprivation income decile. Ultimately, this was not included in the final main model for the following reasons:

- There is a very high correlation between the IMD income decile and the overall IMD rank. This implies that one is a very good substitute for the other and both cannot be used simultaneously in the analysis.
- As other alternatives were available for exploring income, the decision was taken to retain the IMD decile which could be used to consider the relationship between personal well-being and aspects of where we live.
- The income indicator of the IMD income decile is based on the percentage of individuals receiving one or more income or employment benefits. It was therefore not viewed as a good proxy of the average LSOA household or individual income.

5.3.3 Details of different models of health and disability

The regression analyses were conducted using either health or disability on its own or both together to see how the results changed. Additionally, the self-assessed disability variable was also replaced in one model by a proxy for disability based on whether the person reported receipt of any disability-related benefits. This was thought to be a more objective indication of disability that could be compared to the results obtained from using people's views about whether they have a disability. Finally, if people gave disability-related reasons for being out of work, this was also used in some of the analyses.

The justification for putting both self-reported health and disability in the model is that the two are related but do not overlap entirely. However when both are included in the model, the disability effect almost disappears (indicating strong multi-collinearity).

When self-reported disability is included on its own, it picks up some of the impacts of self reported health, but the size effects are not as big as the health variables. Also the explanatory power of the models is smaller than the models which include self-reported health.

The key findings of the alternative models are summarised below, but the overall conclusion is clear: even accounting for the problems of causality, correlations between the variables capturing health and disability and issues of self-reported versus objective data, our views about our health have a large effect on ratings of personal well-being.

Key findings from the alternative approaches tried are as follows:

- When self reported health was not included in the analysis but a variable indicating whether an individual receives a sickness or disability benefit was, the results show that those who do not receive this type of benefit have higher levels of well-being than those who do (between 0.3 and

0.6 points higher). This reinforces the findings that health is important to well-being whether it is measured by asking people their views about their health or by looking at whether they say they receive health-related benefits

- Another model was estimated using a dummy variable indicating whether an individual has reported a current disability or not to see if a self-reported measure of health would produce different results than the more objective measure of disability benefit receipt. It was found that the results were very similar regardless of the measure used. Similar to disability benefit recipients there is a significant relationship between the disability status and the four personal well-being measures.
- Analysis was also carried out including the self-reported health variable but not self-reported disability. As expected, the association between self-reported health and well-being is very strong (much more than the disability variables, even on their own) both in terms of the size and the importance.

Based on this evidence, the regression analysis has taken into account both subjective and more objective health measures found in the Annual Population Survey and a number of specifications have been estimated using these measures. The only potential 'objective' health assessment in the survey is the type of benefit an individual receives. However, it should be noted that benefit receipt is also self-reported on the Annual Population Survey so this is not truly objective data and it may not capture all the individuals in the survey who have a disability or illness. On the other hand, the APS includes two 'subjective' health measures: 'self-reported health' and self-reported 'current disability'. Several studies have used the second of those as an 'objective' variable measuring health but the justification for doing so is unclear.

How much difference does disability make to our well-being?

All other things being equal, people who said they have a disability rated their personal well-being lower than people who did not report a disability. When the models included self-reported disability only (without the self reported health), the effects were around 0.6 points for 'life satisfaction' and 'happy yesterday', and around 0.4 points for 'worthwhile', e.g., average 'life satisfaction' scores of the people who reported a disability were 0.6 points lower than people who did not report a disability. On the other hand, average 'anxious yesterday' scores of the people who reported a disability were around 0.7 points higher than the people who did not report a disability. This suggests disability is associated more with anxiety than the other measures of personal well-being.

Similarly, when the regressions were estimated using an 'objective' variable for disability/health (i.e. disability/sickness benefit claimants), the size effects for 'life satisfaction', 'happy yesterday' and doing things that are 'worthwhile' were very similar to the regressions which included self-reported disability variable. The coefficient of the 'anxious yesterday' was also around 0.6 points (a little less than the models which included self-reported disability only).

5.4 Methodological findings on mode of interview

The Annual Population Survey data is collected either by telephone interview or face to face in the respondent's home. The possibility of people giving different responses in these different interview contexts was the subject of a working paper for the National Statistician's Technical Advisory Group on Measuring National Well-being (December 2011). The paper explored the impact of these methods on the answers to the personal well-being questions and concluded that:

"There is a trade-off between the likelihood of errors caused by the telephone method and the fact that the telephone allows more privacy and confidentiality when answering. However studies have shown substantial differences in responses to scalar questions when asked by telephone versus visual modes, in that more positive responses are given in the telephone mode (Dillman et al., 2009). In addition the evidence gathered from the present study suggests the telephone is associated with misunderstanding and decreased rapport with the interviewer along with a decreased desire to take part". (Ralph, K., Palmer, K., Olney, J., 2011)

In order to hold constant the possible impacts of different interview modes when exploring the relationship of other variables to well-being as well as examining the possible impacts of interview mode on responses to the personal well-being questions, the regression models included method of the interview.

The findings of this analysis show that people interviewed face to face give lower well-being ratings on average than people interviewed by telephone. However, the size effects are small. For example, being interviewed face to face is associated with a reduction of about 0.2 points in 'life satisfaction' ratings compared to being interviewed over the telephone. The differences are similar for ratings of 'happy yesterday' and feelings that our activities are 'worthwhile'. The difference in ratings for 'anxious yesterday' among those having a telephone or personal interview is smaller still. These findings are shown in **Table 12**.

Table 12: Effects of interview mode on ratings of personal well-being after controlling for individual factors

Great Britain

Coefficients

	Life satisfaction	Worthwhile	Happy yesterday	Anxious yesterday
Reference group: Telephone Interview[1]				
Face to Face Interview	-0.171*	-0.165*	-0.132*	0.054*

Table source: Office for National Statistics

Table notes:

1. The reference group for interview mode is 'telephone interviews'.
2. * shows that the relationship is statistically significant at the 5% level.

Download table

XLS XLS format
(29.5 Kb)

Notes

1. However, they can be used to calculate probabilities which require further calculations and selecting ‘representative’cases.

About the ONS Measuring National Well-being Programme

NWB logo 2

This article is published as part of the ONS Measuring National Well-being Programme.

The programme aims to produce accepted and trusted measures of the well-being of the nation - how the UK as a whole is doing.

Measuring National Well-being is about looking at 'GDP and beyond'. It includes headline indicators in areas such as health, relationships, job satisfaction, economic security, education, environmental conditions and measures of 'subjective well-being' (individuals' assessment of their own well-being).

Find out more on the Measuring National Well-being website pages.

Background notes

1. These statistics are experimental in nature and published at an early stage to gain feedback from users. Should users have comments on the ONS approach to the measurement of subjective well-being and or the presentation of the subjective well-being questions they can email ONS at national.well-being@ons.gov.uk. It is the role of the UK Statistics Authority to designate these statistics as National Statistics and this is one of the aspirations of the National Well-being programme is to see these statistics gain National Statistics status.

2. The data analysed in this report are derived from a customised weighted 12 month APS microdataset. This dataset is not part of the regularly produced APS datasets and was produced specifically for the analysis of subjective well-being data. ONS is making the experimental APS microdata available to approved researchers to allow them to undertake further analysis of these experimental questions at an early stage and to provide further feedback to ONS.

3. Details of the policy governing the release of new data are available by visiting the UK Statistics Authority or from the Media Relations Office.

4. This article is published as part of the ONS Measuring National Well-being Programme. The programme aims to produce accepted and trusted measures of the well-being of the nation - how the UK as a whole is doing. It is about looking at 'GDP and beyond' and includes:

   - Greater analysis of the national economic accounts, especially to understand household income, expenditure and wealth.
   - Further accounts linked to the national accounts, including the UK Environmental Accounts and valuing household production and 'human capital'.
   - Quality of life measures, looking at different areas of national well-being such as health, relationships, job satisfaction, economic security, education environmental conditions.
   - Working with others to include the measurement of the well-being of children and young people as part of national well-being.
   - Measures of 'subjective well-being' - individuals' assessment of their own well-being.
   - Headline indicators to summarise national well-being.

   The programme is underpinned by links with Cabinet Office and policy departments, international developments, the public and other stakeholders. The programme is working closely with Defra on the measurement of 'sustainable development' to provide a complete picture of national well-being, progress and sustainable development.

6. Details of the policy governing the release of new data are available by visiting www.statisticsauthority.gov.uk/assessment/code-of-practice/index.html or from the Media Relations Office email: media.relations@ons.gsi.gov.uk

Copyright

This document is also available on our website at www.ons.gov.uk.

References

1. Alcock, I., Wheeler, B., Depledge, M. (2013). 'Green Spaces May Boost Well-being for City Slickers', Association for Psychological Science, Press Release April 22, 2013

2. Boarini, R. Comola, M., Smith, C., Manchin, R. and de Keulenaer, F. (2012), 'What Makes for a Better Life?: The Determinants of Subjective Well-Being in OECD Countries – Evidence from the Gallup World Poll', OECD Statistics Working Papers, 2012/03, OECD

3. Blanchflower, D.G. and Oswald, A.J.(1999), 'Well-Being, Insecurity and the Decline of American Job Satisfaction'

4. Brown, D., Smith, C. and Woolf J. (2010), 'The Determinants of Subjective Wellbeing in New Zealand: An Empirical Look at New Zealand's Social Welfare Function', New Zealand Association of Economists Conference 2010, Statistics New Zealand

5. Clark, A.E (2003), 'Unemployment as a Social Norm: Psychological evidence from Panel Data' , Journal of Labor Economics, 2003, Vol 21 (2)

6. Clark, A., Frijters, P., & Shields, M. A. (2008). A survey of the income happiness gradient. Journal of Economic Literature, 46 (1), March 2008, pp. 95-144 cited by Dolan et al., 2008

7. DeNeve, K. M. and Cooper, H. (1998). 'The happy personality: A meta-analysis of 137 personality traits and subjective well-being', Psychological Bulletin, 124, 197–229

8. Department for Communities and Local Government, 2011. English indices of deprivation 2010. London: Department for Communities and Local Government

9. Diener E. (2000). 'Subjective well-being: the science of happiness, and a proposal for a national index', American Psychologist, 55(1):34–43

10. Diener, E. (1996). 'Traits can be powerful but are not enough: Lessons from subjective well-being', Journal of Research in Personality, 30, 389-399.

11. Diener, E., Lucas, R. E., Oishi, S., and Suh, E. (2003), 'Personality, Culture, and subjective well-being: Emotional and Cognitive Evaluations of Life', Annual Review of Psychology, 54:403–25

12. Diener, E., Suh, E. M., Lucas, R. E. and Smith, H. L. (1999). 'Subjective well-being: Three decades of progress', Psychological Review, 125, 276–302

13. Dillman, D. A., Smyth, J. D., & Christian, L. M. (2009). 'Internet, mail, and mixed-mode surveys: The tailored design method'. Hoboken, NJ: Wiley

14. Dolan, P., Peasgood, T. and White, M. (2008). 'Do we really know what makes us happy/? A review of the economic literature on the factors associated with subjective well-being', Journal of Economic Psychology, 29, 94-122

15. Ferrer-i Carbonell, A. and Frijters, P. (2004). 'How important s methodology for the estimates of the determinants of happiness?', The Economic Journal, 114 (July), 641-659

16. Findlay, A.M., Gayle, V., van Ham, M. and Nowok, B. (2011), 'Does Migration Make You Happy? A Longitudinal Study of Internal Migration and Subjective Well-Being', IZA Discussion Papers, No.6140

Measuring National Well-being - Self reported financial situation, 2013

Author Name(s): **Jen Beaumont, Office for National Statistics**

Abstract

This article analyses by age two of the current measures of national well-being: 'satisfaction with income' and 'those who are finding their financial situation quite or very difficult' and their relationship to well-being. There will also be some indication of change in perceived financial situation over time and by other characteristics of individuals. The data used are from Understanding Society, the UK Household Longitudinal Study.

Introduction

The Office for National Statistics' Measuring National Well-being Programme measures of well-being are organised into ten domains with a total of 40 headline measures.

This article analyses two measures from the Personal Finance domain: 'Somewhat, mostly or completely satisfied with the income of their household' and 'Finding it quite or very difficult to get by financially' together with contextual information. Analysis is by age group and over time. There is also a discussion of some potential reasons for the observed differences.

More information about all the measures can be found in the 'National Well-being wheel of measures' (see section 'About the ONS Measuring National Well-being Programme'). Throughout this article 'relatively satisfied' refers to those who reported being completely, mostly or somewhat satisfied and 'relatively dissatisfied' refers to those who reported being completely, mostly or somewhat dissatisfied.

Key points

- In 2009–10 and 2010–11, 57% of those aged 16 and over in the UK were relatively satisfied with their household income: satisfaction with income varied from about 58% to 66% between 2002 and 2008.
- 11.5% of people aged 16 and over reported that they were finding their financial situation quite or very difficult in 2010–11 a slight decrease compared to 12.4% in 2009–10.
- In 2010–11 about a fifth (19%) of respondents reported that they expected their financial situation to get worse in the next year, while a quarter (25%) expected it to get better.

- There was a large increase between 2007 and 2008 in the percentage of respondents expecting their financial situation to get worse as awareness of the potential economic downturn increased.
- There was a considerable increase in those reporting their financial situation to be quite or very difficult between 2008 and 2009–10.
- In 2010–11 a higher proportion of those aged 60 and over reported that they were relatively satisfied with their household income but a higher percentage also expected their financial situation to get worse next year when compared to those aged less than 60.
- In 2010–11 a much lower percentage of those aged 60 and over reported that they were finding their financial situation quite or very difficult when compared to those aged less than 60.
- The analysis suggests that some of the changes between the younger age groups and those aged 60 and over may be related to a reduction in financial commitments, including those related to dependent children and household costs, and change from most income from paid employment to income from relatively fixed pensions.

Satisfaction with income

Figure 1: Relative satisfaction with income by age group, 2010–11

United Kingdom

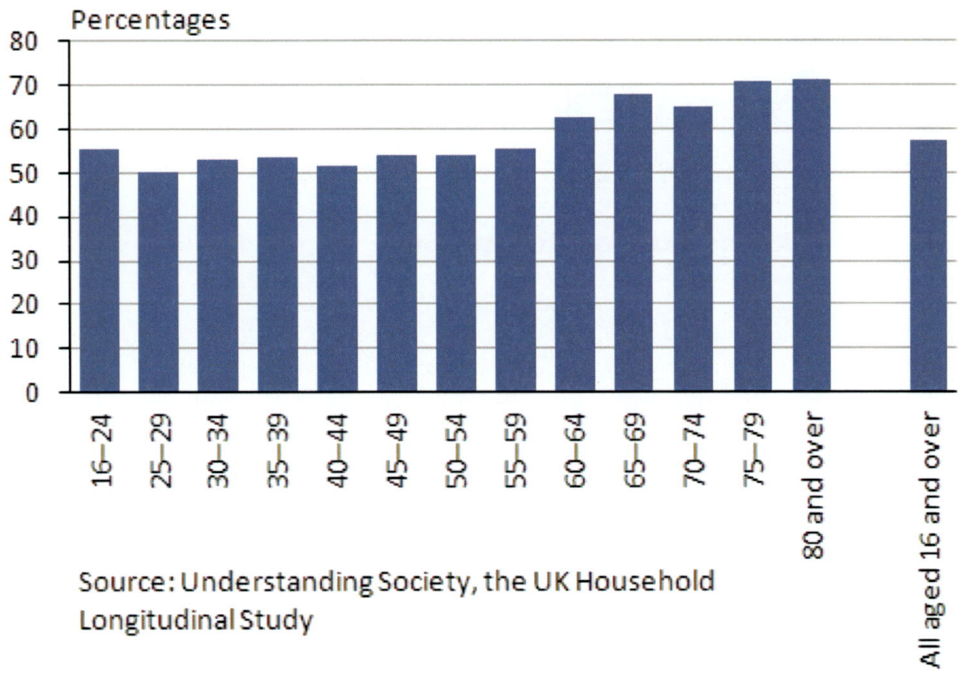

Download chart

XLS XLS format
(29.5 Kb)

In 2010–11, 57% of those aged 16 and over were relatively satisfied with their household income. In each age group from 16 to 24 to 55 to 59 a lower percentage than the average of those aged 16 and over reported that they were relatively satisfied with their household income. In each age group from 60 to 64 to 80 and over a higher percentage than the average said that they were relatively satisfied with their household income. (**Figure 1**)

Figure 2: Relative satisfaction with income (1), 2001–2002 to 2010–11 (2)

United Kingdom

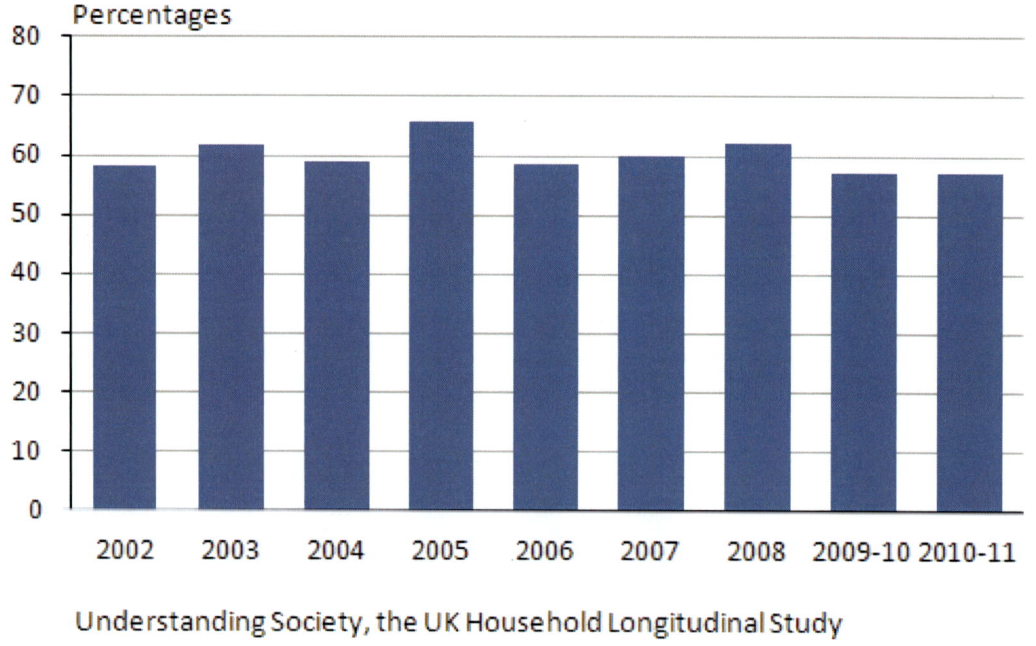

Notes:

1. Respondents were asked how they felt about the income of their household and responded on a seven point scale from 'completely dissatisfied' to 'completely satisfied'. Relative satisfaction refers to those who responded completely, mostly or somewhat satisfied.
2. Data up to 2008 is from the British Household Panel Survey and from 2009 it changed to Understanding Society.

Download chart

XLS XLS format
(28.5 Kb)

The percentage of respondents who were relatively satisfied with their income has changed a little over time, varying between 58% and 66% between 2001 and 2008. In both 2009–10 and 2010–11, 57% of those aged 16 and over were relatively satisfied with their income (**Figure 2**).

Figure 3: Relative satisfaction with life overall (1) by level of satisfaction with income (2), 2010–11

United Kingdom

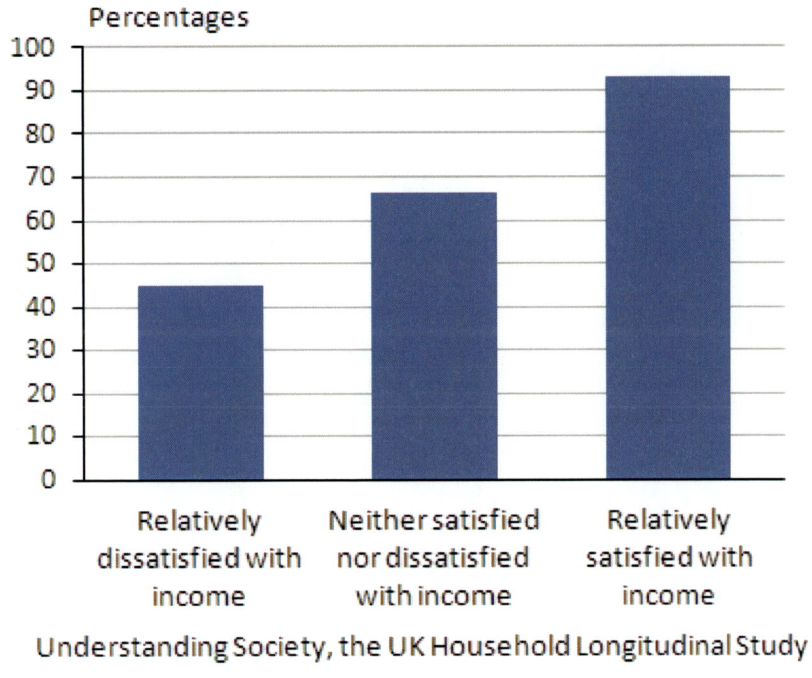

Notes:

1. Respondents were asked how satisfied they were with their lives overall and responded on a seven point scale from completely satisfied to completed dissatisfied.
2. Respondents were asked how they felt about the income of their household and responded on a seven point scale from 'completely dissatisfied' to 'completely satisfied'.

Download chart

XLS XLS format
(28 Kb)

Satisfaction with income is closely related to satisfaction with life overall. In 2010–11 about 93% of those who were relatively satisfied with their income were also relatively satisfied with their lives overall compared to only 45% of those who were relatively dissatisfied with their income (**Figure 3**).

Finding the financial situation quite or very difficult

Figure 4: Finding the financial situation quite or very difficult by age group and sex (1), 2010–11

United Kingdom

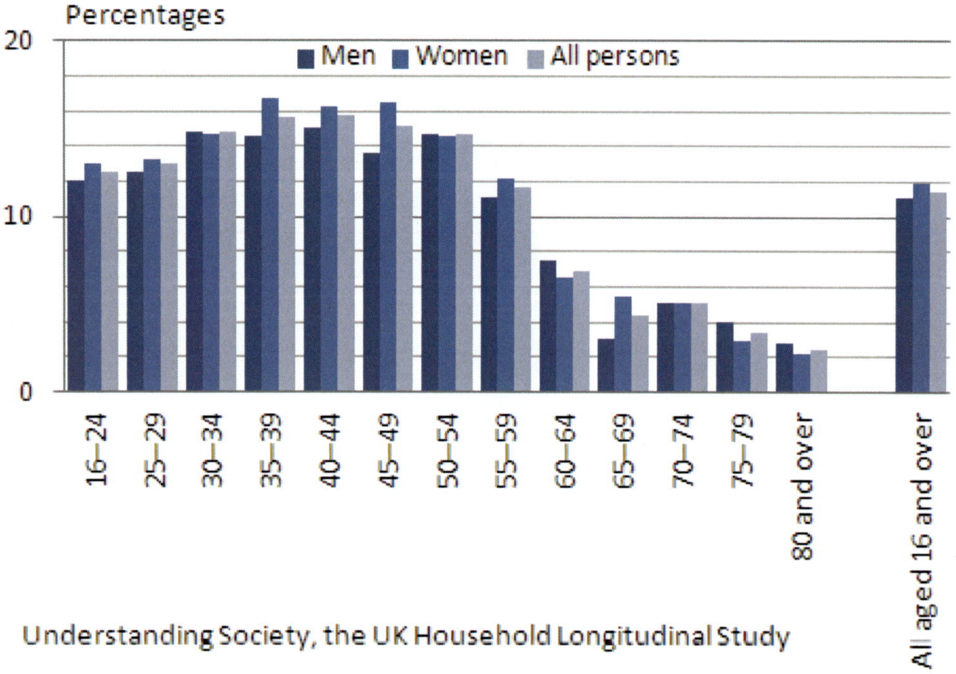

Notes:

1. Respondents were asked how well they were managing financially these days with responses 'living comfortably, doing alright, just about getting by, finding it quite difficult or finding it very difficult.

Download chart

XLS XLS format
(29 Kb)

In 2010–11, 11.5% of those aged 16 and over reported that they were finding their financial situation quite or very difficult (**Figure 4**). The percentage finding their financial situation quite or very difficult varied considerably between the age groups. A higher percentage of each age group from 16 to 24 to 55 to 59 reported finding their financial situation quite or very difficult than the average for all aged 16 and over, with noticeably higher proportions of those between the ages of 30 and 54. For those aged 60 and above, a considerably smaller proportion of each age group reported that they were finding their financial situation quite or very difficult. There were differences between men and women in some age groups: a higher proportion of women than men reported difficulties in the 16 to 24, 35 to 39, 40 to 44, 45 to 49 and 65 to 69 age groups while a higher proportion of men than women reported difficulties in the two oldest age groups.

Figure 5: Relative satisfaction with life overall (1) by reported financial situation (2), 2010-11

United Kingdom

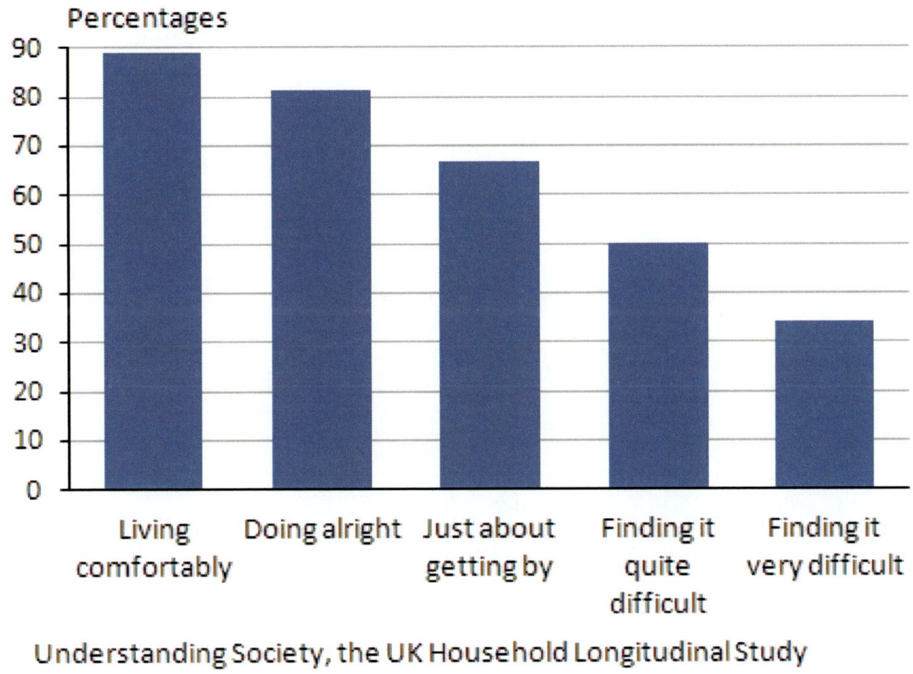

Notes:

1. Respondents were asked how they felt about and their life overall and responded on a seven point scale from 'completely dissatisfied' to 'completely satisfied'. Relative satisfaction refers to those who responded completely, mostly or somewhat satisfied.
2. Respondents were asked how well they were managing financially these days with responses 'living comfortably, doing alright, just about getting by, finding it quite difficult or finding it very difficult.

Download chart

XLS XLS format
(28.5 Kb)

The level at which individuals report their financial situation is closely related to satisfaction with life overall. About 89% of those who reported that they were living comfortably were also relatively satisfied with their lives overall (**Figure 5**). This compares with a half (50%) of those who reported finding it quite difficult and around a third (34%) who reported finding it very difficult who were relatively satisfied with their lives overall.

Expectations for financial situation next year

Figure 6: Expectation of being financially worse off in the next year by age group and sex (1), 2010–11

United Kingdom

Notes:

1. Respondents were also asked how they thought they would be financially a year from now with responses better off, worse than now, or about the same.

Download chart

XLS XLS format
(19 Kb)

Respondents were also asked whether they expected to be better off, about the same or worse off next year. **Figure 6** shows the percentage of individuals who reported that they expected to be worse off next year. Overall in 2010–11 nearly 19% of those aged 16 and over reported that they thought they would be worse off next year. This varied by age. The percentage was similar for the youngest two age groups (10%) but increased with age up to the 70 to 74 age group (32%) and then decreased in the two older age groups. There were some differences between men and women particularly for those aged 70 and over where a higher percentage of men reported that they thought they would be worse off next year.

Expectations for next year compared with financial situation now

Figure 7: Expectations of financial situation next year (1) by reported level of current financial situation (2), 2011–12

United Kingdom

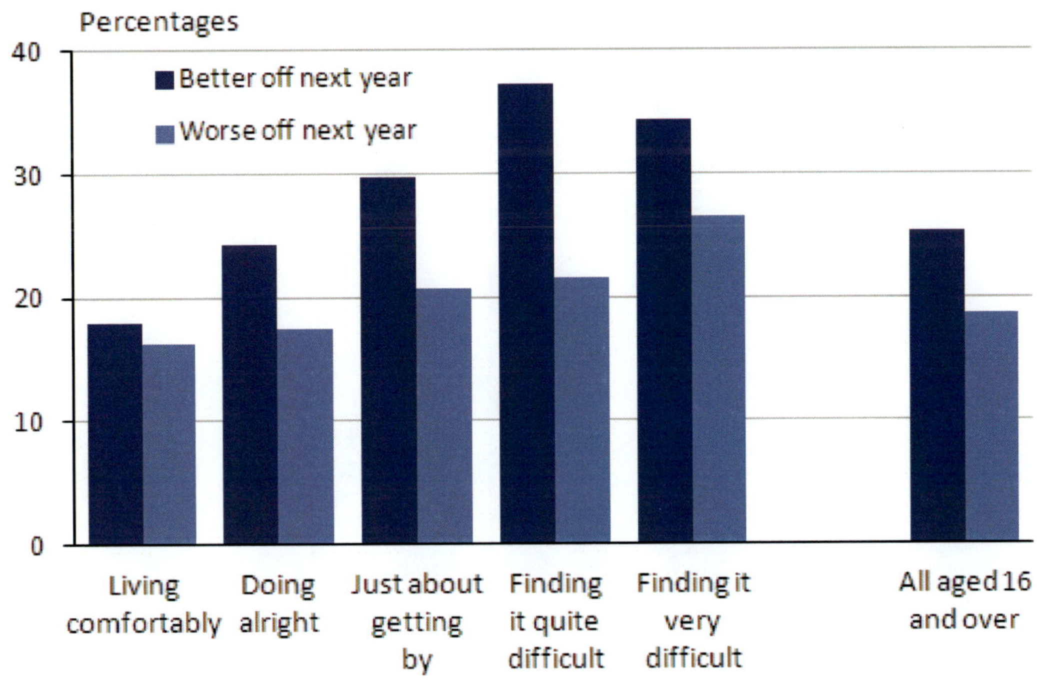

Notes:

1. Respondents were also asked how they thought they would be financially a year from now with responses better off, worse than now, or about the same.
2. Respondents were asked how well they were managing financially these days with responses 'living comfortably, doing alright, just about getting by, finding it quite difficult or finding it very difficult.

Download chart

XLS XLS format
(19 Kb)

As reported earlier in this article about 19% of respondents reported that they expected their financial situation to get worse next year in 2010–11. However, about 25% reported that they expected it to get better (**Figure 7**). For each level of reported current financial situation a higher percentage of respondents reported that they expected their financial situation to be better next year than those who reported that they expected their financial situation to get worse in the next year. For example, of those who reported that they were just about getting by, about 2 in every 10 (21%) also reported that they expected their financial situation to get worse next year while 3 in 10 (30%) reported that they expected it to get worse.

Figure 8: Those with a quite or very difficult financial situation (1) and those who expect worse next year (2), 2001 to 2010–11 (3)

United Kingdom

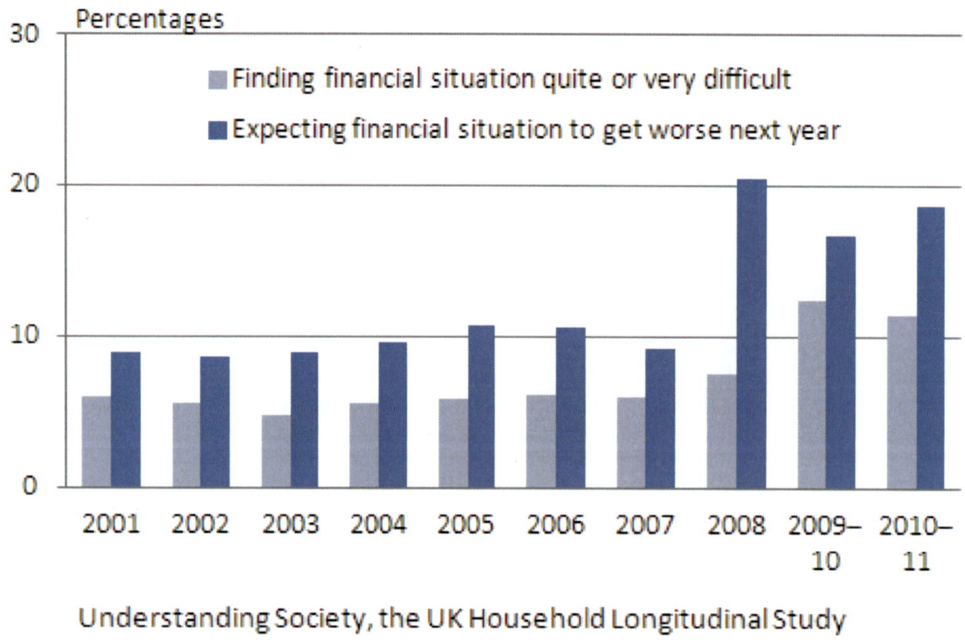

Notes:

1. Respondents were asked how well they were managing financially these days with responses 'living comfortably, doing alright, just about getting by, finding it quite difficult or finding it very difficult.
2. Respondents were also asked how they thought they would be financially a year from now with responses better off, worse than now, or about the same.
3. Data up to 2008 is from the British Household Panel Survey and from 2009 it changed to Understanding Society.

Download chart

XLS XLS format
(20 Kb)

Between 2001 and 2007 the percentage of those aged 16 and over who reported that they expect their financial situation to be worse in the next year varied between 8.7% (2002) and 10.8% (2005) of respondents (**Figure 8**). There was a steep increase to 20.5% in 2008, presumably in response to growing awareness of the potential effects of the economic downturn. In 2009–10, 16.8% and in 2010–11, 18.7% of respondents reported that they expect their financial situation to be worse in the next year.

Between 2001 and 2007 the percentage aged 16 and over who reported finding their financial situation quite or very difficult varied between 4.8% (in 2003) and 6.0% (in 2001 and 2007). There was an increase to 7.5% in 2008. Larger percentages of respondents reported finding their financial situation quite or very difficult in 2009–10 (12.4%) and 2010–11 (11.5%) as would be expected during the current economic climate.

Reasons for change by age group

Table 1: Comparison of those aged 16 to 64 and 60 and over, 2010-11

United Kingdom (Percentages)

		16–59	Over 60	All aged 16 and over
Satisfaction with income	Completely, mostly or somewhat satisfied	54	67	57
	Neither satisfied nor dissatisfied	14	13	14
	Completely, mostly or somewhat dissatisfied	33	20	29
Financial situation now	Living comfortably	23	40	28
	Doing alright	34	32	33
	Just about getting by	29	23	27
	Finding it quite difficult	10	3	8
	Finding it very difficult	4	1	4
Expectation of financial situation	Better off	33	6	25
	Worse off than now	16	26	19
	About the same	52	67	56
Number of children responsible for under 18	0	75	100	82
	1 or more	25	0	18

	16–59	Over 60	All aged 16 and over
In paid employment	71	17	56
Pension from any source	3	89	27

Source: Understanding Society, the UK Household Longitudinal Study

Download table

XLS XLS format
(29 Kb)

All three measures analysed above show a change around the age of 60 and this age pattern exists for all the years for which data are available.

After the age of 60 the proportion reporting that they are satisfied with income increases. One reason for lower satisfaction with income in the younger age groups could be greater financial commitments, such as housing costs including mortgage payments. A recent publication by ONS (The Burden of Property Debt in Great Britain, 2006/08 & 2008/10, 13 May 2013) analysed the Wealth and Assets Survey for liabilities related to property debt. Of those who had such debt both the average debt and the proportion of the age group who had property debt decreased with increasing age. Younger individuals are also more likely to be supporting a family: 25% of those aged 59 or younger had responsibility for a child under the age of 18 compared with none of those aged 60 and over **(Table 1)**.

After the age of 60 the proportion reporting that their current household financial situation is being quite or very difficult decreases. The lower percentage after the age of 60 may also relate to the reduction in family and financial commitments. It appears that many individuals in this age group have sufficient income to allow them to meet their financial commitments or have tailored their commitments to allow them to live well. In 2010–11 nearly three quarters of those aged 60 and over reported that they were either living comfortably or doing alright compared with less than three in five of those aged 59 or less (**Table 1**).

After the age of 60 the proportion reporting that that they expect to be worse off in the next year tends to increase. The higher percentage of those 60 and over reporting that they expect their financial situation to get worse in the next year, even for those who are not finding their financial situation quite or very difficult now, may be related to the proportion who have income from pensions or other relatively fixed sources. The expectation may be that there may be rises in the costs of living which overtake any potential rise in their income. Also, many older people use savings interest to supplement their income and as interest rates have remained low the expectation of any rise in this income may be also be low. By contrast those aged less than 60 are more likely to have income from paid employment: 71% of this age group are in paid employment compared to only 17% of those aged 60 and over. While in employment individuals may see the possibility of supplementing or increasing income by pay increases, taking on more hours or finding a better paid job (**Table 1**).

About Understanding Society, the UK Household Longitudinal Study

Understanding Society is a unique and valuable academic study that captures important information every year about the social and economic circumstances and attitudes of people living in 40,000 UK households. It also collects additional health information from around 20,000 of the people who take part.

Information from the longitudinal survey is primarily used by academics, researchers and policy makers in their work, but the findings are of interest to a much wider group of people including those working in the third sector, health practitioners, business, the media and the general public.

Key facts

- 40,000 households – 2,640 postcode sectors in England, Scotland and Wales – 2,400 addresses from Northern Ireland.
- £48.9 million funding (until 2015).
- Approximately 3 billion data points of information.
- Innovation Panel of 1,500 respondents.
- Participants aged 10 and older.
- Building on 18 years of British Household Panel Survey.
- 35 to 60 minutes: the average time to complete each face to face interview.

How does it work?

Interviews began in 2009 with all eligible members of the selected households.

- Adults are interviewed every 12 months either face to face or over the phone using Computer Assisted Interviewing.
- 10 to 15 year olds fill in a paper self-completion questionnaire.

From 2010 some 20,000 participants aged over 16 also received nurse visits and provided a blood sample and some basic physical measurements (height, weight, blood pressure, grip strength).

Data used in this analysis

The data in this analysis is mainly from the adult self completion questionnaire of Wave 2 of the Survey and has been weighted using the interview with self completion individual cross-sectional weight (a_indscus_xw). Throughout this article relatively satisfied refers to those who report being completely, mostly or somewhat satisfied and relatively dissatisfied refers to those who report being completely, mostly or somewhat dissatisfied.

About the ONS Measuring National Well-being Programme

NWB logo 2

This article is published as part of the ONS Measuring National Well-being Programme.

The programme aims to produce accepted and trusted measures of the well-being of the nation - how the UK as a whole is doing.

Measuring National Well-being is about looking at 'GDP and beyond'. It includes headline indicators in areas such as health, relationships, job satisfaction, economic security, education, environmental conditions and measures of 'subjective well-being' (individuals' assessment of their own well-being).

Find out more on the Measuring National Well-being website pages.

Background notes

1. Details of the policy governing the release of new data are available by visiting www.statisticsauthority.gov.uk/assessment/code-of-practice/index.html or from the Media Relations Office email: media.relations@ons.gsi.gov.uk

References

1. ONS (2012) National Well-being interactive wheel of measures. Accessed at National Well-being interactive wheel of measures [Adobe Flash]

2. University of Essex. Institute for Social and Economic Research and National Centre for Social Research, Understanding Society: Wave 1-2, 2009-2011[computer file]. 4th *Edition*. Colchester, Essex: UK Data Archive [distributor], December 2012. SN: 6614, http://dx.doi.org/10.5255/UKDA-SN-6614-4.

Measuring National Well-being - Health, 2013

Author Name(s): **Jen Beaumont, Helen Lofts - Office for National Statistics**

Abstract

This article analyses by age and other variables two of the current measures of national well-being: 'satisfaction with health' and 'evidence of mental ill-health (GHQ)' and their relationship to well-being. There is also contextual information about other variables related to health which may affect an individual's well-being. The data used are from Understanding Society, the UK Household Longitudinal Study (UKHLS) 2010–11.

Introduction

The Office for National Statistics measures of well-being are organised into ten domains with a total of 40 headline measures.

The World Health Organisation (WHO) defines health as 'a state of complete physical, mental and social well-being and not merely the absence of disease or infirmity' (WHO, 1946). Good physical health is important for good mental health and vice versa.

This article focuses on information about health from the UKHLS 2010–11. Respondents were asked how dissatisfied or satisfied they were with their health, if their health limited moderate activity and to answer questions which gave some indication of their mental health (GHQ). The UKHLS collects information each year about the social and economic circumstances and attitudes of people. For more information see the section; About Understanding Society, the UK Household Longitudinal Study.

Throughout this article relatively satisfied refers to those who reported being completely, mostly or somewhat satisfied and relatively dissatisfied refers to those who were completely, mostly or somewhat dissatisfied.

Key points

In the UK in 2010–11 for those aged 16 and over:

- Two thirds (66%) of people were satisfied with their health with a slightly higher proportion of men than women.

- Satisfaction with health reduced to 53% of those aged 80 and over.
- Around a fifth (19%) of individuals had some indication of anxiety or depression with a higher proportion of women than men and a higher proportion of those aged between 40 and 59 or aged 80 and over.
- Some evidence of anxiety and depression occurred in a higher percentage of those who were divorced or not in paid work or dissatisfied with their health or who were caring for someone else in the household or who were living on their own.
- Around three in ten (28%) reported restrictions in moderate daily activities: the percentage reporting restrictions increased considerably with age from 13% of those aged 16 to 24 to 77% of those aged 80 and over.
- About 14% of those who reported no limitation in moderate activities showed some symptoms of anxiety or depression compared to 26% of those with a little limitation and nearly 41% of those with a lot of limitation.

Satisfaction with health

Overall two thirds (66%) of respondents aged 16 and over reported that they were satisfied with their health in 2010–11. There was a slight downward trend in people's satisfaction with their health between the ages of 16 and 59 followed by a small increase around retirement age and a sharp decline after the age of 69. Three quarters (75%) of those aged 16 to 24 in the UK were relatively satisfied with their health compared with just over half (53%) of those aged 80 and over. The largest percentage differences in men and women's health satisfaction were in the youngest and oldest age groups. About 77% of men were satisfied with their health compared to 73% of women in the 16 to 24 age group. In the 80 and over age group 57% of men were satisfied with their health compared to 50% of women **(Figure 1)**.

Figure 1: Relative satisfaction with health by age group and sex (1), 2010–11

United Kingdom

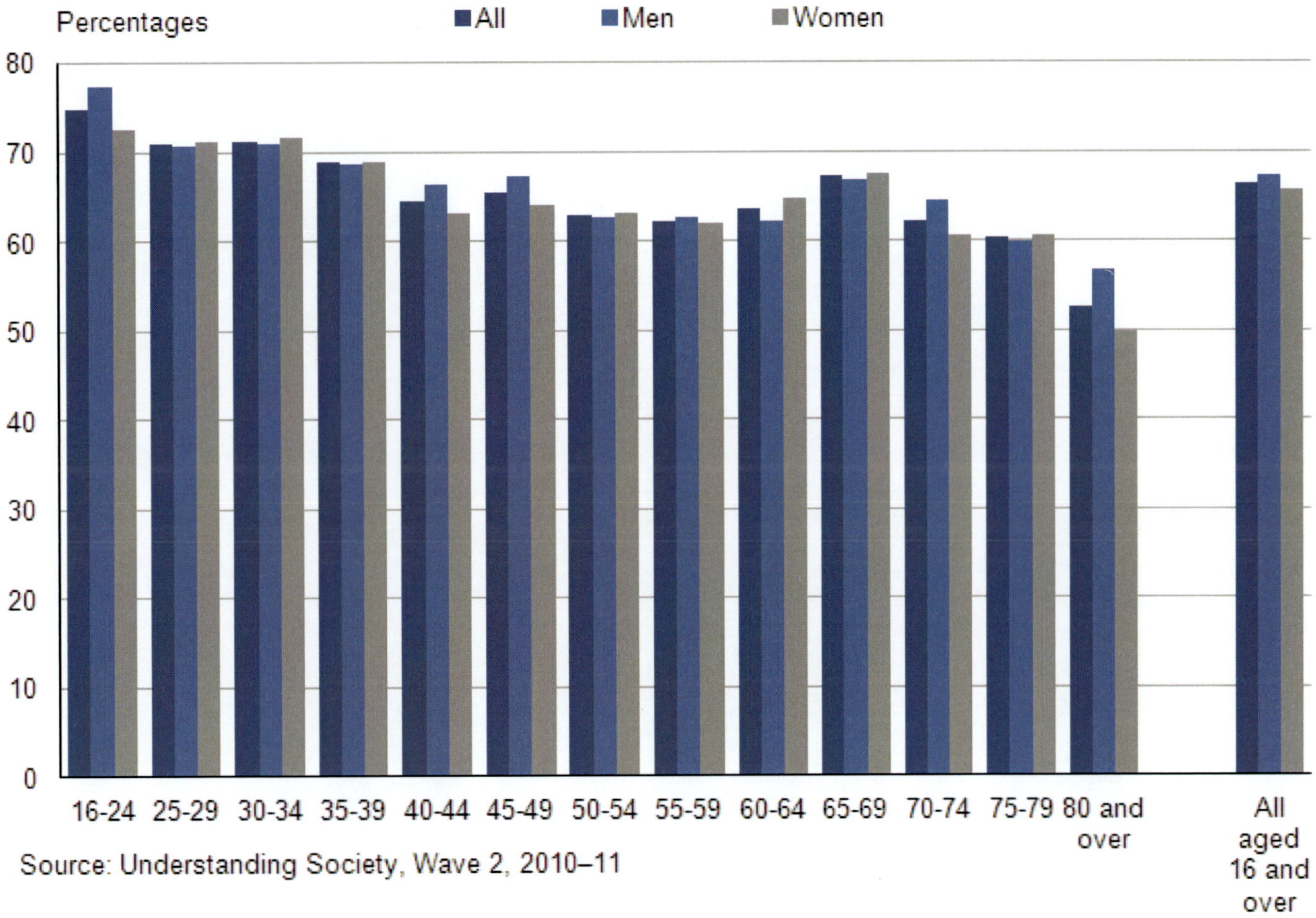

Notes:

1. Respondents were asked 'How satisfied or dissatisfied you are with your health' and responded 'Completely satisfied' to 'Completely dissatisfied'

Download chart

XLS XLS format
(28.5 Kb)

There was a relationship between levels of overall life satisfaction and satisfaction with health. About 90% of those who were relatively satisfied with their health were also satisfied with their life compared to about 44% of those who were relatively dissatisfied with their health. (**Figure 2**).

Figure 2: Relative satisfaction with life overall (1): by level of satisfaction with health (2), 2010–11

United Kingdom

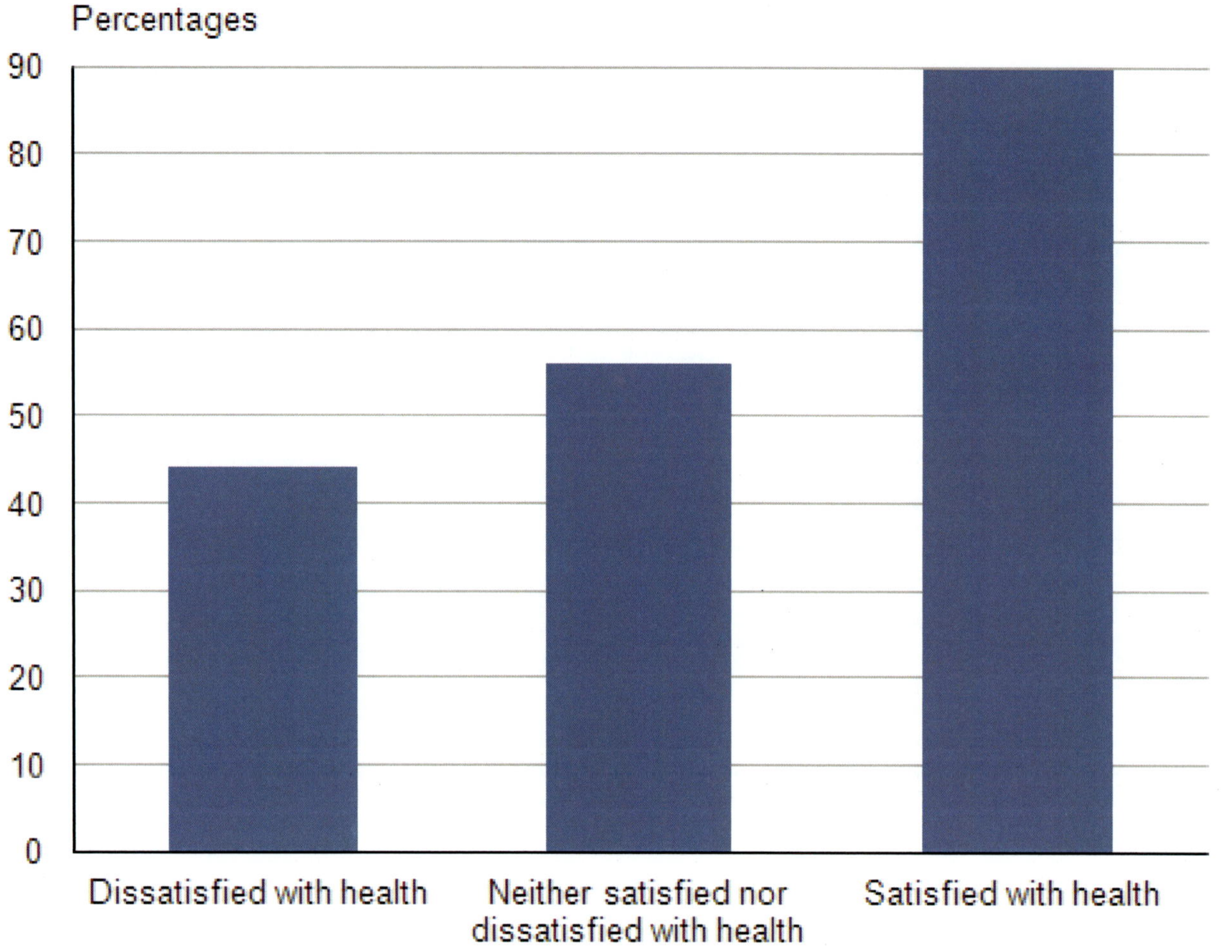

Source: Understanding Society, Wave 2, 2010–11

Notes:

1. Respondents were asked 'How satisfied or dissatisfied you are with your life overall' and responded 'Completely satisfied' to 'Completely dissatisfied'
2. Respondents were asked 'How satisfied or dissatisfied you are with your health' and responded 'Completely satisfied' to 'Completely dissatisfied'

Download chart

XLS XLS format
(18 Kb)

Evidence of mental ill-health

Another current measure of national well-being is the percentage of those with some indication of anxiety and depression. This uses the General Health Questionnaire (GHQ) which asks respondents 12 questions about their recent feelings (for more details see section 'More about the General Health Questionnaire'). A high score on the GHQ indicates that the respondent may have a mild to moderate mental illness - the types of mental illness which might be indicated on this scale **do not** include severe mental disorder characterised by derangement of personality, loss of contact with reality or deterioration of normal social functioning.

Nearly 1 in 5 (19%) of people in the UK aged 16 and over had a GHQ score of four or more indicating some evidence of anxiety or depression with a higher percentage of women (21%) than men (16%). In 2010–11 there was variation by age: the lowest indication of anxiety or depression was in the youngest age group and highest in those aged 50 to 54, the percentage with a score of four or more reduces from the age of 55 with the lowest in the 65 to 69 age group, and then increases after the age of 70. In each age group a higher percentage of women than men have some indication of anxiety and depression **(Figure 3)**. The same distribution by age group is evident in earlier data from both the UKHLS and the British Household Panel Survey (BHPS).

Figure 3: Respondents with some indication of anxiety and depression (1), 2010–11

United Kingdom

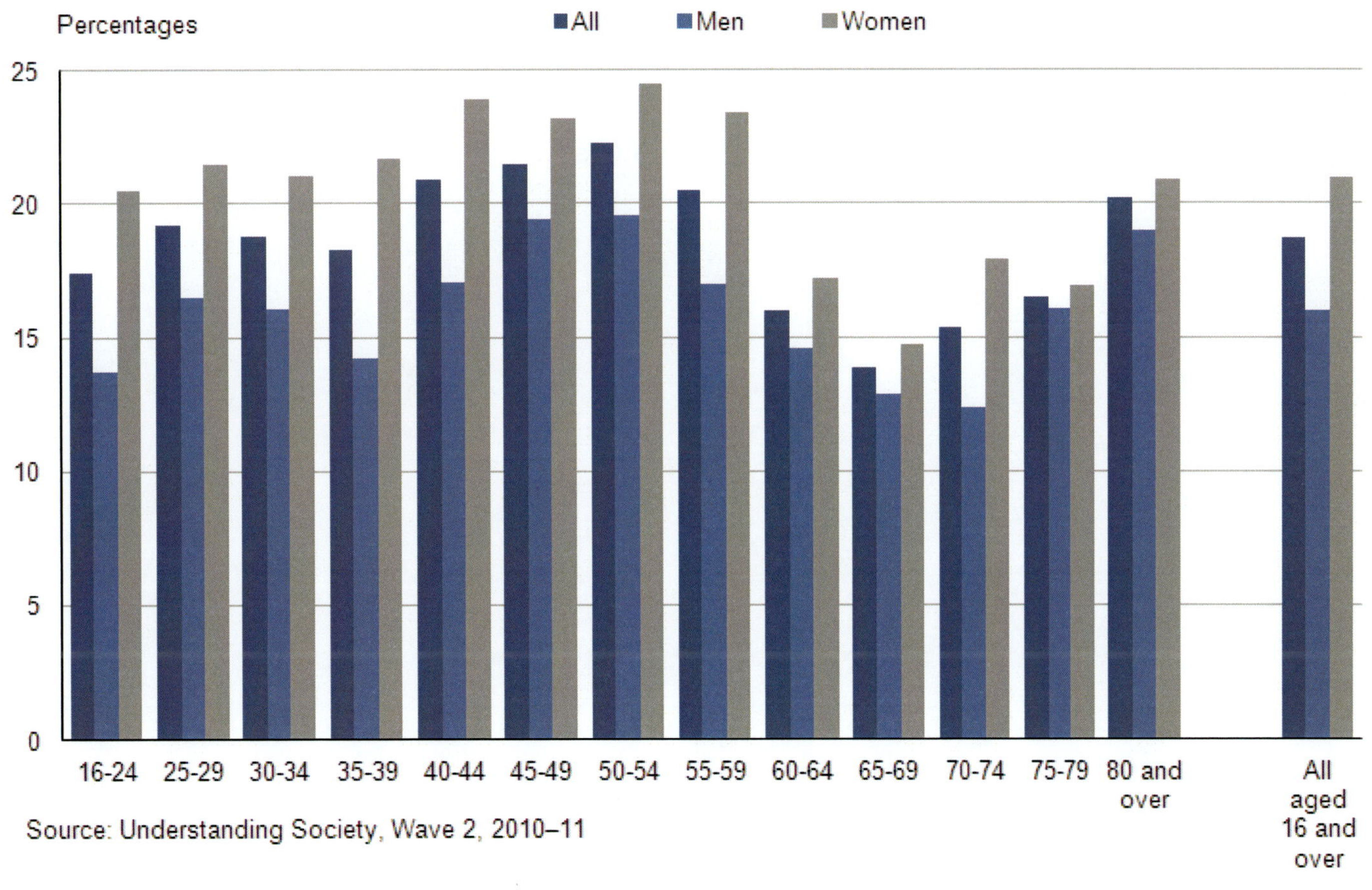

Source: Understanding Society, Wave 2, 2010–11

Notes:

1. For more information about questions used in the General Health Questionnaire, the responses and how the score for each individual is calculated see the section: More about the General Health Questionnaire

Download chart

XLS XLS format
(28 Kb)

The cross-government mental health outcomes strategy sets shared objectives to improve the mental health and well-being of people of all ages and to improve services for people with mental health problems. "Mental health is everyone's business – individuals, families, employers, educators and communities all need to play their part. Good mental health and resilience are fundamental to our physical health, our relationships, our education, our training, our work and to achieving our potential." (No Health Without Mental Health: a cross-government mental health outcomes strategy for people of all ages, 2011).

There are differences in mental ill health by characteristics of individuals as can be seen in **Table 1.** Of those who had some indication of mild to moderate mental ill health (GHQ score of 4-12):

- 27% were divorced or separated compared to 20% who were single, cohabiting or widowed and 16% who were married or in a civil partnership.
- A higher percentage were not in paid work (23%) compared to 15% in paid employment.
- 38% reported relative dissatisfaction with their health compared to 11% who were relatively satisfied with their health.
- 25% cared for someone else in their household compared to 17% who did not provide such care.
- 22% lived alone compared to 19% of all aged 16 and over.

Table 1: Respondents with some indication of anxiety and depression (1), 2010–11 (Percentages)

United Kingdom

		GHQ score (2)	
		0–3	4–12
All aged 16 and over		81	19
Marital status	Married or civil partnership	84	16
	Single	80	20
	Cohabiting	80	20
	Widowed	79	21
	Divorced/separated	73	27
Employment status	In paid work	85	15
	Not in paid work	77	23
Satisfaction with health	Completely, mostly or somewhat satisfied	89	11
	Neither satisfied or dissatisfied	78	22
	Completely, mostly or somewhat dissatisfied	62	38
Cares for elderly/sick/ disabled in household	Yes	75	25
	No	83	17
	Inapplicable as lives alone	78	22

Table notes:

1. For more information about questions used in the General Health Questionnaire, the reponses and how the score for each individual is calculated see the section: More about the General Health Questionnaire
2. A score of 4 to 12 indicates some symptoms of anxiety and depression

Download table

XLS [XLS format](#)
(29 Kb)

To find out more about the number of carers see: 2011 Census Analysis - Provision of Unpaid Care in England and Wales, 2011

Limitations in activities of daily living

Respondents to the UKHLS were also asked if their health limited moderate activities such as pushing a vacuum cleaner. About 28% of people aged 16 and over said that their health limited moderate activities a little or a lot. As would be expected this varied by age and increased from 13% of those aged 16 to 24 to 77% of those aged 80 and over. In each age group a higher percentage of women than men reported their daily activities were limited a little or a lot (**Figure 4**).

Figure 4: Health limitations on moderate activities: by age group and sex (1), 2010–11

United Kingdom

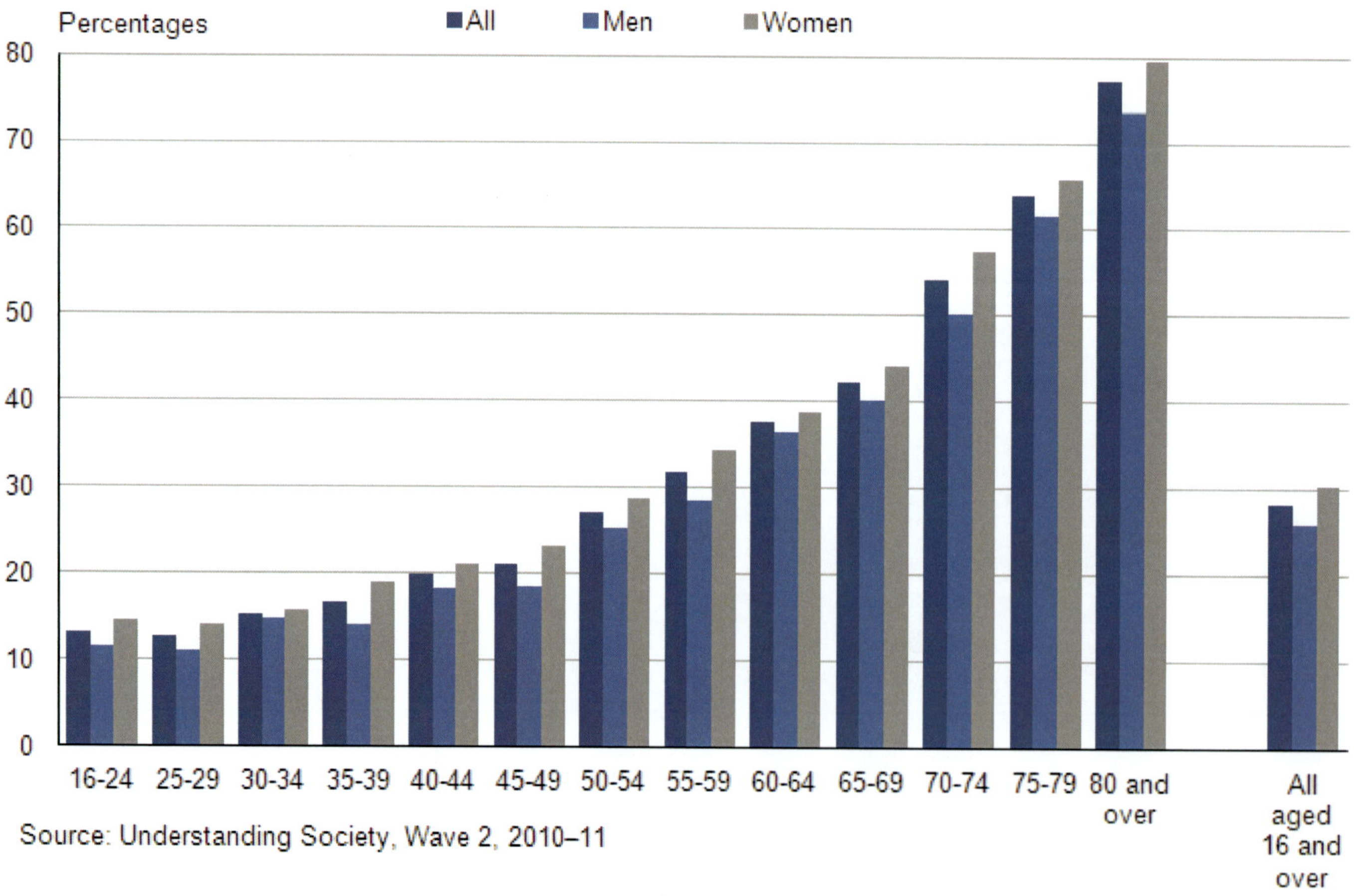

Source: Understanding Society, Wave 2, 2010–11

Notes:

1. Respondents were asked whether their health limited moderate activities such as moving a table, pushing a vacuum cleaner, bowling or playing golf. Responses were 'Yes - limited a lot', 'Yes, limited a little' or 'No, not limited at all'. For this analysis those who said either limited a lot or limited a little are aggregated

Download chart

XLS XLS format
(19 Kb)

Having anxiety and depression has been shown to be related to limitations in daily activities. An analysis of well-being and health related issues based on data from respondents to the English Longitudinal Study of Ageing showed that limitations in activities of daily living (ADL) were a major correlate of well-being as measured by elevated depressive symptoms in middle-aged and older people (Demakakos, McMunn and Steptoe, 2010). The differences in depressive symptoms associated with impaired ADL were among the greatest observed in this analysis irrespective of age.

Figure 5 shows the percentage of respondents with some evidence of anxiety or depression (a score of 4-12 in the GHQ) by their reported limitation in moderate activities. About 14% of those who reported no limitation showed some symptoms of anxiety or depression. This compares to 26% of those with a little limitation and nearly 41% of those who reported a lot of limitation.

Figure 5: Showing symptoms of anxiety and depression (1): by level of limitation of moderate activities (2), 2010–11

United Kingdom

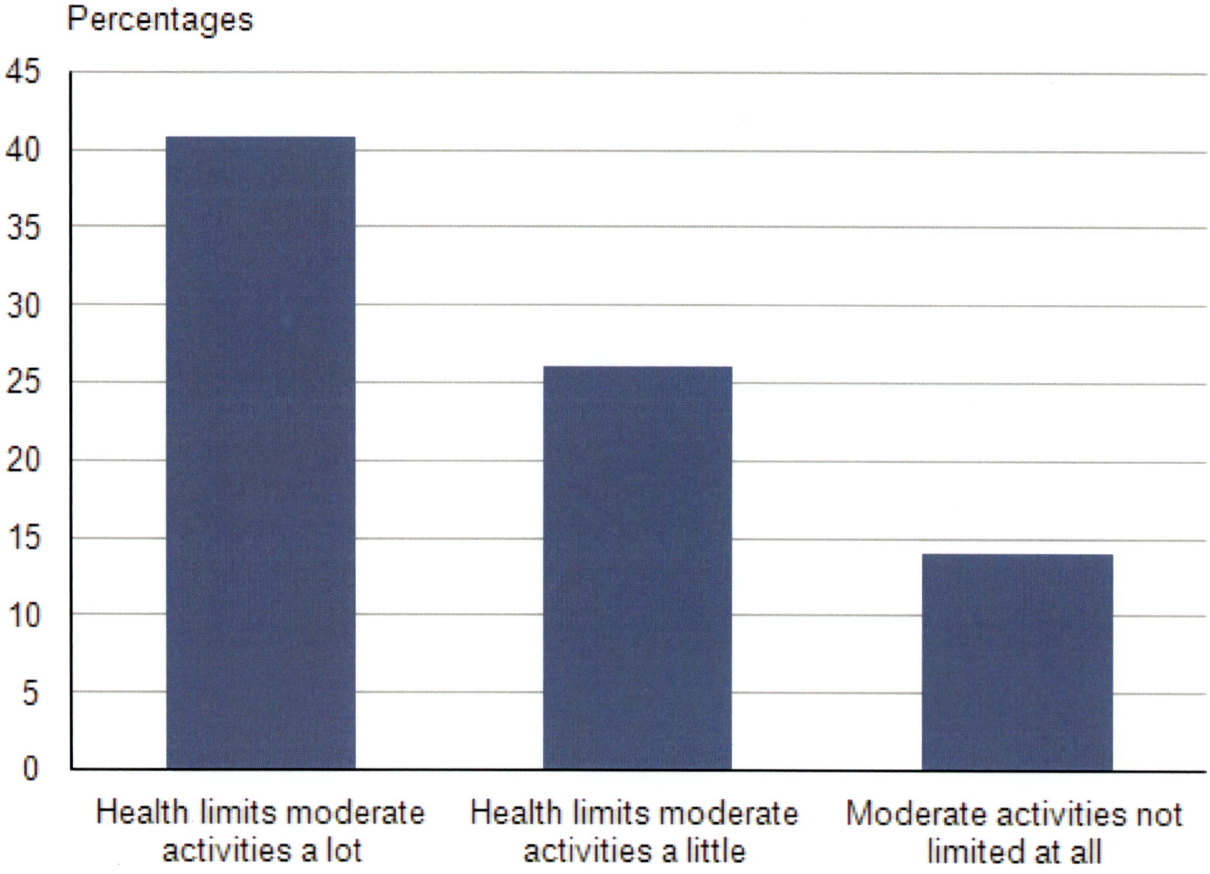

Source: Understanding Society, Wave 2, 2010–11

Notes:

1. For more information about the questions used in the General Health Questionnaire, the responses and how the score for each individual is calculated see the section: More About General Health Questionnaire
2. Respondents were asked whether their health limited moderate activities such as moving a table, pushing a vacuum cleaner, bowling or playing golf. Responses were 'Yes – limited a lot, 'Yes, limited a little' or 'No, not limited at all'. For this analysis those who said either limited a lot or limited a little are aggregated

Download chart

XLS XLS format
(19 Kb)

About the ONS Measuring National Well-being Programme

NWB logo 2

This article is published as part of the ONS Measuring National Well-being Programme.

The programme aims to produce accepted and trusted measures of the well-being of the nation - how the UK as a whole is doing.

Measuring National Well-being is about looking at 'GDP and beyond'. It includes headline indicators in areas such as health, relationships, job satisfaction, economic security, education, environmental conditions and measures of 'subjective well-being' (individuals' assessment of their own well-being).

Find out more on the Measuring National Well-being website pages.

About Understanding Society, the UK Household Longitudinal Study

Understanding Society is a unique and valuable academic study that captures important information every year about the social and economic circumstances and attitudes of people living in 40,000 UK households. It also collects additional health information from around 20,000 of the people who take part.

Information from the longitudinal survey is primarily used by academics, researchers and policy makers in their work, but the findings are of interest to a much wider group of people including those working in the third sector, health practitioners, business, the media and the general public.

Key facts

- 40,000 households – 2,640 postcode sectors in England, Scotland and Wales – 2,400 addresses from Northern Ireland.
- £48.9 million funding (until 2015).
- Approximately 3 billion data points of information.
- Innovation Panel of 1,500 respondents.
- Participants aged 10 and older.
- Building on 18 years of British Household Panel Survey.
- 35 to 60 minutes: the average time to complete each face to face interview.

How does it work

Interviews began in 2009 with all eligible members of the selected households.

- Adults are interviewed every 12 months either face to face or over the phone using Computer Assisted Interviewing.
- 10 to 15 year olds fill in a paper self-completion questionnaire.

From 2010 some 20,000 participants aged over 16 also received nurse visits and provided a blood sample and some basic physical measurements (height, weight, blood pressure, grip strength).

Wave 2 field work occured in 2010–11

Data used in this analysis

The data in this analysis is from the adult self completion questionnaire of Wave 2 of the Survey and has been weighted using the interview with self completion individual cross-sectional weight (a_indscus_xw).

For more information about the UKHLS see Understanding Society

More about the General Health Questionnaire

The GHQ asks 12 questions regarding the way an individual has been feeling over the last few weeks with responses which vary with the question. The areas which are covered are:

- concentration on whatever you are doing.
- loss of sleep over worry.
- feeling that you are playing a useful part in things.
- feeling capable of making decisions.
- feeling constantly under strain.
- feeling that you can overcome your difficulties.
- being able to enjoy your day-to-day activities.
- being able to face up to problems.
- feeling unhappy or depressed.
- losing confidence in yourself.
- thinking of yourself as a worthless person.
- feeling reasonably happy all things considered.

Each of the answers for a question is then scored as 0 for the two most positive responses and 1 for the two least positive responses **(Table 2)**.

Table 2: Example of scoring a question

Question	Response	Score
Have you recently been losing confidence in yourself?	Not at all	0
	Not more than usual	0
	Rather more than usual	1
	Much more than usual	1

Table notes:

1. Respondents were asked to only tick one answer

Download table

XLS XLS format
(28.5 Kb)

Once all 12 questions are scored, these scores are added so that each individual has a score which ranges from 0 to 12. A score of four or more has been shown to indicate that the individual has symptoms of mild to moderate illness such as anxiety or depression. The types of mental illness which might be indicated by a high score on this scale **do not** include severe mental disorder characterised by derangement of personality, loss of contact with reality or deterioration of normal social functioning – these are known as psychoses.

Background notes

1. Details of the policy governing the release of new data are available by visiting www.statisticsauthority.gov.uk/assessment/code-of-practice/index.html or from the Media Relations Office email: media.relations@ons.gsi.gov.uk

Copyright

References

1. Demakakos, P., McMunn, A. & Steptoe, A., (2010). Well-being in older age: a multidimensional perspective. In Financial circumstances, health and well-being of the older population in England: ELSA 2008 (Wave 4). ISBN: 978-1-903274-80-4. Institute for Fiscal Studies, October 2010. Accessed at http://www.ifs.org.uk/ELSA/reportWave4

2. No Health Without Mental Health: a cross-government mental health outcomes strategy for people of all ages, 2011. Accessed at: https://www.gov.uk/government/uploads/system/uploads/attachment_data/file/135457/dh_124058.pdf.pdf

3. ONS (2012) National Well-being interactive wheel of measures. Accessed at National Well-being interactive wheel of measures [Adobe Flash]

4. University of Essex, Institute for Social and Economic Research and National Centre for Social Research, *Understanding Society: Wave 1-2, 2009-2011* [computer file]. 4th *Edition*. Colchester, Essex: UK Data Archive [distributor], December 2012. SN: 6614, http://dx.doi.org/10.5255/UKDA-SN-6614-4.

5. World Health Organisation (1946): definition of health, International Health Conference, New York, 19-22 June, 1946 . Accessed at http://www.who.int/about/definition/en/print.html

Valuing Informal Adultcare in the UK

Author Name(s): **Rosemary Foster and Valerie Fender, Office for National Statistics**

Abstract

This article reports on the measurement and valuation of informal adult care. Informal adult care is an output of household production – the unpaid goods and services produced by households for themselves. Household production includes any non-formal care of those aged over 16, this could include care given by household members, relatives or neighbours. This article looks at those being cared for (the number of adults looked after, differentiated by the type and frequency of the care that they receive), rather than the carers. It is the second in a series of articles to update the full Household Satellite Account (HHSA) for the UK. The methodology remains under development and any estimates reported here, or in forthcoming publications, should be considered experimental and interpreted with caution.

Key Points

- The number of adults receiving informal care in the UK remained broadly stable between 2000 and 2010 at just over 2 million people
- The total number of hours of informal adult care received increased by 2.4 billion hours between 1995 and 2010
- Between 2000 and 2010, the number of adults receiving informal continuous care has grown, while those receiving less frequent care has fallen
- In 2010 the value of informal adult care in the UK was £61.7 billion, this is equivalent to 4.2% of GDP
- The total value of informal adult care in the UK has almost tripled in 15 years, from £21.5 billion in 1995 to £61.7 billion in 2010

Introduction to the Household Satellite Account (HHSA)

In 2002 the Office for National Statistics (ONS) published the first Household Satellite Account (HHSA) for the UK, which measured and valued the unpaid goods and services produced by households (ONS, 2002; Holloway, Short & Tamplin, 2002).

Following the publication of the Report by the Commission for the Measurement of Economic Performance and Social Progress (2009), there has been fresh interest in valuing household production. As such, as part of the Measuring National Well-being programme, ONS is currently updating the HHSA which measures household production in the UK. The value of informal adult care is the second of the eight HHSA modules to be updated.

Household production is all unpaid goods and services produced by households in the UK. Conventional National Accounts measurements, such as GDP, do not fully take into account these goods and services. However, if these goods and services are paid for they are included as part of the National Accounts. For example, if I were to iron my own clothes this service would not be included, however if I were to pay someone to do it for me it would.

The HHSA provides a means by which the influence of changing patterns of unpaid work on the economy can be measured. The information will also be of use to policy makers who need to take significant amounts of unpaid work into account.

This work falls outside the scope of the UK National Accounts. This is because the inclusion of all activity which is productive (in the economic sense) but which does not have a monetary value would swamp the monetary flows, obscure what is happening in the markets, and reduce the usefulness of National Accounts data for analysis. HHSA is therefore separate from, but conceptually consistent with, the UK National Accounts.

The HHSA extends the National Accounts boundary to include all activity that could be delegated to another person. This activity is divided into several principal functions; providing housing, transport, nutrition, clothing, laundry services, adult care, child care and voluntary work. The approach being taken by the ONS is to focus on the outputs of these principal functions.

The methodology remains under development and any estimates reported here, or in forthcoming publications, should be considered experimental and interpreted with caution. ONS welcomes comments and feedback on all aspects of the methodology used and the assumptions made, and seek suggestions for further/alternative data sources. A more detailed description of the methodology can be found in the appendices of this article.

What is informal adult care?

As most of the adult care carried out by household members or their networks (family members or neighbours) could be delegated to another person, it is deemed to be part of the productive role of households.

Informal adult care is defined in the HHSA as any help received either from members of one's own household, or from members of other households. We shall refer to this group as informal carers. The HHSA does not aim to measure the help provided by members of voluntary organisations, as this will be recorded separately in our estimates households' voluntary activity.

The output of adult care is therefore the number of adults (individuals aged 16 and over) receiving informal care in the UK. There must be some adjustment for the amount, quality and regularity of the care given for it to be relevant to the HHSA. The type of care varies from specialised care, such as lifting or changing dressings, to "keeping an eye" on someone or doing their shopping. The amount of care received also varies from a visit once a week to continuous care. As the cost of providing 24 hour nursing care for an elderly person is very different from the cost of providing a meal once a day or doing the shopping for an elderly neighbour once a week, it is clear why the data needs to be sufficiently adjusted to enable valuation using the market rate of an equivalent service. A full account of the methodology can be found in the appendices of this article.

The output of informal care is therefore the number of adults looked after, differentiated by the type and frequency of the informal care that they receive.

Notes

1. In the HHSA voluntary activity is defined as unpaid work undertaken for or on behalf of an organisation or group which benefits other people or the environment

People receiving informal adult care

The number of adults receiving informal care in the UK has remained relatively stable since 2000 at around 2 million, following a period of growth between 1995 and 2000 (Chart 1). In spite of this the total number of hours of informal care received has increased, and was up by 2.4 billion hours in 2010 when compared with 1995.

Chart 1: Total number of adults and hours 1995-2010

United Kingdom

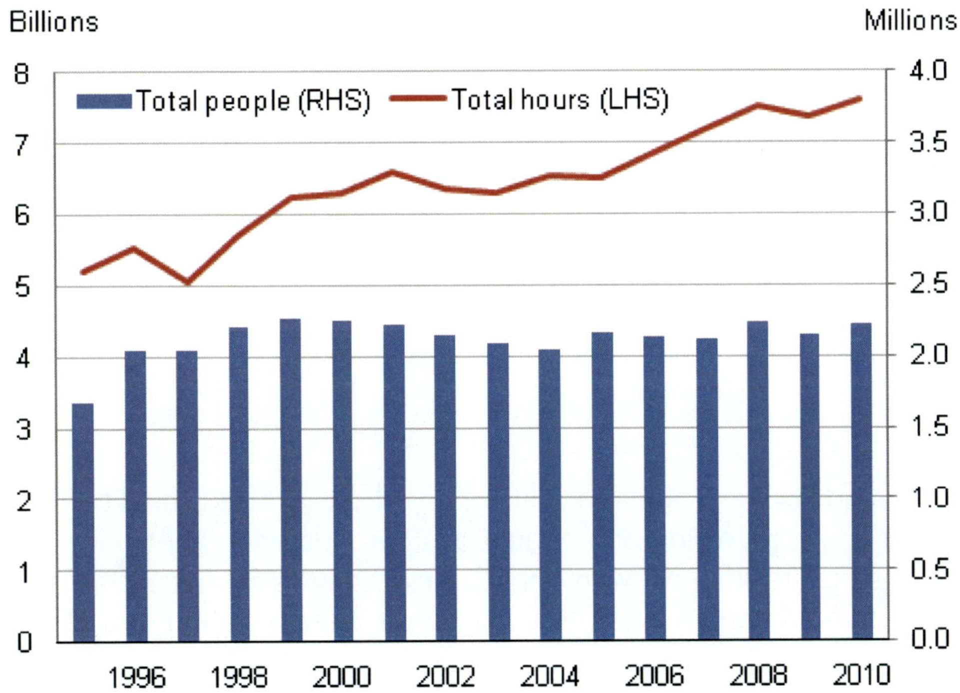

Source: Family Resources Survey - Office for National Statistics, Work and Pensions

Download chart

XLS XLS format
(28 Kb)

The divergence between the growth in the number of adults receiving care and the number of hours they receive can be explained by changes in the frequency of care over the period. Chart 2 shows the growth in the number of people receiving informal continuous care relative to non-continuous care. Continuous care is classified in this case as full-time care given by a household member.

Chart 2: Number of adults receiving care by frequency

United Kingdom

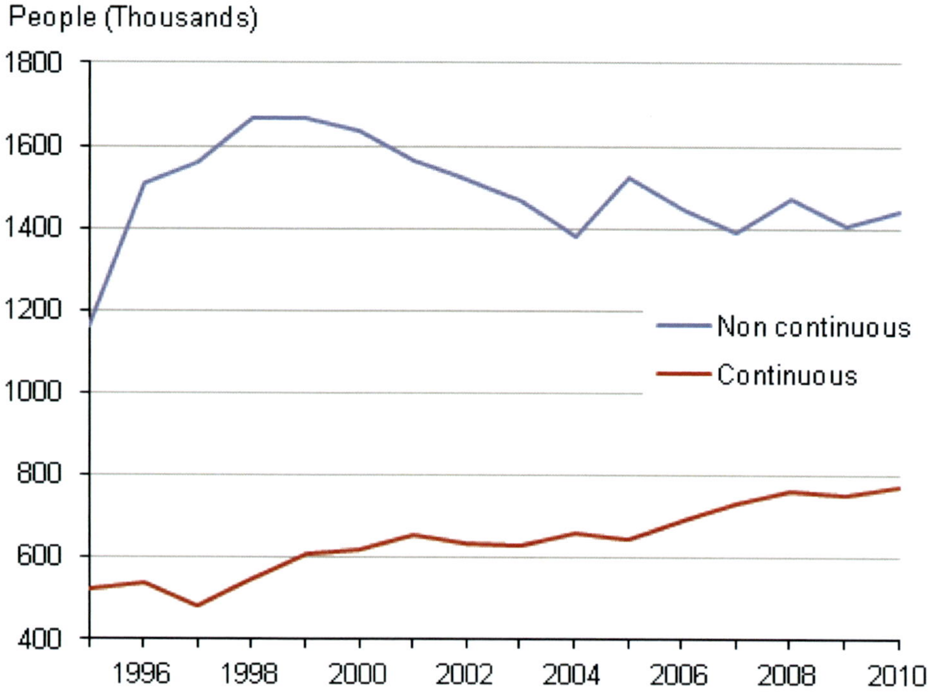

Source: Family Resources Survey - Office for National Statistics, Work and Pensions

Download chart

XLS XLS format
(27.5 Kb)

Between 1995 and 2010, the number of adults receiving informal continuous care has grown by 252,000. In comparison, the number of adults receiving non-continuous care increased between 1995 and 2000, but has since fallen from 1.6 million to 1.4 million. Chart 2 shows that despite this fall the number of adults receiving non-continuous care is much higher than those in need of continuous care.

This has resulted in a change in the proportion of informal adult care which can be attributed to each frequency between 2000 and 2010 (Chart 3). In line with the trend in Chart 2, continuous care accounts for a greater proportion of total care in 2010 than 2000. None of the other frequencies have seen a rise in their share of total care. In 2000 approximately 1 in 4 people that were receiving care were being looked after continuously (27%), a similar proportion to those receiving care several times a week. In 2010, the number of people receiving continuous care had increased to approximately 1 in 3 (35%). That increase is equivalent to over a billion hours of informal care.

Chart 3: Proportion of people receiving care by frequency - 2000 and 2010

United Kingdom

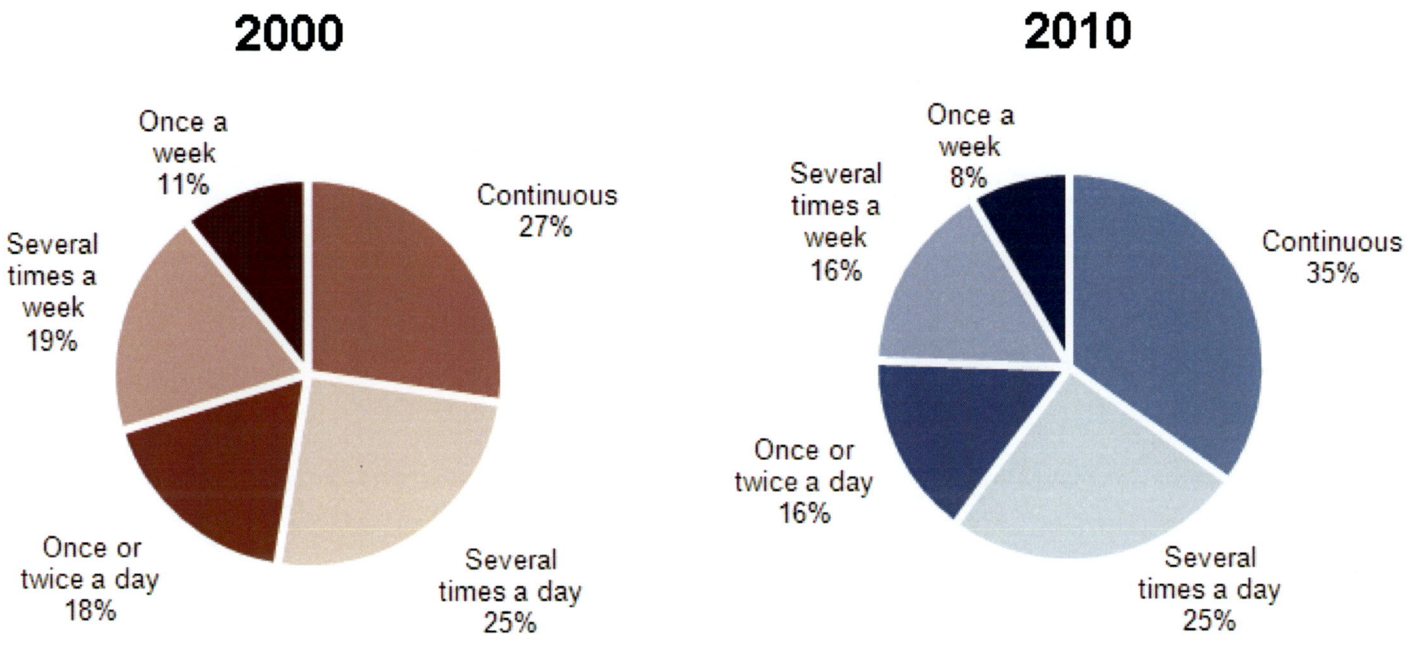

Source: Family Resources Survey - Office for National Statistics, Work and Pensions

Download chart

XLS XLS format
(28 Kb)

This change in the proportions could be as a result of either relatively stronger growth in continuous care or a decline in demand for the other frequencies of care. Therefore it is important to look at the number of people being looked after by the frequency. Chart 4 shows that the growth in continuous care is supported by movement away from less frequent care - the number of people receiving less frequent care has decreased, rather than just experiencing low growth in comparison to continuous care.

Chart 4: Number of people receiving care by frequency - 1995-2010

United Kingdom

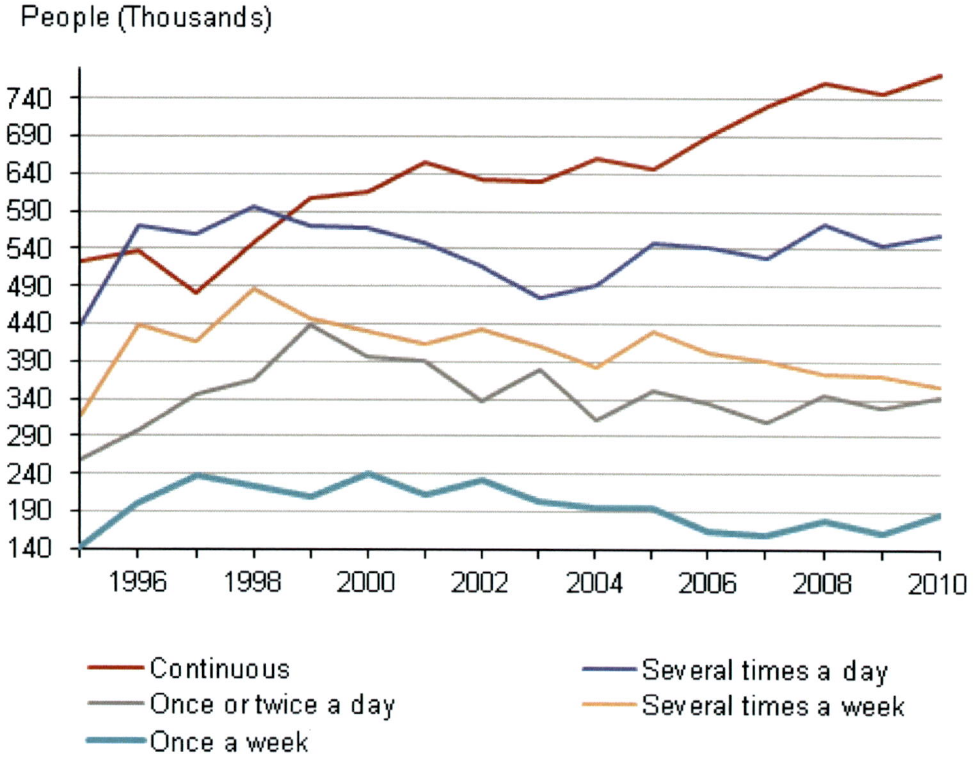

Source: Family Resources Survey - Office for National Statistics, Work and Pensions

Download chart

XLS XLS format
(27 Kb)

The UK population has grown over the decade and in 2010 was 6% bigger than in 2000. As the UK population has increased, the proportion of the adults receiving care has gone down. Chart 5 shows how the number adults receiving informal care has changed, and 2010 stood at 4.4% of the adult population. However the chart also shows that even though the number of adults has increased, the proportion of UK adults receiving continuous care has gone up.

Chart 5: Proportion of UK adults receiving care by frequency - 1995-2010

United Kingdom

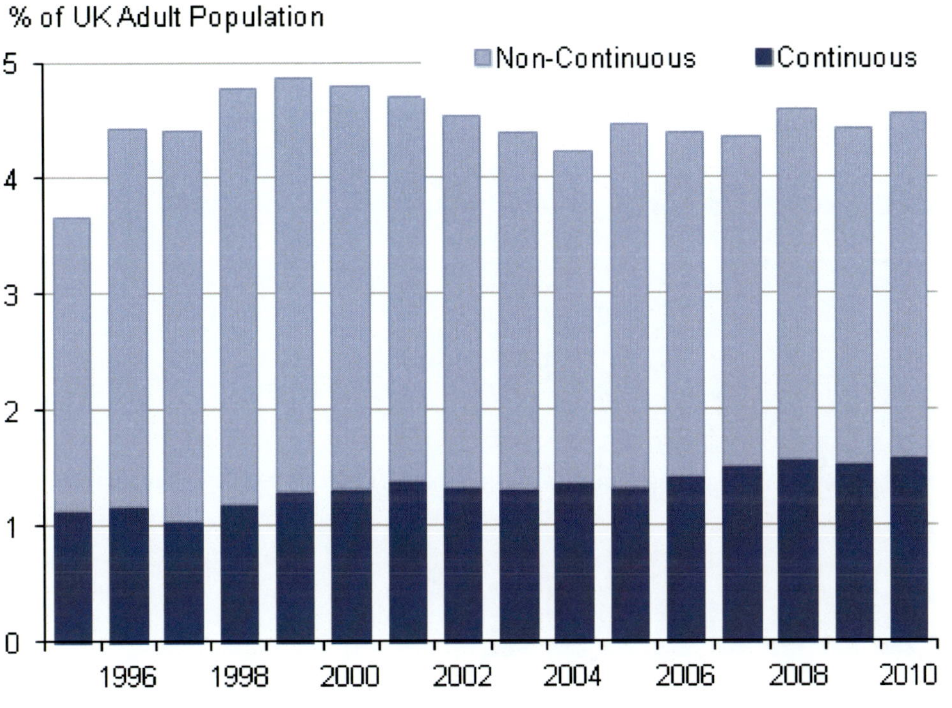

Source: Family Resources Survey - Office for National Statistics, Work and Pensions

Download chart

XLS XLS format
(26.5 Kb)

Those receiving informal care by age

The population of the UK is ageing: the number of adults has grown relative to the population as a whole and four in every five people in the UK are now adults. This can be seen in Chart 6 as the population share of the older three age groups increases over the period.

Chart 6: Adult population change by age group - 1995-2010

United Kingdom

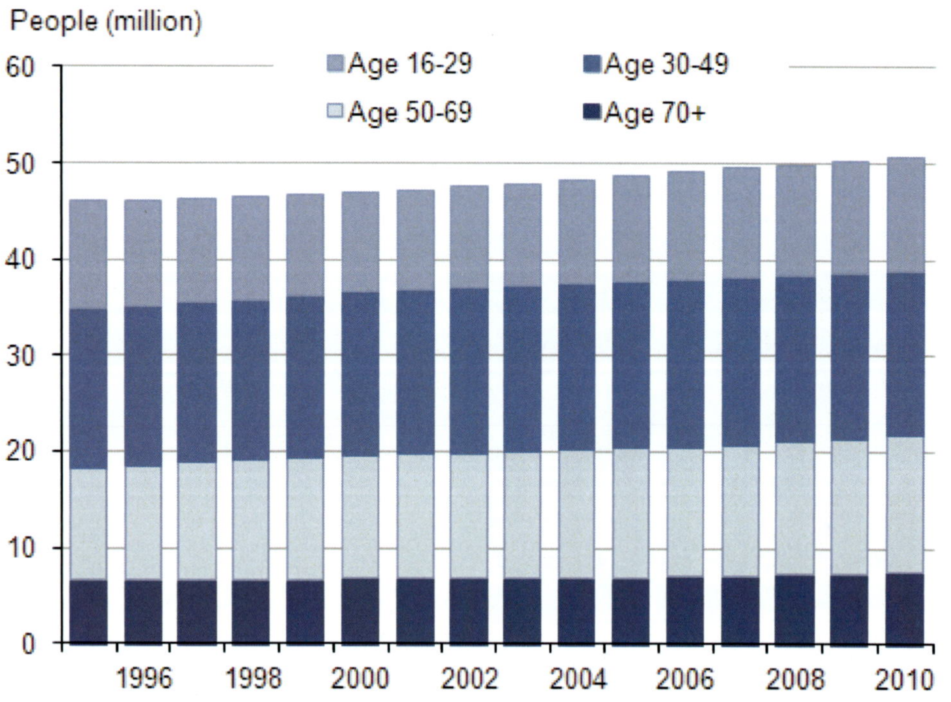

Source: Family Resources Survey - Office for National Statistics, Work and Pensions

Download chart

XLS XLS format
(36 Kb)

An aging population is likely to have an impact on adult care, as those who are over 70 years old make up just under half of all of those receiving informal adult care in the UK (Chart 7). It is not surprising that the over 70s receive the most care, however it is interesting to see that the same group's share of care has not increased as their share of the population has increased.

Chart 7: Adults receiving care by age group - 1995-2010

United Kingdom

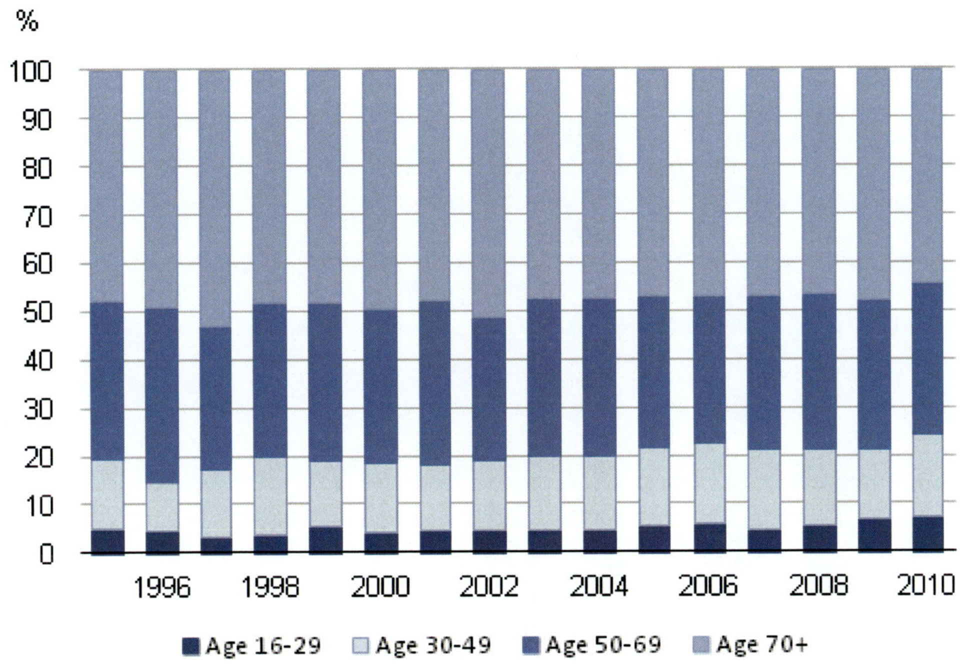

Source: Family Resources Survey - Office for National Statistics, Work and Pensions

Download chart

XLS XLS format
(36 Kb)

Chart 8 shows the split between continuous and non-continuous care, for all four age groups, between 1995 and 2010. The resulting chart shows that as the age of the group increases, the share of their care that is non-continuous also increases.

In 1995 approximately two in three people receiving care between the ages of 16 and 29 needed continuous care. This has fallen to just over half in 2010. In comparison, the proportion of those in the over 70s age group that receive continuous care has risen.

Chart 8: Adult care by age group and frequency - 1995-2010

United Kingdom

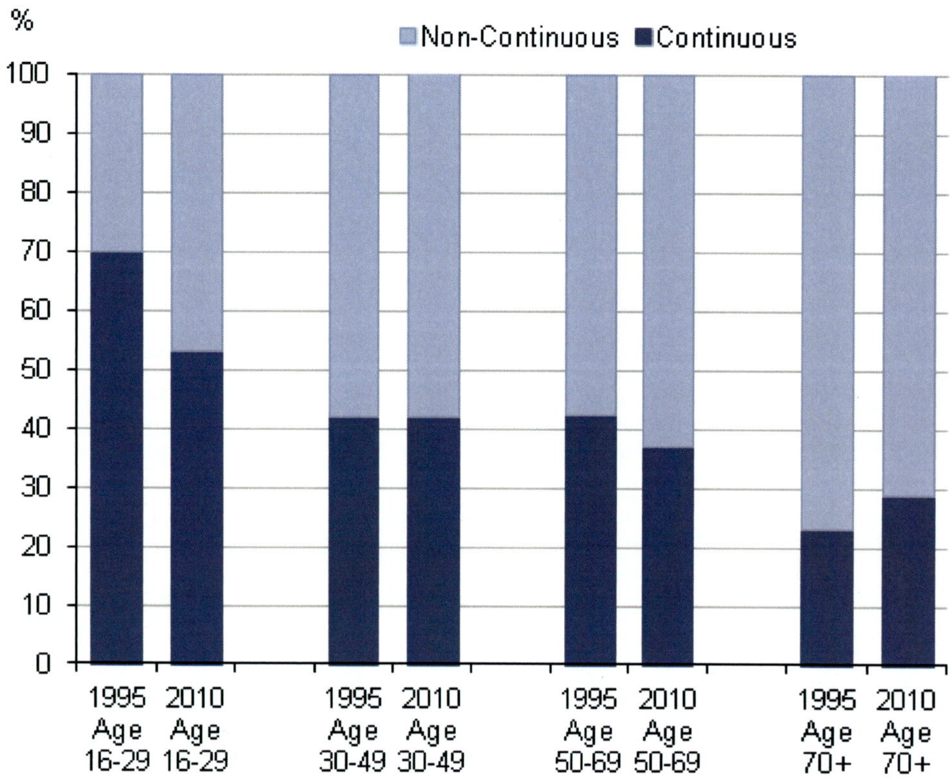

Source: Family Resources Survey - Office for National Statistics, Work and Pensions

Download chart

XLS [XLS format](#)
(36 Kb)

Hours of informal care

Having considered the number of people receiving care, we will now turn to look at the number of hours of care that are received. The total number of hours of informal care received has increased and, as shown by Chart 1, was up by 2.4 billion hours in 2010 when compared with 1995.

As continuous care counts for 168 hours per week (24 hours a day multiplied by 7 days), movements in the number of people receiving continuous care can have huge effects on the number of hours of informal care received. This is clear in Chart 9, which shows the proportion of total care hours that can be attributed to each frequency. Continuous care makes up 89% of total hours of informal care in the UK in 2010.

Chart 9: Total hours of care by frequency - 2010

United Kingdom

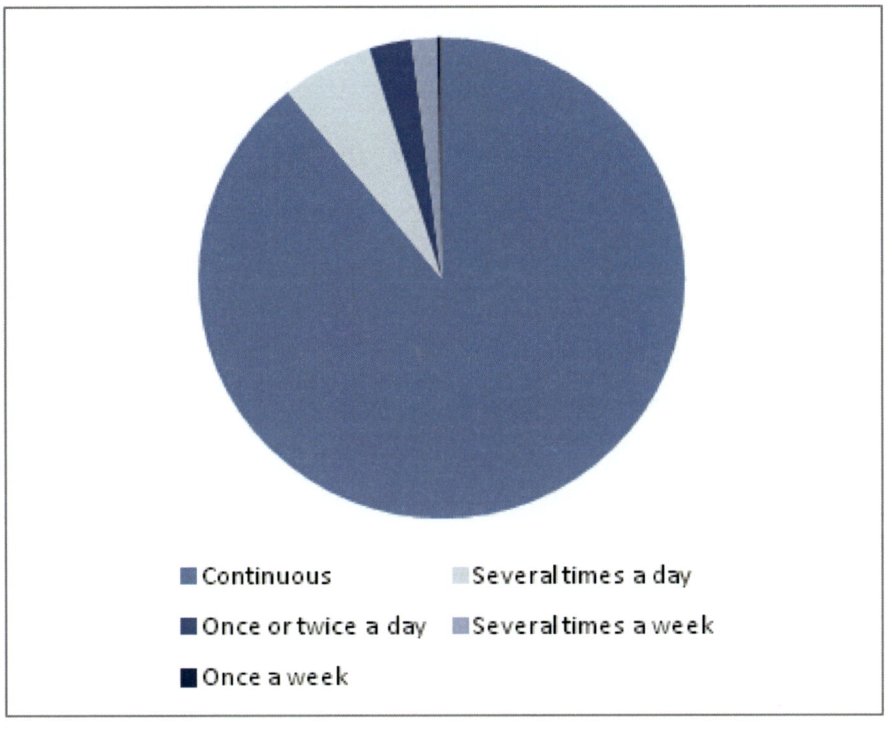

Source: Family Resources Survey - Office for National Statistics, Work and Pensions

Download chart

XLS XLS format
(28 Kb)

Chart 10 shows the total number of hours of care received by adults in the UK split into non-continuous and continuous care from 1995 to 2010. This spilt shows that the change in total hours has followed the rise in continuous care hours. Non-continuous care hours have remained low in comparison, at just under 1 billion hours for the whole period. It is clear that continuous care has seen the most change over the period and that this change has had the greatest affect on total care.

Chart 10: Total hours of care by frequency - 1995-2010

United Kingdom

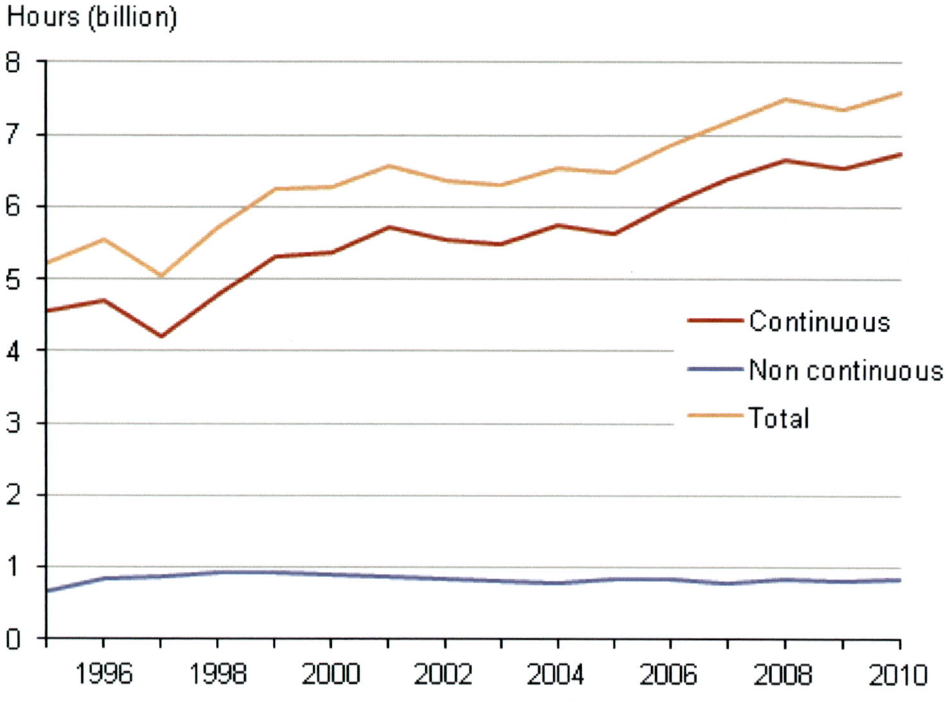

Source: Family Resources Survey - Office for National Statistics, Work and Pensions

Download chart

XLS XLS format
(26.5 Kb)

Notes

1. HHSA assumes that any household member caring for an adult 112 hours a week is also passively caring for that adult, so the hours are made up to 168. See methodology section for further details.

Value of informal adult care

We value informal adult hours using the wage rate for an equivalent service – how much it would cost if you had to employ someone else to do it for you. This differs between personal and practical care, and the frequency of care. For a full explanation of the valuation method used, please see the methodology section of the paper.

In 1995 the total value of UK adult care was £21.5 billion, or equivalent to 2.9% of GDP. This has almost tripled over 15 years: taking the value to £61.7 billion or the equivalent of 4.2% of GDP.

Chart 11 shows growth in both the hours and the value of informal adult care from 1995 to 2010. Both hours and the value follow an upward trend over the 15 years, however the total value of UK adult care has grown at a faster rate than total hours.

Chart 11: Total hours received and valuation of informal adult care - 1995-2010

United Kingdom

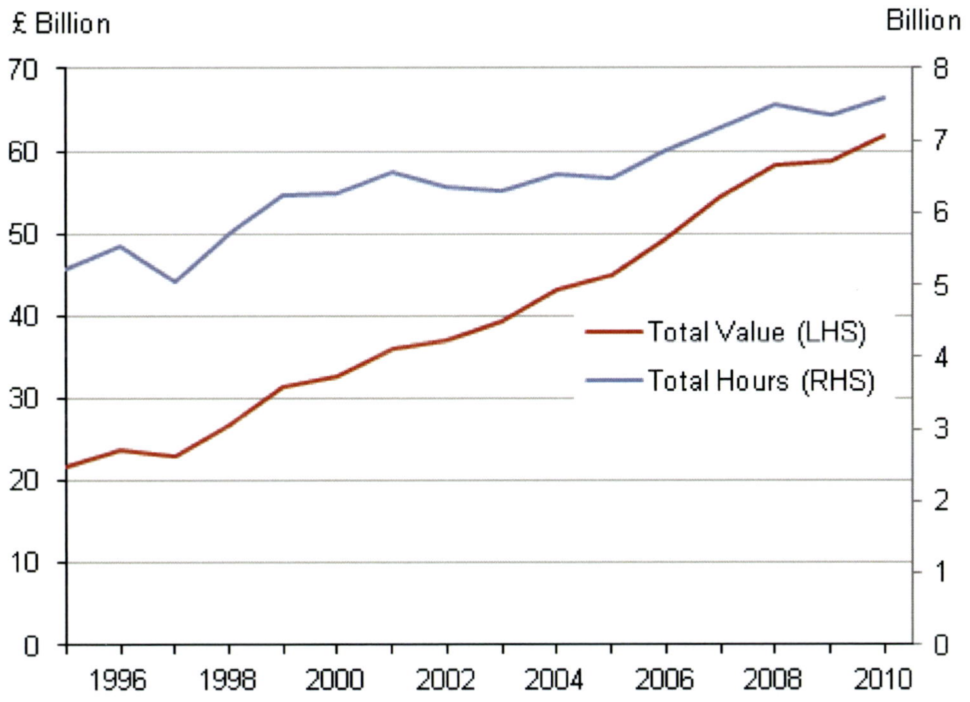

Source: Family Resources Survey - Office for National Statistics, Work and Pensions

Download chart

XLS XLS format
(28 Kb)

This indicates that while the growth in the value of UK adult care can be partially attributed to the increase in hours, it is also as a result of increases in the cost of UK adult care over the period.

Annex 1: Methodology

The main data source used for the estimation of informal adult care is the Family Resource Survey (FRS) (commissioned by the Department for Work and Pensions, DWP) which collects information on the number of adults receiving care and whether this care is on a weekly, daily or continuous basis. The FRS is currently the best data source available for the estimation of the household production of adult care, but is known to underestimate the number of adults receiving care.

The FRS defines adults as the members of the population who are over 16 years of age and care as all help or assistance given to others because of physical or mental need. It ranges from odd jobs e.g. helping an elderly neighbour/relative with shopping or gardening, to full-time nursing care of the sick, disabled or elderly.

The questions provide information on the number of adults receiving help and give the respondent's perception of the help received. This perception may include active care (direct interaction or supervision) or passive care (i.e. available on call if needed).

The total number of adults receiving help includes those who are helped by people working for organisations, e.g. visiting social workers, nurses, specialist teachers and volunteers. For simplicity, we will refer to this group as formal carers. For HHSA purposes, we exclude any episodes of care which are provided by formal carers. For this reason our estimates will differ from those published in the FRS report, which give an overall valuation of care.

We can also identify the number of cases where an adult is helped exclusively formally or informally. In the cases were there is only informal care, people tend to be helped by spouses, their children, neighbours, friends and other relatives. These cases are valued by our estimates, whereas the cases that are exclusively formal care are not.

However, there are cases where an adult receives both formal and informal care. In some cases an adult is being cared for by an outside helper and the informal carer is supplementing this help, e.g. an adult may be attending a day care home for the majority of the day and receive informal help from a neighbour when they get home. In other cases an adult could be predominantly cared for by a household member, but could receive more specialised care, such as changing a dressing etc, from an outside helper. For the HHSA it is important that we include all adults who are helped by an informal carer, even if they are also receiving help from a formal care provider. In order to include these cases, we need to adjust the type and length of the help received. This will enable estimation the help from informal carers only.

Frequency of help received

For valuation purposes we need to differentiate between continuous and less frequent episodes of care, as these are associated with different market rates. Using the FRS, we have some information on how often the adult receives help. The frequencies are broken down into the following categories:

1. Continuously
2. Several times a day
3. Several times a week
4. Once or twice a week
5. Once a week

However, this is dependent on the respondent’s perception of what constitutes each frequency type.

The equivalent market price of informal care is based on an hourly rate rather than on an episode of care or an independent measure of the output, e.g. bathing an elderly person. Therefore we have had to make an assumption about the approximate the number of hours in each episode of care.

Estimating the number of hours in each frequency type

To estimate the number of hours that correspond to each frequency, we examined the cases where an adult is helped by informal carers only. When we examined the hours of help given and the frequency of help received, there was a considerable range in the total number of hours helped and the frequency type. This suggests a difference in respondents' perception of frequency. This can be accounted for by the fact that frequencies are undefined and that no distinction is made in the question between active and passive care. The modal number of hours was used to approximate the number of hours, which correspond to each frequency. Sensitivity tests have been calculated to see the effect of using the mean number of hours for each frequency. The discrepancy between reported care given and care received is not ideal for creating relevant and reliable estimates. Our experimental statistics are attempting to create estimates to gauge the magnitude of the value of informal adult care.

Measuring passive care

In the HHSA we define productive activity as anything that could be delegated to another person - the "third party criterion" developed by Margaret Reid (1934). The important point is that if no unpaid carer were available, someone would have to be paid to take his or her place. We should therefore measure passive as well as active care wherever possible. This could just be keeping an eye on an elderly parent, or being available to help during the night.

In the FRS, an adult has the option of reporting that they receive continuous care. We assume this is 168 hours per week: 24 hours a day multiplied by 7 days.

There are cases where an adult reports that they need continuous help (active plus passive care), but the total number of hours of help given by informal carers is only a few hours a week (active care only). Similarly, there are cases where a helper reports giving care 168 hours a week (active and passive care), yet the frequency of help received is reported as several times a week (active care only).

In order to include passive care, whether it is reported or not, we have re-coded the frequency of help received. This now includes not only those cases where the recipient records a need for continuous care, but also those cases where at least one household member gives more than 112 hours a week (or 100 hours a week in the later years of the estimates due to changes in the FRS questionnaire). Our underlying assumption is that, if a household member is caring for an adult 16 hours a day (the average waking day), 7 days a week (112 hours) then they are also likely to be caring for the adult at night - even if this is passive care. This is not the case when the informal carer is not a member of the same household as the adult receiving care, in which case they must be giving 168 hours of care for it to be considered continuous.

Reclassifying the frequency of help received by those adults who have both formal and informal carers

All formal care needs to be excluded, whether provided by paid carers or by volunteers working on behalf of an organisation. We have information on the total number of hours of help given by just formal carers or informal carers and can exclude the number of hours given formally. We can use this estimate of informal hours of help given as a proxy for the frequency of help received. By using our earlier assumption about the number of hours which correspond to each frequency, we can then reclassify the frequency of help received.

There are limitations in this approach, as the number of hours of help given will not always correspond to the frequency of help received. This could be due to different perceptions of what constitutes care (passive or active), different perceptions of what constitutes each frequency type, two or more carers helping simultaneously or reporting errors in the survey itself. However, to reclassify this help an assumption has to be made about the relationship of the frequency of help received to the hours of help given.

In order to inform this assumption, we examined the cases where adults receive help only from informal carers and compared the total number of hours given by those carers with the reported frequency of help received. We calculated an average of the modal values of hours given corresponding to each frequency category. We used this in order to re-categorise the frequency of help received once formal care hours were excluded. As before, an adult is considered to be receiving continuous help only if 112 hours or more are given by one household member.

Examples of this reclassification follow. An adult may report they receive continuous help and a total of 168 hours of help are given. This could be provided equally by a volunteer and a relative. By removing the hours of help given by the volunteer, the total number of hours given by the relative is reduced to 84. This corresponds with the several times a day category, and so the frequency of help received is re-categorised. Similarly an adult could report they receive continuous help and a total of 132 hours are given. This could be provided by a spouse who gives 112 hours and a relative who gives 20 hours a week. Because one household member is giving 112 hours we assume that this person is receiving continuous care.

Other cases also need to be re-categorised. For example, an adult could receive 10 hours of help and report that the frequency of help is several times a week. If 8 of these 10 hours of help are provided by a district nurse, then we would re-categorise the frequency to once a week, as only 2 hours of help are being provided by an informal carer.

There are many cases where the number of hours given do not correspond to the frequency of help the person reports they receive. Only in the cases of re-categorising help received from both formal and informal carers do we use the number of hours giving help, rather than the reported frequency of help received.

Type of help received

For non-continuous care (several times a day, once or twice a day, several times a week, and once a week) it is important to distinguish between the types of help received, so that we can value the care at different appropriate market prices. Respondents are asked "what kind of things does [X] usually receive help with?", the responses include "getting into and out of bed" (physical help), "keeping an eye on them" (other physical help), and "giving medicines" (other personal help). Respondents are given a show card to help prompt their answers, and can respond with one or more of the following:

- Help with personal care e.g. dressing, bathing, washing, shaving, feeding, using the toilet
- Physical help e.g. walking, getting up and down the stairs getting into and out of bed
- Other sorts of personal help e.g. preparing meals, giving medicines change dressings
- Help with paperwork or financial matters e.g. writing letters dealing with bills handling money, banking filling in forms

- Other practical help e.g. shopping laundry housework gardening doing odd-jobs, taking out for a walk, keeping an eye on him/her

Due to small sample sizes in each category, we have reclassified this help into three categories:

- personal help (help with personal care, other sorts of personal help),
- practical help (physical help, help with paper work or financial matters and other practical help)
- both personal and practical help

Reclassifying the type of help received by those adults who have both formal and informal carers

Analysis shows formal and informal carers give different types of help. When adults are helped by informal carers only, approximately 60% receive both personal and practical help. In contrast, in cases where adults are helped by formal carers only, approximately 60% receive help with personal tasks only and only 30% with both personal and practical tasks. The proportion receiving help with practical tasks is similar in both cases. This seems to suggest that formal carers help more often with only one specific type of task, while informal carers provide are more likely to help with a range of activities.

The majority of adults who receive help from both formal and informal carers also are helped with both practical and personal tasks. However, it is hard to come to any conclusion about whether these adults use formal carers to support the help given by household members (e.g. an extra pair of hands to lift, bath etc.) or to provide additional, more specialised help. In cases where we have excluded the help by formal carers, adjustments have been made to the number of hours received using the gender of the individual and the frequency of care.

Grossing to the UK population

Data was not available on a UK basis before the end of 2002. Therefore we needed to gross the data for England, Scotland and Wales to account for Northern Ireland as well. A UK total allows the estimates to be consistent with the rest of the HHSA. Post 2002, the FRS includes Northern Ireland and therefore no grossing has been necessary.

Valuation

In order to value informal care, we need to use the cost of the nearest equivalent service provided by the market. As already noted it is important to try and encapsulate the different types of help received, taking into account how often the care is received and the type of care given.

Non-continuous personal care includes help with dressing, bathing, changing dressings and feeding. We have chosen the average wage of an assistant nurse or nursing auxiliary as the most appropriate market rate for valuing this care, as they would usually provide this type of specialised care outside the home.

For non-continuous practical care we have used the hourly rate of care assistants and attendants in health and related occupations. The wage rates used are median hourly wages from the Annual

Survey of Hours and Earnings. Data from this survey is not available for 1995 and 1996, so these figures have been imputed.

In 2002, the valuation of continuous care was estimated using the residential care weekly fee from the Care of Elderly People Market Survey 2001, conducted by Laing and Buisson. Given the experimental nature of the HHSA estimates published in 2002, the process of consultation remained ongoing. Following publication of the estimates, the use of this valuation approach for continuous care was reconsidered. Using the cost of a nursing home as a market equivalent ignores the economies of scale in a nursing home, which result in it not being a market equivalent to informal care at home. (Hirst, 2002) . In these estimates we have therefore used the same valuation technique as practical care, but for all 168 hours. This is considered to be a more appropriate market equivalent.

This has an impact on the magnitude of the value of informal care, and therefore we have conducted sensitivity analysis to show the difference.

Data Sources

Family Resources Survey

The FRS is a continuous survey that consults households in the UK using a stratified multi-stage probability sample. The questions and answers that we are interested in appear in the care module:

1. In some households, there are people who receive help or being looked after, for example because they are sick, disabled or elderly. Is there anyone in this household who receives any of these kinds of help or looking after? This could be from outside or anyone who lives here.

Yes / No

2. How frequently does (X) receive such help?

1 - Continuously

2 - Several times a day

3 - Once or twice a day

4 - Several times a week

5 - Once a week

6 - Less frequently

3. Who looks after, or provides help for (X)? Anyone else?

14 - Named person

15 - Relative

16 - Friend

17 - Helpers

4. About how many hours a week, on average does (name of helper) spend actually providing help for or looking after (X)?

Number of hours given.

5. What kind of things does (X) usually receive help with?

1. Personal care (dressing, bathing, washing, shaving, feeding, using the toilet)

2. Physical care (walking, getting into and out of bed, and getting up and down stairs)

3. Other sorts of personal care (preparing meals, giving medicines, changing dressings)

4. Help with paper works or financial matters (writing letters, dealing with bills, handling money, and banking)

5. Other practical help (shopping, laundry, housework, gardening, doing odd jobs, taking out for walks, visiting, talking to, keeping an eye on)

'Care of the Elderly: People Market Survey'

This is a postal survey 42 of all for-profit homes with 4 or more places in the UK. The homes were asked to give their minimum and maximum single and sharing fees for nursing and residential care. The average was calculated as the mean of the minimum and maximum fees, weighted by bed numbers. The response rate for 2000 was 24% of all for-profit homes. The residential rate was chosen because the services provided by a residential home involve daily help with personal and practical care, as well as being on call.

Annual Survey of Hours and Earnings

The Annual Survey of Hours and Earnings replaced the New Earnings Survey in 2004, and back dated the series using the new methodology to 1997. The Annual Survey of Hours and Earnings (ASHE) provides information about the levels, distribution and make-up of earnings and hours worked for employees in all industries and occupations. ASHE is based on a one per cent sample of employee jobs taken from HM Revenue & Customs (HMRC) PAYE records.

Annex 2: Sensitivity Analysis

The estimates of adult care are subject to a number of assumptions. This section of the article considers some alternatives to the assumptions made, and the resulting changes on the value of adult care.

Estimating the number of hours in each frequency type

As discussed in the methodology, the frequency of care that individuals receive is recategorised and then the modal number of hours for each frequency is applied to estimate the number of hours of informal care. Sensitivity tests have been calculated to see the effect of using the mean number of hours for each frequency (see table 1).

Table 1: Sensitivity to hours assumption

United Kingdom

£million

	Value using mode reported hours	Value using mean reported hours	% Difference
1995	21,520	23,829	10.7
1996	23,626	26,665	12.9
1997	22,943	26,154	14.0
1998	26,811	30,356	13.2
1999	31,377	35,069	11.8
2000	32,627	36,403	11.6
2001	36,086	39,938	10.7
2002	36,875	40,683	10.3
2003	39,375	43,149	9.6
2004	43,062	47,015	9.2
2005	45,028	49,599	10.2
2006	49,248	53,845	9.3
2007	54,362	59,059	8.6
2008	58,334	63,613	9.0
2009	58,736	63,948	8.9
2010	61,703	67,173	8.9

Table source: Office for National Statistics

Download table

XLS XLS format
(19 Kb)

This sensitivity analysis shows that using the mean reported hours rather than the modal reported hours results in a higher value of adult care for the UK in all years between 1995 and 2010. The extent of this difference varies from year-to-year, in 2000 using mean hours gave an estimate that was 11.6% higher.

Valuation

In the 2002 estimates, weekly residential home fees were used to value continuous care. After methodological consultation, the HHSA now uses the hourly wage of a care assistant, or home carer, to value the 168 hour week. Included below are the estimations for the value of informal adult care using the weekly cost of residential care. For this we use the average of all weekly residential care.

Table 2: Sensitivity to valuation approach

United Kingdom

£million

	Value using residential care	Value using wage rate	% Difference
1996	14,593	23,626	-38.2
1997	14,637	22,943	-36.2
1998	15,945	26,811	-40.5
1999	20,161	31,377	-35.7
2000	20,112	32,627	-38.4
2001	21,582	36,086	-40.2
2002	22,244	36,875	-39.7
2003	23,377	39,375	-40.6
2004	26,657	43,062	-38.1
2005	28,236	45,028	-37.3
2006	32,534	49,248	-33.9
2007	33,966	54,362	-37.5
2008	43,243	58,334	-25.9
2009	45,615	58,736	-22.3
2010	47,467	61,703	-23.1

Table source: Office for National Statistics

Download table

XLS XLS format
(29 Kb)

The hourly wage of a care assistant has been included as the value of continuous care as it is deemed as the most appropriate alternative to home care. Residential care, although full-time, has many economies of scale that enable the providers to offer it a cheaper rate than it would be on an individual level. As a result, this has not been chosen as the market alternative rate used for valuation.

Notes

1. Average weekly residential care data are provided by the National Health Service.

About the ONS Measuring National Well-being Programme

National well-being

This article is published as part of the ONS Measuring National Well-being Programme.

The programme aims to produce accepted and trusted measures of the well-being of the nation - how the UK as a whole is doing.

Measuring National Well-being is about looking at 'GDP and beyond'. It includes headline indicators in areas such as health, relationships, job satisfaction, economic security, education, environmental conditions and measures of 'subjective well-being' (individuals' assessment of their own well-being).

Find out more on the Measuring National Well-being website pages.

Background notes

1. Revisions

   The data in 2002 HHSA (1995 -2000) have undergone some revisions. These revisions come from:

   - The use of a more recent estimate of the grossing factor from the Family Resources Survey, which grosses up the sample to represent the whole population. This has changed to reflect the availability of more recent and accurate population estimates.
   - Methodological improvements in the valuation of adult care.

   Although these revisions make subtle changes to each individual year, the long term trend implied by the data remains the same.

2. Details of the policy governing the release of new data are available by visiting www.statisticsauthority.gov.uk/assessment/code-of-practice/index.html or from the Media Relations Office email: media.relations@ons.gsi.gov.uk

Copyright

Supporting Information

Further information

About the Household Satellite Account
Further information about the ONS Household Satellite Account (HHSA) (experimental)

Household Satellite Accounts
Experimental statistics on the output of the household production. This release is part of a programme of work within the Measuring National Well-being Programme to develop and update the Household Satellite Account for the UK originally published by the Office for National Statistics in 2002.

References

1. Stiglitz, J. Sen, A. Fitoussi, J.P. (2009). Commission on the Measurement of Economic Performance and Social Progress.

2. Holloway, Short and Tamplin (2002). Household Satellite Account (Experimental) Methodology. Office for National Statistics.

3. Office for National Statistics (2002). Complete Household Satellite Accounts.

4. Hirst, M.(2002).Costing Adult Care. SPRU. University of York.

5. Reid, M. (1934): Economics of Household Production, New York, John Wiley.

Statistical Bulletin

EXPERIMENTAL STATISTICS

Personal Well-being in the UK, 2012/13

Coverage: **International**
Date: **30 July 2013**
Geographical Area: **UK**
Theme: **People and Places**

Key Points

- According to the latest findings from the ONS Annual Population Survey, there were small improvements in personal well-being in the UK between 2011/12 and 2012/13.
- The percentage of people reporting higher levels of life satisfaction, feeling that the things they do in life are worthwhile and happiness levels all increased while the percentage reporting higher levels of anxiety declined.
- Between 2011/12 and 2012/13 the proportion of people rating their life satisfaction as 7 or more out of 10 rose from 75.9% to 77.0%. There was also a reduction in the proportion of people rating their anxiety at a higher level of 6 or more out of 10 falling from 21.8% to 20.9%.
- The data show differences in personal well-being between groups of the population. For example, people aged 45 to 49 rated their life satisfaction lower than any other age group and Black people lower than any other ethnic group. There were no significant changes between the years for unemployed people whose average life satisfaction remained below those in employment.
- Other non-official sources show an improvement in personal well-being for similar periods. They also show that life satisfaction in the UK changed less between 2007 and 2011 than other European countries.

Background

This bulletin presents annual findings for personal well-being in the UK for April 2012 to March 2013. It compares the latest results to those of the previous year, published by the Office for National Statistics (ONS) in July 2012.

Personal well-being, people's thoughts and feelings about their own quality of life, is an important aspect of national well-being and is used by ONS to supplement other economic, social and environmental statistics to provide a statistical picture of the nation's well-being.

The estimates in this bulletin are based on data from the Annual Population Survey (APS) which includes responses from around 165,000 people. This provides a large representative sample of adults aged 16 and over who live in residential households in the UK.

Since April 2011, the APS has included four questions which are used to monitor personal well-being in the UK:

1. Overall, how satisfied are you with your life nowadays?
2. Overall, to what extent do you feel the things you do in your life are worthwhile?
3. Overall, how happy did you feel yesterday?
4. Overall, how anxious did you feel yesterday?

People are asked to give their answers on a scale of 0 to 10 where 0 is 'not at all' and 10 is 'completely'. These questions allow people to make an assessment of their life overall, as well as providing an indication of their day-to-day emotions. Although 'yesterday' may not be a typical day for any one individual, the large sample means that these differences 'average out' and provide a reliable assessment of the anxiety and happiness of the adult population in the UK over the year.

This bulletin also explores differences in personal well-being estimates by sex, age, ethnicity, relationship status, health, disability, and employment status. Breaking down overall findings in this way is useful for looking at how well-being differs across society and can help to show how policies can be developed to improve people's well-being.

The large sample of the APS also allows estimates for regional and local geographies to be produced, but this bulletin focuses on the UK as a whole. A separate bulletin will be published by ONS in October 2013 which will present personal well-being across the UK, including estimates for Local Authority Districts.

ONS personal well-being estimates are 'Experimental Statistics' and are published at an early stage to gain feedback from users in their development before being designated as National Statistics. We would welcome feedback on this bulletin and would be particularly interested in hearing about how the data are used. Please contact us via email: nationalwell-being@ons.gsi.gov.uk or telephone Dawn Snape on 01633 45 5674.

Overview

Personal Well-being 2012/2013

National Well-being

Office for National Statistics

Key Figures

The latest findings from the ONS Annual Population Survey show a small improvement in personal well-being in the UK between 2011/12 and 2012/13. **Table 1** provides a summary of the key findings.

In Table 1 and throughout the bulletin, two different methods are used to help explain the findings. These are:

- **Distributions** showing how people responded to the personal well-being questions based on the scale from 0 to 10, particularly focusing on the percentage of people who rated their well-being at the higher or lower end of the scale;
- **Averages** based on ratings for each aspect of personal well-being on the 0 to 10 point scale. This provides another summary measure that allows comparisons using a single number for each aspect of personal well-being.

Table 1: Overall personal well-being, 2011/12 & 2012/13 (1)

United Kingdom

	Life Satisfaction	Worthwhile	Happy yesterday		Anxious yesterday
					Percentages
% Rating 7-10				**% Rating 0-3**	
2011/12	75.9	80.0	71.1	2011/12	60.1
2012/13	77.0	80.7	71.6	2012/13	61.5
Annual % point change	*1.2**	*0.7**	*0.5**	*Annual % point change*	*1.4**
% Rating 0-4				**% Rating 6-10**	
2011/12	6.6	4.9	10.9	2011/12	21.8
2012/13	5.8	4.4	10.3	2012/13	20.9
Annual % point change	*-0.9**	*-0.5**	*-0.5**	*Annual % point change*	*-0.9**
					Averages
Average				**Average**	
2011/12	7.4	7.7	7.3	2011/12	3.1
2012/13	7.5	7.7	7.3	2012/13	3.0

Annual point change	*0.04**	*0.03**	*0.01*	*Annual point change*	*-0.11**

Table source: Office for National Statistics

Table notes:

1. * indicates change is significant at the 0.05 level.

Download table

XLS XLS format
(34 Kb)

Changes between 2011/12 and 2012/13

Overall, between 2011/12 and 2012/13 there was a small improvement in personal well-being in the UK.

Distributions

One way to present personal well-being data is to look at the percentage of people who gave particular ratings to each of the personal well-being questions on the 0 to 10 scale where 0 is ‘not at all’ and 10 is ‘completely’. Comparisons can then be made about how these have changed between 2011/12 and 2012/13.

Figure 1 below provides these estimates for each aspect of personal well-being and ONS have developed an interactive tool to illustrate this information.

Figure 1: Distribution of responses for personal well-being, 2011/12 & 2012/13 (1)

United Kingdom

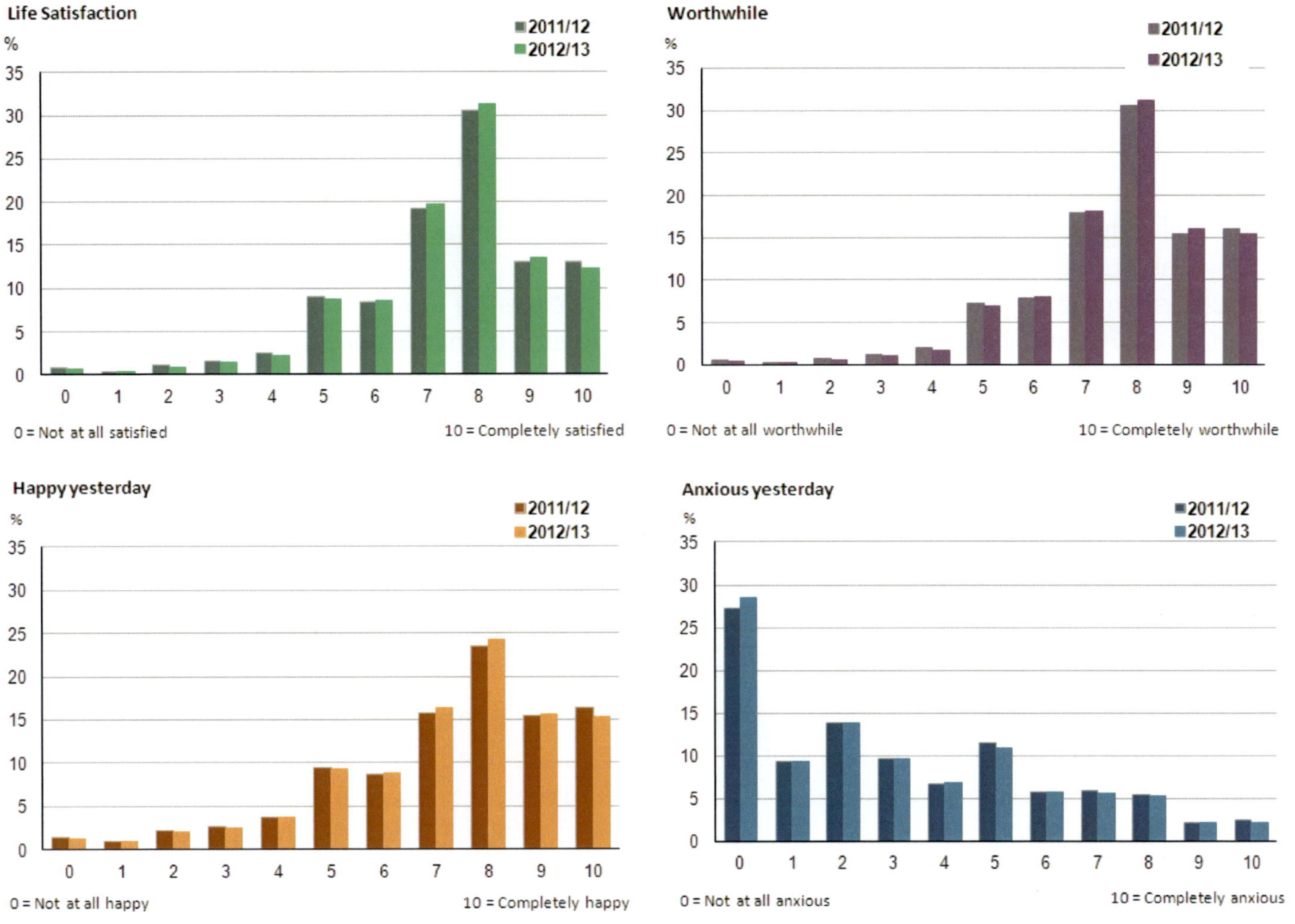

Source: Annual Population Survey (APS) - Office for National Statistics

Notes:

1. Adults aged 16 and over were asked 'Overall, how satisfied are you with your life nowadays?', 'Overall, to what extent do you feel the things you do in your life are worthwhile?', 'Overall, how happy did you feel yesterday?' and 'Overall, how anxious did you feel yesterday?' where 0 is 'not at all' and 10 is 'completely'.

Download chart

XLS XLS format
(29.5 Kb)

In order to summarise the information in Figure 1, the different ratings on the scale are grouped and the percentages of the UK adult population giving a range of ratings is then presented.

Higher personal well-being

Higher levels of personal well-being for life satisfaction, worthwhile and happiness are defined as 7 or more out of 10. However, for anxiety 3 or less out of 10 is used because lower levels of anxiety indicate better personal well-being.

Summary findings in relation to changes in personal well-being between 2011/12 and 2012/13 on this basis show:

- an overall improvement in life satisfaction. The proportion of people rating their life satisfaction as 7 or more out of 10 rose from 75.9% to 77.0%;
- an overall reduction in anxiety levels. The proportion of people rating their anxiety at a low level of 3 or less out of 10 increased from 60.1% to 61.5%;
- an increase in the percentage of people giving higher ratings for worthwhile and happiness, from 80.0% to 80.7% and 71.1% to 71.6% respectively. The size of these increases was smaller than for the other questions, but they were statistically significant.

Lower personal well-being

It is equally important to look at whether there were changes in the proportion of people giving lower ratings of life satisfaction, worthwhile and happiness or higher ratings of anxiety. This helps to clarify whether improvements in the personal well-being of some were off-set by deterioration in the well-being of others.

For life-satisfaction, worthwhile and happiness ratings, 0 to 4 out of 10 are used to indicate lower well-being. However for anxiety, ratings of 6 to 10 out of 10 are used because higher ratings for this question suggest greater anxiety (10 out of 10 being 'completely anxious') and therefore indicate worse personal well-being. A reduction in the percentage of people rating anxiety as 6 to 10 out of 10 would therefore show an improvement in anxiety levels.

Key findings in relation to changes in lower personal well-being between 2011/12 and 2012/13 include:

- a decrease in people rating their life satisfaction as 4 or less out of 10. This fell from 6.6% to 5.8%;
- a decrease in people rating their anxiety at 6 or more out of 10. This fell from 21.8% to 20.9%;
- for both worthwhile and happiness, the proportions of people giving ratings of 4 or less out of 10 also fell - from 4.9% to 4.4% for worthwhile and from 10.9% to 10.3% for happiness.

Average ratings of personal well-being

As well as presenting estimates in this way, it is also possible to provide the average (mean) rating as a summary measure for each aspect of personal well-being and comparisons between 2011/12 and 2012/13 can then be made.

On this basis key points to note include:

- the average ratings for life satisfaction increased by 0.04 points, worthwhile by 0.03 points and happiness 0.01 points;
- the annual increases in average life satisfaction and worthwhile were statistically significant, but the change in happiness was not;
- the largest change was in average ratings for anxiety which decreased by 0.11 points and was statistically significant.

The change in context

The overall improvement in personal well-being is small but is consistent across the four aspects of personal well-being measured. The reasons for the small improvement between 2011/12 and 2012/13 are not fully understood at this stage.

The factors affecting personal well-being are complex and will differ from person to person and further analysis and research is required to better understand the drivers of personal well-being at the national level. This includes understanding how wider economic and social circumstances and events affect people's assessments of personal well-being.

Recent ONS analysis on 'What matters most to personal well-being?' (ONS, 2013a) found that after taking other possible influences into account, the factors most associated with personal well-being are health, employment situation and relationship status.

The labour market picture worsened during 2011 but has generally been improving since then. Unemployment peaked in the autumn of 2011 but then decreased steadily throughout most of 2012. The number of job vacancies remained close to its record low during 2011 but began to rise in early 2012 and this has continued through to spring 2013 when it reached its highest since autumn 2008 (ONS, 2013b).

The period of 2012/13 also included several special events in the UK, such as the Queen's Diamond Jubilee (in June 2012) which included a special bank holiday and the 2012 Summer Olympic and Paralympic games (July to early September 2012). These events could also have potentially influenced people's assessment of their personal well-being in the 2012/13 period.

In addition, data for similar periods from non-official sources seem to be in keeping with the ONS estimates from the APS:

- the Gallup World Poll found a 2 percentage point increase in the proportion of people in the UK deemed to be 'thriving' in July to August 2012 compared to the previous year (Gallup World Poll, 2012);
- the Which? Consumer Insight Tracker found that people were also more satisfied with their lives in the period from January to March 2013 than they had been in the previous quarter despite 'strong pessimism about personal finances and the economy' (Which?, 2013);

- estimates from the World Database of Happiness also showed a small increase in average life satisfaction from 7.15 to 7.26 out of 10 between autumn 2011 and autumn 2012 (Veenhoven, R, 2012).

The data from the World Database of Happiness also provides estimates of life satisfaction in the UK between 2002 and 2012. This provides a useful context for understanding life satisfaction in the UK over a longer period of time than is available from the APS.

Figure 2: Average life satisfaction in the UK, 2002 - 2012 (1)

United Kingdom

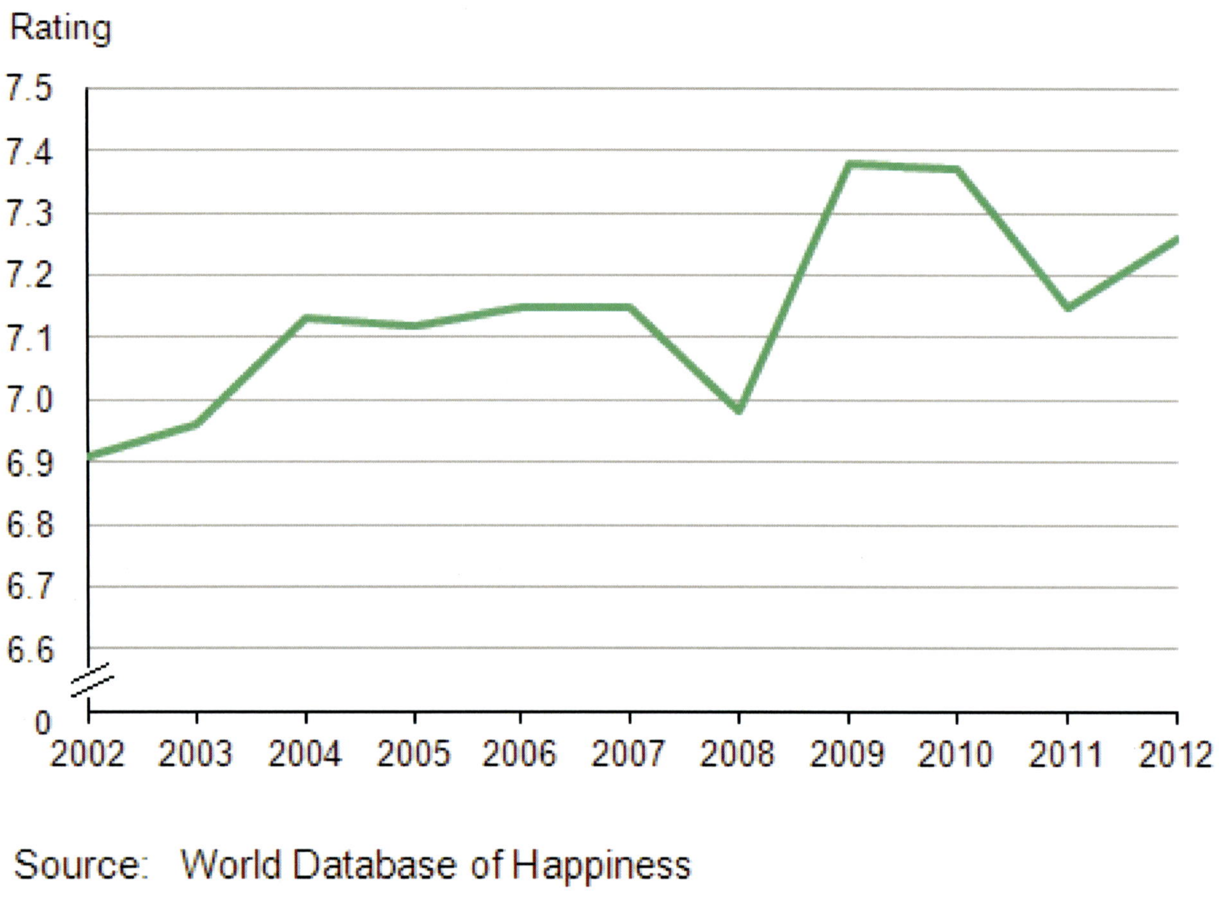

Notes:

1. Life satisfaction data are as a proportion of Great Britain respondents who stated that they were fairly or very satisfied when answering the question: 'On the whole how satisfied are you with the life you lead?' – with the responses 1) not at all satisfied; 2) not very satisfied; 3) fairly satisfied; 4) very satisfied. This was then increased to a 10 point scale by linear stretch. The data used is for the Autumn quarter where available.

Download chart

XLS XLS format
(30 Kb)

Key points to note from **Figure 2**:

- a decrease in life satisfaction associated with the recession in 2008;
- the average level of life satisfaction in the UK recovered between 2008 and 2009 and reached a high point in 2009 and 2010 after which it began to fall again;
- in keeping with the latest findings from the APS, average life satisfaction increased in 2012 compared with 2011.

European comparisons

In order to put the findings from the 2011-13 period into context, it is helpful to look at how personal well-being in the UK compares to other European countries. To do this estimates from the European Quality of Life Survey have been used for 2007 and 2011.

Figure 3 shows how life satisfaction in the UK has changed since the year before the recession and how this compares to other European countries. Key points to note:

- life satisfaction in the UK is high on average compared to many other countries. The UK ranked tenth for life satisfaction out of the 27 European Union countries, with an average rating of 7.3 out of 10 in 2011;
- life satisfaction in the UK was the same in 2007 as it was in 2011;
- however, over the same period, there was a fall in life satisfaction among all the other countries ranked higher than the UK for life satisfaction in 2011;
- the majority of countries ranked lower than the UK in 2011 experienced an increase in life satisfaction over this period, although there were exceptions such as Greece.

The picture of stability in life satisfaction in the UK from 2007 to 2011 stands in contrast to the changes in life satisfaction among many other European countries over the same period.

Figure 3: Average life satisfaction, by European country, 2007 & 2011 (1,2)

EU27

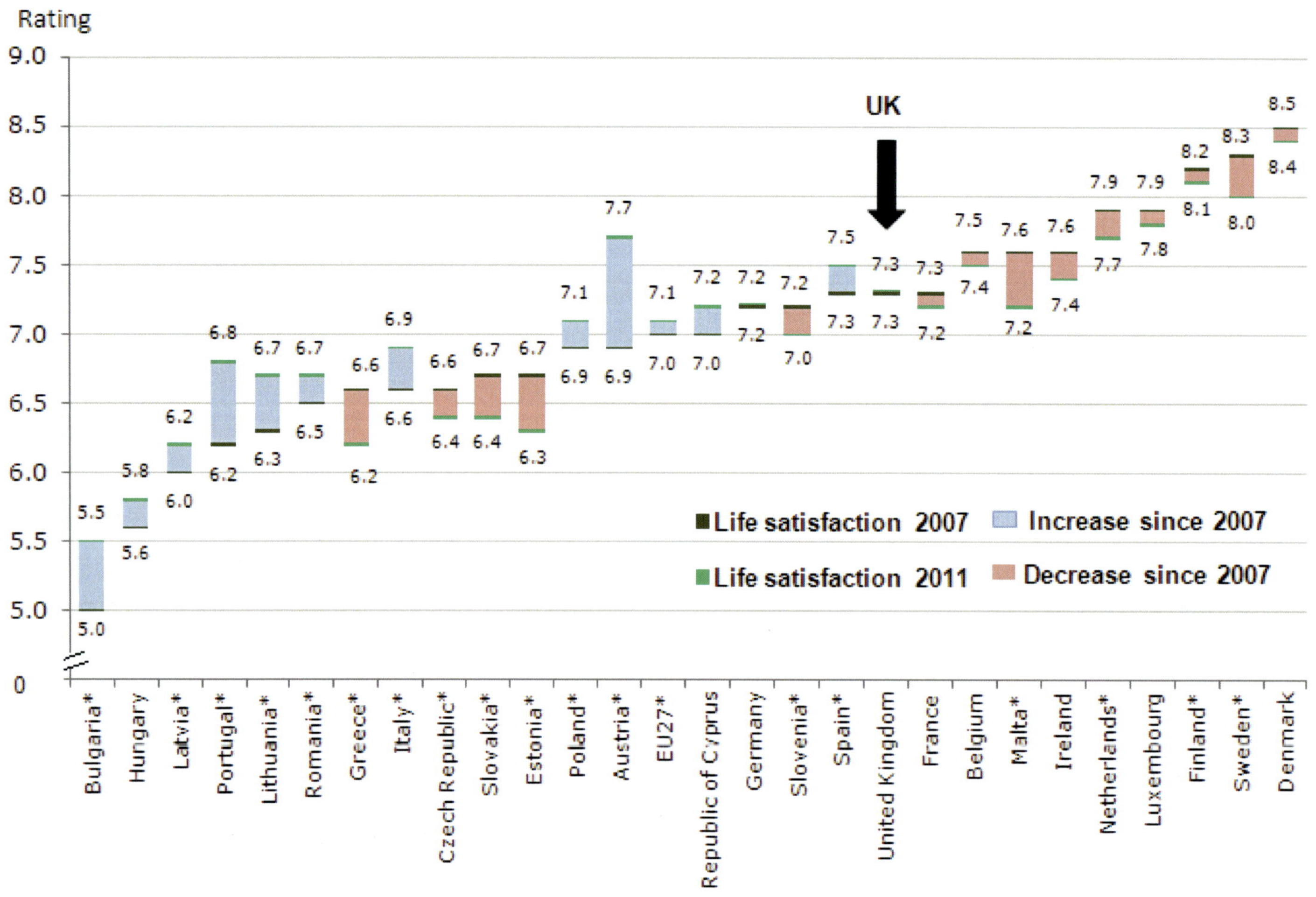

Source: Third European Quality of Life Survey

Notes:

1. Measured on a 1 - 10 scale.
2. * indicates change is significant at the 0.05 level.

Download chart

XLS XLS format
(19.5 Kb)

Sex, age and ethnicity

Overall personal well-being estimates differ by people's personal characteristics including sex, age and ethnicity.

Personal well-being of men and women

Consistent with findings from other studies and previous ONS analysis, there are small but statistically significant differences in how men and women rate their personal well-being. For example, the 2012/13 APS data show:

- on average, women have higher life satisfaction, consider their activities to be more worthwhile and rate their happiness slightly higher than men;
- women also rate their anxiety levels significantly higher than men. The average anxiety rating for women is 3.1 compared with 2.9 for men.

In terms of changes between 2011/12 and 2012/13, both men and women reported a small reduction in their levels of anxiety. Additionally, both sexes reported small improvements in life satisfaction, worthwhile activities and happiness levels, none of these were statistically significant.

Age and personal well-being

Previous research has found that older and younger people rate their life satisfaction more highly than those in mid life (Dolan et al., 2008; ONS, 2013a). Life satisfaction ratings also decline among those in their late seventies onwards.

The 2012/13 APS results, shown in **Figure 4**, are consistent with these findings and show:

- average levels of life satisfaction, worthwhile activities and happiness levels were lowest for people aged 45 to 54;
- younger people gave higher average ratings than those in mid life and those aged 65 to 79 had significantly higher average ratings than any other age group for both worthwhile and happiness;
- those aged 80 and over gave lower average ratings for life satisfaction, worthwhile and happiness than those aged 65 to 79.

Recent analysis by ONS looked at factors associated with well-being among older people (ONS, 2013c) and one possible reason for the lower average levels of life satisfaction, worthwhile activities and happiness levels for those aged 80 and over could be related to feeling lonely. Those in this age group report higher levels of loneliness and those who feel lonely are more likely to report lower life satisfaction levels on average.

Figure 4 also shows that:

- those in their early thirties to late fifties rated their anxiety levels highest;
- younger people rated their anxiety at lower levels than those in mid life. Although the lowest average levels of anxiety appear to be among those aged 65 and over, they were not significantly different to the anxiety levels of those aged 16 to 19 (the latter are not shown as a separate group in Figure 4);
- interestingly, those aged 80 and over did not have higher levels of anxiety on average than those aged 65 to 79.

A growing body of research (Dolan et al, 2008) consistently finds this relationship between age and well-being. Two possible explanations have been suggested:

- personal well-being may change as we move through life and have different experiences, responsibilities and circumstances which change our perspectives,
- this may be a 'cohort' effect in which people born in different eras have different experiences and expectations which shape their well-being.

Work in this area is ongoing and there is still no definitive explanation as to why people's well-being typically decreases in mid life.

Figure 4: Average personal well-being, by age group, 2012/2013

United Kingdom

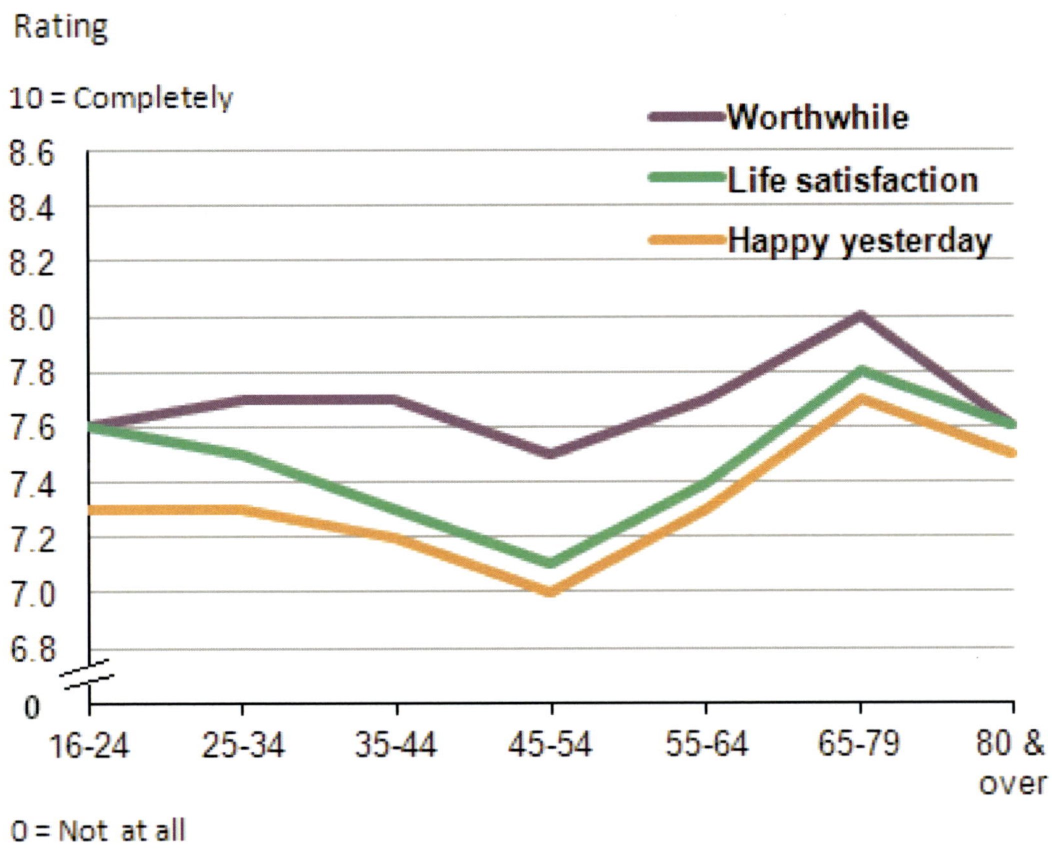

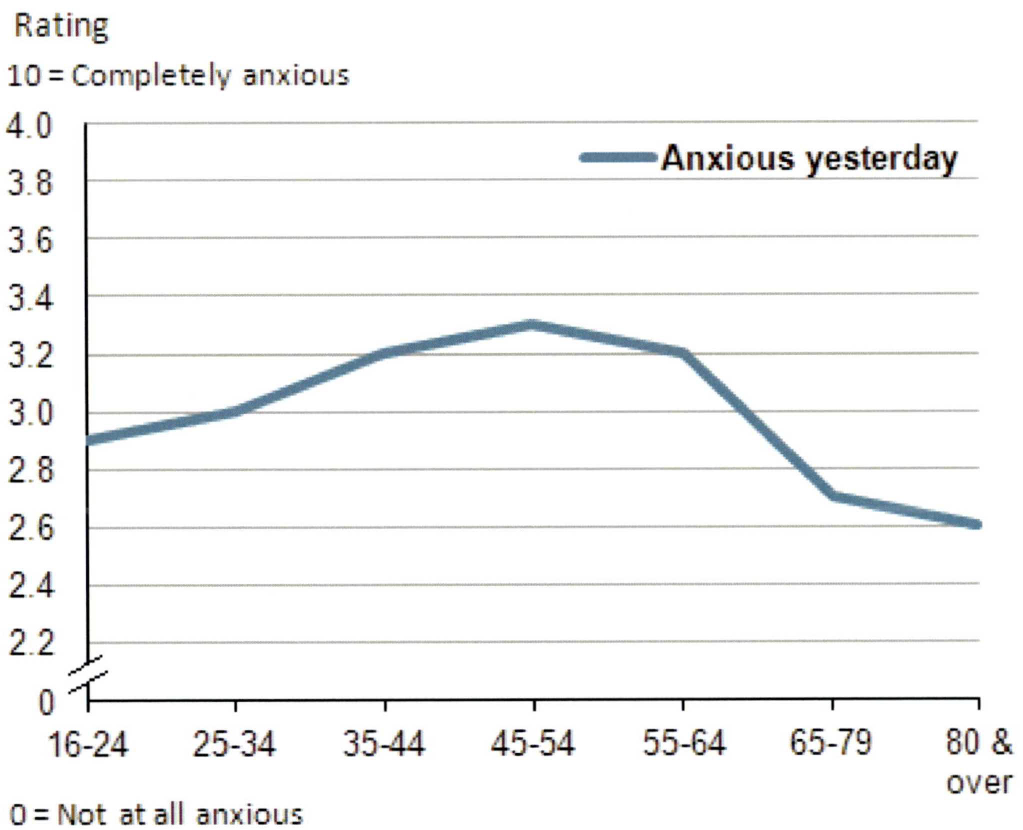

Source: Annual Population Survey (APS) - Office for National Statistics

Download chart

XLS XLS format
(29 Kb)

Between 2011/12 and 2012/13, there have been some small changes in how people of different ages rate their well-being. For example, between 2011/12 and 2012/13:

- there were reductions in anxiety levels across most age groups but those aged 80 and over reported the largest decrease. The average rating for anxiety among this group fell from 2.9 to 2.6 out of 10.

Personal well-being and ethnicity

Table 2 shows the average personal well-being ratings across ethnic groups for 2012/13. Key findings to note are that:

- the White and Indian respondents are on average the most satisfied with their lives while the Black/African/Caribbean/Black British respondents are the least satisfied. There is a statistically significant difference in life satisfaction between these groups. The average life satisfaction rating for both the White and Indian groups is 7.5, compared to 6.9 for the Black/African/Caribbean/Black British group.

The distinct differences in personal well-being ratings between ethnic groups may be due to:

- differences in the life experiences, circumstances and perspectives of people from different ethnic groups; or
- cultural or linguistic differences in the way people interpret the personal well-being questions or the meaning of the 0 to 10 scale or both.

These are areas where further research would be helpful in clarifying why personal well-being differs between ethnic groups.

Table 2: Average personal well-being, by ethnic group, 2012/13

United Kingdom

Rating

	Life satisfaction	Worthwhile	Happy yesterday	Anxious yesterday
White	7.5	7.7	7.3	3.0
Gypsy, Traveller or Irish Traveller[1]	..	..	..	..
Mixed/Multiple ethnic groups	7.0	7.5	7.0	3.4
Indian	7.5	7.7	7.4	3.3
Pakistani	7.3	7.5	7.2	3.2
Bangladeshi	7.2	7.5	7.3	3.1
Chinese	7.4	7.4	7.4	3.0
Any other Asian background	7.4	7.6	7.3	3.3
Black/African/Caribbean/Black British [2]	6.9	7.5	7.1	3.1
Arab	7.1	7.1	6.7	3.3
Other ethnic group	7.2	7.4	7.1	3.4

Table source: Office for National Statistics

Table notes:

1. Sample sizes too small for reliable estimates.
2. Differences in the terminology and data collection of the country specific Scotland question makes these categories difficult to compare. The 'African' categories in the Scottish question is presented in a separate section to the 'Caribbean' or 'Black' category, however, under the harmonised output these two categories are combined as part of 'Black/African/Caribbean/Black British'. The African categories used in Scotland could potentially capture 'White/Asian/Other African' in addition to 'Black' identities.

Download table

XLS XLS format
(30.5 Kb)

Changes were made to the APS ethnicity questions in 2011 as a result of harmonisation and to bring them in line with the Census data collection on this topic. The implementation of this may account for some of the differences found in the personal well-being of ethnic groups between 2011-12 and 2012-13. For this reason, no direct year on year comparisons should be made.

Health and disability

There is a strong association between how people rate their health and how they rate their personal well-being. This has been noted both in academic research and in recently published ONS analysis which found that people's assessment of their health matters more than any other factor to their personal well-being (ONS, 2013a; Dolan et al, 2008).

The findings for 2012/13 are consistent with this. In general, the better people say their health is, the higher they rate their life satisfaction, worthwhile and happiness and the lower they rate their anxiety. (See **Figure 5**)

Figure 5: Average personal well-being, by self reported health, 2012/13

United Kingdom

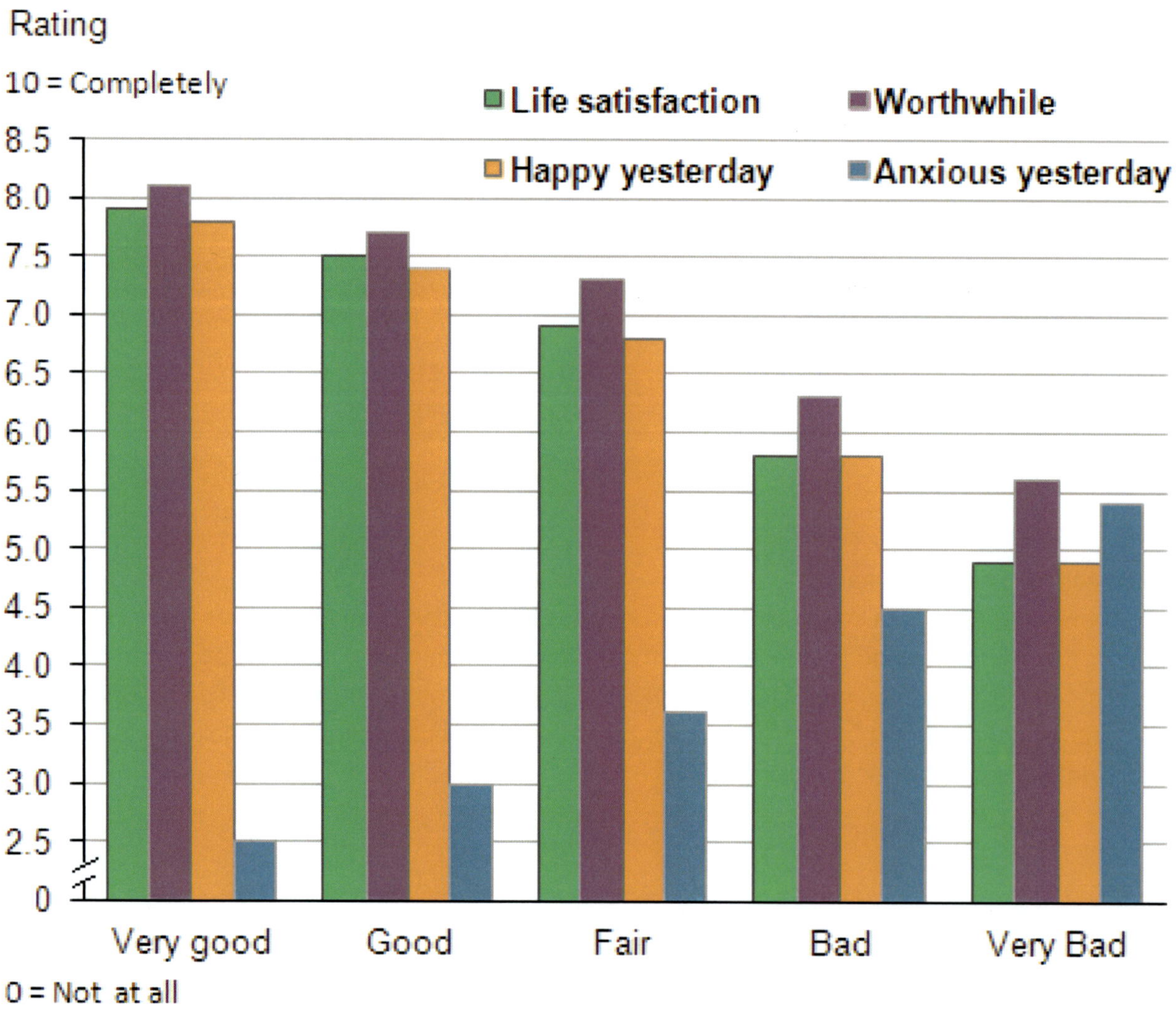

Source: Annual Population Survey (APS) - Office for National Statistics

Download chart

XLS XLS format
(19.5 Kb)

In terms of change between 2011/12 and 2012/13:

- there were no significant changes in average ratings for life satisfaction, worthwhile or happiness for any of the self-reported health groups;
- there was a small but significant improvement in average anxiety levels among those rating their health 'very good', 'good' or 'fair';
- there was no significant change for any of the personal well-being measures among those rating their health as 'bad' or 'very bad'.

It is important to highlight that the measure of health used here is based on people's views of their health rather than on objective information about people's health. As such, it is likely to reflect people's emotional as well as physical state and the degree of optimism they have about their health. Similarly, people's ratings of their well-being reflect their emotional state and optimism about life. For this reason, it is perhaps not surprising that people's perceptions of their health are strongly related to their perceptions of their life.

Disability and personal well-being

This section focuses on how disabled people rate their personal well-being compared to those without a disability. It is important to note that people who report a disability are a diverse group which includes those with a disability which substantially limits their day-to-day activities, as well as those with a disability which limits the type or amount of work they do, but does not limit their day-to-day activities.

The findings for 2012/13 show that people who report that they have a disability rate their life satisfaction, worthwhile and happiness yesterday lower than those who do not report a disability (see **Figure 6**). The anxiety levels of people with a disability are also higher on average than those of people without a disability.

Figure 6: Average personal well-being, by disability status, 2012/13

United Kingdom

Source: Annual Population Survey (APS) - Office for National Statistics

Download chart

XLS [XLS format](#)
(28.5 Kb)

In terms of change between 2011/12 and 2012/13, there were improvements in average personal well-being for both disabled and non-disabled people including:

- a small increase in average ratings of life satisfaction for both disabled and non-disabled people;
- a small decrease in average ratings of anxiety for both disabled and non-disabled people.

Relationships

Previous research into personal well-being has found that being in a stable relationship is linked to higher personal well-being (Dolan et al., 2008; ONS, 2013a). By contrast, people who are not in a relationship report lower life satisfaction, worthwhile and happiness, and higher anxiety.

Figure 7 shows the most recent findings for life satisfaction across people in different relationship situations.

- people who are married or in civil partnerships rate their life satisfaction highest, with the average score at 7.8 out of 10. This is significantly higher than for cohabiting couples who reported an average of 7.6 out of 10;
- single people rated their life satisfaction significantly lower than those who are married, in a civil partnership or a cohabiting couple, or widowed at an average of 7.2 out of 10;
- people who are divorced or separated, including those who have dissolved civil partnerships rated their life satisfaction lowest, at an average of 6.8 out of 10.

Although these findings suggest that divorced people have the worst life satisfaction of all the relationship groups, previous analysis by ONS shows that widowed people have lower well-being on average when other influences on well-being such as age group are taken into account (ONS, 2013a).

Figure 7: Average life satisfaction, by relationship status, 2012/13

United Kingdom

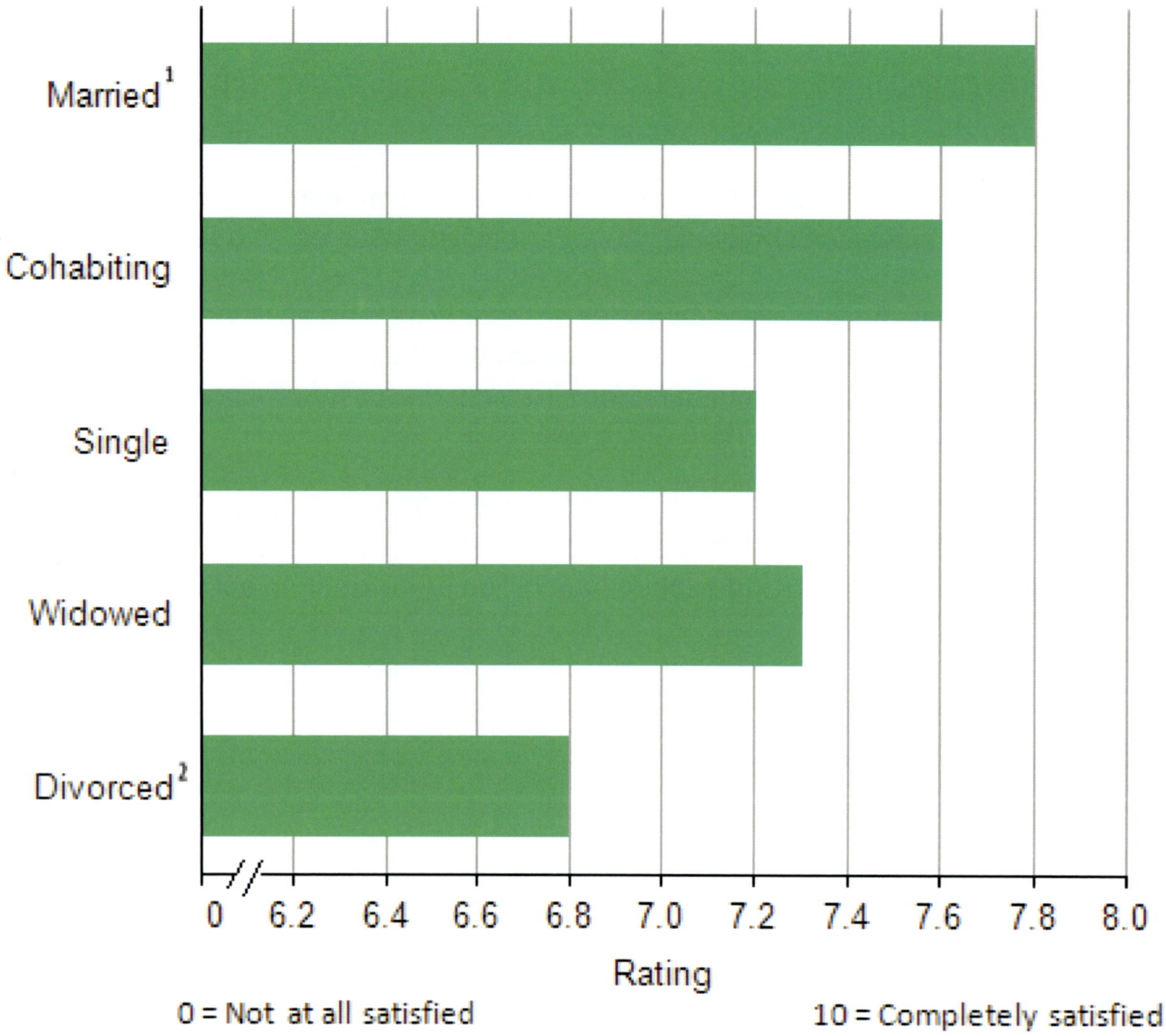

Source: Annual Population Survey (APS) - Office for National Statistics

Notes:

1. 'Married' includes people in civil partnerships.
2. 'Divorced' includes people who are separated and people in dissolved civil partnerships.

Download chart

XLS [XLS format](#)
(29 Kb)

Changes between 2011/12 and 2012/13 include:

- an improvement in average ratings for life satisfaction among those who are divorced or separated;
- a reduction in average ratings for anxiety among those who are married or civil partners, divorced, separated or widowed.

Work situation

Work is clearly an important aspect of life for many of us. As well as providing obvious material benefits such as income and a pension, employment can also provide psychological benefits such as a sense of purpose, social status, social interaction and a daily routine. This section looks at the relationship between work and personal well-being.

The findings here focus on employment status, that is, whether people are employed, unemployed or economically inactive. People are referred to as 'economically inactive' if they are not participating in the labour market.

Employment status and personal well-being

Previous research has shown that unemployment has a negative effect on personal well-being (Dolan et al., 2008) and this is supported by analysis of the most recent ONS data and by regression analysis published by ONS earlier this year (ONS, 2013a). As **Figure 8** shows, average ratings for life satisfaction, worthwhile and happiness are all lower for those who unemployed than for those in employment. Taking one example:

- Unemployed people rate their life satisfaction significantly lower on average than employed people. The average life satisfaction rating of unemployed people is 6.6 out of 10 compared to 7.6 for employed people.

Unemployed people also have significantly higher anxiety levels than those in employment:

- The average anxiety rating of unemployed people is 3.4 out of 10 compared to 3.0 for people in employment.

Figure 8: Average personal well-being, by employment status, 2012/13

United Kingdom

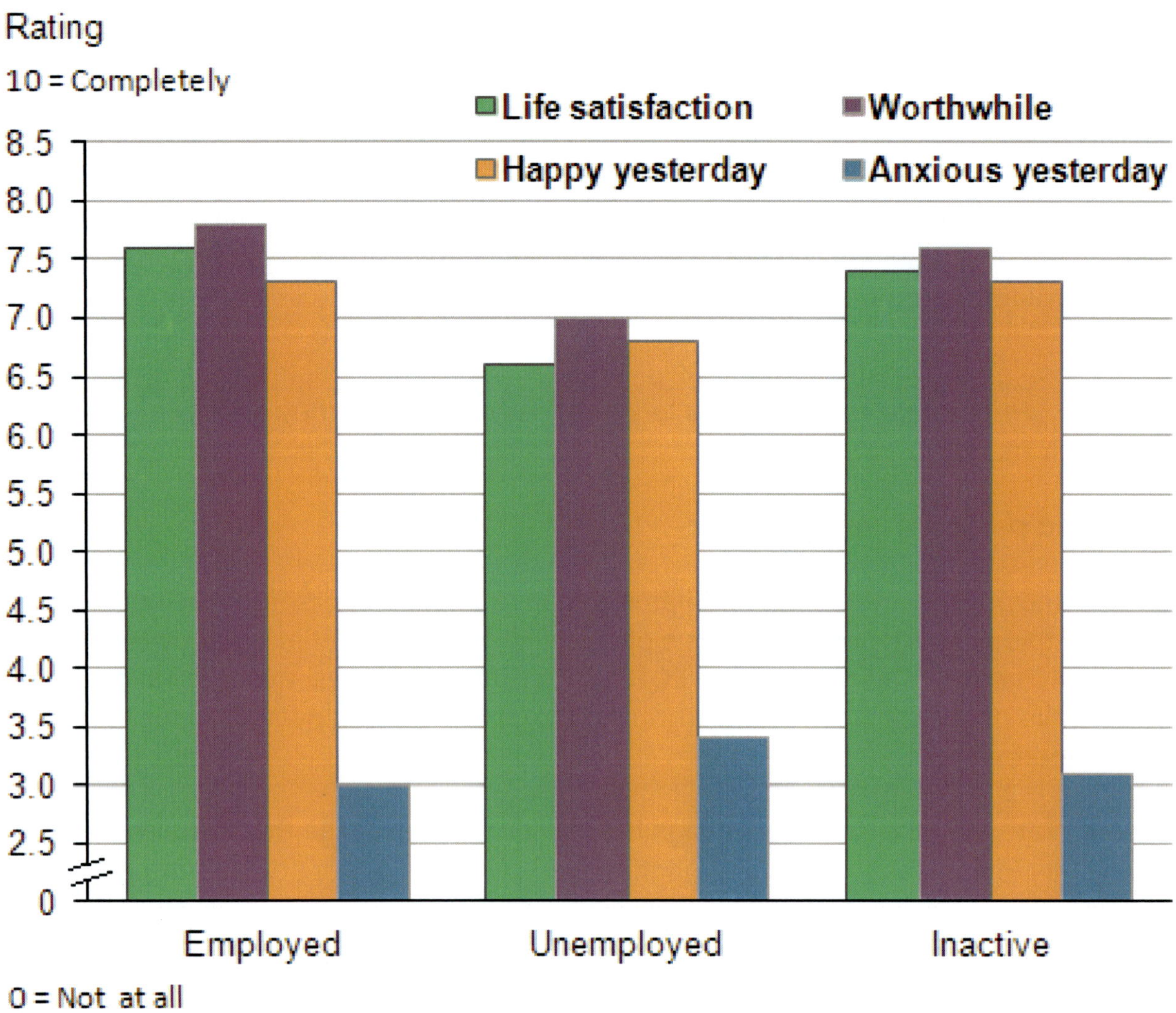

Source: Annual Population Survey (APS) - Office for National Statistics

Download chart

XLS XLS format
(28.5 Kb)

As Figure 8 shows, people who are unemployed also have lower personal well-being than those who are economically inactive. Specifically:

- Unemployed people rate their life satisfaction, worthwhile and happiness lower on average than people who are economically inactive. They also rate their 'anxiety' higher than those who are economically inactive.

In terms of changes between 2011/12 and 2012/13:

- there was a small increase in average life satisfaction ratings among people who are employed;
- there was a reduction in average ratings for anxiety among those who are employed or economically inactive;
- there were no statistically significant changes in average personal well-being ratings among unemployed people.

These findings suggest that it will be important to continue to monitor the personal well-being gap between unemployed people and others over time to see whether it is widening. This is particularly so in the context of recent increases in long-term unemployment in the UK.

Economic inactivity and personal well-being

Given that there are a wide range of reasons why people are economically inactive, it is useful to look at whether well-being differs depending upon people's reason for economic inactivity. **Figure 9** shows that life satisfaction ratings vary greatly depending on the reason for economic inactivity.

Figure 9: Average life satisfaction, by reason for economic inactivity, 2012/13

United Kingdom

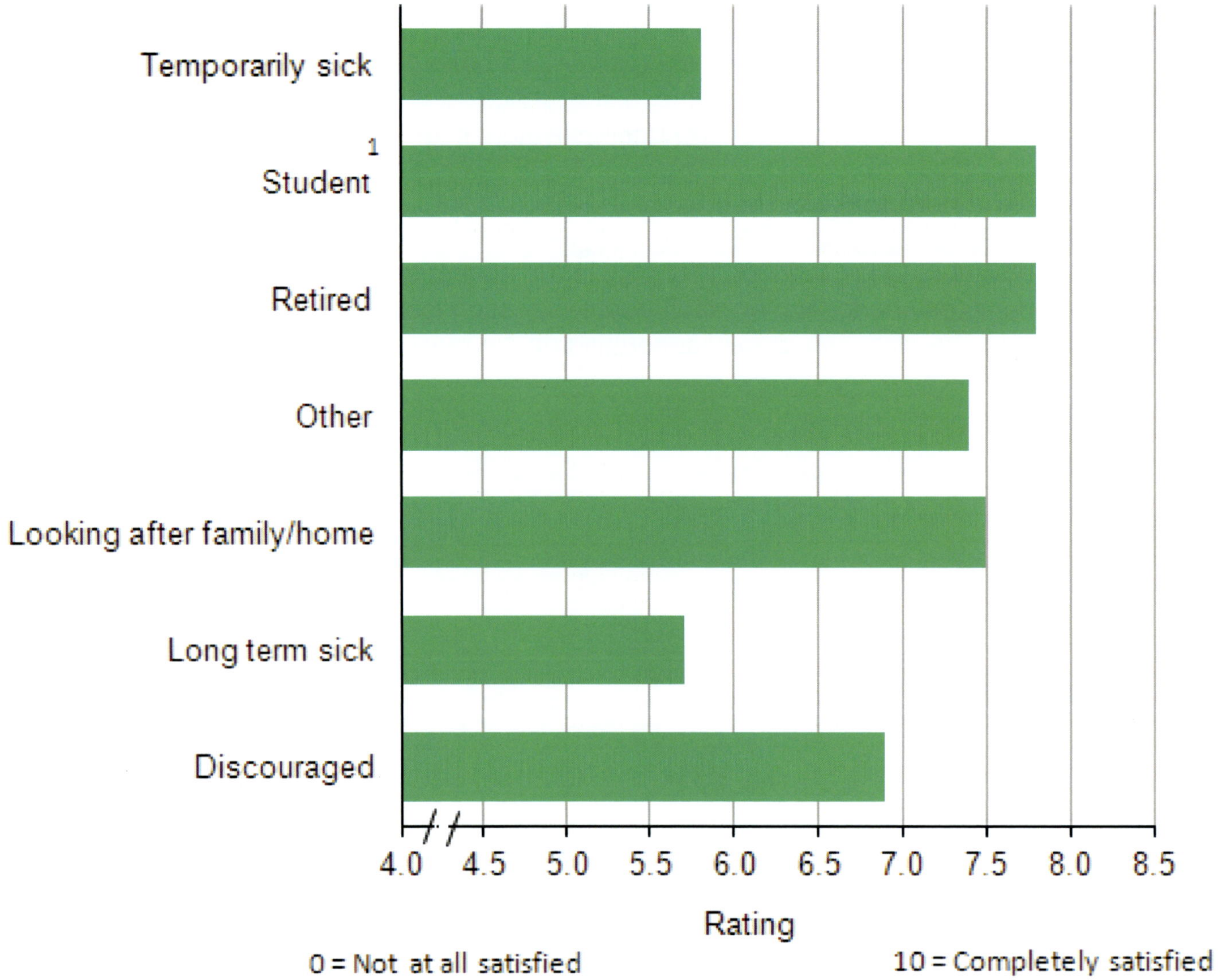

Source: Annual Population Survey (APS) - Office for National Statistics

Notes:

1. The 'student' category refers specifically to those students who are economically inactive.

Download chart

XLS XLS format
(29.5 Kb)

Key findings to note are that:

- among the economically inactive groups, retired people and students are the most satisfied with their lives on average. The life satisfaction ratings of people in these two groups were significantly higher than for all the other economic inactivity groups;
- ratings for worthwhile were significantly higher among those looking after a home or family than for all other groups except retired people;
- those who are not in work due to temporary or long term sickness are least satisfied with their lives. They also have higher anxiety on average and lower levels of worthwhile and happiness than those giving other reasons for economic inactivity;
- the 'discouraged worker' group is comprised of those who said their main reason for not seeking work was because they believed there were no jobs available. Apart from those who are not working due to temporary or long term sickness, their life satisfaction is lower on average than other economically inactive groups.

These findings are consistent with those of other ONS analysis which found particularly low average ratings for all four well-being questions among the group who were sick or disabled. The same study found that after taking into account other factors that may affect well-being, retired people who said that they do not need to work have even higher personal well-being than people who are working (ONS, 2013a).

Full-time or part-time work and personal well-being

Previous studies have found no difference in life satisfaction between those working full-time or part-time (Bardasi and Francesconi, 2004). However, the recent findings from the APS show that those working part-time rate their life satisfaction, worthwhile and happiness slightly higher on average than those working full-time and the differences are statistically significant. There are no differences in the average anxiety levels of those working full or part-time. (See **Figure 10**)

Figure 10: Average personal well-being, by full-time and part-time employment, 2012/13

United Kingdom

Source: Annual Population Survey (APS) - Office for National Statistics

Download chart

XLS XLS format
(19 Kb)

As noted in relation to economic inactivity, there are a variety of reasons why people may work full or part-time. If their reasons are to do with positive choices rather than perceived constraints, we would expect this to be reflected in higher personal well-being. **Figure 11** shows how personal well-being differs among those working part-time depending upon their reasons for doing so.

Figure 11: Average personal well-being, by reason for part-time work, 2012/13

United Kingdom

Source: Annual Population Survey (APS) - Office for National Statistics

Download chart

XLS XLS format
(28.5 Kb)

Key findings to note are that on average:

- those who work part-time because they are students and those who did not want a full-time job had higher levels of life satisfaction on average than those working part-time for other reasons;
- those who work part-time because they are ill or disabled have a similar level of life satisfaction on average as those who could not find a full-time job, but they have much higher anxiety than other groups;
- those working part-time because they did not want a full time job had the highest sense that their activities are worthwhile. Their anxiety levels are very similar to those of students;
- those working part-time because they could not find a full time job had a similar personal well-being profile to those who work part-time due to illness or disability for life satisfaction, worthwhile and happiness.

The findings again suggest that on average, those who make a positive choice to work part-time either because they are students or because they do not want a full-time job have a greater sense of personal well-being. By contrast, those whose choices have been constrained by illness, disability, or perceived inability to get a full-time job have lower average personal well-being.

Methodology

The data analysed in this release are derived from customised weighted 12 month Annual Population Survey (APS) microdatasets. These datasets are not part of the regularly produced APS datasets and were produced specifically for the analysis of personal well-being data. ONS is making the experimental APS microdatas available to approved researchers to allow them to undertake further analysis of these experimental questions at an early stage and to provide further feedback to ONS.

Choice of questions

The experimental questions included in the Annual Population Survey were developed with expert academic advice (Dolan et al. 2011) as well as benefiting from discussions between members of the National Statistician's Measuring National Well-being Advisory Forum and Technical Advisory Group. They represent a balanced approach to the measurement of personal well-being drawing on the three main theoretical approaches identified in the academic literature on the subject (Dolan et. al. 2011, ONS, 2011a) and are designed to collect information on different aspects of people's personal well-being. The three different approaches to measuring personal well-being are:

- the 'evaluative' approach in which people are asked to reflect on their life and make a cognitive assessment of how their life is going overall or of how specific aspects of their life are going;
- the 'eudemonic' approach, sometimes referred to as the psychological or functioning/flourishing approach, which draws on self-determination theory and measures people's sense of meaning and purpose in life, connections with family and friends, a sense of control and whether they feel part of something bigger than themselves;
- the 'experience' approach which measures people's positive and negative experiences (or affect) over a short timeframe to capture people's personal well-being on a day-to-day basis.

The questions that ONS has asked on its household surveys include:

- Overall, how satisfied are you with your life nowadays? (evaluative approach)
- Overall, to what extent do you feel the things you do in your life are worthwhile? (eudemonic approach)
- Overall, how happy did you feel yesterday? (experience approach)
- Overall, how anxious did you feel yesterday? (experience approach).

All are answered using a 0 to 10 scale where 0 is 'not at all' and 10 is 'completely'.

Further information on the ONS approach to measuring personal well-being can be found in the paper 'Measuring Subjective Well-being' (240.8 Kb Pdf) published by ONS in July 2011.

Survey design

The Annual Population Survey (APS), first conducted in 2004, combines results from waves one and five of the Labour Force Survey (LFS) and the English, Welsh and Scottish LFS boosts. The survey asks 155,000 households and 360,000 people per dataset about their own circumstances and experiences regarding a range of subjects including housing, employment and education. The survey provides enhanced data on key social and socio-economic variables. For the personal well-being questions, responses by proxy are not collected. That is only people who respond directly to the survey are included rather than including responses made on behalf of other people. For this reason the sample size for the personal well-being data is around 165,000 people.

One of the benefits of collecting personal well-being data on a large scale survey such as APS is that large sample sizes, all else being equal, produce smaller standard errors. The standard error is an indication of the accuracy of an estimate and gives users an indication of how close the sample estimator (in this case the personal well-being estimates) is to the population value: the larger the standard error, the less precise the estimator. Large sample sizes also allow for comparisons across population groups and areas.

The APS is a mixed mode survey and uses both face-to-face and telephone interviews. Different collection modes can affect responses and personal well-being estimates are no exception. For example in the Annual Population Survey it appears from the aggregate estimates that on average people responding face-to-face with an interviewer in their home give different ratings to those responding via the telephone (see **Table 3**). Further investigation is required to ascertain why this may be the case.

Higher average ratings for the life satisfaction, worthwhile, happy yesterday questions and a slightly lower average for the anxious yesterday question were provided by respondents interviewed via the telephone compared with those who are asked personal well-being questions face-to-face, as can be seen in Table 3.

Table 3: Average personal well-being, by mode of interview, 2012/13

United Kingdom

Average

	Telephone	Face-to-face
Life satisfaction	7.6	7.4
Worthwhile	7.8	7.6
Happy yesterday	7.4	7.2
Anxious yesterday	3.1	3.0

Table source: Office for National Statistics

Download table

XLS XLS format
(28.5 Kb)

This issue is particularly important for the APS as all interviews in Scotland north of the Caledonian Canal are administered by telephone only, rather through than a combination of telephone and face-to-face interviews, as is the case in other areas of the UK.

There are a number of other methodological issues which have been or are being tested on the Opinions Survey, for more information see (ONS, 2011b). These include:

- **Contextual effects** - responses to evaluative questions can be affected by the respondent's current mood and by the immediate context, however, the idiosyncratic effects of recent events are likely to average out in a large, representative population sample like the APS.
- **Question order** – responses to personal well-being questions have been shown to be affected by earlier questions in the survey (for example, questions about health or labour market status). Prior to April 2011, ONS carried out small scale cognitive testing of the placement of the personal well-being questions. As a result it was decided that the placement of the overall monitoring questions would be fairly early on in the questionnaire after the basic questions on household and individual demographics. This allows time for rapport to be built up between the interviewer without allowing later questions, such as those on employment, to influence response to the personal well-being questions.
- **Response scales** - different response scales for personal well-being questions have been used on different surveys. Differences in scaling and labeling of scale points require careful consideration as they are likely to affect how people respond. Additionally the use of different scales in different surveys means that it is more difficult to compare across different sources of data. It appears that the way the scales are labelled can also have an impact on these estimates and that is something that needs further investigation. ONS decided that an 11 point scale from 0–10 where 0 is 'not at all' and 10 is an absolute value such as 'completely' should be used for all the APS personal well-being questions. The reason for this decision was to ensure that the scales between the questions are consistent in order to help respondents answer the questions more easily and also to aid analysis across the separate questions. Further to this, 11 point scales are commonly used across other similar surveys, particularly internationally, and using the same type of scale will aid comparisons with these estimates.
- **Question wording** - it is not only response scales that differ from survey to survey but also question wording, including the use of time frames. ONS has used both cognitive testing techniques and split trial testing of data collected on the Opinions Survey to ascertain the impact these differences have on estimates. This is especially important with respect to issues such as harmonisation of question wording across surveys in order to gain comparable results.

Interpreting personal well-being estimates

When comparing differences between average ratings for groups it is important to realise that these comparisons are made using aggregate statistics based on samples with those characteristics. Just because the average of the sample has a certain rating of personal well-being does not necessarily mean that all people with that certain characteristic have that particular outcome. For example, even though women on average have higher life satisfaction than men, it is important not to infer that all women are more satisfied with their lives than men. Looking at the percentage below or above different thresholds goes some way in addressing this. However, it is also important not to infer that what is true for part of the sample with a certain characteristic is true for all people with that characteristic.

It is also important to note that although personal well-being estimates in this bulletin have been analysed by different personal characteristics and circumstances, this should not be taken to imply causation. Although some groups are more likely to give higher life satisfaction ratings on average it may not be the particular characteristic that is causing them to have higher personal well-being. There are other factors that could also be influencing their ratings which would need to be controlled for in a regression model, and even then causation is often difficult to infer. For example, although married people on average give higher levels of happiness it is difficult to say with certainty that marriage increases happiness or whether actually people who are happy are more likely to marry.

The size of differences between average ratings of personal well-being for groups of people with certain characteristics or in different circumstances can appear fairly small. These differences must be interpreted in light of the fact that personal well-being is affected by many different life circumstances with a variety of factors having a bearing on a person's personal well-being. For example, if someone is in poor health, that is only one aspect of their lives so when making a cognitive judgment about how satisfied they are with their lives overall, although their poor health may have a bearing, other factors may mitigate against that and mean they do not give such a low score as we may perhaps first expect.

Additionally it should be noted that the health measure used is this bulletin is self-reported health, and like the four personal well-being questions relies on the person's own perceptions. This could be a factor in the reason for the strong association between these measures.

Uses of the data

Personal well-being data is useful for better decision making, for policy makers, individuals, communities, business and civil society. It complements other measures of progress and quality of life such as unemployment and household income and is used by the Office for National Statistics to better monitor and understand national well-being.

One of the main benefits of personal well-being data is that it is based on people's views of their own individual well-being. Without it, assumptions need to be made about how objective conditions, such as people's health and income, might influence their individual well-being. Personal well-being measures, on the other hand, are grounded in individuals' preferences and take account of what matters most to them by allowing them to decide what is important when providing an assessment of their own quality of life.

The uses of personal well-being data are varied, but in particular four main uses have been identified:

- overall monitoring of national well-being,
- use in the policy making process,
- international comparison,
- public decision making.

Overall monitoring of national well-being

Collected regularly, personal well-being data can provide an indication of how the well-being of a nation is changing. However, to get a full picture of national well-being, ONS believe it is important to use this information to supplement existing objective information. ONS have identified different aspects (or domains) of well-being that sit alongside the personal well-being domain. These include such areas as health, our relationships, what we do, where we live, personal finance, education and skills, the economy, the environment and governance.

The National Well-being wheel of measures includes indicators for all these aspects of national well-being, and personal well-being estimates from the APS are used with other indicators to monitor the overall well-being of the UK.

Use in the policy making process

Personal well-being data, within the framework of wider measures to understand national well-being is intended to inform policy development so that it focuses on what matters most in people's lives. How people think and feel about their lives is an important addition to official statistics from which policy makers can draw to make more rounded decisions focussed on quality of life. There is an emerging demand for personal well-being information to support policy development and the government has begun to use the experimental data to better account for well-being in policy development.

Identifying need and targeting policies

The large sample size of this experimental personal well-being dataset from the Annual Population Survey allows for comparisons between different groups of the population (for example, different age groups or different ethnic groups) and between different areas within the UK (for example, countries and local authority districts). This can help policy-makers target policy at the groups or areas with highest need in terms of personal well-being.

Analysis can also be carried out to look at how different objective domains relate to personal well-being and which have the biggest impact on personal well-being. This can help in identifying which policy measures could improve personal well-being. In May 2013, ONS published analysis looking at 'What matters most to personal well-being?' (ONS 2013a) and this identified health, relationship status and employment status as the factors most highly associated with personal well-being in the Annual Population Survey.

Policy appraisal

Another use is in cost-benefit analysis in policy appraisal. Personal well-being estimates can provide an alternative method to value the costs and benefits of different policies. This process could also help inform decisions around which forms of spending will lead to the largest increases in personal well-being (Dolan et al, 2011).

The Green Book is HM Treasury's guide for government departments on the appraisal of the costs and benefits of projects through social cost-benefit analysis. A Green Book discussion paper (Fujiwara & Campbell, 2011), produced jointly by HM Treasury and the Department for Work and Pensions, looks at the potential uses of personal well-being measures in social cost-benefit analysis. Another recent example of the use of personal well-being data in this area has been to produce a method for the monetary valuation of volunteering (Fujawara et al, 2013).

Evaluation and monitoring of policy

Personal well-being data can also be used to evaluate and monitor the effectiveness of policy interventions. A recent example is the National Citizen Service where a pilot evaluated the personal well-being of young people before and after their participation in the service. The results show increases in personal well-being among participants, before and after involvement, compared with a control group of peers over the same period. As well as government interventions, other civil society and third sector interventions could be evaluated in a similar way.

Added to this, looking at policies through a 'well-being lens' and using data to inform not only the formulation of policy but also how policy could be better implemented with people's well-being in mind is also important. The Social Impacts Taskforce (SITF), comprising of senior analysts from across government, has been working to make use of personal well-being data and share approaches and findings across government. The Cabinet Office has also convened a cross-Whitehall steering group of senior policy makers to encourage the consideration of well-being in policy. Separate initiatives to investigate well-being are being undertaken by the devolved governments. These include: the National Performance Framework, which forms part of the 'Scotland performs' initiative and the recently published 'Analysis of subjective well-being in Wales: Evidence from the Annual Population Survey'. These initiatives reflect the specific needs of the countries they represent.

Further information, including case studies of how personal well-being data is beginning to be used in the policy process is available in recent government evidence submitted by the Cabinet Office to the Environmental Audit Committee as part of their inquiry on well-being.

International comparisons

The benefit of understanding where the UK is placed compared to other nations is an important reason for the collection of personal well-being data.

There is increasing demand from international organisations to develop personal well-being estimates and increasing recognition internationally that this should be included in official data collection.

Eurostat (the Statistical Office of the European Union) have started to collect personal well-being statistics from member states as part of the European Statistics on Income and Living Conditions (EU-SILC) in an ad-hoc well-being module in 2013. Eurostat's Quality of Life Indicators, currently being developed, will also include personal well-being information to supplement objective information already collected across Europe.

The Organisation of Economic Co-operation and Development (OECD) has also recently developed guidance on the measurement of personal well-being. This can be seen as a first step towards harmonised international standards for the measurement of personal well-being.

Public decision making

ONS personal well-being data could also be used by the public in a number of ways. These include:

- informing public debate and discussion about what matters most,
- using well-being data to make a judgement on how the government is doing in terms of increasing the well-being of the nation,
- informing life-style choices and making better decisions in terms of how they impact on personal well-being, for example the 'five ways to well-being' that stress the importance of social connections, being active, taking notice of surroundings, learning and giving of time and money.

ONS is committed to making personal well-being data accessible and engaging and the ONS Measuring National Well-being web-page has links to interactive charts and maps to enable people to explore the data further.

About the ONS Measuring National Well-being Programme

NWB logo 2

This statistical bulletin is published as part of the ONS Measuring National Well-being Programme.

The programme aims to produce accepted and trusted measures of the well-being of the nation - how the UK as a whole is doing.

Measuring National Well-being is about looking at 'GDP and beyond'. It includes headline indicators in areas such as health, relationships, job satisfaction, economic security, education, environmental conditions and measures of 'subjective well-being' (individuals' assessment of their own well-being).

Find out more on the Measuring National Well-being website pages.

References

Bardasi, E. & Francesconi, M., (2004). The impact of atypical employment on individual well-being. Evidence from a panel of British workers. Journal of Social Science and Medicine; 58.

Cabinet Office (2013), Evidence to the Environmental Audit Committee.

Dolan P, Layard R and Metcalfe R, Office for National Statistics (2011). Measuring Subjective Well-being for Public Policy (99.8 Kb Pdf).

Dolan P, Peasgood T and White M (2008). Do we really know what makes us happy? A review of the economic literature on the factors associated with subjective well-being. Journal of Economic Psychology; 29:94-122.

European Quality of Life Survey (2012).

Eurostat (2013), Quality of Life Indicators.

Fujiwara D and Campbell R, HM Treasury and Department for Work and Pensions (2011). Valuation Techniques for Social Cost-Benefit Analysis: Stated Preference, Revealed Preference and Subjective Well-Being Approaches.

Fujiwara, D, Oroyemi, P & McKinnon, E. Cabinet Office and Department for Work and Pensions (2013), Well-being and Civil Society; Estimating the value of volunteering using subjective wellbeing data.

Gallup World Poll (2012). Gallup Worldview.

New economics foundation (nef), Five Ways to Well-being.

OECD (2013), Guidelines on measuring subjective well-being.

Office for National Statistics (2011a). Measuring Subjective Well-being (240.8 Kb Pdf).

Office for National Statistics (2011b). Initial investigation into Subjective Well-being data from the ONS Opinions Survey.

Office for National Statistics (2012). First Annual ONS Experimental Subjective Well-being Results.

Office for National Statistics (2013a). Measuring National Well-being – What matters most to Personal Well-being?.

Office for National Statistics (2013b). Labour Market Statistics.

Office for National Statistics (2013c). Measuring National Well-being - Older people and loneliness.

The Scottish Government (2012), National Performance Framework, Scotland performs.

Veenhoven, R. Trends in Nations, World Database of Happiness, Erasmus University Rotterdam, Happiness Economics Research Organization (2002-2012).

Welsh Government (2012), An Analysis of Subjective Wellbeing in Wales: Evidence from the Annual Population Survey.

Which? (2013) 'Which? Consumer Insight Tracker'.

Background notes

1. These statistics are experimental in nature and published at an early stage to gain feedback from users. Should users have comments on the ONS approach to the measurement of personal well-being and or the presentation of the personal well-being questions they can email ONS at nationalwell-being@ons.gsi.gov.uk. It is the role of the UK Statistics Authority to designate these statistics as National Statistics and one of the aspirations of the National Well-being programme is to see these statistics gain National Statistics status.

2. Data analysed in this report relates to APS data from April 2012 to March 2013 unless stated otherwise.

3. The data analysed in this bulletin was collected from the Annual Population Survey (APS). The sample size of the 12 month APS personal well-being dataset is 165,000 adults aged 16 and over and living in residential accommodation in the UK (England, Scotland, Wales and Northern Ireland). Data used are weighted to be representative of the population, unless otherwise stated.

4. A list of the job titles of those given pre-release access to the contents of this Statistical Bulletin is available on the website.

5. Details of the policy governing the release of new data are available by visiting the UK Statistics Authority or from the Media Relations Office.

6.

Information Policy Team, The National Archives, Kew, London TW9 4DU, or email: psi@nationalarchives.gsi.gov.uk.

7. Details of the policy governing the release of new data are available by visiting www.statisticsauthority.gov.uk/assessment/code-of-practice/index.html or from the Media Relations Office email: media.relations@ons.gsi.gov.uk

Copyright

This document is also available on our website at www.ons.gov.uk.

Statistical contacts

Name	Phone	Department	Email
Dawn Snape	+44 (0)1633 455674	Measuring National Well-being	dawn.snape@ons.gsi.gov.uk
Lucy Tinkler	+44 (0)1633 455713	Measuring National Well-being	lucy.tinkler@ons.gsi.gov.uk

Issuing Body:
Office for National Statistics

Media Contact Details:
Telephone: 0845 604 1858
(8.30am-5.30pm Weekdays)

Emergency out of hours (limited service): 07867 906553

Email:
media.relations@ons.gsi.gov.uk

Measuring National Well-being - What we do - September 2013

Author Name(s): **Chris Randall, Office for National Statistics**

Abstract

This article is published as part of the Office for National Statistics Measuring National Well-being Programme (MNWB). The 'What we do' domain contains six measures which cover unemployment, employment, volunteering, leisure time and participation in arts and culture and sports. This article summarises these measures and also looks at associated data such as stress at work, work-life balance and free time activities.

Introduction

The Office for National Statistics measures of national well-being are grouped into ten domains with a total of 41 headline measures. More information about all the measures can be found here - National Well-being

This article summarises the six measures under the 'What we do' domain, which include:

- Unemployment rate.
- Percentage who were somewhat, mostly or completely satisfied with their job.
- Percentage who volunteered in the last 12 months.
- Percentage who were somewhat, mostly or completely satisfied with their amount of leisure time.
- Percentage of people who have engaged with, or participated in, arts or cultural activity at least three times in the last year.
- Adult participation in 30 minutes of moderate intensity sport, once a week.

It also looks at associated data such as stress at work, work-life balance and free time activities.

Key points

- The percentage of the workforce aged 16 and over in the UK who were unemployed was 7.8% in April to June 2013, equivalent to 2.51 million people, a fall of 4,000 from January to March 2013.
- In 2010/11, 78.5% of adults aged 16 and over in the UK who were in work reported being somewhat, mostly or completely satisfied with their job.
- 16.8% of adults aged 16 and over in the UK reported they had done voluntary work several times a year or more in 2010/11, while 81.5% had never or almost never done any voluntary work.

- Just over 6 in 10 (60.9%) of adults aged 16 and over in the UK were somewhat, mostly or completely satisfied with their amount of leisure time in 2010/11.
- Over 8 in 10 (83.2%) adults aged 16 and over in England engaged with, or participated in, arts or cultural activity at least three times in the year prior to interview in 2012/13.
- Between October 2011 and October 2012, 36.0% of adults aged 16 and over in England participated in at least 30 minutes of sport at moderate intensity at least once a week, equivalent to 15.51 million people.

Unemployment and employment

'There is a strong evidence base showing that work is generally good for physical and mental health and well-being. Worklessness is associated with poorer physical and mental health and well-being'. - Gordon Waddell, A Kim Burton - Is Work Good for your Health and Well-being?

According to the Labour Force Survey, the percentage of the workforce aged 16 and over in the UK who were unemployed in April to June 2013 was 7.8%, equivalent to 2.51 million people[1,2]. This was a fall of 4,000 in the number of unemployed people from January to March 2013 and 49,000 lower than April to June 2012. Despite these falls, unemployment remains much higher than a decade ago when the unemployment rate was 4.9% in April to June 2003 (ONS, 2013).

In April to June 2013 there were 29.78 million people in work in the UK, a rise of 69,000 compared to January to March 2013 and 301,000 higher than April to June 2012. The employment rate, which measures the percentage of people aged 16 to 64 in work, was 71.5% in April to June 2013[3] (ONS 2013).

Job satisfaction is an important factor in the well-being of employees. In 2010/11 just under 8 in 10 (78.5%) adults aged 16 and over in the UK who had a job reported being somewhat, mostly or completely satisfied with their job according to the UK Household Longitudinal Study(UKHLS)[4]. This compares with 14.3% who reported being somewhat, mostly or completely dissatisfied with their job (UKHLS, 2010/11).

Figure 1: Satisfaction with aspects of job (1)

Great Britain

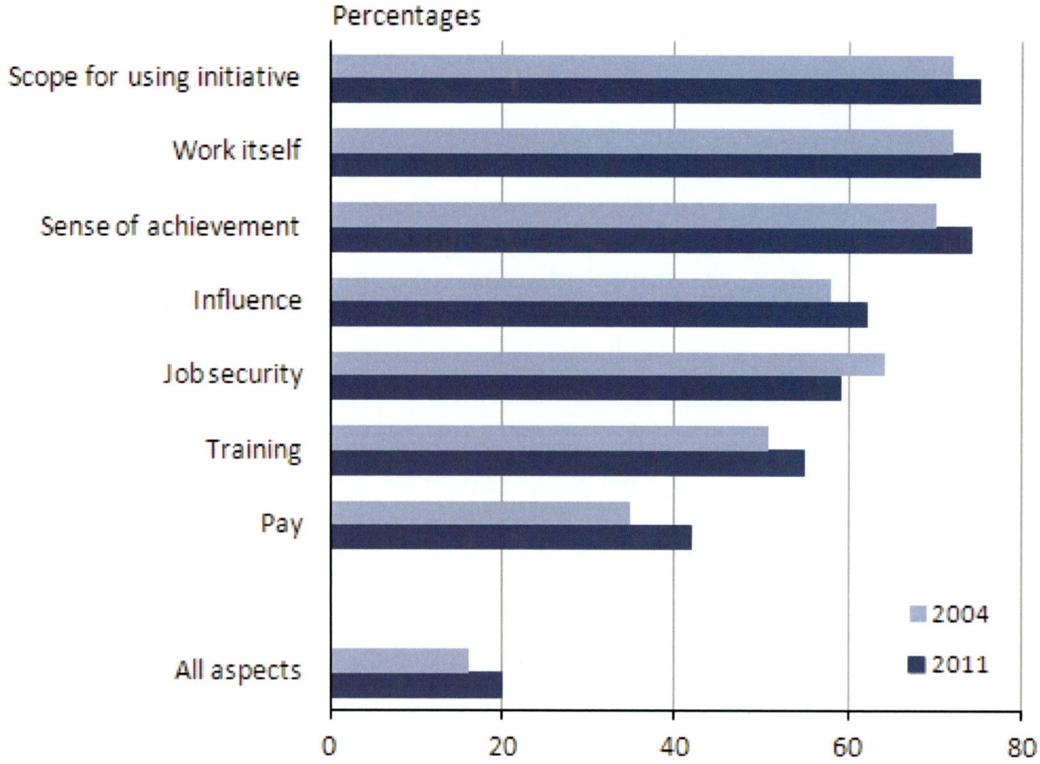

Source: The 2011 Workplace Employment Relations Study: First Findings (third edition), Department for Business Innovation & Skills

Notes:

1. Employees were asked 'How satisfied are you with the following aspects of your job'? The percentages in the chart include those who reported 'very satisfied' or 'satisfied'.

Download chart

XLS XLS format
(32.5 Kb)

According to the 2011 Workplace Employment Relations Study (WERS), 20% of employees in Great Britain were either satisfied or very satisfied with all the seven facets of their job explored in the study and included in **Figure 1** compared with 16% in 2004. The percentage of employees saying that they were satisfied or very satisfied rose for all the categories individually except for job security where the percentage fell from 64% in 2004 to 59% in 2011. In 2011, around three-quarters of employees were either satisfied or very satisfied with the scope for using their own initiative, the work itself or feeling a sense of achievement (WERS, 2011).

Work can have a positive impact on a person's health and well-being. A survey from Populus conducted in March 2013 asked working adults aged 18 and over in England and Wales how stressed their work life made them feel. Just over a third (34%) reported that their working life made them feel very or quite stressful, while just under a third (32%) reported that their working life was not very or not at all stressful (Populus, 2013).

Figure 2: Reasons for stress at work, 2013 (1)

England and Wales

Notes:

1. 1,939 respondents aged 18 and over were asked in March 2013 'In your current job, how stressful, if at all, are the following?' Those who reported 'A little stressful' are not included in the chart.

Download chart

XLS XLS format
(33.5 Kb)

The same survey asked respondents who were employed how stressful aspects of their current job were. Nearly a third (32%) reported that they felt very or quite stressful with their frustration with poor management **(Figure 2)**. Around a quarter reported feeling very or quite stressful about excessive workloads or unrealistic targets or not enough support from managers or job insecurity (Populus, 2013).

Getting the right balance between work and leisure may also be important to a person's well-being. Work-life balance is a concept which involves prioritising between work and a person's lifestyle which could include health, leisure and family. In a survey conducted by YouGov in November 2011 over three-quarters (76%) of adults in the UK reported that having a good work-life balance was an important indicator of a good employer (YouGov, 2011).

In June 2011, adults aged 16 and over in Great Britain were asked by the ONS Opinions Survey how satisfied they were on a scale of 0 to 10[5] with the balance between the time spent on paid work and the time spent on other aspects of their life. The average (mean) rating of satisfaction was 6.4. When broken down by age group the average mean for those aged 16 to 24 was 7.1, for those 25 to 49 it was 6.1 and for those 50 and over it was 6.7.

Table 1: Proportion of employees agreeing they achieve the right balance between their work and home lives: by sex and work sector, 2013 (1)

United Kingdom (Percentages)

	All	Men	Women	Private sector	Public sector	Voluntary sector
Strongly agree	10	8	13	11	9	4
Agree	47	45	48	46	46	57
Neither agree nor disagree	15	17	14	15	15	17
Disagree	19	22	17	20	19	13
Strongly disagree	8	9	8	8	11	9
Not sure	1	0	1	1	1	1

Source: Employee Outlook, Chartered Institute of Personnel and Development

Table notes:

1. March 2013. Due to rounding figures may not add up to 100%.

Download table

XLS XLS format
(32.5 Kb)

According to a survey conducted in March 2013 by the Chartered Institute of Personnel and Development (CIPD), over half (57%) of employees in the UK agreed or strongly agreed that they achieved the right balance between their work and home lives **(Table 1)**. Men are less likely than women to agree or agree strongly that they achieve the right balance (53% and 61% respectively).

Voluntary sector employees were most likely to agree or strongly agree that this was the case (61%), compared to 57% and 55% respectively for those in the private and public sector (CIPD, 2013).

Notes

1. This is a measure under the 'What we do' domain.

2. The unemployment rate is the number of unemployed people (aged 16 and over) divided by the economically active population (aged 16 and over).

3. The employment rate is the number of people aged 16 to 64 in employment divided by the population aged 16 to 64.

4. This is a measure under the 'What we do' domain.

5. Where nought is 'not at all' and 10 is 'completely'.

Volunteering

Apart from paid employment individuals spend time on things which might be considered as 'unpaid work' or voluntary work.

'Volunteering is vital to charities and civil society, helps to strengthen local communities, and improves the wellbeing of individuals who participate' - Daniel Fujiwara, Paul Oroyemi and Ewen McKinnon - Wellbeing and Civil Society.

Figure 3: Frequency of unpaid voluntary work (1), 2010/11

United Kingdom

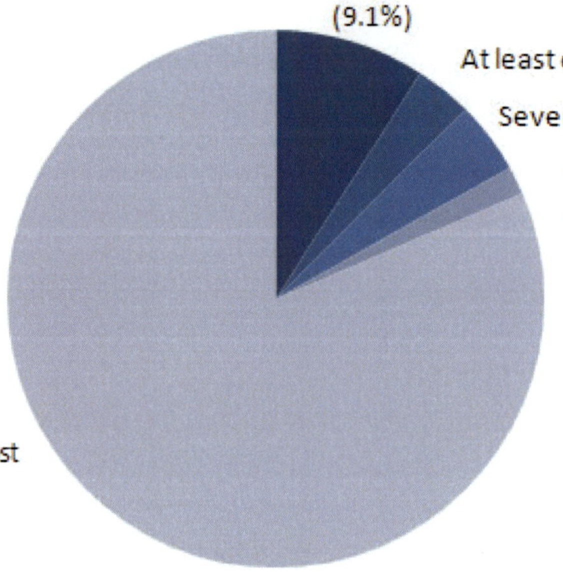

Source: Understanding Society, the UK Household Longitudinal Study, 2010/11

Notes:

1. Respondents aged 16 and over were asked "How frequently do you do unpaid voluntary work?"
2. The percentages are of those who responded.

Download chart

XLS XLS format
(33 Kb)

According to the 2010/11 UK Household Longitudinal Survey (UKHLS), 16.8% of adults aged 16 and over had done voluntary work several times a year or more[1] **(Figure 3)**. Over 8 in 10 (81.5%) had never or almost never done any voluntary work, while 1 in 10 (9.1%) worked voluntarily at least once a week (UKHLS, 2010/11).

Another survey that records the frequency of volunteering is the Community Life Survey (CLS) run by the Cabinet Office. In this survey, two measures of volunteering are covered, formal and informal[2]. Volunteering both formally and informally has generally risen over the past few years. In August 2012 to April 2013, 29% of adults aged 16 in England and over said they had volunteered formally at least once a month in the 12 months prior to being interviewed. This is a significant increase in the level seen in 2010 –11 (25%) and in all years from 2007–08, before which there had been a downward trend since 2005[3]. In August 2012 to April 2013, 44% of people said that they had volunteered formally at least once in the last year prior to being interviewed. This has significantly increased from 39% in 2010-11 and is also significantly higher than levels in 2008–09 and 2009–10 (CLS, 2012/13).

Over a third (36%) of people said they had volunteered informally at least once a month in the 12 months prior to being interviewed. This has significantly increased from 29% in both 2009–10 and 2010–11. In August 2012 to April 2013, 62% of people said they had volunteered informally at least once in the last year prior to being interviewed. This has significantly increased from 55% in 2010–11 and is also higher than the level seen in 2009–10 (54%) (CLS, 2012/13).

Notes

1. This is a measure under the ‘What we do’ domain.

2. Formal volunteering – giving unpaid help through groups, clubs or organisations. This could be a small community group consisting entirely of volunteers, or through major organisations such as Health Trusts or national voluntary organisations. Informal volunteering – giving unpaid help as an individual to people who are not relatives. This could be babysitting for a friend or checking on an elderly neighbour.

3. Data for earlier years are sourced from the Citizenship Survey which was run by the Department for Communities and Local Government.

Leisure, arts, culture and sport

‘Participation in both physical and non-physical leisure activities has been shown to reduce depression and anxiety, produce positive moods and enhance self-esteem and self-concept, facilitate social interaction, increase general psychological wellbeing and life satisfaction, and improve cognitive functioning’ (Haworth - Life, Work, Leisure and Enjoyment: the role of social institutions).

Having the right amount of leisure time is important, as it gives people the time to spend doing things they choose to do rather than the things they must do. According to the 2010/11 UK Household Longitudinal Survey (UKHLS) just over 6 in 10 (60.9%) adults aged 16 and over were somewhat, mostly or completely satisfied with their amount of leisure time[1]. This compares to just over a quarter (25.4%) that were somewhat, mostly or completely dissatisfied with their amount of leisure time (UKHLS, 2010/11).

Table 2: Engagement or participation in an arts or cultural activity: by sex and age, 2008/09 to 2012/13 (1)

England (Percentages)

	All aged 16 and over	Male	Female	16–24	25–44	45–64	65–74	75 and over
2008/09	80.8	78.9	82.6	78.3	83.4	83.6	79.4	67.8
2009/10	81.6	81.6	81.6	81.0	85.2	83.7	81.1	63.9
2010/11	81.0	78.6	83.3	79.2	84.0	82.2	82.2	68.1
2011/12	83.9	82.0	85.8	85.3	85.7	85.3	83.1	71.7
2012/13	83.2	81.3	85.0	82.8	85.0	83.6	86.3	72.0

Source: Taking Part: The National Survey of Culture, Leisure and Sport, Department for Culture, Media and Sport

Table notes:

1. At least three times in the year prior to interview. This covers engagement or participation in the arts (excluding reading for pleasure), museums and galleries, libraries, archives and heritage sites.

Download table

XLS XLS format
(32.5 Kb)

According to the Taking Part Survey (TPS) run by the Department for Culture, Media and Sport over 8 in 10 (83.2%) adults aged 16 and over in England engaged with, or participated in, arts or cultural activity at least three times in the year prior to interview in 2012/13[2] **(Table 2)**. More women than men participate or engage at 85.0% and 81.3% respectively. Since 2008/09, the proportion of engagement and participation has risen in most age groups, most notably by 6.9 percentage points for those aged 65 to 74[3] (TPS, 2012/13).

In the same survey, respondents were shown a list of activities and asked to pick the things they did in their free time. Table 3 shows the results by age-group.

Table 3: Free time activities: by age, 2012/13

England (Percentages)

	16–24	25–44	45–64	65–74	75 and over	All aged 16 and over
Watch TV	84.1	88.6	91.6	92.5	93.9	89.8
Spend time with friends/ family	88.6	87.7	86.8	87.0	84.8	87.2
Listen to music	88.3	80.7	76.7	70.5	67.5	78.2
Shopping	71.6	77.1	74.9	78.4	76.4	75.7
Eat out at restaurants	70.5	74.7	74.8	73.7	66.8	73.2
Read	53.7	68.4	73.7	76.3	74.6	69.3
Days out or visits to places	59.7	71.3	69.3	72.7	57.5	67.8
Internet/ emailing	80.4	80.1	66.3	48.6	22.7	67.0
Sport/ exercise	65.1	62.2	55.7	49.4	34.4	56.6
Go to cinema	73.3	63.3	49.7	36.1	25.0	54.0
Go to pubs/ bars/ clubs	58.2	56.4	51.5	39.0	26.3	50.4

Source: Taking Part: The National Survey of Culture, Leisure and Sport, Department for Culture, Media and Sport

Table notes:

1. Respondents were shown a list of activities and asked to pick the things they did in their free time.

Download table

XLS XLS format
(33 Kb)

Watching television has been a common pastime for decades. The latest data from the Taking Part Survey showed that in 2012/13 watching television in free time continued to be the most common activity reported by adults aged 16 and over in England **(Table 3)**. Nine in 10 (89.8%) of all adults watched television in their free time and it was the most popular activity for age groups from 25 upwards (TPS, 2012/13).

For those aged 16 to 24, spending time with friends or family and listening to music was reported by the highest proportion of respondents (88.6% and 88.3% respectively). Overall, for adults aged 16 and over, spending time with friends and family was the second most popular activity at 87.2%, followed by listening to music (78.2%) and shopping (75.7%). The activities which were reported less frequently as age increased were listening to music, internet and emailing, sport and exercise, going out to pubs, clubs or bars and going out to the cinema (TPS, 2012/13).

Sport and physical activity can enhance individual quality of life and well-being by improving physical and mental health, educational attainment, and providing opportunities for positive social interaction that give a sense of belonging and inclusion.

Figure 4: At least 30 minutes of sport participation at moderate intensity at least once a week, 2005–06 to 2011–12 (1)

England

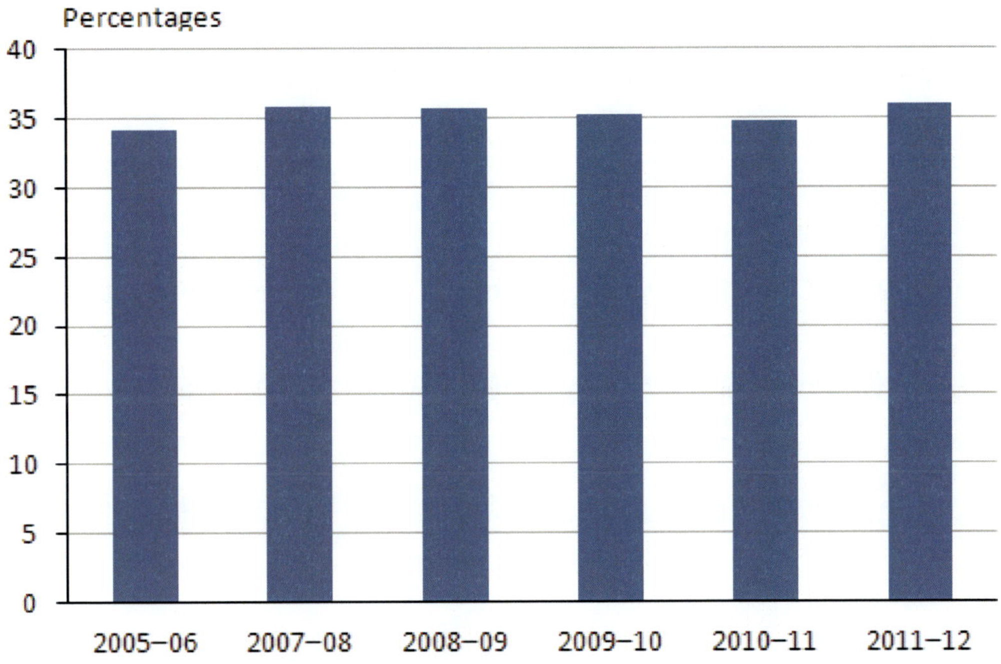

Source: Active People Survey, Sport England

Notes:

1. Adults aged 16 and over. One session a week (at least four sessions of at least moderate intensity for at least 30 minutes in the previous 28 days). Data are October to October.

Download chart

XLS XLS format
(32.5 Kb)

Between October 2011 and October 2012, over a third (36.0%) of adults aged 16 and over in England participated in at least 30 minutes of sport at moderate intensity at least once a week[4] according to the Active People Survey (APS) **(Figure 4)**. This was equivalent to 15.51 million people, over 750,000 more people than in 2010–11 and 1.6 million increase on 2005–06. During the period October 2011 and October 2012, men were more likely than women to participate once a week (41.1% and 31.1% respectively). When analysed by age group over the same period, 3.79 million young people (54.0%) aged 16 to 25 participated once a week compared with 11.72 million adults (32.4%) aged 26 and over[5] (APS, 2011–12).

Notes

1. This is a measure under the 'What we do' domain.

2. This is a measure under the 'What we do' domain. The measure excludes 'reading for pleasure' as this was thought to have covered most people.

3. Similar data for arts and culture for the devolved administrations can be found here:

   Scotland's People Annual Report: Results from 2012 Scottish Household Survey, 13: Culture and Sport

   www.scotland.gov.uk/Publications/2013/08/6973/13

   The Arts Council of Wales, 2012 Omnibus Survey, Report on Main Findings (Art attendance and participation)

   www.artswales.org.uk/what-we-do/research/annual-surveys/wales-omnibus-survey

   Arts and Culture in Northern Ireland 2012

   www.artscouncil-ni.org/the-arts/literature-language-and-culture/traditional-arts/publications

4. This is a measure under the 'What we do' domain.

5. Similar data for sport participation for the devolved administrations can be found here:

   Scotland's People Annual Report: Results from 2012 Scottish Household Survey, 13: Culture and Sport

   www.scotland.gov.uk/Publications/2013/08/6973/13

   Active adults 2012, Sports Wales

   www.sportwales.org.uk/research--policy/surveys-and-statistics/active-adults-survey.aspx

   Experience of sport and physical activity by adults in Northern Ireland".

   Findings from the 2012/13 Continuous Household Survey.

   www.northernireland.gov.uk/index/media-centre/news-departments/news-dcal/news-dcal-120913-sport-and-physical.htmm

Background notes

1. Details of the policy governing the release of new data are available by visiting www.statisticsauthority.gov.uk/assessment/code-of-practice/index.html or from the Media Relations Office email: media.relations@ons.gsi.gov.uk

Copyright

References

1. APS, 2011–12 - Active People Survey

2. CIPD, 2013 - Employee Outlook, Chartered Institute of Personnel and Development available at www.cipd.co.uk/hr-resources/survey-reports/employee-outlook-spring-2013.aspx

3. CLS, 2012/13 - Cabinet Office Community Life survey

4. Fujiwara, Oroyemi and McKinnon - Wellbeing and Civil Society available at www.gov.uk/government/publications/wellbeing-and-civil-society-estimating-the-value-of-volunteering-using-subjective-wellbeing-data-wp112

5. Haworth - Life, Work, Leisure and Enjoyment: the role of social institutions available at www.wellbeing-esrc.com/developments.html

6. ONS, 2013 - Labour Market Statistics

7. Populus, 2013 - Populus

8. TPS, 2012/13 - DCMS - Taking Part Survey

9. UKHLS, 2010/11 - Understanding Society

10. Waddell and Burton - Is Work Good for your Health and Well-being? available at www.gov.uk/government/publications/is-work-good-for-your-health-and-well-being

11. WERS, 2011 - BIS: Workplace Employment Relations Survey

12. YouGov, 2011 - Yougov archives

About the ONS Measuring National Well-being Programme

NWB logo 2

This article is published as part of the ONS Measuring National Well-being Programme.

The programme aims to produce accepted and trusted measures of the well-being of the nation - how the UK as a whole is doing.

Measuring National Well-being is about looking at 'GDP and beyond'. It includes headline indicators in areas such as health, relationships, job satisfaction, economic security, education, environmental conditions and measures of 'subjective well-being' (individuals' assessment of their own well-being).

Find out more on the Measuring National Well-being website pages.

Measuring National Well-being - Domains and Measures - September 2013

Author Name(s): **Ann Corp, Office for National Statistics**

Abstract

This article is published as part of the ONS Measuring National Well-being Programme. The programme aims to produce accepted and trusted measures of the well-being of the nation - how the UK as a whole is doing. The article outlines the latest changes to the measures of national well-being and is part of the ongoing refinement of measures. Also published today is an updated National Well-being Wheel of Measures and National Well-being interactive graphs.

Introduction

The aim of the MNW programme is to 'develop and publish an accepted and trusted set of National Statistics which help people to monitor national well-being'. Critical to achieving this aim is the development of an agreed set of domains and measures.

The initial list of national well-being domains and measures was developed based on responses to the National Debate (which took place between November 2010 and April 2011), existing research and international initiatives.

The measures were the subject of a public consultation which ran between October 2011 and January 2012. A summary and discussion of responses received was published in July 2012, Measuring National Well-being: Report on consultation responses on proposed domains and measures. (524.4 Kb Pdf) No significant changes were made to the set of measures at that time.

In May 2013 Measuring National Well-being – Review of domains and measures, 2013 was published. This honoured a commitment made in November 2012 in Measuring National Well-being: Life in the UK, 2012 that ONS would 'review and further refine domains and measures of well-being and the criteria used to select them'. Feedback was invited on the changes made in this review, resulting in the further refined set of measures published today.

ONS seek and welcome feedback about the national well-being domains and measures. Please send comments to nationalwell-being@ons.gsi.gov.uk

Summary of changes to measures

This section summarises the changes made to national well-being measures since the last publication in May 2013.

- A 'Population mental well-being' measure has been added to the personal well-being domain.
- A 'Median household income' measure has been added to the personal finance domain and the 'Real household actual income per head' measure has been removed from the economy domain.
- The calculation has changed for the 'Has a spouse, family member or friend to rely on if they have a serious problem' measure in the Our relationships domain.
- In the Natural environment domain, the source for 'Energy consumed within the UK from renewable sources' has changed so the measure is on a UK territory basis.

Explanation of changes to measures

This section explains the changes made to national well-being measures since the last publication in May 2013.

1. A 'Population mental well-being' measure has been added to the personal well-being domain.

ONS has previously committed to the inclusion of a measure of mental well-being from the Warwick-Edinburgh Mental Well-being Scale (WEMWBS). The addition of this new measure honours this commitment and is supported by the Department of Health.

2. A 'Median household income' measure has been added to the personal finance domain and the 'Real household actual income per head' measure has been removed from the economy domain.

There is support for using median household income as the preferred measure for indicating how changes in GDP per capita affect average households, for example in the London School of Economics (LSE) Growth Commission report 'Investing for prosperity'[1].

With the inclusion of median household income, it was decided to remove real household actual income per head to avoid any confusion between these measures of household income.

3. The calculation has changed for the 'Has a spouse, family member or friend to rely on if they have a serious problem' measure in the Our relationships domain.

The current measure includes those who have either a spouse or family member or friend who they can rely on 'a lot'. The calculations used for the May 2013 release included responses of 'a little', 'somewhat' or 'a lot' but resulted in a lower figure as respondents were only included where they had a spouse and family member and friend who they could rely on.

4. In the Natural environment domain, the source for 'Energy consumed within the UK from renewable sources' has changed so the measure is on a UK territory basis.

For the May 2013 publication this measure was sourced from AEA Energy and Environment and ONS and was on a resident basis. The source has been changed to the Department for Energy and Environment (DECC) so the measure is now on a UK territory basis, consistent with the 'Total green house gas emissions' measure, also sourced from DECC.

Details of which measures data has been updated since the May 2013 publication can be found in the Measuring National Well-being Domains and Measures, September 2013 (1.56 Mb Excel sheet) spreadsheet.

Notes

1. http://www.lse.ac.uk/researchAndExpertise/units/growthCommission/documents/home.aspx

Where to find domains and measures data

There are now 41 measures of national well-being split across 10 domains. Information and data for the latest release of domains and measures is available in various formats:

- National Well-being wheel of measures (445.1 Kb Pdf) – includes the latest data for all measures (as available at August 2013) in PDF 'print and keep' format
- National Well-being interactive wheel of measures – an interactive tool which includes the latest data for all measures (as available at August 2013) and a previous period for comparison
- Measuring National Well-being Domains and Measures, September 2013 (1.56 Mb Excel sheet) – an Excel file with time series data and information about sources for the measures
- National Well-being interactive graph – an interactive tool showing a range of measures by region and country

Further national well-being analysis and articles are available from the Measuring National Well-being pages on the ONS website at Measuring National Well-being

About the ONS Measuring National Well-being Programme

NWB logo 2

This article is published as part of the ONS Measuring National Well-being Programme.

The programme aims to produce accepted and trusted measures of the well-being of the nation - how the UK as a whole is doing.

Measuring National Well-being is about looking at 'GDP and beyond'. It includes headline indicators in areas such as health, relationships, job satisfaction, economic security, education, environmental conditions and measures of 'subjective well-being' (individuals' assessment of their own well-being).

Find out more on the Measuring National Well-being website pages.

Background notes

1. Details of the policy governing the release of new data are available by visiting www.statisticsauthority.gov.uk/assessment/code-of-practice/index.html or from the Media Relations Office email: media.relations@ons.gsi.gov.uk

Copyright

Statistical Bulletin

EXPERIMENTAL STATISTICS

Personal Well-being Across the UK, 2012/13

Coverage: **UK**
Date: **23 October 2013**
Geographical Areas: **Country, Local Authority and County, Region**
Theme: **People and Places**

Key Points

- Personal well-being improved in the UK between 2011/12 and 2012/13. Ratings for life satisfaction and feeling that the things we do in life are worthwhile increased on average, whilst anxiety levels fell.

- The proportions rating their personal well-being as very high or very low fell between 2011/12 and 2012/13 in the UK, while the proportion rating their well-being around 7 or 8 out of 10 increased.

- Among the countries of the UK, Northern Ireland had the highest average ratings for life satisfaction, worthwhile and happiness in 2012/13. A greater proportion of people in Northern Ireland rated their life satisfaction, worthwhile and happiness as very high (9 or 10 out of 10) than in any other country.

- Among the English regions, the South West and the South East had some of the highest levels of average life satisfaction and worthwhile ratings in 2012/13. The South West also had proportionately more people than any other region rating life satisfaction, worthwhile and happiness as 9 or 10 out of 10.

- The relationship between personal well-being and local circumstances is complex and the reasons why different areas of the UK have different levels of personal well-being is not yet fully understood. ONS plan to publish further analysis later this year looking in detail at how different aspects of where we live contribute to personal well-being.

Background

This is the first statistical bulletin from ONS exploring how personal well-being varies across the countries, regions and more local areas of the UK. The estimates in this bulletin are based on data from the Annual Population Survey (APS) from April 2012 to March 2013 which includes responses from around 165,000 people. This provides a large representative sample of adults aged 16 and over who live in residential households in the UK.

A separate bulletin published by ONS in July 2013 provided estimates of personal well-being for the UK as a whole, broken down by sex, age, ethnicity, relationship status, health, disability and employment status.

The four questions which are used to monitor personal well-being in the UK are:

1. Overall, how satisfied are you with your life nowadays?
2. Overall, to what extent do you feel the things you do in your life are worthwhile?
3. Overall, how happy did you feel yesterday?
4. Overall, how anxious did you feel yesterday?

The findings reported here are based on people's responses to these four questions. People are asked to give their answers on a scale of 0 to 10 where 0 is 'not at all' and 10 is 'completely'. These questions allow people to make an assessment of their life overall, as well as providing an indication of their day-to-day emotions. Although 'yesterday' may not be a typical day for any one individual, the large sample means that these differences 'average out' and provide a reliable assessment of the anxiety and happiness of the adult population in the UK over the year.

In response to user demand, the data released with this bulletin are available for the first time at a range of different geographical levels. Please see Methodology section for full details.

Definitions

Two different methods are used to help explain the findings.

- **Averages** based on ratings for each aspect of personal well-being on the 0 to 10 point scale. This provides another summary measure that allows comparisons using a single number for each aspect of personal well-being.
- **Distributions** focusing particularly on the proportions of people rating each aspect of their well-being at the highest and lowest levels.

The highest levels of life satisfaction, worthwhile and happiness include ratings of 9 or 10 out of 10. For anxiety, ratings of 0 or 1 out of 10 indicate the lowest levels of anxiety and therefore the highest well-being.

The lowest levels of life satisfaction, worthwhile and happiness include ratings of 0 to 4 out of 10. For anxiety, ratings of 6 or more out of 10 indicate the highest levels of anxiety and therefore the lowest well-being.

It should be noted that 'highest' and 'lowest' well-being are more narrowly defined here than in the release of data in July (ONS, 2013a). This will help highlight more clearly the differences between areas. The reference tables provide the data for both 2011/12 and 2012/13, broken down by the same thresholds to allow consistent comparisons.

Throughout the bulletin, only findings that are statistically significant are commented upon. Two methods of determining statistical significance have been used in this bulletin: p-values for change over time and non-overlapping confidence intervals for cross-sectional comparisons between an area estimate and the UK estimate. The reference tables contain full details of each.

Personal well-being in the UK, 2012/13

Figure 1 shows how people in the UK rated each aspect of their personal well-being out of 10 in 2011/12 and 2012/13.

Figure 1: Distribution of responses for personal well-being, 2011/12 & 2012/13

United Kingdom

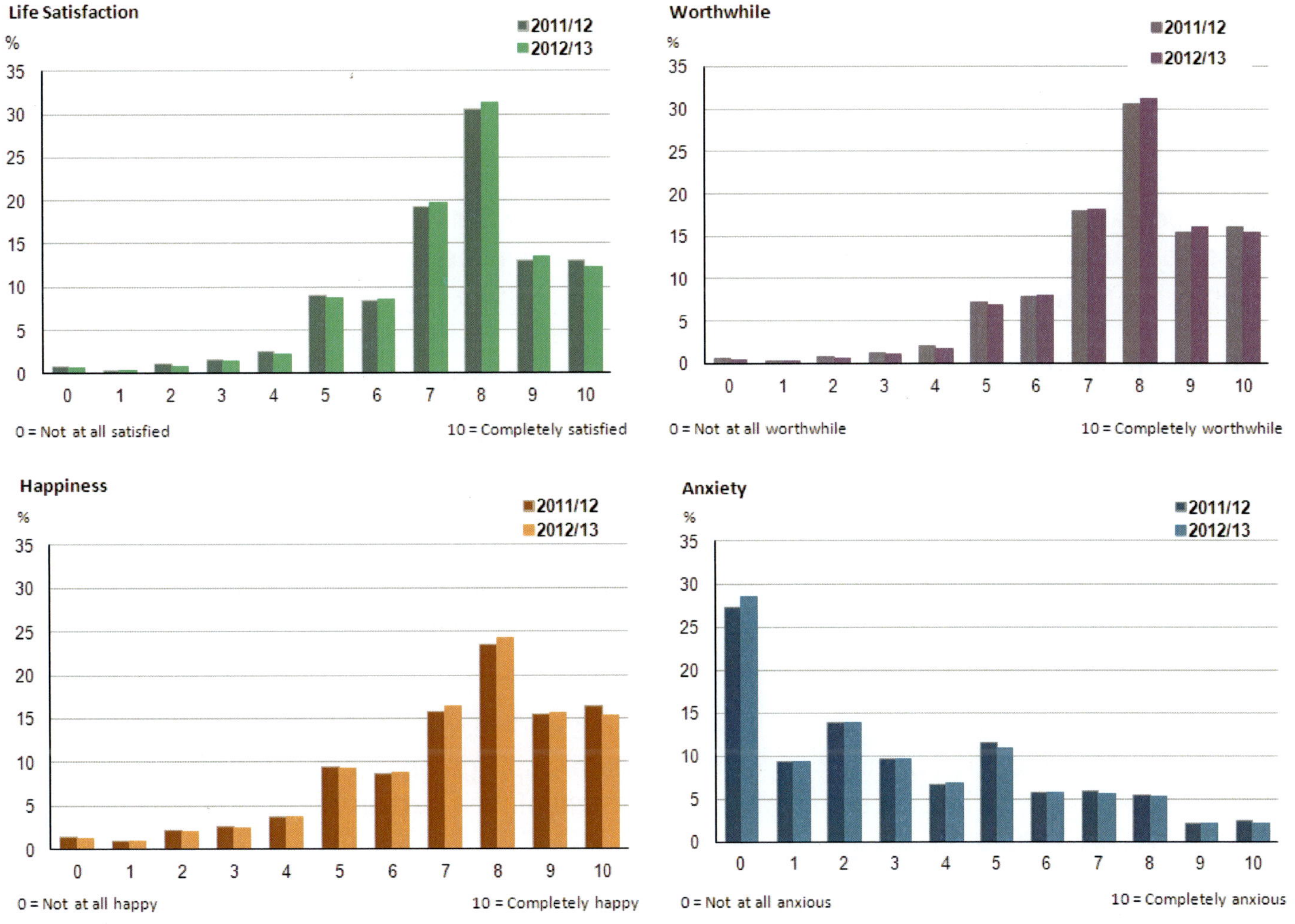

Source: Annual Population Survey (APS) - Office for National Statistics

Notes:

1. Adults aged 16 and over were asked 'Overall, how satisfied are you with your life nowadays?', 'Overall, to what extent do you feel the things you do in your life are worthwhile?', 'Overall, how happy did you feel yesterday?' and 'Overall, how anxious did you feel yesterday?' where 0 is 'not at all' and 10 is 'completely'.

Download chart

XLS XLS format
(30 Kb)

You can explore the data further using interactive graphs showing different levels of personal well-being and overall averages.

Key findings to note about personal well-being in the UK (see **Table 1**) include:

- Small improvements in the average ratings of life satisfaction, worthwhile and anxiety between 2011/12 and 2012/13
- A fall in the proportion of people in the UK reporting very low personal well-being across all four measures in 2012/13 compared with the previous year
- A fall in the proportion of people reporting very high happiness levels in 2012/13 compared with the previous year
- An increase in the proportion of people reporting very low anxiety in 2012/13 compared with the previous year.

The small decreases in the proportions of people reporting very high life satisfaction, worthwhile and happiness have been off-set by small increases in the proportions reporting more moderate levels of well-being in the range of 7-8 out of 10.

The findings in context

Reasons for the small improvement in personal well-being between 2011/12 and 2012/13 are not fully understood.

Recent ONS analysis on 'What matters most to personal well-being?' (ONS, 2013b) found that the factors most associated with personal well-being are health, employment situation and relationship status. Where possible, these factors will be referred to to help contextualise differences in personal well-being across different areas of the UK.

At the UK level, improvements in the labour market picture and special events such as the Queen's Diamond Jubilee and the 2012 Summer Olympic and Paralympic games were suggested as factors which could have positively influenced people's assessment of their personal well-being during the 2012/13 period (ONS, 2013a).

Table 1: Overall Personal Well-being in the UK, 2011/12 and 2012/13

United Kingdom

	Life Satisfaction	Worthwhile	Happiness		Anxiety
					Percentages
High Well-being				**High Well-being**	
% Ratings 9-10				**% Ratings 0-1**	
2011/12	26.1	31.4	31.8	2011/12	36.6
2012/13	26.0	31.4	30.9	2012/13	38.0
Annual % point change	*-0.16*	*-0.01*	*-0.82**	*Annual % point change*	*1.42**
Low Well-being				**Low Well-being**	
% Ratings 0-4				**% Ratings 6-10**	
2011/12	6.6	4.9	10.9	2011/12	21.8
2012/13	5.8	4.4	10.3	2012/13	20.9
Annual % point change	*-0.88**	*-0.49**	*-0.54**	*Annual % point change*	*-0.90**
					Averages
Average				**Average**	
2011/12	7.4	7.7	7.3	2011/12	3.1
2012/13	7.5	7.7	7.3	2012/13	3.0
Annual point change	*0.04**	*0.03**	*0.01*	*Annual point change*	*-0.11**

Table source: Office for National Statistics

Table notes:

1. * Indicates significant at the 0.05 level.
2. Final percentage point change rounded to 2 decimal places.

Download table

XLS XLS format
(30.5 Kb)

Personal well-being in the UK countries, 2012/13

This section provides average ratings for each measure of personal well-being across the countries of the UK in 2012/13. It also considers the proportions of people rating each aspect of well-being at the highest and lowest levels and changes between 2011/12 and 2012/13.

Maps 1 and 2 show the differences in personal well-being across the countries of the UK. You can explore the data further using interactive maps showing personal well-being findings across the UK.

Map 1: Percentages of high personal well-being, by country, 2012/13

United Kingdom

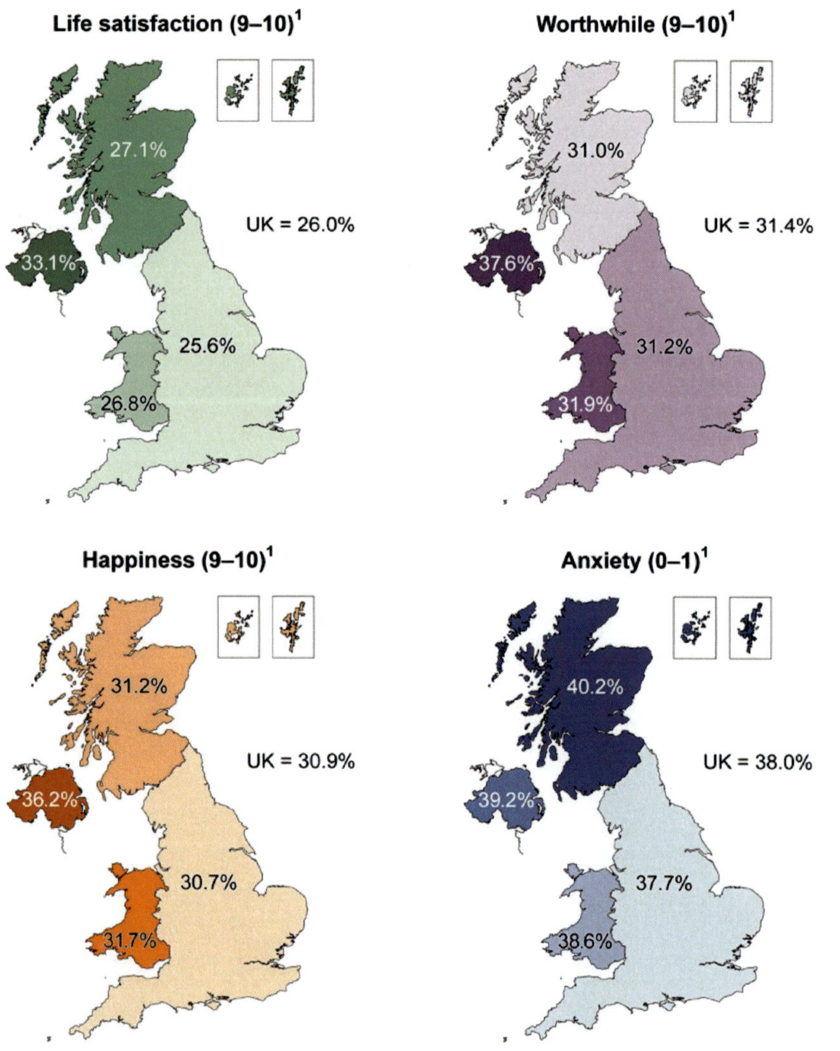

1 Adults aged 16 and over were asked 'Overall, how satisfied are you with your life nowadays?', 'Overall, to what extent do you feel the things you do in your life are worthwhile?', 'Overall, how happy did you feel yesterday?' and 'Overall, how anxious did you feel yesterday?' where 0 is 'not at all' and 10 is 'completely'.
Source: Office for National Statistics

Source: Annual Population Survey (APS) - Office for National Statistics

Download map

PNG PNG format
(358.4 Kb)

Map 2: Percentages of low personal well-being, by country, 2012/13

United Kingdom

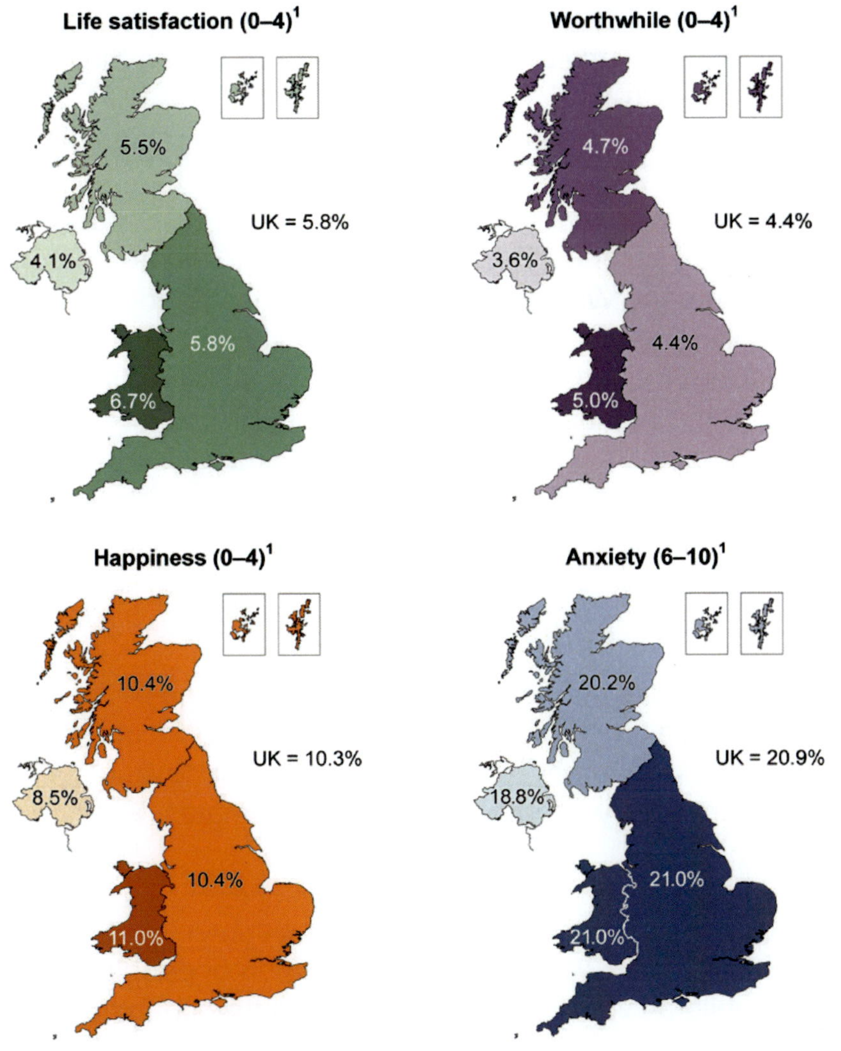

1 Adults aged 16 and over were asked 'Overall, how satisfied are you with your life nowadays?', 'Overall, to what extent do you feel the things you do in your life are worthwhile?', 'Overall, how happy did you feel yesterday?' and 'Overall, how anxious did you feel yesterday?' where 0 is 'not at all' and 10 is 'completely'.
Source: Office for National Statistics

Source: Annual Population Survey (APS) - Office for National Statistics

Download map

PNG PNG format
(350.8 Kb)

The personal well-being picture in 2012/13: UK countries

Key points to note about personal well-being in the UK countries in 2012/13 (see **Tables 2-4**):

- In 2012/13, Northern Ireland had proportionately more people than any other country rating their life satisfaction, worthwhile and happiness as very high (9 or 10 out of 10). Average ratings of life satisfaction, worthwhile and happiness were higher in Northern Ireland than in the UK as a whole. Wales had proportionately more people than any other country in the UK rating their life satisfaction and worthwhile as very low (0-4 out of 10).
- Scotland had proportionately more people than any other country in the UK rating their anxiety as very low (0-1 out of 10) in 2012/13.
- Between 2011/12 and 2012/13, the proportion of people reporting very low anxiety (0-1 out of 10) increased in England, Scotland and Northern Ireland. Over the same period, the proportion reporting very high anxiety in England, Scotland and Wales (6-10 out of 10) decreased.
- Between 2011/12 and 2012/13, the proportions of people reporting very low life satisfaction (0-4 out of 10) fell in England, Scotland and Northern Ireland. Only Northern Ireland saw an increase in the proportion rating their life satisfaction at the highest levels (9-10 out of 10).
- Although the average ratings of happiness remained unchanged in England and Wales between 2011/12 and 2012/13, proportionately fewer people in each country rated their happiness levels as very high (9-10 out of 10).

The findings in context

This section considers how findings based on people's own ratings of their personal well-being relate to circumstances in the areas in which they live. It shows that traditional measures of social progress such as unemployment rates, gross value added per head and life expectancy may sometimes present a different picture to that presented by personal well-being estimates. For example:

- During the period from February to April 2013, Wales had the highest unemployment rate among the countries of the UK at 8.4% (ONS, 2013c). In 2012/13, a greater proportion of people in Wales rated their life satisfaction and worthwhile as very low, compared with other countries in the UK and the UK as a whole.
- Gross value added (GVA) per head is an economic indicator that divides total economic output in the area by the population of the area. It is a measure of the economic competitiveness of an area and is also related to deprivation.
- In 2011, England had the highest GVA per head (£21,349) among the UK countries, but was among the countries with the lowest average personal well-being ratings. In the same year, Northern Ireland had the third lowest GVA per head (£16,531) but the highest personal well-being average rating (ONS, 2012a). The two countries with the lowest life expectancy rates at birth (Northern Ireland and Scotland) had the highest average personal well-being ratings (ONS, 2011a).

Table 2 summarises the average ratings out of 10 for each country and the UK in 2012/13 and shows the change in each measure since 2011/12.

Table 2: Average ratings of Personal Well-being, by UK countries, 2011/12 and 2012/13

United Kingdom

Ratings

	Life Satisfaction	Worthwhile	Happiness	Anxiety
UK				
2011/12	7.4	7.7	7.3	3.1
2012/13	7.5	7.7	7.3	3.0
Annual point change	*0.04**	*0.03**	*0.01*	*-0.11**
England				
2011/12	7.4	7.7	7.3	3.2
2012/13	7.4	7.7	7.3	3.1
Annual point change	*0.04**	*0.02**	*0.00*	*-0.1**
Wales				
2011/12	7.4	7.7	7.3	3.1
2012/13	7.4	7.7	7.3	3.0
Annual point change	*0.04*	*0.00*	*0.00*	*-0.07*
Scotland				
2011/12	7.5	7.7	7.3	3.1
2012/13	7.5^{+}	7.7	7.3	2.9^{+}
Annual point change	*0.03*	*0.03*	*0.04*	*-0.14**
Northern Ireland				
2011/12	7.5	7.8	7.4	3.1
2012/13	7.7^{+}	7.9^{+}	7.6^{+}	2.9
Annual point change	*0.17**	*0.10*	*0.20**	*-0.18**

Table source: Office for National Statistics

Table notes:

1. * Indicates significant at the 0.05 level.
2. \+ Indicates significantly different to the UK estimate for 2012/13.
3. Final point change rounded to 2 decimal places.

Download table

XLS [XLS format](#)
(29.5 Kb)

Table 3 summarises how the UK countries compared in terms of highest personal well-being in 2012/13. The change in each measure since 2011/12 is also provided.

Table 3: High Personal Well-being, by UK countries, 2011/12 and 2012/13

United Kingdom

Percentages

	Life Satisfaction (9-10)	Worthwhile (9-10)	Happiness (9-10)	Anxiety (0-1)
UK				
2011/12	26.1	31.4	31.8	36.6
2012/13	26.0	31.4	30.9	38.0
Annual % point change	*-0.16*	*-0.01*	*-0.82**	*1.42**
England				
2011/12	25.8	31.2	31.6	36.4
2012/13	25.6	31.2	30.7	37.7
Annual % point change	*-0.25*	*0.01*	*-0.90**	*1.32**
Wales				
2011/12	26.9	32.7	33.1	38.6
2012/13	26.8	31.9	31.7	38.6
Annual % point change	*-0.09*	*-0.80*	*-1.42**	*0.04*
Scotland				
2011/12	27.6	31.1	32.2	38.1

2012/13	27.1	31.0	31.2	40.2+
Annual % point change	*-0.45*	*-0.13*	*-1.05*	*2.10**
Northern Ireland				
2011/12	30.1	36.9	33.0	34.5
2012/13	33.1+	37.6+	36.2+	39.2
Annual % point change	*2.97**	*0.73*	*3.20**	*4.72**

Table source: Office for National Statistics

Table notes:

1. * Indicates significant at the 0.05 level.
2. + Indicates significantly different to the UK estimate for 2012/13.
3. Final percentage point change rounded to 2 decimal places.

Download table

XLS XLS format
(32 Kb)

Table 4 summarises how the UK countries compared in terms of lowest personal well-being in 2012/13. The proportionate change in each measure since 2011/12 is also provided.

Table 4: Low Personal Well-being, by UK countries, 2011/12 and 2012/13

United Kingdom

Percentages

	Life Satisfaction (0-4)	Worthwhile (0-4)	Happiness (0-4)	Anxiety (6-10)
UK				
2011/12	6.6	4.9	10.9	21.8
2012/13	5.8	4.4	10.3	20.9
Annual % point change	*-0.88**	*-0.49**	*-0.54**	*-0.90**
England				
2011/12	6.7	4.9	10.8	21.8
2012/13	5.8	4.4	10.4	21.0
Annual % point change	*-0.88**	*-0.51**	*-0.48**	*-0.84**
Wales				
2011/12	7.2	5.0	11.6	22.3
2012/13	6.7+	5.0+	11.0	21.0
Annual % point change	*-0.54*	*0.02*	*-0.55*	*-1.28**
Scotland				
2011/12	6.3	5.3	11.2	21.5
2012/13	5.5	4.7	10.4	20.2
Annual % point change	*-0.75**	*-0.54*	*-0.79*	*-1.24**
Northern Ireland				
2011/12	6.3	4.4	9.8	19.9
2012/13	4.1+	3.6	8.5+	18.8+
Annual % point change	*-2.20**	*-0.74*	*-1.30*	*-1.09*

Table source: Office for National Statistics

Table notes:

1. * Indicates significant at the 0.05 level.
2. + Indicates significantly different to the UK estimate for 2012/13.

3. Final percentage point change rounded to 2 decimal places.

Download table

XLS XLS format
(30 Kb)

Personal well-being in the English regions, 2012/13

This section looks at personal well-being in the English regions in 2012/13, focusing on the average ratings of personal well-being and the proportions of people in each region rating their well-being at the highest and lowest levels. Changes in personal well-being between 2011/12 and 2012/13 for each region are also discussed.

You can explore the data further using interactive graphs comparing all the regions, for different levels of personal well-being and overall averages. Interactive maps are also available.

The personal well-being picture in 2012/13: English regions

The findings show that in 2012/13, the South West region had the highest personal well-being ratings and the North East the worst. The West Midlands had the biggest improvement in personal well-being between 2011/12 and 2012/13.

Other key points to note about personal well-being in the English regions have been taken from **Tables 5 – 7** and include:

- English regions with some of the highest average personal well-being ratings were the South West and the South East. Average life satisfaction and worthwhile were higher in these two regions than the averages for the UK as a whole.
- The South West had the highest proportions of people giving the highest ratings of 9 or 10 out of 10 for life satisfaction and worthwhile, and both were higher than the UK figures.
- London had the lowest average rating for life satisfaction and the highest average rating for anxiety, both higher than the UK average.
- In the North East proportionately more people rated their life satisfaction, worthwhile and happiness as 4 or less out of 10, more than in any other region. Additionally, proportionately more people rated their anxiety levels at a high level than in any other region, indicating lower well-being.
- The region with the biggest change between 2011/12 and 2012/13 for the average ratings was the West Midlands. Life satisfaction and worthwhile increased significantly in 2012/13 and anxiety levels fell.
- The West Midlands also had the largest fall in the proportions of people giving a low rating of 4 or less for life satisfaction, worthwhile and happiness.

The findings in context

Research into why well-being varies across different regional areas is ongoing. Characteristics which may help explain higher ratings of average well-being in the South West include:

- The South West had the lowest unemployment rate among the English regions at 6.2% in the period from February to April 2013 (ONS, 2013c).
- The South West has a higher proportion of older people than any other English region. Previous ONS research has found that overall older people have higher than average personal well-being (ONS, 2012b).
- Among the English regions, the South West had the second highest life expectancy rates at birth for both males and females in 2009-2011 (ONS, 2013d).
- The South West has the lowest population density across the English regions (ONS, 2012b).

Characteristics which may explain why the North East had the lowest average personal well-being among the English regions include:

- The North East had the highest unemployment rate among the English regions at 10.1% in the period from February to April 2013 (ONS, 2013c).
- Looking at economic and financial measures, the North East ranked last among the nine English regions on GVA per head (ONS, 2012a). Gross disposable household income is also lower in the North East than in any other region (ONS, 2013e).
- Among the English regions, the North East and the North West fared least well on life expectancy, both at birth and at age 65 (ONS, 2013d).
- Among the regions, healthy life expectancy was lowest in the North East for both males and females compared to all other regions (ONS, 2013f).

London also had low average personal well-being ratings, but different issues may explain the well-being picture here including:

- London has the highest gross disposable income per head among the regions and the highest GVA per head. However, London also has the greatest range of GVA per head of any region with large differences between areas of Inner London and Outer London (ONS, 2012a).
- Among the regions, London has the highest population density and had the highest population growth between 2011 and 2012. It also has the highest crime rates (ONS, 2013e).
- Compared to the other regions, London has the lowest proportion of the population aged 65 and over (11.3% compared to 20.3% in the South West).

Table 5 summarises the average ratings for each aspect of personal well-being in each region in 2012/13 and also shows the point change out of 10 in each measure since the previous year.

Table 5: Average Ratings of Personal Well-being, by English Regions, 2011/12 and 2012/13

England

Ratings

		Life Satisfaction	Worthwhile	Happiness	Anxiety
North East	2012/13	7.4+	7.6+	7.2+	3.1
	Annual point change	*-0.06*	*0.00*	*-0.01*	*-0.16**
North West	2012/13	7.4+	7.7	7.2+	3.1
	Annual point change	*0.04*	*0.01*	*-0.02*	*-0.09**
Yorkshire and The Humber	2012/13	7.5	7.7	7.3	3.0
	Annual point change	*0.07**	*0.02*	*0.03*	*-0.08*
East Midlands	2012/13	7.5	7.7	7.4	3.0
	Annual point change	*0.03*	*0.04*	*0.03*	*-0.17**
West Midlands	2012/13	7.4	7.6+	7.3	2.9+
	Annual point change	*0.14**	*0.09**	*0.05*	*-0.18**
East	2012/13	7.5	7.7	7.3	3.0
	Annual point change	*0.04*	*0.02*	*-0.03*	*-0.08*
London	2012/13	7.3+	7.6+	7.2+	3.3+
	Annual point change	*0.01*	*0.05*	*0.02*	*-0.16**
South East	2012/13	7.5+	7.8+	7.3	3.0
	Annual point change	*0.03*	*0.02*	*-0.01*	*-0.04*
South West	2012/13	7.5+	7.8+	7.3	3.0

	Annual point change	*0.02*	*-0.01*	*-0.04*	*0.01*

Table source: Office for National Statistics

Table notes:

1. * Indicates significant at the 0.05 level.
2. + Indicates significantly different to the UK estimate for 2012/13.
3. Final percentage point change rounded to 2 decimal places.

Download table

XLS XLS format
(31 Kb)

Table 6 summarises how the English regions compared in terms of highest personal well-being in 2012/13. The proportionate change in each measure since 2011/12 is also provided.

Table 6: High Personal Well-being, by English Regions, 2011/12 and 2012/13

England

Percentages

		Life Satisfaction (9-10)	Worthwhile (9-10)	Happiness (9-10)	Anxiety (0-1)
North East	2012/13	26.1	30.8	30.7	40.4+
	Annual % point change	*-1.01*	*-0.01*	*0.22*	*3.41**
North West	2012/13	26.3	31.6	30.6+	37.9
	Annual % point change	*0.45*	*0.19*	*-0.57*	*1.68**
Yorkshire and The Humber	2012/13	26.9	32.7	31.7	39.3
	Annual % point change	*0.62*	*0.37*	*-0.10*	*1.37*
East Midlands	2012/13	26.4	33.0	32.3	39.9+
	Annual % point change	*-0.53*	*0.86*	*-0.73*	*3.29**
West Midlands	2012/13	25.0	29.2+	30.2	41.3+

	Annual % point change	*0.51*	*0.32*	*-1.01*	*3.02**
East	2012/13	26.5	31.2	31.2	37.8
	Annual % point change	*0.23*	*-0.97*	*-1.15*	*0.70*
London	2012/13	21.0+	27.7+	28.1+	32.2+
	Annual % point change	*-1.42**	*0.27*	*-1.08*	*1.28*
South East	2012/13	25.9	32.3	30.7	37.2
	Annual % point change	*-0.50*	*0.13*	*-1.50**	*-0.30*
South West	2012/13	27.9+	33.0+	32.3	38.0
	Annual % point change	*-0.61*	*-1.01*	*-1.22*	*-0.28*

Table source: Office for National Statistics

Table notes:

1. * Indicates significant at the 0.05 level.
2. + Indicates significantly different to the UK estimate for 2012/13.
3. Final percentage point change rounded to 2 decimal places.

Download table

XLS XLS format
(31.5 Kb)

Table 7 shows how the English regions compared in terms of lowest personal well-being in 2012/13. The change in each measure since 2011/12 is also provided.

Table 7: Low Personal Well-being, by English Regions, 2011/12 and 2012/13

England

Percentages

		Life Satisfaction (0-4)	Worthwhile (0-4)	Happiness (0-4)	Anxiety (6-10)
North East	2012/13	7.0+	5.7+	12.6+	22.5+
	Annual % point change	*0.38*	*0.44*	*0.39*	*-0.98*
North West	2012/13	6.5+	5.0+	11.3+	21.8
	Annual % point change	*-0.53*	*-0.15*	*-0.14*	*-0.79*
Yorkshire and The Humber	2012/13	6.3	4.7	10.9	21.3
	Annual % point change	*-0.91**	*-0.25*	*-0.92*	*-0.47*
East Midlands	2012/13	5.3	4.3	10.1	20.6
	Annual % point change	*-1.55**	*-0.55*	*-0.86*	*-0.84*
West Midlands	2012/13	6.0	4.6	10.4	19.6+
	Annual % point change	*-2.58**	*-1.26**	*-1.07**	*-0.84*
East	2012/13	5.2	4.1	9.3+	19.9
	Annual % point change	*-0.62*	*-0.43*	*-0.32*	*-1.22*
London	2012/13	6.3	4.2	10.3	22.4+
	Annual % point change	*-0.67*	*-0.96**	*-0.84*	*-1.57**
South East	2012/13	4.9+	3.6+	9.5+	20.7
	Annual % point change	*-0.66**	*-0.52*	*-0.38*	*-0.69*
South West	2012/13	5.3	4.0	10.2	20.3

Annual % point change	*-0.53*	*-0.31*	*0.11*	*0.10*

Table source: Office for National Statistics

Table notes:

1. * Indicates significant at the 0.05 level.
2. + Indicates significantly different to the UK estimate for 2012/13.
3. Final percentage point change rounded to 2 decimal places.

Download table

XLS XLS format
(31 Kb)

Personal well-being in English UA/County areas, 2012/13

This section looks at personal well-being within the Unitary Authorities and Counties (UA/County) in England in 2012/13, focusing both on average ratings and the highest and lowest levels of personal well-being.

The personal well-being picture in 2012/13: English UA/Counties

Hampshire and Cornwall had some of the highest levels of personal well-being among the English UA/County areas in 2012/13. Among the areas with the lowest personal well-being were Stoke-on-Trent, Blackburn with Darwen and Inner London. The points below focus on areas which had the highest or lowest personal well-being on more than one measure and where the area estimate differs significantly to the UK estimate. The key points are taken from **Tables 8-11**.

Key points to note about the English UA/County areas with the **highest** personal well-being include the following :

- Hampshire had some of the highest average levels of personal well-being across all four personal well-being questions. Additionally, Hampshire had the second highest proportion of people reporting their anxiety levels as 1 or less out of 10.
- Cornwall was among the highest for average life satisfaction, worthwhile and happiness. Additionally, when we look at the proportions of people giving the highest ratings of 9 or 10 out of 10 Cornwall was among the highest for life satisfaction and happiness.
- Rutland had some of the highest average ratings for life satisfaction and worthwhile.
- Bath and North East Somerset had among the highest average life satisfaction and happiness.

Key points to note about the English UA/County areas with the **lowest** personal well-being include the following :

- Stoke-on-Trent had among the lowest averages ratings for life satisfaction, worthwhile and happiness. Additionally, Stoke-on-Trent had high proportions of people reporting low ratings of 4 or less for life satisfaction, worthwhile and happiness, indicating low well-being.
- Inner London had some of the lowest averages for life satisfaction and high anxiety.
- Blackburn with Darwen had some of the lowest averages for life satisfaction and worthwhile.
- County Durham had proportionately more people than most other areas rating life satisfaction, worthwhile and happiness as very low at 4 or less out of 10, coupled with high anxiety levels. This suggests low overall low well-being.
- Merseyside Met County also had high proportions of people reporting low happiness and high anxiety indicating low well-being.
- Interestingly, some areas that were not among those with the lowest average ratings of life satisfaction, worthwhile and happiness had high average ratings for anxiety such as Brighton and Hove and Milton Keynes.

The findings in context

This section examines how circumstances in each area relate to how people rate their personal well-being. It also highlights how traditional measures of social progress relate to the personal well-being measures.

Many areas of higher personal well-being also have comparatively low unemployment rates. For example, in the period from February to April 2013, Dorset, Cornwall, Bath and North East Somerset all had low unemployment rates ranging from 4.3% in Dorset to 5.9% in Cornwall and all had very high personal well-being ratings (ONS, 2013c).

This can be compared with some of the areas identified as having particularly low personal well-being which have very high unemployment rates such as Stoke-on-Trent and Blackburn with Darwen. In these areas, unemployment over the same period ranged from 8.5% in Stoke-on-Trent to 10.1% in Blackburn with Darwen (ONS, 2013c).

Looking at how life expectancy relates to the personal well-being findings among the UA/ Counties in England, areas with higher personal well-being ratings also have some of the highest average life expectancy rates. These include Dorset, Cornwall, and Bath and North East Somerset (ONS, 2013d).

This can be compared to much lower life expectancy at birth in some of the areas with some of the lowest personal well-being ratings such as Stoke-on-Trent, Blackburn with Darwen (ONS, 2013d).

As noted in relation to the London region, the well-being picture for London looks different to many other areas. Inner London had some of the lowest average ratings of life satisfaction and high anxiety, but also has the highest disposable household income per head among the English UA/ county area (ONS, 2012d).

Within Inner London there are large variations in local characteristics. For example, average life expectancy rates at birth ranged from 78.8 years in Tower Hamlets to 84.0 years in Kensington and Chelsea (ONS, 2013d).

Table 8: Highest Average Personal Well-being, by English Unitary Authorities/Counties, 2012/13

England

Ratings

	Life Satisfaction	Worthwhile	Happiness	Anxiety
1	Wokingham UA (7.8)+	Dorset (7.9)+	Cheshire East UA (7.6)+	North Yorkshire (2.6)+
2	Hampshire (7.7)+	Rutland UA (7.9)+	Bath and North East Somerset UA (7.5)+	Hampshire (2.6)+
3	Cornwall UA (7.7)+	Cornwall UA (7.9)+	Hampshire (7.5)+	Nottinghamshire (2.7)+
4	Rutland UA (7.7)+	Hampshire (7.9)+	Wokingham UA (7.5)+	Warwickshire (2.7)+
5	Bath and North East Somerset UA (7.7)+	North Yorkshire (7.9)+	Cornwall UA (7.5)+	Central Bedforshire UA (2.7)

Table source: Office for National Statistics

Table notes:

1. + Indicates significantly different to the UK estimate for 2012/13.

Download table

XLS XLS format
(28 Kb)

Table 9: High Personal Well-being, by English Unitary Authorities/Counties, 2012/13

England

Percentages

	Life Satisfaction (9-10)	Worthwhile (9-10)	Happiness (9-10)	Anxiety (0-1)
1	Dorset (32.1)+	Dorset (37.0)+	Cornwall UA (37.2)+	Hartlepool UA (46.4)+
2	Redcar and Cleveland UA (31.0)+	Redcar and Cleveland UA (36.2)+	Lincolnshire (36.0)+	Hampshire (45.7)+
3	Cornwall UA (30.6)+	East Riding of Yorkshire UA (35.8)+	North Lincolnshire UA (35.5)+	Nottinghamshire (45.4)+
4	Cumbria (30.5)+	North Yorkshire (35.7)+	Central Bedfordshire UA (34.7)	Nottingham UA (44.6)+
5	Wokingham UA (30.4)+	North East Lincolnshire UA (35.6)+	Isle of Wight UA (34.6)+	North Yorkshire (44.3)+

Table source: Office for National Statistics

Table notes:

1. + Indicates significantly different to the UK estimate for 2012/13.

Download table

XLS XLS format
(29 Kb)

Table 10: Lowest Average Personal Well-being, by English Unitary Authorities/Counties, 2012/13

England

Ratings

	Life Satisfaction	Worthwhile	Happy Yesterday	Anxious Yesterday
1	Stoke-on-Trent UA (7.2)+	Stoke-on-Trent UA (7.2)+	Bedford UA (7.0)	Reading UA (3.4)+
2	Inner London (7.2)+	Nottingham UA (7.5)+	Merseyside Met County (7.0)+	Slough UA (3.4)+
3	Blackburn with Darwen UA (7.2)+	Blackburn with Darwen UA (7.5)+	Stoke-on-Trent UA (7.0)+	Milton Keynes UA (3.4)+
4	County Durham UA (7.3)+	Bristol, City of UA (7.5)	County Durham UA (7.1)+	Brighton and Hove UA (3.4)+
5	Southend-on-Sea UA (7.3)	Blackpool UA (7.5)+	Halton UA (7.1)+	Inner London (3.4)+

Table source: Office for National Statistics

Table notes:

1. + Indicates significantly different to the UK estimate for 2012/13.

Download table

XLS XLS format
(28 Kb)

Table 11: Low Personal Well-being, by English Unitary Authorities/Counties, 2012/13

England

Percentages

	Life Satisfaction (0-4)	Worthwhile (0-4)	Happiness (0-4)	Anxiety (6-10)
1	County Durham UA (8.8)+	Stoke-on-Trent UA (8.2)+	Stoke-on-Trent UA (14.9)+	Merseyside (Met County) (25.8)+
2	Hartlepool UA (8.5)+	County Durham UA (6.4)+	County Durham UA (14.8)+	Rutland UA (25.4)
3	Stoke-on-Trent UA (8.3)+	Tyne and Wear (Met County) (6.4)+	North East Lincolnshire UA (14.6)+	Brighton and Hove UA (25.4)+
4	Kingston upon Hull, City of UA (8.2)+	Blackpool UA (6.0)	Halton UA (14.3)+	Milton Keynes UA (25.4)+
5	Thurrock UA (8.1)	Herefordshire, County of UA (5.9)	Merseyside Met County (14.2)+	County Durham UA (25.4)+

Table source: Office for National Statistics

Table notes:

1. + Indicates significantly different to the UK estimate for 2012/13.

Download table

XLS XLS format
(43 Kb)

Personal well-being in Welsh Unitary Authorities, 2012/13

This section looks at personal well-being within the Unitary Authorities (UAs) in Wales in 2012/13, focusing both on average ratings and the highest and lowest levels of personal well-being.

The personal well-being picture in 2012/13: Unitary Authorities in Wales

Gwynedd, the Isle of Anglesey and Pembrokeshire were areas with some of the highest personal well-being in Wales. Among the areas with lower personal well-being were Newport, Blaenau Gwent and Caerphilly. The points below focus on areas which had the highest or lowest personal well-being on more than one measure and where the area estimate differs significantly to the UK estimate. The key points are taken from **Tables 12- 15**.

Key points to note about the UAs in Wales with the **highest** personal well-being include the following:

- Gwynedd had some of the highest average ratings of personal well-being across all four questions.
- The Isle of Anglesey and Gwynedd were among the areas with the highest average life satisfaction, worthwhile and happiness. The Isle of Anglesey and Gwynedd also had high proportions of people rating life satisfaction as 9 or 10 out of 10.
- Pembrokeshire had the lowest average anxiety and Carmarthenshire had the highest proportion of people rating their anxiety level as 1 or less out of 10.

Key points to note about the UAs in Wales with the **lowest** personal well-being include the following:

- Newport was among the areas that had lowest average ratings of life satisfaction and worthwhile.
- Caerphilly had the lowest average happiness rating and and was one of the areas with the highest average anxiety ratings as well as a high proportion of people rating their anxiety as 6 or more out of 10. Caerphilly also had one of the highest proportions of people reporting very low levels of worthwhile.
- Newport had a high proportion of people reporting 4 or less out of 10 for life satisfaction and happiness and Blaenau Gwent was also among the areas with the highest proportions of people rating their life satisfaction, worthwhile and happiness as very low.
- Merthyr Tydfil had the highest average anxiety and was also among the areas with the highest proportions of people rating their life satisfaction as 4 or less out of 10.

The findings in context

The following points show how the personal well-being findings in Wales relate to local circumstances and to other traditional measures of social progress such as unemployment and life expectancy rates.

- Areas in Wales with the highest unemployment rates were also among those with the lowest personal well-being. They included: Blaenau Gwent (15.2%) and Merthyr Tydfil (11.4%) (ONS, 2013c).

- Areas of Wales with higher personal well-being had much lower unemployment rates ranging from 6.6% in Carmarthenshire to 6.7% in Gwynedd and 7.4% in the Isle of Anglesey (ONS, 2013c).
- Blaenau Gwent and Merthyr Tydfil which have some of the lowest personal well-being ratings in Wales also have the lowest average life expectancy rates at birth. Average life expectancy at birth in Blaenau Gwent was 77.75 years and in Merthyr Tydfil 78.05 years (ONS, 2011a).

Table 12: Highest Average Personal Well-being, by Welsh Unitary Authorities, 2012/13

Wales

Ratings

	Life Satisfaction	Worthwhile	Happiness	Anxiety
1	Isle of Anglesey (7.7)+	Isle of Anglesey (7.9)+	Gwynedd (7.6)+	Pembrokeshire (2.7)+
2	Ceredigion (7.7)+	Gwynedd (7.9)+	Monmouthshire (7.6)+	Flintshire (2.8)
3	Gwynedd (7.6)+	Flintshire (7.9)+	Flintshire (7.5)+	Gwynedd (2.8)+
4	Conwy (7.6)	Ceredigion (7.8)	Pembrokeshire (7.5)+	Ceredigion (2.8)
5	Pembrokeshire (7.6)	Monmouthshire (7.8)	Isle of Anglesey (7.5)+	Carmarthenshire (2.8)

Table source: Office for National Statistics

Table notes:

1. + Indicates significantly different to the UK estimate for 2012/13.

Download table

XLS XLS format
(27.5 Kb)

Table 13: High Personal Well-being, by Welsh Unitary Authorities, 2012/13

Wales

Percentages

	Life Satisfaction (9-10)	Worthwhile (9-10)	Happiness (9-10)	Anxiety (0-1)
1	Isle of Anglesey (34.1)$^{+}$	Wrexham (34.0)	Isle of Anglesey (38.6)$^{+}$	Carmarthenshire (44.3)$^{+}$
2	Gwynedd (30.4)$^{+}$	Conwy (33.9)	Conwy (34.6)	Pembrokeshire (43.4)$^{+}$
3	Ceredigion (30.2)	Monmouthshire (33.4)	Monmouthshire (34.5)	Neath Port Talbot (42.0)
4	Denbighshire (29.2)	Denbighshire (33.0)	Gwynedd (34.2)	Swansea (41.9)
5	Merthyr Tydfil (28.4)	Bridgend (32.4)	Powys (34.0)	Torfaen (41.8)

Table source: Office for National Statistics

Table notes:

1. + Indicates significantly different to the UK estimate for 2012/13.

Download table

XLS XLS format
(27.5 Kb)

Table 14: Lowest Average Personal Well-being, by Welsh Unitary Authorities, 2012/13

Wales

Ratings

	Life Satisfaction	Worthwhile	Happiness	Anxiety
1	Newport (7.2)+	Newport (7.5)+	Caerphilly (7.1)+	Merthyr Tydfil (3.4)+
2	Torfaen (7.3)+	Torfaen (7.6)	Newport (7.1)	Caerphilly (3.4)+
3	Blaenau Gwent (7.3)	Rhondda Cynon Taf (7.6)	Cardiff (7.1)	Cardiff (3.3)+
4	Merthyr Tydfil (7.3)	Swansea (7.6)	Torfaen (7.2)	Bridgend (3.2)
5	Swansea (7.3)	Cardiff (7.6)	Blaenau Gwent (7.2)	Denbighshire (3.2)

Table source: Office for National Statistics

Table notes:

1. + Indicates significantly different to the UK estimate for 2012/13.

Download table

XLS XLS format
(27.5 Kb)

Table 15: Low Personal Well-being, by Welsh Unitary Authorities, 2012/13

Wales

Percentages

	Life Satisfaction (0-4)	Worthwhile (0-4)	Happiness (0-4)	Anxiety (6-10)
1	Newport (9.6)+	Blaenau Gwent (6.9)+	Newport (14.9)+	Caerphilly (25.7)+
2	Blaenau Gwent (9.4)+	Swansea (6.9)+	Caerphilly (14.7)+	Merthyr Tydfil (25.6)
3	Swansea (9.1)+	Caerphilly (6.5)+	Blaenau Gwent (13.4)	Denbighshire (23.0)
4	Merthyr Tydfil (8.5)+	Newport (5.9)	Merthyr Tydfil (13.2)	Bridgend (22.6)
5	Torfaen (8.1)+	Conwy (5.9)	Torfaen (13.0)	Neath Port Talbot (22.2)

Table source: Office for National Statistics

Table notes:

1. + Indicates significantly different to the UK estimate for 2012/13.

Download table

XLS XLS format
(30.5 Kb)

Personal well-being in Scottish Local Authorities, 2012/13

This section looks at personal well-being within the Local Authorities in Scotland in 2012/13, focusing both on average ratings and the highest and lowest levels of personal well-being.

The personal well-being picture in 2012/13: Local Authorities in Scotland

Eilean Siar, Orkney and Shetland, Dumfries and Galloway and Highland were areas with some of the highest personal well-being in Scotland. Among the areas with lower personal well-being were North Ayrshire, Dundee City and Glasgow City. The points below focus on areas which had the highest or lowest personal well-being on more than one measure and where the area estimate differs significantly to the UK estimate. The key points are taken from **Tables 16-19**.

Key points to note about the Local Authorities in Scotland with the **highest** personal well-being include the following :

- Eilean Siar, Orkney and Shetland had the highest average life satisfaction, worthwhile and happiness, and the second lowest average rating of anxiety. Additionally, Eilean Siar, Orkney and Shetland had the highest proportion of people rating their happiness as 9 or 10 out of 10.
- The area with the lowest average anxiety was Dumfries and Galloway, which also had high average life satisfaction and happiness. Dumfries and Galloway also had one of the highest proportions of people giving a high rating of 9 or 10 out of 10 for life satisfaction, worthwhile and happiness, and one of the highest proportions of people giving a low rating for their anxiety levels of 0 or 1 out of 10.
- Highland also had some of the highest average life satisfaction, worthwhile and happiness ratings.

Key points to note about the Local Authorities in Scotland with the **lowest** personal well-being include the following:

- North Ayrshire had the lowest average life satisfaction and the highest average anxiety, and was among the areas with the lowest average ratings for worthwhile. Additionally, North Ayrshire had one of the highest proportions of people rating worthwhile and happiness as 4 or less out of 10.
- Dundee City and Glasgow City had the lowest average ratings for worthwhile.

The findings in context

The section considers how the personal well-being for Local Authorities in Scotland relate to local circumstances and to other traditional measures of social progress such as unemployment and life expectancy.

- In 2012, some of the areas with the highest unemployment rates in Scotland also had some of the lowest levels of personal well-being. This included: North Ayrshire with an unemployment rate of 12.2% (ONS, 2013c).
- Areas with some of the lowest unemployment rates during the same period had some of the highest levels of personal well-being in Scotland including Shetland Islands (3.7%), Orkney Islands (3.5%) and Highland (5.2%).
- Some of the lowest average life expectancy rates at birth in Scotland were in areas with the lowest average personal well-being ratings. This included Dundee City with an average life expectancy at birth of 76.55 years and West Dunbartonshire (75.95 years) (ONS, 2011a).
- Some of the highest average life expectancy rates in Scotland were in areas with the highest average personal well-being ratings including the Orkney Islands (79.35 years).

Table 16: Highest Average Personal Well-being, by Scottish Local Authority, 2012/13

Scotland

Ratings

	Life Satisfaction	Worthwhile	Happiness	Anxiety
1	Eilean Siar, Orkney & Shetland (8.0)+	Eilean Siar, Orkney & Shetland (8.1)+	Eilean Siar, Orkney & Shetland (7.9)+	Dumfries and Galloway (2.2)+
2	Highland (7.9)+	Highland (8.0)+	Dumfries and Galloway (7.7)+	Eilean Siar, Orkney & Shetland (2.5)+
3	Dumfries and Galloway (7.8)+	Clackmannanshire (8.0)+	Highland (7.7)+	Clackmannanshire (2.5)+
4	Scottish Borders (7.8)+	Moray (7.9)+	Perth and Kinross (7.6)+	Aberdeen City (2.6)+
5	Stirling (7.7)+	Scottish Borders (7.9)+	Argyll & Bute (7.6)+	Angus (2.6)+

Table source: Office for National Statistics

Table notes:

1. + Indicates significantly different to the UK estimate for 2012/13.

Download table

XLS XLS format
(29 Kb)

Table 17: High Personal Well-being, by Scottish Local Authority, 2012/13

Scotland

Percentages

	Life Satisfaction (9-10)	Worthwhile (9-10)	Happiness (9-10)	Anxiety (0-1)
1	Dumfries and Galloway (33.6)+	Dumfries and Galloway (36.0)+	Eilean Siar, Orkney & Shetland (43.3)+	Clackmannanshire (51.8)+
2	Scottish Borders (33.4)+	Inverclyde (35.6)	Highland (39.2)+	Dumfries and Galloway (50.6)+
3	Argyll & Bute (29.8)+	Argyll & Bute (35.1)+	Dumfries and Galloway (38.4)+	Eilean Siar, Orkney & Shetland (46.0)+
4	Angus (28.6)	Perth and Kinross (33.1)	Clackmannanshire (37.1)	Angus (45.8)+
5	North Lanarkshire (28.3)	Fife (31.4)	Argyll and Bute (36.1)+	Renfrewshire (45.7)+

Table source: Office for National Statistics

Table notes:

1. + Indicates significantly different to the UK estimate for 2012/13.

Download table

XLS XLS format
(29.5 Kb)

Table 18: Lowest Average Personal Well-being, by Scottish Local Authority, 2012/13

Scotland

Ratings

	Life Satisfaction	Worthwhile	Happiness	Anxiety
1	North Ayrshire (7.3)+	Dundee City (7.4)+	North Lanarkshire (7.0)+	North Ayrshire (3.3)+
2	Dundee City (7.3)	Glasgow City (7.4)+	East Ayrshire (7.1)	South Ayrshire (3.3)+
3	West Dunbartonshire (7.3)	North Ayrshire (7.5)+	Glasgow City (7.1)+	East Ayrshire (3.3)
4	Glasgow City (7.3)	Renfrewshire (7.5)+	West Dunbartonshire (7.1)	City of Edinburgh (3.3)+
5	East Ayrshire (7.3)	West Dunbartonshire (7.6)	Dundee City (7.1)	West Lothian (3.2)

Table source: Office for National Statistics

Table notes:

1. + Indicates significantly different to the UK estimate for 2012/13.

Download table

XLS XLS format
(27.5 Kb)

Table 19: Low Personal Well-being, by Scottish Local Authority, 2012/13

Scotland

Percentages

	Life Satisfaction (0-4)	Worthwhile (0-4)	Happiness (0-4)	Anxiety (6-10)
1	Inverclyde (9.7)+	Dundee City (8.1)+	North Lanarkshire (14.7)+	North Ayrshire (26.0)+
2	Dundee City (8.6)+	Glasgow City (7.6)+	Glasgow City (13.8)+	West Dunbartonshire (24.8)+
3	West Dunbartonshire (8.0)	North Ayrshire (7.3)+	North Ayrshire (13.6)+	East Ayrshire (24.7)+
4	North Ayrshire (7.9)	South Ayrshire (7.2)+	East Ayrshire (13.3)	South Ayrshire (23.9)+
5	South Ayrshire (7.5)	Inverclyde (6.9)+	Renfrewshire (13.3)	City of Edinburgh (23.7)+

Table source: Office for National Statistics

Table notes:

1. + Indicates significantly different to the UK estimate for 2012/13.

Download table

XLS [XLS format](#)
(29 Kb)

Methodology

ONS personal well-being estimates are 'Experimental Statistics' and are published at an early stage to gain feedback from users in their development before being designated as National Statistics. We would welcome feedback on this bulletin and would be particularly interested in hearing about how the data are used. Please contact us via email: nationalwell-being@ons.gsi.gov.uk or telephone Dawn Snape on 01633 45 5674.

The data analysed in this bulletin are derived from customised weighted 12 month Annual Population Survey (APS) microdatasets. They are not part of the regularly produced APS datasets and were created specifically for the analysis of personal well-being data. ONS is also making the experimental APS microdata available to approved researchers to allow them to undertake further analysis of the data at an early stage and to provide further feedback to ONS.

Choice of questions

The experimental questions included in the Annual Population Survey were developed with expert academic advice (Dolan et al. 2011) as well as benefiting from discussions between members of the National Statistician's Measuring National Well-being Advisory Forum and Technical Advisory Group. They represent a balanced approach to the measurement of personal well-being drawing on the three main theoretical approaches identified in the academic literature on the subject (Dolan et. al. 2011, ONS, 2011b) and are designed to collect information on different aspects of people's personal well-being. The three different approaches to measuring personal well-being are:

- The 'evaluative' approach in which people are asked to reflect on their life and make a cognitive assessment of how their life is going overall or of how specific aspects of their life are going.
- The 'eudemonic' approach sometimes referred to as the psychological or functioning/flourishing approach, which draws on self-determination theory and measures people's sense of meaning and purpose in life, connections with family and friends, a sense of control and whether they feel part of something bigger than themselves.
- The 'experience' approach which measures people's positive and negative experiences (or affect) over a short timeframe to capture people's personal well-being on a day-to-day basis.

The personal well-being questions that ONS asks on its household surveys are:

- Overall, how satisfied are you with your life nowadays? (evaluative approach)
- Overall, to what extent do you feel the things you do in your life are worthwhile? (eudemonic approach)
- Overall, how happy did you feel yesterday? (experience approach)
- Overall, how anxious did you feel yesterday? (experience approach)

All are answered using a 0 to 10 scale where 0 is 'not at all' and 10 is 'completely'.

Further information on the ONS approach to measuring personal well-being can be found in the paper 'Measuring Subjective Well-being' (240.8 Kb Pdf) published by ONS in July 2011.

Survey design

The Annual Population Survey (APS), first conducted in 2004, combines results from waves one and five of the Labour Force Survey (LFS) and the English, Welsh and Scottish LFS boosts. The survey asks 155,000 households and 360,000 people per dataset about their circumstances and experiences regarding a range of subjects including housing, employment and education. The survey provides enhanced data on key social and socio-economic variables. For the personal well-being questions, responses by proxy are not collected. This means that only people who respond directly to the survey are included rather than including responses made on behalf of other people. For this reason the sample size for the personal well-being dataset is around 165,000 people.

The APS is a mixed mode survey and uses both face-to-face and telephone interviews. Different collection modes can affect responses and personal well-being estimates are no exception. For example in the Annual Population Survey it appears that on average people responding face-to-face with an interviewer in their home give different ratings to those responding via the telephone (see **Table 20**). Further investigation is required to ascertain why this may be the case.

Higher average ratings for the life satisfaction, worthwhile, happy yesterday questions and a slightly lower average for the anxious yesterday question were provided by respondents interviewed via the telephone compared with those who are asked personal well-being questions face-to-face, as can be seen in Table 20.

Table 20: Average personal well-being, by mode of interview, 2012/13

United Kingdom

Average

	Telephone	Face-to-face
Life satisfaction	7.6	7.4
Worthwhile	7.8	7.6
Happy yesterday	7.4	7.2
Anxious yesterday	3.1	3.0

Table source: Office for National Statistics

Download table

XLS XLS format
(28.5 Kb)

This issue is particularly important for the APS as all interviews in Scotland north of the Caledonian Canal are administered by telephone only, rather than through a combination of telephone and face-to-face interviews, as is the case in other areas of the UK.

There are a number of other methodological issues which have been or are being tested on the Opinions Survey, for more information see the 'Initial Investigation into Subjective Well-being data from the ONS Opinions Survey' (ONS, 2011c). These include:

- **Contextual effects** - responses to evaluative questions can be affected by the respondent's current mood and by the immediate context, however, the idiosyncratic effects of recent events are likely to average out in a large, representative population sample like the APS.
- **Question order** – responses to personal well-being questions have been shown to be affected by earlier questions in the survey (for example, questions about health or labour market status). Prior to April 2011, ONS carried out small scale cognitive testing of the placement of the personal well-being questions. As a result it was decided that the placement of the overall monitoring

questions would be fairly early on in the questionnaire after the basic questions on household and individual demographics. This allows time for rapport to be built up between the interviewer without allowing later questions, such as those on employment, to influence response to the personal well-being questions

- **Response scales** - different response scales for personal well-being questions have been used on different surveys. Differences in scaling and labeling of scale points require careful consideration as they are likely to affect how people respond. Additionally the use of different scales in different surveys means that it is more difficult to compare across different sources of data. It appears that the way the scales are labelled can also have an impact on these estimates and that is something that needs further investigation. ONS decided that an 11 point scale from 0–10 where 0 is 'not at all' and 10 is an absolute value such as 'completely' should be used for all the APS personal well-being questions. The reason for this decision was to ensure that the scales between the questions are consistent in order to help respondents answer the questions more easily and also to aid analysis across the separate questions. Further to this, 11 point scales are commonly used across other similar surveys, particularly internationally, and using the same type of scale will aid comparisons with these estimates.
- **Question wording** - it is not only response scales that differ from survey to survey but also question wording, including the use of time frames. ONS has used both cognitive testing techniques and split trial testing of data collected on the Opinions Survey to ascertain the impact these differences have on estimates. This is especially important with respect to issues such as harmonisation of question wording across surveys in order to gain comparable results.

This work is ongoing but the results of the most recent split trial testing can be found here (519.1 Kb Pdf).

Interpreting personal well-being estimates

When comparing the average personal well-being ratings of people living in different areas it is important to bear in mind that these comparisons are made using aggregate statistics based on samples. Just because the average of the sample has a certain rating of personal well-being does not necessarily mean that all people living in that area have that particular outcome. For example, even though people may report higher life satisfaction on average in Area A than in Area B, it is important not to infer that all people living in Area A have higher well-being than those living in Area B. Looking at the percentage who rate aspects of their well-being below or above a certain level goes some way in addressing this. However, it is also important not to infer that what is true for those who have reported the highest or lowest levels of well-being in a given area is true for all people living in that area.

It is also important to note that although personal well-being estimates in this bulletin have been analysed by area, this should not be taken to imply causation. In other words, differences in the results between areas should not be taken to directly indicate differences in people's satisfaction with their local area. This is because where an individual lives is just one aspect that influences an individual's response to the personal well being questions. Other factors such as the individual's health, relationships and employment situation will also influence their response.

Therefore, although people in some areas are more likely to give higher life satisfaction ratings on average it may not be living in that area that causes them to have higher personal well-being. There are other, possibly more important factors that may influence their ratings[1].

Levels of geography included in the dataset

In response to user demand, the personal well-being data from the APS is being made available at a range of geographical levels including: the UK, countries of the UK, regions of England, Unitary Authorities in Wales, Local Authorities in Scotland, District Council Areas in Northern Ireland, Unitary Authorities and Counties in England, and Local Authority District Level in England.

Although this report has focused on findings from UA/ County level and above, the data have been broken down to each of the levels listed and are available in the reference tables for both 2011/12 and 2012/13. At each level, the estimates are provided for:

- the mean average response to each personal well-being question for each area; and
- the percentage of responses in each area across the 11 point response scale, broken down into four levels of well-being.

Both averages (means) and percentages across the different levels of well-being have been used for analysing the data in this bulletin. Whilst the mean provides a useful summary statistic about the population of interest overall, the percentages tell us more about the distribution of responses.

Data quality

Standard errors, coefficients of variation and confidence intervals are provided in the reference tables to enable users to fully assess the quality of the data available for any given area. The following points provide information and guidance about these measures and how they are presented in the reference tables.

- The standard errors provide a measure of the precision of an estimate that is computed from a sample, as opposed to from a census- it is a measure of the sampling error. The standard error forms the basis for the calculation of the margin of error, a confidence interval and the coefficient of variation.
- A confidence interval gives the range in which the true population value is likely to fall, with a stated level of confidence. All supporting reference tables to this bulletin contain 95% confidence intervals. Half the width of a confidence interval defines the margin of error of an estimate.
- The coefficient of variation (CV) is a measurement of the relative variability of an estimate, expressed as a percentage. It allows the comparison of the precision of estimats across groups and different parameters
- Areas with smaller sample sizes will inevitably have a higher margin of error. We urge users to consider this carefully both when conducting cross-sectional analysis and when analyzing changes over time. Furthermore, in areas with smaller sample sizes, it may be more appropriate to use the mean (or average) to summarise the data across the sample as a whole rather than the proportions across the different levels of well-being.

- Data with a coefficient of variation (CV) of 20% or above have been suppressed in the tables for quality purposes.
- The data in the reference tables are colour coded to reflect the relative quality of the estimates according to the size of the CV. A key to the colour coding is provided in the reference tables. The size bands used to rank the CVs are as follows:

  - CV <= 5% - Precise

  - 5% < CV <= 10% - Reasonably precise

  - 10% < CV <= 20% - Acceptable

  - 20% < CV - Unreliable (these estimates are not published, being considered too unreliable for practical purposes)

- Confidentiality is maintained by applying standard ONS criteria that require estimates to have a minimum of three respondents contributing to it. Estimates that fail to meet this standard are also suppressed.

Notes for Methodology

1. Evidence from a previous ONS regression study (ONS, 2013b) suggests it is some of these other factors, namely personal characteristics such as health, employment and relationship status, that were most strongly associated with the well-being ratings provided by an individual. The region in which an individual lived was only found to be weakly associated with personal well-being in the regression study.

   Local area effects such as the characteristics of the local built up area or of neighbours were not considered in this initial regression study. Therefore, to investigate the extent to which the local area may directly impact on personal well-being, a follow up ONS regression study examining this issue will be published later in the year.

The Measuring National Well-being Programme

NWB logo 2

This statistical bulletin is published as part of the ONS Measuring National Well-being Programme.

The programme aims to produce accepted and trusted measures of the well-being of the nation - how the UK as a whole is doing.

Measuring National Well-being is about looking at 'GDP and beyond'. It includes headline indicators in areas such as health, relationships, job satisfaction, economic security, education, environmental conditions and measures of personal well-being (individuals' assessment of their own well-being).

Find out more on the Measuring National Well-being website pages.

References

Dolan P, Layard R and Metcalfe R, Office for National Statistics (2011). Measuring Subjective Well-being for Public Policy (99.8 Kb Pdf).

Office for National Statistics (2011a) Life expectancy at birth and at age 65 by local areas in the United Kingdom, 2004–06 to 2008–10

Office for National Statistics (2011b). Measuring Subjective Well-being (240.8 Kb Pdf).

Office for National Statistics (2011c) Initial investigation into Subjective Well-being data from the ONS Opinions Survey.

Office for National Statistics (2012a) Regional Gross Value Added (Income Approach), December 2012

Office for National Statistics (2012b) Regional Profiles - Social Indicators - South West - February 2012

Office for National Statistics (2012c) First Annual ONS Experimental Subjective Well-being Results

Office for National Statistics (2012d) Household Disposable Income Across the UK, 2010

Office for National Statistics (2013a) Personal Well-being in the UK, 2012/13

Office for National Statistics (2013b) What Matters Most to Personal Well-being?

Office for National Statistics (2013c) Regional Labour Market Statistics, September 2013

Office for National Statistics (2013d) Life expectancy at birth and at age 65 for local areas in England and Wales, 2009-11

Office for National Statistics (2013e) Regional and Country Profiles: Key Statistics Tables, October 2013

Office for National Statistics (2013f) Healthy Life Expectancy at birth for Upper Tier Local Authorities: England 2009-11

Background notes

1. These statistics are experimental in nature and published at an early stage to gain feedback from users. Should users have comments on the ONS approach to the measurement of personal well-being and or the presentation of the personal well-being questions they can email ONS at nationalwell-being@ons.gov.uk. It is the role of the UK Statistics Authority to designate these statistics as National Statistics and one of the aspirations of the National Well-being programme is to see these statistics gain National Statistics status.

2. Data analysed in this report relates to APS data from April 2012 to March 2013 unless stated otherwise.

3. The data analysed in this report was collected from the Annual Population Survey (APS) which is the largest constituent survey of the Integrated Household Survey. The sample size of the 12 month APS dataset is 165,000 adults aged 16 and over and living in residential accommodation in the UK (England, Scotland, Wales and Northern Ireland). Data used are weighted to be representative of the population, unless otherwise stated.

4. Details of the policy governing the release of new data are available by visiting the UK Statistics Authority or from the Media Relations Office.

5.

6. Details of the policy governing the release of new data are available by visiting www.statisticsauthority.gov.uk/assessment/code-of-practice/index.html or from the Media Relations Office email: media.relations@ons.gsi.gov.uk

Copyright

This document is also available on our website at www.ons.gov.uk.

Statistical contacts

Name	Phone	Department	Email
Dawn Snape	+44 (0)1633 455674	Measuring National Well-being	dawn.snape@ons.gsi.gov.
Lucy Tinkler	+44 (0)1633 455713	Measuring National Well-being	lucy.tinkler@ons.gsi.gov.uk

Issuing Body:
Office for National Statistics

Media Contact Details:
Telephone: 0845 604 1858
(8.30am-5.30pm Weekdays)

Emergency out of hours (limited service): 07867 906553

Email:
media.relations@ons.gsi.gov.uk

12 December 2013

Human Capital Estimates, 2012

Author Name(s): **Valerie Fender, Office for National Statistics**

Abstract

This article presents experimental statistics on the valuation of the UK's Human Capital Stock from 2004 to 2012. This release is part of a programme of work within the Measuring National Well-being Programme and updates previous estimates released by ONS in December 2011.

Key points

- Following substantial falls in 2010 and 2011, the value of the UK's human capital stock began to stabilise in 2012.
- In 2012 the value of the UK's employed human capital was £17.15 trillion; £68 billion lower than in 2011 (a fall of 0.4%).
- The gap between the UK's full human capital and employed human capital was the largest since estimates began in 2004 at £754 billion.
- 34.7% of the human capital stock was embodied in the 25.3% of the population whose highest educational attainment was a degree or equivalent.
- The total value of women's human capital was around 59% of men's.
- The stock of human capital is disproportionately concentrated in younger workers.

What is Human Capital?

'The most valuable of all capital is that invested in human beings', Alfred Marshall - Principles of Economics (Marshall, 1890).

Human capital is most easily understood when put in the context of its contribution to economic output. Growth in an economy can be driven by increases or improvements in either:

- land - the natural resources that we have at our disposal, for example coal, wood etc;
- labour - our workforce; and
- capital - the buildings and machines we use to produce goods and services.

In this context human capital refers to the labour, one of the factors used in the production process, and captures both the number of people in the workforce and the abilities they bring with them.

At the individual level we can think about human capital as measuring a person's competencies, knowledge, social attributes, personality and health attributes, including creativity. All of these factors enable them to work, and therefore produce something of economic value.

We place a value on the machines that we use to produce goods and services. However, these machines would be almost useless without the knowledge of how to use and maintain them; this is human capital and also needs to be valued.

In general, human capital is considered to be linked to education, although this is not the only influence on human capital. The technical definition adopted by ONS is that provided by the Organisation for Economic Co-operation and Development (OECD). It defines human capital as: "the knowledge, skills, competencies and attributes embodied in individuals that facilitate the creation of personal, social and economic well-being".

These activities can take place throughout an individual's life and in a range of environments. OECD (2001) identifies four main ways human capital can be developed:

- Learning within family and early childcare settings.
- Formal education and training.
- Workplace training.
- Informal learning (e.g. through daily living, civic participation and on the job training).

Although a consensus on this definition of human capital is beginning to be formed by the international statistical community, it is a concept that is difficult to measure. The concept of human capital is broad and encompasses a range of personal attributes, such as people's health conditions. However, in practical terms the focus of measurement has been limited to people's skills, knowledge and competencies, and in particular on the role of formal education and training in enhancing them.

The value of Human Capital

Figure 1: Employed and Full Human Capital 2004 - 2012

United Kingdom

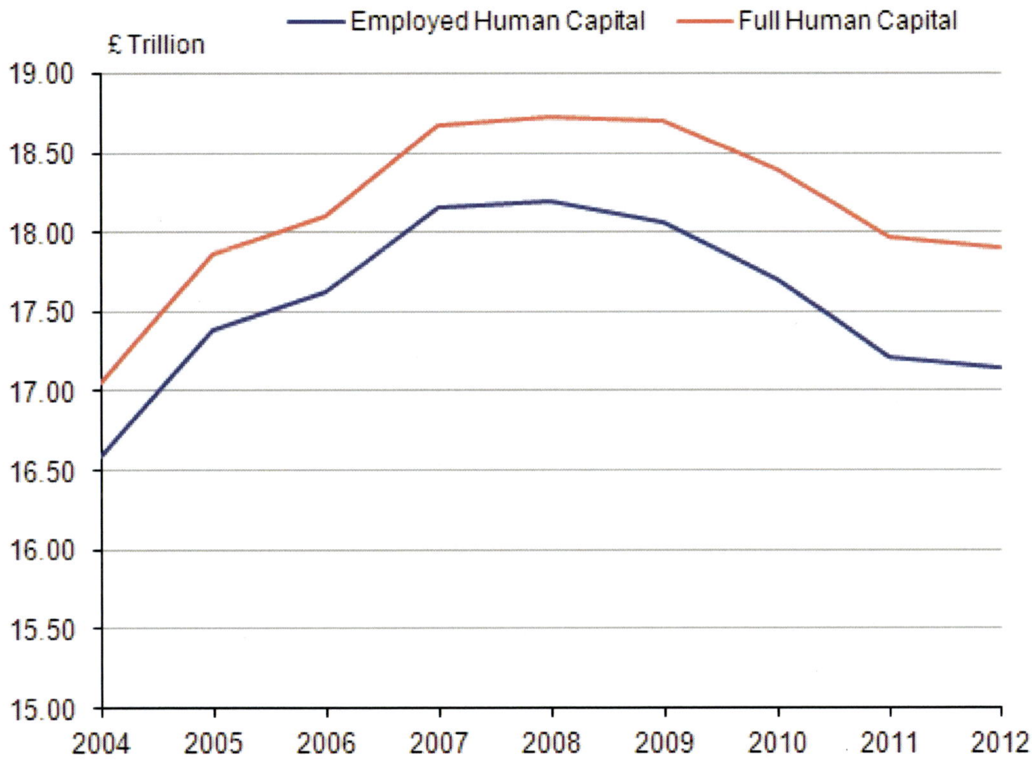

Source: Annual Population Survey (APS) - Office for National Statistics

Notes:

1. Figures in 2012 prices.
2. Labour productivity growth rate = 2%.
3. Discount rate = 3.5%.

Download chart

XLS XLS format
(27 Kb)

Figure 1 illustrates the effect of the economic downturn on the UK's employed human capital stock. In the years 2004 to 2007 the value of the UK's human capital stock increased steadily, at an average of 3.1% per year. This was driven by an increase in the employed working-age population and an increase in the skills level of the population (with the proportion of the working age population with a degree qualification or higher increasing and the proportion of the population with no qualifications decreasing). Other things being equal, this would have been expected to increase the human capital stock as higher educational attainment tends to be associated with higher productivity and higher earnings. Another important driver of the increase in the value of the UK's human capital stock is earnings growth, which generally grew in real terms between 2004 and 2007.

Growth in employed human capital slowed into 2008 (0.2%) before falling slightly in 2009 (-0.7%) beginning to reflect the effect of the economic downturn on the UK's human capital stock. With falling employment rates and falls in real earnings, 2010 and 2011 saw further falls in the value of the UK's human capital stock (of 2.0% and 2.8% respectively). Following these substantial falls in 2010 and 2011, the value of the UK's human capital stock began to stabilise in 2012. In 2012 the value of employed human capital was £17.15 trillion. This is a fall of £68 billion from £17.22 trillion in 2011.

The value of the UK's full human capital stock (including the unemployed) was £17.50 trillion in 2012. Both employed and full human capital show a similar trend since 2004. In recent years, the decline in the UK's full human capital stock has not been as severe as the decline in the UK's employed human capital stock reflecting the impact of unemployment on the estimates of employed human capital. As a result, in 2012 the gap between the UK's full human capital and employed human capital was the largest since estimates began in 2004 at £754 billion.

Figure 2: Employed and Full Human Capital Per Head (working age population) 2004-2012

United Kingdom

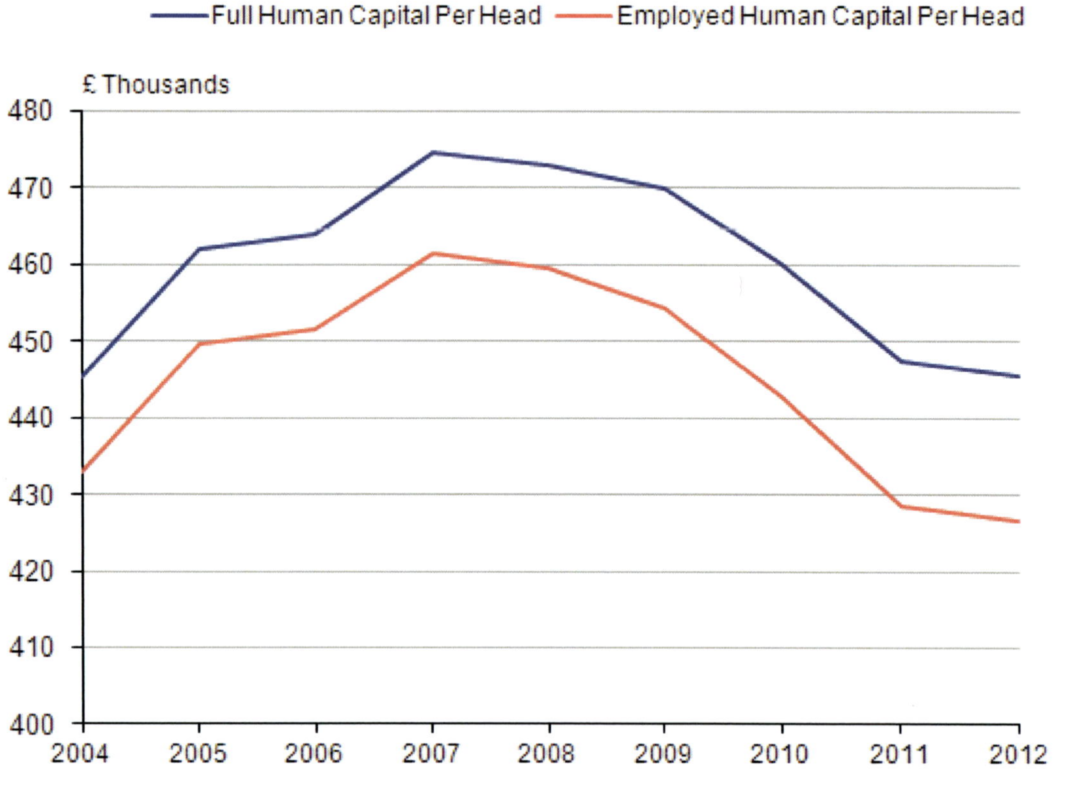

Source: Annual Population Survey (APS) - Office for National Statistics

Notes:

1. Figures in 2012 prices.
2. Labour productivity growth rate = 2%.
3. Discount rate = 3.5%.

Download chart

XLS XLS format
(27 Kb)

Figure 2 shows the evolution of the stock of human capital per head of working-age population (for both full and employed human capital). Similar to the results for the total stock, there was a steady accumulation of human capital per capita between 2004 and 2007. In 2008, the per capita figure began to decline, and has been in decline ever since. This is despite growth in the total stock of human capital. This is a result of growth in the size of the working age population. In 2012, the average full human capital stock per head of working age population was £445,479, a decrease of £1,922 on the 2011 estimate.

The distribution of Human Capital

This section considers the distribution of employed human capital in 2012 by age, highest qualification and gender.

Figure 3: Employed Human Capital by Highest Qualification - 2012

United Kingdom

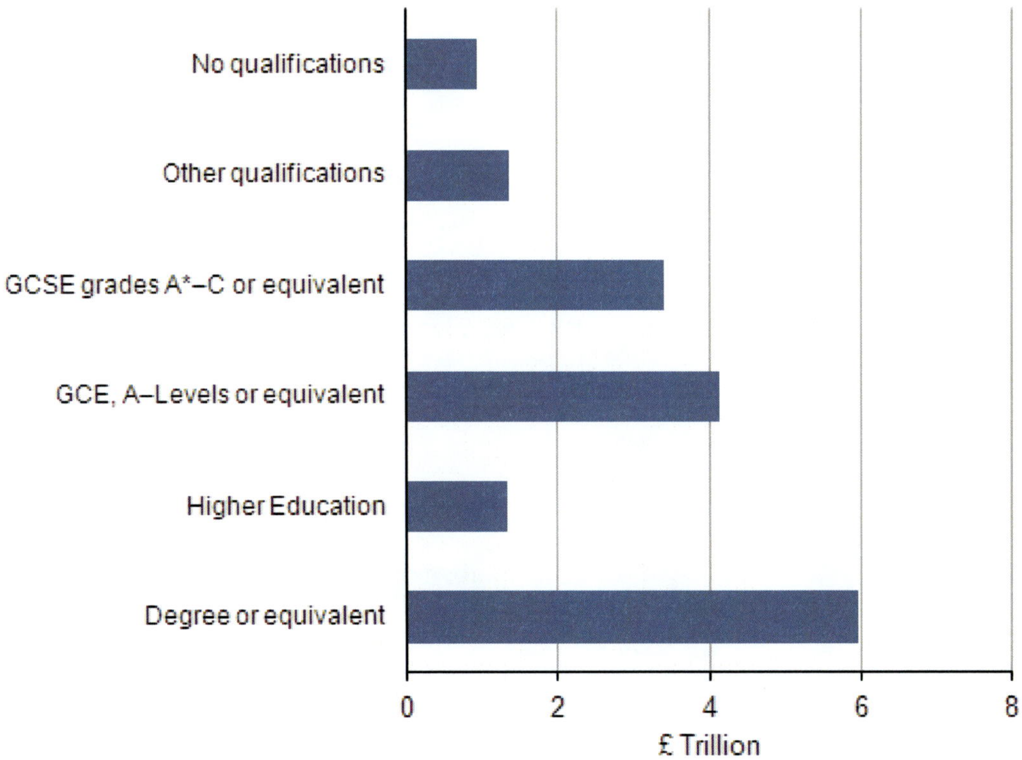

Source: Annual Population Survey (APS) - Office for National Statistics

Notes:

1. Components may not sum to total due to rounding.
2. Labour productivity growth rate = 2%.

3. Disount rate = 3.5%.

Download chart

XLS XLS format
(28 Kb)

Figure 3 shows that in 2012 34.7% of the human capital stock was embodied in the 25.3% of the population whose highest educational attainment was a degree or equivalent. In contrast, only 5.5% of the UK's human capital stock was embodies in the 9.9% of the working age population who have no formal qualifications.

Less time in paid employment over their lifetime and lower average labour market earnings means that the total value of women's human capital (£6.35 trillion) was around 59% of men's (£10.80 trillion).

Figure 4: Employed Human Capital by Age Group - 2012

United Kingdom

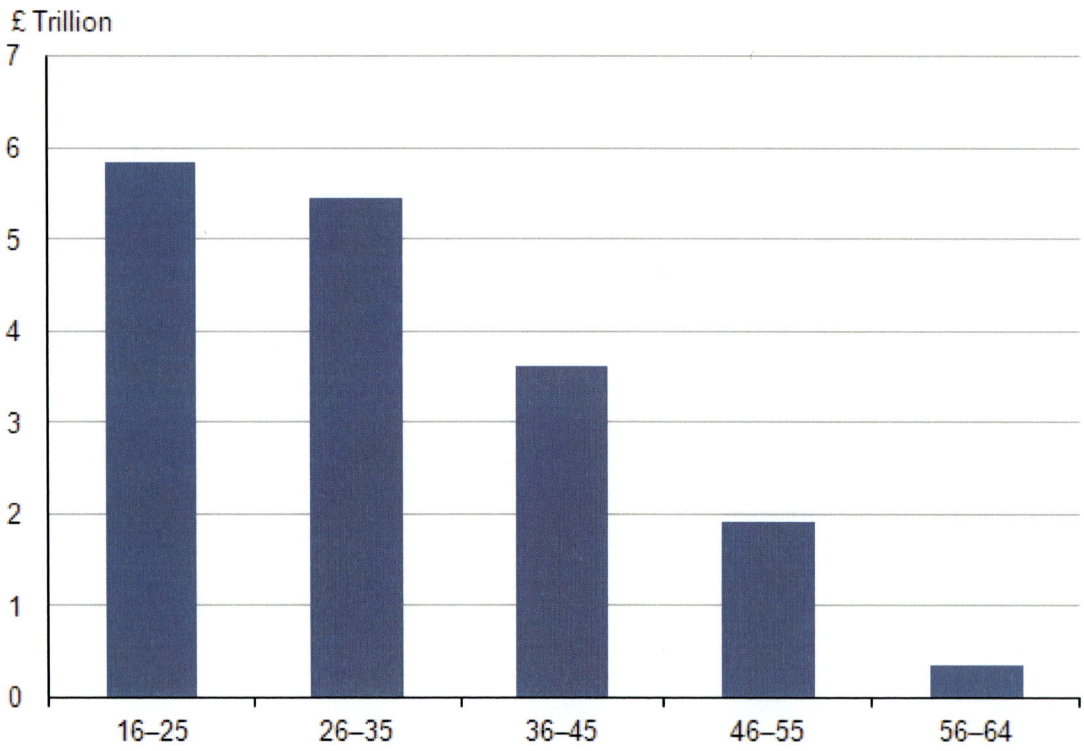

Source: Annual Population Survey (APS) - Office for National Statistics

Notes:

1. Components may not sum to total due to rounding.
2. Labour productivity growth rate = 2%.
3. Discount rate = 3.5%.

Download chart

XLS XLS format
(27.5 Kb)

Figure 4 shows that the stock of human capital is disproportionately concentrated in younger workers. For example, 41.2% of the working age population are aged between 16 and 35 but this group embodies 65.9% of the human capital stock, showing that being relatively young and having more years of paid employment remaining more than offsets the effect of having higher earnings whilst being relatively old.

Sensitivity analysis

Estimates of human capital are sensitive to a number of assumptions. Holding everything else constant, each assumption can be varied individually to show the impact. The three key assumptions analysed here are:

- the discount rate
- the labour productivity growth rate
- the upper age boundary

The results are shown in **Table 1.**

Table 1: Employed Human Capital in 2012 (£ trillion, current prices)

United Kingdom

Labour Productivity Growth Rate	Discount rate	Upper Age Limit	Employed Human Capital in 2012
1	3.5	64	14.94
1.5	3.5	64	15.99
2	**3.5**	**64**	**17.15**
2.5	3.5	64	18.43
3	3.5	64	19.86
2	2	64	21.45
2	2.5	64	19.84
2	3	64	18.42
2	**3.5**	**64**	**17.15**
2	4	64	16.01
2	4.5	64	14.99
2	5	64	14.07

Labour Productivity Growth Rate	Discount rate	Upper Age Limit	Employed Human Capital in 2012
2	**3.5**	**64**	**17.15**
2	3.5	65	17.30
2	3.5	66	17.41
2	3.5	67	17.49
2	3.5	68	17.53
2	3.5	69	17.57

Table source: Office for National Statistics

Table notes:

1. Labour productivity growth rate in main estimates = 2%.
2. Discount rate in main estimates = 3.5%.
3. Upper age limit in main estimates = 64 years old.

Download table

XLS XLS format
(28 Kb)

Sensitivity analysis shows that increasing the discount rate by one percentage point, to 4.5 per cent, reduces the estimated value of the human capital stock by almost £2.16 trillion. Conversely, reducing the discount rate to 2.5 per cent increases the value of the human capital stock by almost £2.70 trillion. Changing the labour productivity growth rate by one percentage point, leads to changes of a similar magnitude but in the opposite direction in the estimates of the human capital stock.

Restricting the sample to individuals aged between 16 and 64 years is a somewhat arbitrary assumption particularly at the higher end of the age range. **Table 1** illustrates the effects of changes in the upper age bound on estimates of the human capital with a discount rate of 3.5 per cent and a labour productivity growth rate of 2 per cent. As would be expected, increasing the upper age bound increases the estimates of the human capital stock since the human capital of additional workers is included in the estimate and the expected working lives of individuals already in the sample is extended, raising the value of their human capital. The increases become smaller as the upper age bound is increased because the employment rate and total income is lower in each age-year cohort added to the sample.

Revisions

There have been a number of developments since the previous publication of Human Capital in December 2011 which have resulted in revisions. These are:

- Changing the main data source from the Labour Force Survey to the Annual Population Survey (APS). The APS is an annual version of the LFS with annual sample boosts. The larger sample sizes improve the robustness of the estimates. This is expected to have a limited effect.
- Implementation of a new system to estimate Human Capital consistently on an annual basis and improving the robustness.
- In addition, a full review of the methodology has been carried out and a number of procedures have been improved and standardised:

  - Three year moving averages have been used for employment rates to reduce the exposure of the human capital estimates to the business cycle.

  - Improved consistency in the treatment of outliers when cleaning the micro-data.

  - Ten year average transitional rates have been used due to small sample sizes coming from the longitudinal LFS. This replaces the use of the whole dataset in the original methodology, reducing the likelihood of revisions in future.

  - Employment rates and earnings by gender, age and highest qualification have been smoothed to reduce the impact of any outliers.

These revisions have not been quantified individually; however, together they have resulted in an average revision to the estimate of the value of the UK's employed human capital stock of less than 2% between 2004 and 2010.

Table 2: Revisions to Employed Human Capital

United Kingdom

				£ Trillion
	Previously Published Employed Human Capital	Employed Human Capital	Revision	Revision (%)
2001	14.46	-	-	-
2002	15.00	-	-	-
2003	15.32	-	-	-
2004	15.82	15.44	-0.38	-2.0%
2005	16.37	16.19	-0.18	-1.0%
2006	16.71	16.41	-0.30	-2.0%
2007	17.01	16.90	-0.11	-1.0%
2008	17.12	16.94	-0.18	-1.0%
2009	17.25	16.82	-0.43	-3.0%
2010	17.12	16.48	-0.64	-4.0%
2011	-	16.03	-	-
2012	-	15.96	-	-

Table source: Office for National Statistics

Table notes:

1. Figures in 2010 prices.
2. Labour productivity growth rate = 2%.
3. Discount rate = 3.5%.

Download table

XLS XLS format
(28 Kb)

Users and uses of Human Capital estimates

Responses to the recent ONS consultation on measurement of human capital identified that this measure of human capital has several potential policy applications. First, it can be used as a measure of an economy's future well-being as the empirical work on economic growth suggests that countries with higher levels of human capital, other things being equal, have greater potential output and income in the future. The measures can also be used in the assessment of the impact of an ageing population, changes in retirement ages and in the evaluation of the economic benefits of different levels of education.

Background notes

1. The statistics presented in this release are experimental in nature.

2. Full information on data sources and methodology can be found in the Measuring Human Capital Methodology Document available here: http://www.ons.gov.uk/ons/guide-method/user-guidance/well-being/publications/human-capital---methodology-paper.pdf

3. The sources of data used in the analysis are the Annual Population Survey (APS), which is an annual version of the Labour Force Survey (LFS), and the longitudinal LFS. Both surveys are conducted by the Office for National Statistics. The APS and LFS collect household and individual data from a nationally representative sample.

4. Details of the policy governing the release of new data are available by visiting www.statisticsauthority.gov.uk/assessment/code-of-practice/index.html or from the Media Relations Office email: media.relations@ons.gsi.gov.uk

Copyright

References

1. Organization for Economic Cooperation and Development (2001) ‘ Measuring Capital: OECD Manual Measurement of Capital Stocks, Consumption of Fixed Capital and Capital Services’ OECD, Paris.

2. Marshall, A. (1890). Principles of Economics. London: Macmillian and Co.

3. ONS (2012) Consultation on the Measures of Human Capital - available at Consultation on the Measures of Human Capital

4. Jones and Fender (2011) Human Capital Estimates 2010 - available at Human Capital Estimates 2010

12 December 2013

Household Satellite Accounts - Valuing Voluntary Activity in the UK

Author Name(s): **Rosemary Foster ONS**

Abstract

The value of voluntary activity in the UK for 2012 is estimated to be £23.9 billion, approximately 1.5% of GDP. This paper discusses the methodology and the assumptions used in this estimation. It is part of the Household Satellite Account, which attribute monetary values to household production activities that are not included in the National Accounts. These estimates are an update of the voluntary activity estimates published by the Office for National Statistics in 2002 for the year 2000. This paper also provides possible options for valuing the intervening years.

Introduction to Household Satellite Account

In 2002, the Office for National Statistics (ONS) published the first Household Satellite Account (HHSA) for the UK. This measured and valued the goods and services that are produced by households, but are not included in the National Accounts (ONS, 2002; Holloway, Short & Tamplin, 2002).

Following the publication of the Report by the Commission for the Measurement of Economic Performance and Social Progress (2009), there has been fresh interest in estimating the value of household production. As part of the Measuring National Well-being programme, ONS is currently updating the HHSA which measures the aspects of household production in the UK that are not included in the National Accounts.

Household production, in the context of the HHSA, is all the unpaid production of goods and services by households in the UK. Conventional National Accounts measurements, such as GDP, do not fully take into account these goods and services. However, if these goods and services are paid for, they contribute to GDP (for example, paying for clothes to be ironed rather than the task being done by a member of the household).

The HHSA provides a means by which the influence of changing patterns of unpaid work on the economy can be measured. The valuation of unpaid work could prove useful in assessing the impact of policies on households and the voluntary sector. This work falls outside the scope of the UK National Accounts. This is because the inclusion of all activities which are productive (in the economic sense) but which do not have a monetary value would swamp the monetary flows[1], obscure what is happening in the markets, and reduce the usefulness of National Accounts data for analysis. This significance is demonstrated by the HHSA results for 2000, which show the total monetary value of these flows to be close to GDP for that year. The HHSA remains separate from the UK National Accounts; however, they are conceptually consistent.

The HHSA extends the National Accounts boundary to include all activity that could be delegated to another person. This activity is divided into several principal functions:

- childcare
- adult care
- voluntary activity
- housing
- transport
- nutrition
- clothing
- laundry services

ONS aim is to update all the above eight modules as part of the HHSA. This work is being completed as part of the Measuring National Well-being Programme. ONS has published the estimates for Informal Childcare in the UK and Informal Adult Care in the UK in 2013. This paper updates the third module – voluntary activity.

The approach being taken by the ONS to value HHSA is to focus on the outputs of the principal functions except voluntary activity, where the focus has been on input approach due to data restrictions making the output approach challenging. The methodology remains under development and any estimates reported should be considered experimental and interpreted with caution. ONS welcomes comments and feedback on all aspects of the methodology used and the assumptions made, and seek suggestions for further/alternative data sources.

Notes

1. System of National Accounts (SNA) 2008 – Section 1.41: Household Production.

What is Voluntary Activity?

As there is some crossover between volunteering and care it is important that the definitions are clear. Volunteering is defined by the International Labour Organisation (2001)[1] as 'unpaid non-compulsory work; that is time individuals give without pay to activities performed either through an organisation or directly for others outside of the household'. This definition shows that voluntary activity can be classed as formal or informal depending on the nature of the activity. This paper only estimates the value of the activity that occurs through a formal institution – a group or organisation. Informal volunteering, such as helping friends or family members, is included either in the childcare or adult care projects (separate modules within the Household Satellite Account). By not including estimates of informal volunteering we may be underestimating the value of volunteering in the UK.

The output, or product, of voluntary activity is difficult to measure. The goods and services produced by volunteers are generally not sold and, therefore, there is no readily available market price. The voluntary activity was originally published as part of the HHSA by ONS in 2002 and was valued at £13.2 billion for 2000. As with all the other modules of the HHSA the goal was to measure the output independent of the inputs, for example, the number of hours children spend in uniformed organisations rather than the time spent supervising them. However, due to data limitations, the 2002 account valued voluntary activity using the proportion and hours of the people volunteering – an input based methodology.

Notes

1. Outlined in Appendix 2

Approaches to Valuing Formal Voluntary Activity

There are a number of ways to value the hours of formal voluntary activity:

1) The opportunity cost approach values the hours volunteered at an individual's wage rate. This method assesses the value of what the person is willing to give up in order to volunteer: the wage that they could be getting from a job. Therefore, the volunteering must be worth at least that much to the individual for him/her to give up that wage. However, using this method an identical service may have a different value depending on who provides it. For example, a leaflet being handed out by a lawyer could be worth more than the same leaflet being handed out by a pensioner.

2) The well-being approach gauges the positive change in a person's personal well-being that is associated with frequent voluntary activity. This change is then given an approximate value equivalent to the rise in income that would cause the same change in personal well-being. This method again approximates the value to the individual of volunteering - how much someone has to be paid to give up volunteering and still be as happy. A well-being approach to valuing volunteering was published in 2013 and is examined in Appendix 2.

3) The replacement cost approach values each individual hour at a market wage rate to show what would be the cost of paying somebody to do the same job. This wage rate could either be the minimum wage, the mean wage, the median wage or a market wage for the voluntary work. This method assumes that the quality of voluntary work is the same as the quality of paid work and that the volunteers would be replaced with paid workers. However, as we are trying to measure the product of volunteering, the value of the work being done, this method is the most appropriate for valuing voluntary activity. This methodology uses a specific wage from the ONS Annual Survey of Hours and Earnings to value voluntary activity.

Both the opportunity cost approach and the well-being approach value the gain to the contributor, rather than to the recipient of the output. They do not show the value of the output being produced, but the replacement cost approach shows how much the recipient would have to pay to replace the volunteering and therefore the cost that the volunteers are forgoing. This makes the replacement cost method the best available method to value voluntary activity. The replacement cost approach has been recommended by the International Labour Office and is the most comparable to the National Accounts.

The Value of Voluntary Activity in 2012/13

This section estimates the number of hours volunteered in the UK in 2012/13 and values them using the replacement cost approach.

Those who volunteer at least once a month are characterised as frequent volunteers. This paper only estimates the value of frequent volunteering. The exclusion of infrequent volunteering is due to issues with data quality. The infrequent hours data tend to be less consistent and by just using the frequently volunteered hours, the estimates could be more accurate.

From the Community Life Survey[1] it is possible to work out the proportion of the sample who volunteered formally and informally and the hours which they volunteered in 2012/13[2]. The survey estimates that about 29% of those who are over 16 years old frequently take part in formal voluntary activity. This equates to nearly fifteen million people in 2012/13.

The Community Life Survey provides data on twelve specific types of activities which are then split into three general groups. These groups show the type of activity taking place for valuation purposes. All of the volunteering valued within the HHSA is through a formal group or organisation. These are outlined in Table 1.

Table 1: Types of Voluntary Activity

Citizenship Categories	Type of Activity
Raising Money	Clerical and Secretarial
Leading a Group	Professional
Organising an Event	Clerical and Secretarial
Visiting People	Personal and Protective
Befriending or Mentoring People	Personal and Protective
Giving Advice, information or Counselling	Personal and Protective
Secretarial, Admin or Clerical	Clerical and Secretarial
Providing Transport	Personal and Protective
Representing	Professional
Campaigning	Professional
Other Practical Help	Personal and Protective
Any Other Help	Personal and Protective

Table source: Office for National Statistics

Download table

XLS XLS format
(18 Kb)

Median wage rates are used to reduce the effects of outliers which could cause distortion. The data, which have been split into groups dependant on the type of voluntary activity, are valued using gross median hourly earnings[3]. An individual can take part in one form of activity or a combination of two or all three. The median wage is then applied to the number of hours depending on which activity or combination of activities the individual takes part in. The median wages are outlined in Appendix 4.

Results

Table 2 shows the volume and value estimates for Voluntary Activity in 2012/13. UK residents formally volunteered 2.12 billion hours in 2012/13. As mentioned earlier, this paper focuses only on the frequent voluntary activity – that is those who volunteer at least once a month. The value of frequent volunteering was £23.9 billion in 2012/13. This value is an estimate of what the same number of hours would cost if they were being provided by a paid person, in the market.

Table 2: The Hours and Value of Formal Voluntary Activity in 2012/13

Year	Total Hours (billions of hours)	Frequent Hours (billions of hours)	Total Value (£billion)	Frequent Value (£billion)
2012/13	2.29	2.12	25.6	23.9

Table source: Office for National Statistics

Download table

XLS XLS format
(18.5 Kb)

It is more meaningful to analyse the value of volunteering activity as a proportion of GDP. The value of frequent volunteering as a percentage of GDP[4] was just over 1.5% in 2012.

Notes

1. For a full explanation of the data sources please see Appendix 1.
2. The later years of the Citizenship survey (2007/08, 2008/09, 2009/10 and 2010/11) and the Community Life Survey (2012/13) span 2 years.
3. Annual Survey of Hours and Earnings (ASHE).
4. This is Current Price Annual GDP from the ONS UK Economic Accounts.

The Value of Voluntary Activity 2001-2010/11

Voluntary activity was valued for the year 2000 (in the 2002 Household Satellite Account) using the 2001 ONS Omnibus Survey with the replacement cost approach. However, no estimation exists for

2001 – 2010/11. This section discusses options to estimate the number of hours volunteered in the UK between 2001 and 2010/11 which are then also valued using the replacement cost approach.

Between 2001 and 2010/11, the data available on voluntary activity is not as detailed as in the Community Life or Omnibus Surveys and therefore there are challenges involved in estimating the number of hours volunteered between these years. One of the best data sources that could be used is the Citizenship Survey, which preceded the Community Life Survey. This survey measured the proportion of the population that formally and informally volunteered as well as the frequency of volunteering, but not the formal voluntary hours. To value the proportion of the adult population that is volunteering, a proxy needs to be used to estimate the number of hours volunteered.

Three options to estimate the number of hours volunteered are discussed below. All of them use the Citizenship Survey but with different approximated hours. The sources for these three different sets of approximated hours are the 2001 Omnibus Survey, the 2011 Understanding Society Survey and the 2012/13 Community Life Survey. In all three cases, the replacement cost method is used to derive values from the volume estimates.

It should be noted that the Citizenship Survey dataset does not cover all the relevant years. Figure 1 shows the years that are covered by the Citizenship Survey.

Figure 1(1): Proportion of the Sample that Volunteer, 2001- 2012/13

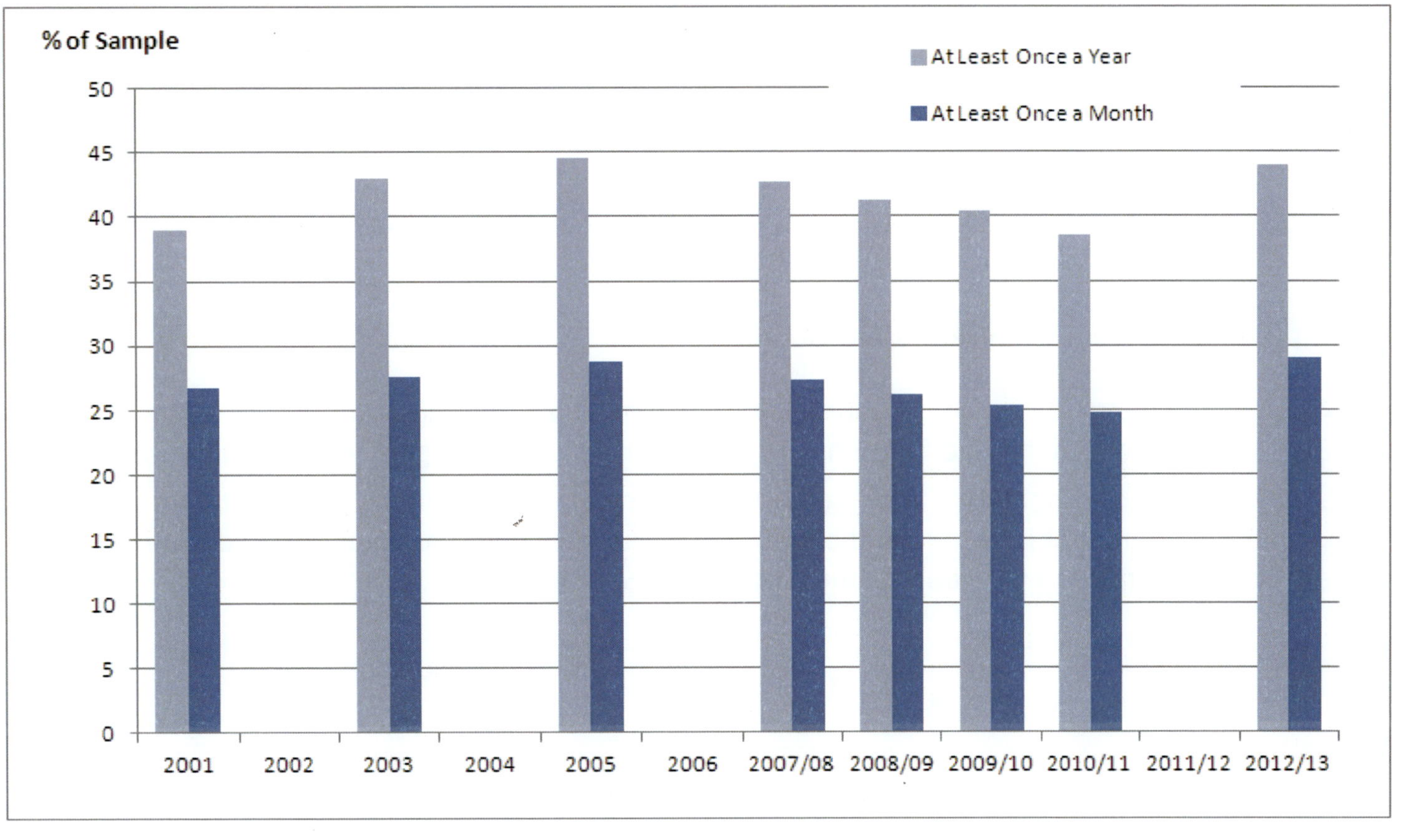

Source: Home Office, Communities and Local Government, Cabinet Office

Notes:

1. Please note that 2012 data is from the Community Life Survey.

Download chart

XLS XLS format
(27 Kb)

Options to estimate the number of hours volunteered

1) Using the hours from the Community Life Survey

Creating proxy hours for each frequency of voluntary activity - weekly, monthly and so on – for each different age group allows the use of hours data in conjunction with the proportions data to create volume estimates for the number of hours volunteered in the UK. The hours from the Community Life survey are given in Table 3.

Table 3: Average Number of Hours per Frequency of Volunteering, 2012/13

Age	Weekly	Monthly	Less often
16 to 29	171	125	5
30 to 49	213	83	4
50 to 69	283	90	5
older than 70	226	93	6
Average	223	98	5

Download table

XLS XLS format
(19 Kb)

2) Using the hours from Understanding Society

Table 4 shows the average number of hours that people from different age groups worked as volunteers. These are split into the frequency of volunteering and average number of hours is calculated for the whole population from the Understanding Society Survey[1]. These data are used to approximate the number of hours worked by the individual, depending on their age and regularity of voluntary activity, in each of the years of the Citizenship Survey.

Table 4: Average Number of Hours Split into Age Group and Frequency, 2011

Age	Weekly	Monthly	Less often	Other	Total
16 to 29	241	89	10	9	87
30 to 49	223	73	7	7	77
50 to 69	314	100	8	12	109
older than 70	332	106	10	4	113
Average	277	92	9	8	97

Download table

XLS XLS format
(18.5 Kb)

3) Using the hours from the Omnibus Survey

In 2002, HHSA used the 2001 Omnibus Survey to estimate the number of volunteers, the hours volunteered in the last four weeks and the type of voluntary activity undertaken. The average number of hours per year in the Omnibus Survey for each activity is given in Table 5. The hours provide a separate estimation to proxy hours provided by the 2011 Understanding Society Survey.

Table 5: Omnibus Hours Data – split by type of volunteering, 2001

	Average Annual Hours
Personal & Protective	165.1
Professional	107.9
Clerical & Secretarial	161.2
Personal and Professional	136.5
Personal and Clerical	163.2
Clerical and Professional	134.6
All	144.7

Download table

XLS XLS format
(32.5 Kb)

Comparison of the Three Options for Valuing Voluntary Activity, 2001-2010/11

Table 6 shows the total frequent hours estimates from each of the three options discussed in the previous section. The range in the estimates is noticeable. All three possible options create estimates of around two million voluntary hours over the decade. The pattern between the years reflects that of the proportions seen in Figure 1.

Table 6: Comparison of Frequent Volunteering, Millions of Hours 2001-2010/11

Year	Understanding Society	Community Life	Omnibus
2001	2.44	2.18	1.91
2003	2.3	2.09	1.91
2005	2.53	2.28	2.14
2007/08	2.54	2.27	2.07
2008/09	2.44	2.19	1.99
2009/10	2.37	2.11	1.94
2010/11	2.29	2.05	1.91

Download table

XLS XLS format
(32 Kb)

These hours are valued using the same replacement cost method used to value the 2012 estimates discussed earlier - splitting the hours into types of activity and using a market replacement wage. This wage, as before, is taken from the Annual Survey of Hours and Earnings and is explained in Appendix 4.

Figure 2 shows a comparison of the valuation of the three different options and the value for 2012. The value of each year is shown at the wage rate of that year. This means that an increase in value is due to wage increases rather than growth in volume.

Figure 2: Value of Voluntary Activity 2001 – 2012/13, Options (£billion)

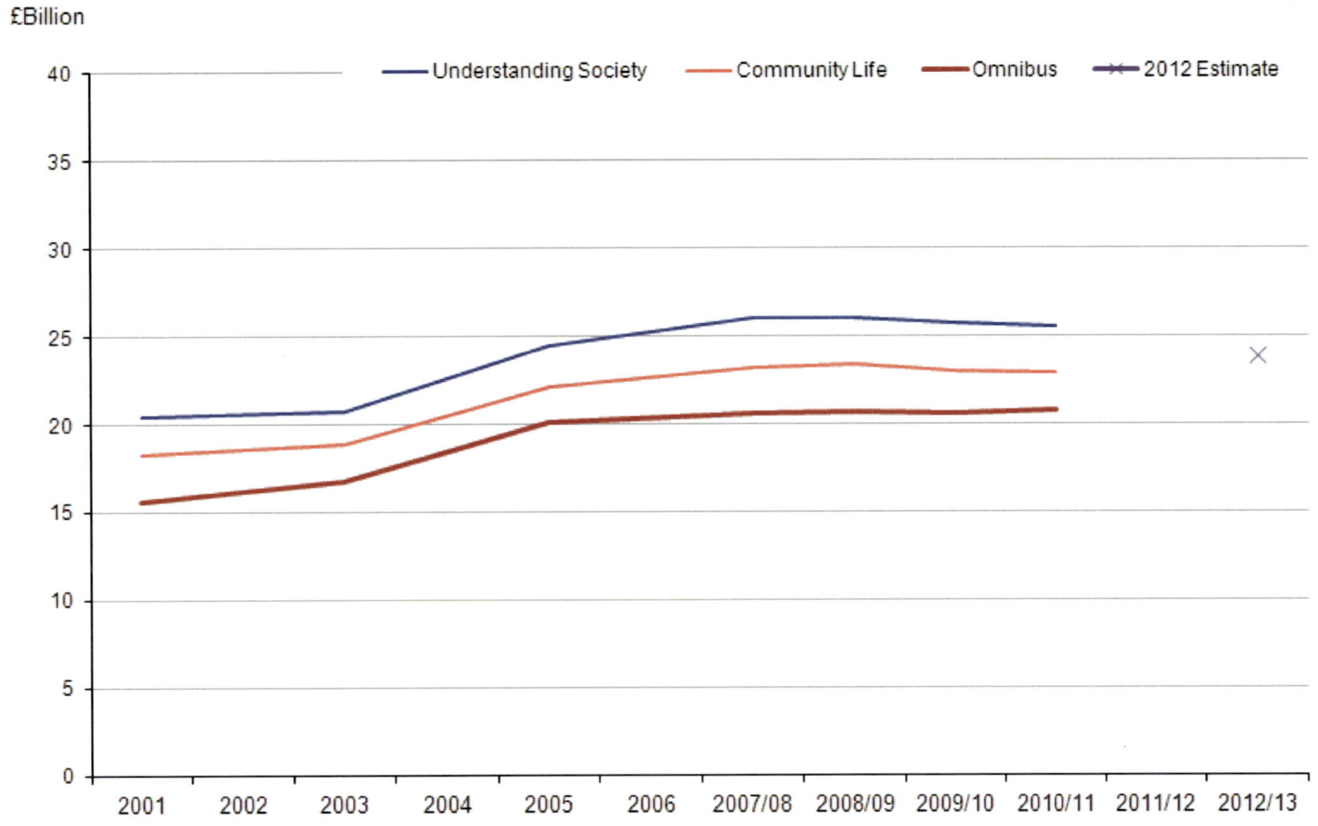

Source: Annual Survey of Hours and Earnings (ASHE) - Home Office, Cabinet Office, Communities and Local Government, Office for National Statistics

Download chart

XLS XLS format
(18.5 Kb)

The highest and the lowest value of voluntary activity derived above using the three options discussed earlier could be used as a range to value voluntary activity. With each of the options, the value of voluntary activity follows a similar pattern. The Community Life Survey is the most comparable to the 2012 estimates due to the proportions used in the methodology. Each of the options gives an experimental estimate of the value of voluntary activity over the decade. Any future improvement in data sources might lead to more accurate estimates.

Notes

1. Data Sources explained in Appendix 1.

Using an Alternative Data Source

The Household Satellite Account (HHSA) is an experimental dataset and therefore the methodology used in this paper to value volunteering activity is under development. This section discusses another data source – the British Household Panel Survey (BHPS) – as opposed to the three data sources used above for valuing formal voluntary activity for 2001 – 2010/11 to show how big the change would be if this data source is chosen.

British Household Panel Survey Proportions

Conducted until 2008, the British Household Panel Survey (BHPS) was a UK wide biennial survey that provided data on the proportion of the sample that formally volunteered. It was replaced after 2008 by the Understanding Society Survey. Both surveys form an alternative data source to the Citizenship and Community Life Survey. The proportion of those volunteering was much lower than that indicated by the Citizenship Survey (see Figure 3). The BHPS goes into much less detail in the questions about voluntary activity than the Citizenship Survey. By asking more questions about volunteering, the citizenship survey collects more information and a more reliable number of those volunteering.

Figure 3: Proportion of Frequent Volunteers, 2001-2010/11

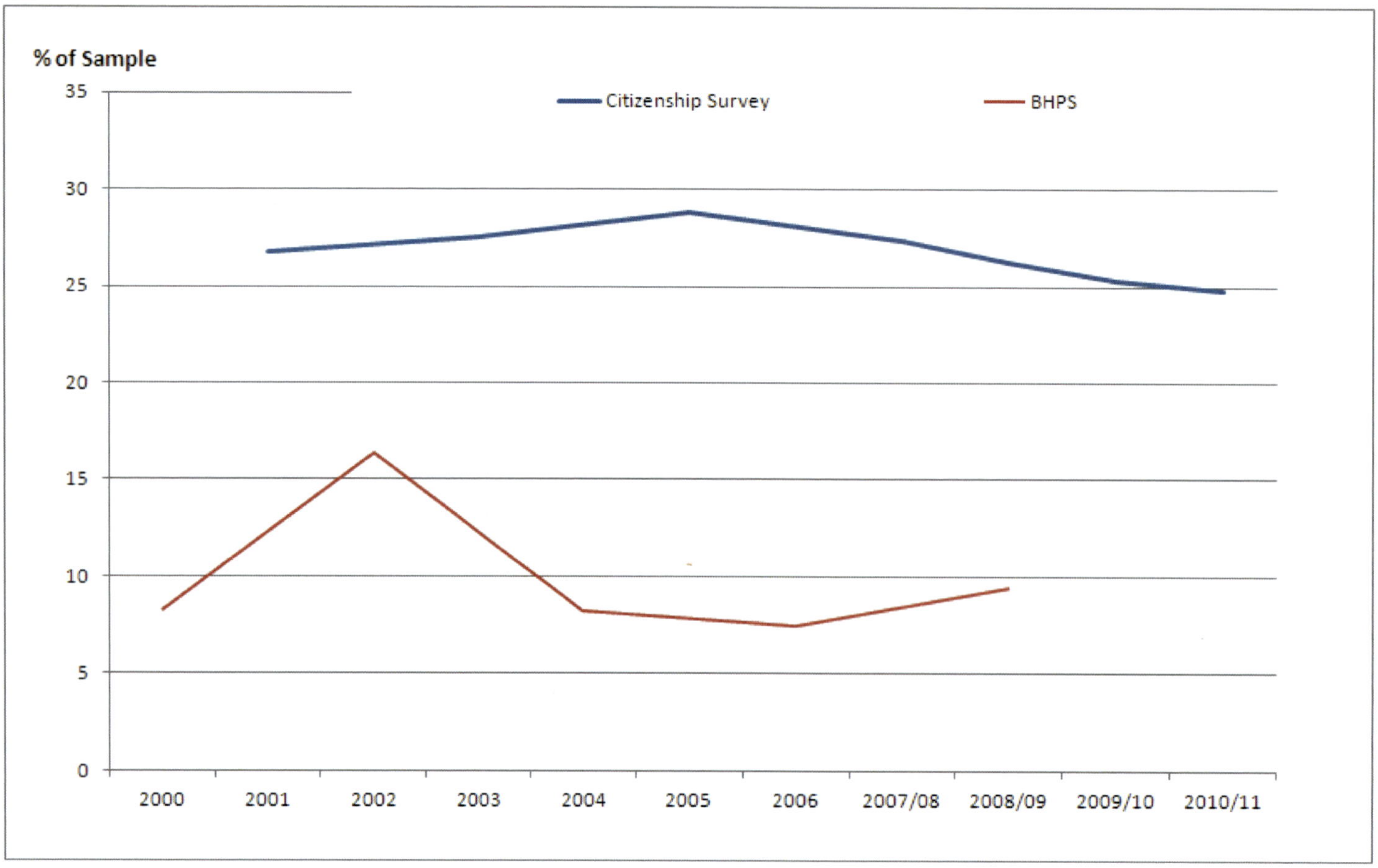

Source: Home Office, Communities and Local Government

Download chart

XLS XLS format
(27.5 Kb)

According to the BHPS, the proportion of the sample that volunteer frequently and formally averages just under 11% in the BHPS (2000, 2002, 2004, 2006, 2008) presented in Figure 3. The methodology used to create the estimates for 2012/13 discussed in the earlier section is replicated to create the volume estimates in this case.

As the BHPS does not differentiate between the different types of activities, the value of volunteering must be estimated using an average wage of the three activity types[1] and the volume data. The results are shown in Table 7.

Table 7: Value of Voluntary Activity – Using BHPS Data

Year	Total Hours (billions of hours)	Frequent Hours (billions of hours)	Total Value (£billions)	Frequent Value (£billions)
2000	1.1	1.0	9.6	9.4
2002	1.0	1.0	10.3	10.1
2004	1.0	1.0	10.7	10.6
2006	1.0	1.0	11.7	11.5
2008	1.1	1.1	13.0	12.7

Download table

XLS XLS format
(32 Kb)

Comparison of BHPS and Community life

A comparison of the BHPS estimates with the other three options is shown in Figure 4.

Figure 4: Options for the Value of Voluntary Activity in the UK, 2000-2010 (£ Billion)

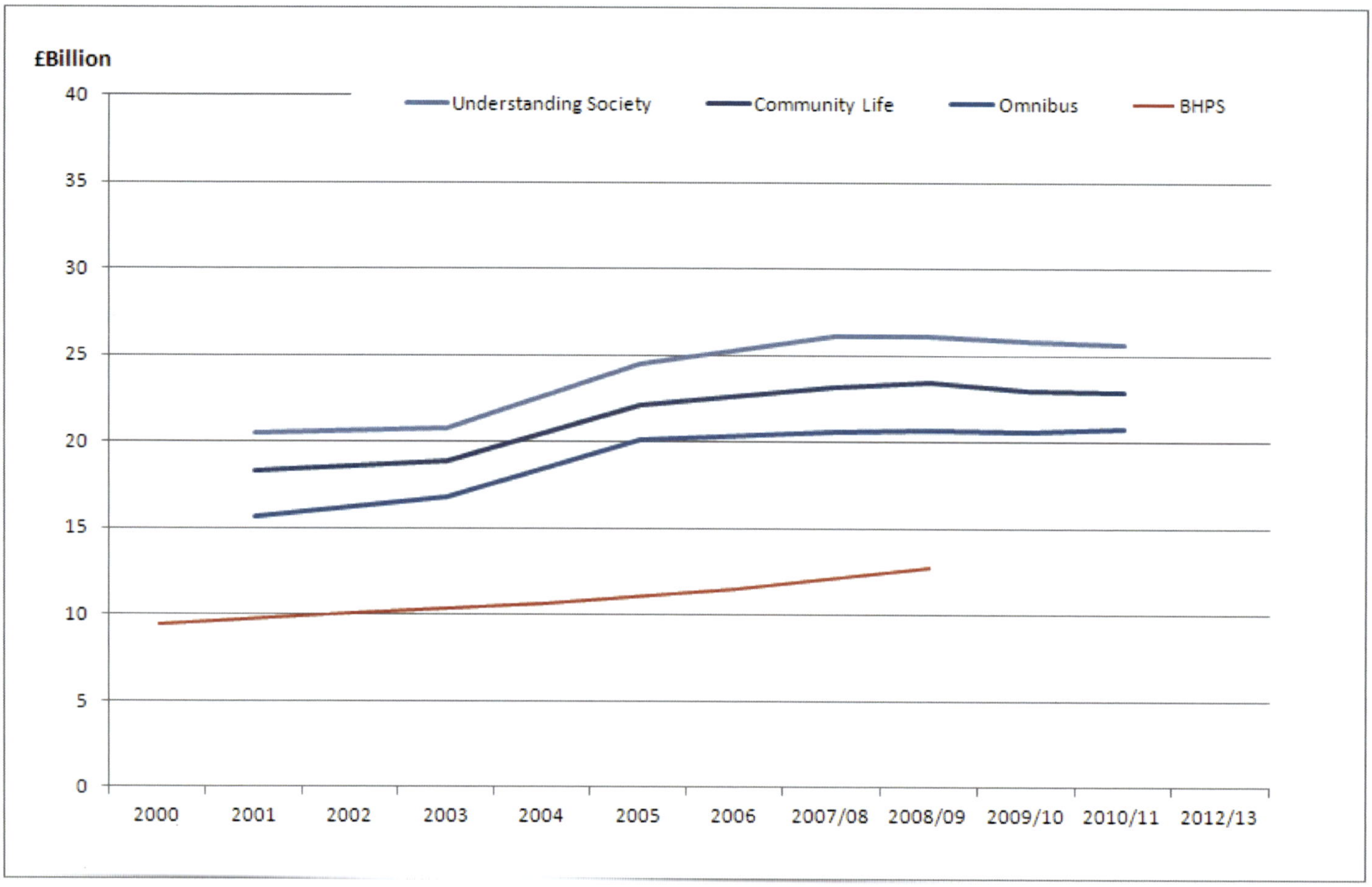

Source: Annual Survey of Hours and Earnings (ASHE) - Home Office, Communities and Local Government, Cabinet Office, Office for National Statistics

Download chart

XLS XLS format
(18.5 Kb)

The BHPS estimates are notably lower than that shown by the three options using the Citizenship Survey. This analysis demonstrates how two different data sources could produce different results and shows the importance of using reliable data sources. As mentioned in the first section, ONS welcomes comments on the different data sources used and seek suggestions for further / alternative data sources.

Notes

1. Clerical and Secretarial, Personal and Protective and Professional.

Appendix 1: Data sources

The estimated number of volunteers varies considerably, depending on the survey used, with different surveys asking different questions at different times of the year. The primary source of information for the estimates in the HHSA is an unpaid work module within the Citizenship Survey.

The Citizenship Survey

The Citizenship survey only has data for the following years: 2001, 2003, 2005, 2007/8, 2008/9, 2009/10, and 2010/11, so it does not present full estimates. The survey covers only England and Wales and was run by the Home Office until 2006. The final four waves of the survey were run by the Department for Communities and Local Government. The survey states that about 40% of the survey's sample formally volunteers at least once a year, and 25% at least once a month. This is higher than proportions from the original data source (Omnibus Survey 2001) and other comparable surveys such as the British Household Panel Survey (BHPS). The possible data sources have been examined and with the input of experts, it has been decided that due to its survey design, the citizenship survey has created the most accurate estimates for the proportion of individuals that volunteer. This is because the questions on the Citizenship and Community Life Surveys go into more detail and have more information about voluntary activity than one question would, as on the BHPS.

The Citizenship Survey has a nationally representative sample of 10,000 adults (16 and over) and an ethnic minority boost sample of 5,000 adults.

The Community Life Survey

This survey covers only England and is run by the Cabinet Office. It is the successor to the Citizenship Survey and covers many of the same questions and, therefore, variables. The survey was carried out for the year 2012/13 and is ongoing. The proportion of the sample that volunteer has slightly increased in 2012/13 compared with the results found within the Citizenship Survey. This may be due to a change in methodology or as a result of the 'Olympic'[1] effect. The Community Life Survey has a representative sample (of England) of 6,600 interviews that take place over three quarters, of 2012/13.

Understanding Society

The survey has published data from two different waves, 2009 and 2011. The Understanding Society Survey is currently being updated for 2013. Only the second wave (2011) contains a full module on volunteering. Understanding Society is a longitudinal survey that captures information annually about the social and economic circumstances and attitudes of people living in 40,000 UK households. It is run by the University of Essex and is UK wide.

Understanding Society has a total of 38,271 households– 26,035 in the General Population sample, 3,959 in the Ethnic Minority Boost sample and 8,277 previously in the BHPS sample. The samples are representative of the UK population.

British Household Panel Survey

The most comparable data source to the Citizenship Survey in terms of coverage is the BHPS. This survey was the predecessor to Understanding Society Survey and, biennially, ran a question on the frequency of volunteering. The proportion of those frequently volunteering is much lower than in the Citizenship Survey and there is no information about the type of activity taking place. This paper compares the results for years 2000, 2002, 2004, 2006 and 2008 with the results gained from the Citizenship Survey. It was also run by the University of Essex and was UK wide. The BHPS originally had a sample of 8167 households. All members of the households were sampled and 'boost' samples were collected from Wales and Scotland. The samples were representative of the UK population.

Notes

1. The Olympic effect can be characterised as the uptake of volunteering after the use of volunteers during the Olympic and Paralympics Games.

Appendix 2: Overview of Valuing Voluntary Activity Literature

International Labour Force Manual on the measurement of volunteer work (2011)

In 2011, the International Labour Office in Geneva published a manual on the measurement of volunteer work. The purpose of the manual was to create 'a guide for countries in generating systematic and comparable data on volunteer work by means of regular supplements to labour force or other household surveys'. The target of this guide was to produce comparable data that could be used to help produce cross-national outputs that would be easy to compare. This would help to fulfil the recommendations made by the United Nations Secretary General's International Year of Volunteers report that aims to 'establish the economic value of volunteering'.

The manual discusses a number of definitions and the use of different variables and measurements in measuring volunteering.

Although data collection is not covered extensively in the manual, the Labour Force Survey comes closest to meeting the recommended rationale and strategy for measuring volunteer work. This is due to the frequency of the Labour Force Surveys, the sample sizes and the fact that they facilitate an accurate valuation of the work itself. The UK has a number of current and recently discontinued household surveys that collected informative data on volunteering.

The manual outlines an interesting 'conservative' estimate that 'the value of contribution of time, i.e., volunteer work, is approximately double the value of contribution of money'. This highlights the need for comparable cross-national information on volunteering becoming readily available, as volunteering is 'an enormous renewable resource for social problem-solving'.

Targeted variables are discussed within the manual. Having similar, if not identical variables, is an important part of making cross-national economic values of volunteering comparable. The Manual pinpoints three key target variables: number of volunteers, number of hours volunteered and the occupation (type of work performed).

The main objective of the manual is to provide a basis for estimating the economic value of volunteering. To ensure international comparability, there should be a common approach by all countries so that all economic values are measured in comparable output units.

The manual recommends using the 'replacement cost approach' rather than the 'opportunity cost approach'. The replacement cost approach is seen as a better method of measuring the economic value of volunteering to the overall economic view point of society, as it measures the value for the recipient of the voluntary effort. The replacement cost approach estimates a value that the recipient would have to pay to hire a person to perform the same job as the volunteer. This is compared to the opportunity cost approach, which measures the economic value of volunteering to the volunteer. More information about the two methods can be found in the manual.

Fujiwara, Oroyemi and McKinnon (2013) 'Estimating the value of volunteering using subjective wellbeing data'

In 2013, a paper was published by the Department for Work and Pensions and the Cabinet Office by Fujiwara, Oroyemi and McKinnon on 'Estimating the Value of Volunteering using Subjective Well-being Data'.

The paper uses the British Household Panel Survey and analyses four waves of the survey; 2000, 2002, 2004 and 2008, for people aged 16 years and above.

The paper is unique in the UK because it develops a Well-being Valuation (WV) approach. The WV approach is being developed as an alternative to the opportunity cost approach and the replacement cost approach, which are currently used in much of the literature surrounding the valuation of non-market costs and benefits.

This approach estimates the increase in self reported well-being associated with a particular good or a service and then calculates the equivalent amount of money necessary to give the same boost to well-being.

To summarise, the paper's key methodological points are that volunteering and well-being are positively correlated and that the WV approach has a number of advantages over traditional preference-based valuation methods for the topic of volunteering.

Appendix 3: Survey Coverage

As the Citizenship Survey covers only England and Wales and the Community Life Survey only covers England, it was important to gauge if the proportions were appropriate for use in Northern Ireland and Scotland before applying the UK population figures. The British Household Panel Survey (BHPS) gives the proportion of those that formally volunteer biennially until 2008. This covers the whole of the UK and can be split into each separate country. This shows us if the difference in the results between England and Wales and the whole of the UK are statistically significant. If they are not, the use of the England and Wales proportions (from the Citizenship survey) as a proxy for the whole of the UK is an acceptable methodology. Table A1 provides the proportions.

Table A1: Frequent volunteering proportions

	2000	2002	2004	2006	2008
England and Wales	10.90%	10.60%	9.90%	9.60%	12.20%
UK	10.90%	10.60%	9.90%	9.60%	12.10%

Download table

XLS XLS format
(32 Kb)

To analyse whether the difference between the proportions in the UK and in England and Wales is not statistically significant, a linear regression was performed separately for both the proportion of the sample that frequently volunteers and all of those that volunteer.

The proportion of people who volunteered in England and Wales was found to be a good approximation of the proportion of people who volunteered in the whole UK and, therefore, data from the Citizenship Survey can be used.

Appendix 4: Median Hourly Earnings from the Annual Survey of Hours and Earnings

Table A2: Median Hourly Wage Rates from ASHE, 2001-2012

£ per hour

Year	Professional	Clerical	Personal	Personal and Professional	Personal and Clerical	Clerical and Professional	Personal, Professional and Clerical
2000	14.9	6.76	5.53	10.22	6.15	10.83	9.06
2001	15.56	7.02	5.73	10.65	6.38	11.29	9.44
2002	16.13	7.55	6.13	11.13	6.84	11.84	9.94
2003	16.7	7.85	6.47	11.59	7.16	12.28	10.34
2004	17.12	8.01	6.74	11.93	7.38	12.57	10.62
2005	18.13	8.33	7.02	12.58	7.68	13.23	11.16
2006	18.43	8.58	7.28	12.86	7.93	13.51	11.43
2007	18.85	8.92	7.53	13.19	8.23	13.89	11.77
2008	19.36	9.18	7.86	13.61	8.52	14.27	12.13
2009	19.86	9.5	8.15	14.01	8.83	14.68	12.5
2010	20.12	9.66	8.26	14.19	8.96	14.89	12.68
2012[1]	19.01	9.95	8.32	13.67	9.14	14.48	12.43

Table source: Office for National Statistics

Table notes:

1. 2012 figures are provisional.

Download table

XLS XLS format
(28 Kb)

References

1. Stiglitz, J. Sen, A. Fitoussi, J.P. (2009). Commission on the Measurement of Economic Performance and Social Progress.
2. Holloway, Short and Tamplin (2002). Household Satellite Account (Experimental) Methodology. Office for National Statistics.
3. Office for National Statistics (2002). Complete Household Satellite Accounts.
4. Fujiwara et al (2013). Estimating the value of volunteering using subjective wellbeing data.
5. International Labour Office (2011). Manual on the measurement of volunteer work.
6. Salamon, L M et al (2011). Measuring the Economic Value of Volunteer Work Globally: Concepts, Estimates, and a Roadmap to the Future. Annals of Public and Cooperative Economics, Vol. 82, Issue 3, pp. 217-252, 2011
7. Gaskin, K. Dobson, B. (1997). The Economic Equation of Volunteering. Joseph Rowntree Foundation.

Background notes

1. Details of the policy governing the release of new data are available by visiting www.statisticsauthority.gov.uk/assessment/code-of-practice/index.html or from the Media Relations Office email: media.relations@ons.gsi.gov.uk

Copyright

National
Well-being

September 2013 release

Measuring what matters:
Understanding the nation's well-being

More data and interactive version available at: **www.ons.gov.uk/well-being**

Data are the latest available at August 2013